The work published in *Phonology and Phonetic Evidence* presents an integrated phonetics–phonology approach in what has now become an established field, laboratory phonology. The volume is divided into three sections: Part I deals with the status and role of features in phonological representations; Part II, on prosody, contains amongst others two papers which present for the first time detailed acoustic and perceptual evidence on the rhythm rule; and Part III, on articulatory organization, includes several papers which from different perspectives test hypotheses derived from articulatory phonology, thereby testifying to the great influence this theory has exerted in recent years.

This, the fourth in the series of *Papers in Laboratory Phonology*, will be welcomed by all those interested in phonetics, phonology, and their interface.

PAPERS IN LABORATORY PHONOLOGY

SERIES EDITORS: MARY E. BECKMAN AND JOHN KINGSTON

Phonology and Phonetic Evidence

Phonology and Phonetic Evidence
Papers in Laboratory Phonology IV

EDITED BY BRUCE CONNELL

Research Associate, Institute of Social and Cultural Anthropology,
University of Oxford

AND

AMALIA ARVANITI

Research Associate, Department of Linguistics,
University of Edinburgh

CAMBRIDGE
UNIVERSITY PRESS

Published by the Press Syndicate of the University of Cambridge
The Pitt Building, Trumpington Street, Cambridge CB2 1RP
40 West 20th Street, New York, NY 10011-4211, USA
10 Stamford Road, Oakleigh, Melbourne 3166, Australia

First published 1995

Printed in Great Britain at the University Press, Cambridge

A catalogue record for this book is available from the British Library

Library of Congress cataloguing in publication data

Phonology and phonetic evidence / edited by Bruce Connell and Amalia
Arvaniti.
       p.   cm. – (Papers in laboratory phonology; 4)
Includes indexes.
ISBN 0 521 48259 3 (hc.) – ISBN 0 521 48388 3 (pbk.)
1. Grammar, Comparative and general – Phonology. 2. Phonetics.
3. Speech perception. I. Connell, Bruce. II. Arvaniti, Amalia.
III. Series.
P217.P556   1995
414 – dc20   94-45669   CIP

ISBN 0 521 48259 3 hardback
ISBN 0 521 48388 3 paperback

Contents

Contents

II. Prosody

III. Articulatory Organization

Contents

Contributors

AMALIA ARVANITI *Department of Linguistics, University of Edinburgh*

MARY E. BECKMAN *Department of Linguistics, The Ohio State University*

CATHERINE P. BROWMAN *Haskins Laboratories*

H. TIMOTHY BUNNELL *ASE Speech Processing Laboratory, AI du Pont*

BRUCE CONNELL *Institute of Social and Cultural Anthropology, University of Oxford*

DIDIER DEMOLIN *Département de Linguistique Générale, Université Libre de Bruxelles*

RANDY L. DIEHL *Psychology Department, University of Texas, Austin*

GERARD J. DOCHERTY *Department of Speech, University of Newcastle-upon-Tyne*

JORDI FONTDEVILA *CEDI, Institut d'Estudis Catalans*

LOUIS GOLDSTEIN *Haskins Laboratories*

ESTHER GRABE *Max Planck Institute for Psycholinguistics*

TARA HOLST *Department of Linguistics, University of Cambridge*

STEVEN HOSKINS *Department of Linguistics, University of Delaware*

KATHLEEN HUBBARD *Department of Linguistics, University of California, San Diego*

KENNETH DE JONG *Department of Linguistics, University of Indiana*

List of contributors

SUN-AH JUN   *Department of Linguistics, University of California, Los Angeles*

JOHN KINGSTON   *Department of Linguistics, University of Massachusetts*

HARUO KUBOZONO   *Department of Japanese, Osaka University of Foreign Studies*

SOOK-HYANG LEE   *Chung-Ang University, Seoul*

JAMES M. MCQUEEN   *Max Planck Institute for Psycholinguistics*

TERRANCE M. NEAREY   *Department of Linguistics, University of Alberta*

FRANCIS NOLAN   *Department of Linguistics, University of Cambridge*

RICHARD OGDEN   *Department of Language and Linguistic Science, University of York*

JOHN J. OHALA   *Department of Linguistics, University of California, Berkeley*

MANJARI OHALA   *Department of Linguistics and Language Development, San Jose State University*

MARIA DOLORS PALLARÈS   *CEDI, Institut d'Estudis Catalans*

DANIEL RECASENS   *CEDI, Institut d'Estudis Catalans and Universite Autonomá de Barcelona*

JAMES M. SCOBBIE   *Department of Speech Pathology, Queen Margaret College, Edinburgh*

STEFANIE SHATTUCK-HUFNAGEL   *Speech Communication Group, Department of Electrical Engineering, Massachusetts Institute of Technology*

CAROLINE L. SMITH   *Audiology and Speech Pathology, West Los Angeles VA Medical Center and Department of Linguistics, Universiy of California, Los Angeles*

BERNARD TRANEL   *Department of Linguistics, University of California, Irvine*

IRENE VOGEL   *Department of Linguistics, University of Delaware*

List of contributors

PAUL WARREN   *Department of Linguistics, Victoria University, Wellington*

ELIZABETH C. ZSIGA   *Department of Linguistics, Georgetown University*

Acknowledgments

This selection of papers is based on the Fourth Conference in Laboratory Phonology, which was held in Oxford in August 1993. The conference was organized by a committee consisting of Bruce Connell, Amalia Arvaniti and Ian Watson, while Gerry Docherty, Bob Ladd, and Francis Nolan reviewed the anonymous abstracts before the final selection was made by the committee. We are grateful to the Oxford University Phonetics Laboratory, the Modern Languages Faculty for providing funds for the conference, and to the Committee for General Linguistics and Comparative Philology, which contributed to the cost of the camera-ready-copy preparation of the present volume. Thanks also go to the Phonetics Laboratory secretary, Celia Glynn, and to two of the Laboratory's graduate students, Jana Dankovicová and Jane Stewart-Smith, who helped with the running of the conference, and to David Zeitlyn for his assistance in preparing the camera-ready-copy.

The papers for this volume were reviewed anonymously by *ad-hoc* referees, too numerous to mention individually. Their contribution to the preparation of this volume is, however, gratefully acknowledged.

As in the previous volume, we have tried to adhere to the 1989 IPA transcription conventions. We would like to thank the contributors for assisting us in this effort, and apologize to readers for any inconsistencies that remain, in this or any other respect.

Last, but not least, we would like to thank Mary Beckman and John Kingston, the series editors, for their helpful advice, interest in the progress of the volume, and much needed encouragement.

Bruce Connell
Amalia Arvaniti

1
Introduction

BRUCE CONNELL and AMALIA ARVANITI

This, the fourth volume in the *Papers in Laboratory Phonology* series, is based on papers originally presented at the Fourth Conference on Laboratory Phonology, held at the University of Oxford in August 1993.

The first Laboratory Phonology conference (LabPhon) was held in June 1987, with its major stated aim the breaking down of barriers between phonetics and phonology. Since that time, laboratory phonology has rapidly become established, if not as mainstream in phonology circles, then certainly as a well respected approach to studying the organization of sound systems. Testament to this can be seen equally in the success of the subsequent LabPhon meetings (in Edinburgh, UCLA, and Oxford), the increasing input from younger scholars at these meetings, and the growing number of papers in major journals reporting research done from the laboratory phonology perspective.

Laboratory based phonology papers can be frequently found in journals such as *Language and Speech* (e.g. de Jong, Beckman & Edwards, 1993), *Journal of Phonetics* (e.g. Zsiga, 1994), *Phonetica* – which has featured theme issues on the relation between phonetics and phonology, and on Articulatory Phonology, a theory whose own growth and development is intimately connected to that of Labphon – and *Phonology* (e.g. Gussenhoven, 1991; Keating, 1988; Maddieson & Precoda, 1992; Trigo, 1991). With the exception of *Phonology*, the slant of these journals has traditionally been towards phonetics, which might suggest that in achieving the desired rapprochement between phonetics and phonology, it is mostly the phoneticians who have taken on board the view that their work would benefit from phonological input. Although this may not be surprising – the methods of laboratory phonology have much in common with those of experimental phonetics – we still look forward to the day when laboratory based studies find their way into a yet larger range of journals, and laboratory phonology is more widely adopted. Moreover, it should be noted, that laboratory phonology incorporates more than the methodology of experimental phonetics; we find, for example, much work being done in a psycholinguistic vein. This variety of approaches can be found in the papers of the present volume.

The volume is divided into three sections, and the order of the papers within each of them follows to a certain extent the order of presentation at the Oxford meeting, though the thematic basis of the three parts here does not match the thematic structure of the conference.

Part I, Features and Perception, deals with the status and role of features in phonological representations, addressing issues such as whether features are accessed in perception directly or via intermediate perceptual categories (Kingston and Diehl, discussed by Nearey), underspecification in lexical representations (Ohala and Ohala, discussion by McQueen), the status of redundant features in terms of Enhancement Theory (de Jong), and the role of the perception of features in shaping sound systems (Ohala).

Part II, Prosody, includes two papers which present for the first time detailed acoustic and perceptual evidence on the Rhythm Rule, an issue which has attracted considerable attention in recent years (Grabe and Warren, and Vogel, Bunnell, and Hoskins, discussion of both by Shattuck-Hufnagel). The other two papers in this section deal with prosodic structure and present in turn perceptual evidence for the existence of the mora in Japanese (Kubozono, discussion by Beckman), and acoustic data that bear on moraic structure in Bantu languages (Hubbard, discussion by Tranel).

Part III, Articulatory Organization, includes several papers which from different perspectives test claims of and hypotheses derived from Articulatory Phonology, thereby testifying to the great influence this theory has exerted in recent years. The topics addressed include temporal coordination for different rhythmic categories (Smith, discussion by Ogden), an analysis of the lenis stop voicing in Korean as a consequence of overlapping glottal gestures (Jun, discussion by Docherty), postlexical palatalization in American English (Zsiga, discussion by Scobbie), place of articulation assimilation as gestural overlap (Holst and Nolan, discussion by Browman), and the role of the jaw in the production of gutturals (Lee, discussion by Nolan). The two remaining papers are less concerned with the claims of Articulatory Phonology; they present detailed articulatory data and diachronic evidence on the nature and feature geometry representation of palatals (Recasens, Fontdevila and Pallarès), and the existence of implosives in Lendu (Demolin, discussion by Goldstein).

This collection of papers is further testimony to the vitality of the LabPhon conferences, in that several of them address issues first raised in earlier meetings: Ohala and Ohala carry on a debate started with Lahiri and Marslen-Wilson at LabPhon II; Holst and Nolan present work which builds on that presented by Nolan at the same meeting; and Lee tests a suggestion put forward by Goldstein in his commentary on McCarthy's LabPhon III contribution.

Introduction

References

de Jong, K. J., M. E. Beckman & J. R. Edwards. 1993. The interplay between prosodic structure and coarticulation. *Language and Speech* 36: 197–212.

Gussenhoven, C. 1991. The English Rhythm Rule as an accent deletion rule. *Phonology* 8: 1–35.

Keating, P. A. 1988. Underspecification in phonetics. *Phonology* 5: 275–292.

Maddieson, I. & K. Precoda. 1992. Syllable structure and phonetic models. *Phonology* 9: 45–60.

Trigo, L. 1991. On pharynx–larynx interactions. *Phonology* 8: 113–136.

Zsiga, E. C. 1994. Acoustic evidence for gestural overlap in consonant sequences. *Journal of Phonetics* 22: 121–140.

Part I
Features and Perception

2
Intermediate properties in the perception of distinctive feature values

JOHN KINGSTON and RANDY L. DIEHL

2.1 Introduction

Any minimal contrast between speech sounds is conveyed by multiple acoustic differences, in part, because some articulations have more than one acoustic consequence, but also because some minimal contrasts are accomplished by multiple, covarying articulations, each with its own array of acoustic consequences. These facts raise two questions. First, how does the resulting array of acoustic properties get mapped into a specific distinctive feature value when a speech sound is identified by listeners? Second, how are the particular sets of covarying articulations that convey contrasting distinctive feature values selected by speakers?

Two kinds of answers have been offered to the first question. Some covarying acoustic properties may cohere perceptually because they have a common articulatory source, as has been suggested for the consequences of VOT differences by Lisker & Abramson (1970). Alternatively, acoustic properties may cohere because they have similar auditory effects (Diehl & Kluender, 1989; Diehl & Kingston, 1991; Kingston, 1991; Kingston & Diehl, 1994; Kingston & Macmillan, submitted); the experiments reported here explore this second possibility. These experiments also test a possible answer to the second question, that speakers covary articulations precisely because their acoustic consequences are auditorily similar enough to be integrated into more comprehensive perceptual properties, intermediate between the acoustic properties and distinctive feature values.

As Nearey observes in the following commentary, the experiments we report here are thus motivated by a "strong auditorist" perspective, in that we seek to demonstrate strong, i.e., robust and transparent, relations between the listeners' auditory experience and the symbolic phonological representation of utterances. As he also observes, our perspective is not "double-strong," in that we doubt that the phonological representation constructed by the listener is strongly related to the speaker's articulations, i.e., we reject the "strong gesturalist" perspective, either in its motor-theoretic or direct-realist versions. From the strong gesturalist perspective, perceptual integration of acoustic properties occurs only when they share an articulatory source.

To exclude such an explanation for the particular cases we consider, as well as the possibility that the acoustic properties integrate simply because listeners have a great deal of experience with their covariation in speech, we used nonspeech analogues of speech sounds. The acoustic properties of these stimuli were covaried in ways that mimic their covariation in speech sounds. Because these stimuli nonetheless do not sound like speech,[1] any perceptual integration of their acoustic properties cannot arise from attributing their covariation to their common articulatory origin – in nonspeech sounds there is no articulatory origin to which such an attribution can be made. Nor, since the stimuli are novel, can listeners have had any experience with the covariation of their properties. Thus, any perceptual integration that occurs must arise from auditory processes not specific to speech.[2]

2.2 The C:V duration ratio and low frequency property

This paper focuses on perceptual interactions among some of the principal acoustic properties of the [voice] contrast in intervocalic stops. Acoustically, a [+voice] stop differs from a [–voice] stop in this context in having: more low-frequency periodic energy in the period in a shorter interval of low-passed, attenuated energy (corresponding to the oral closure), more low-frequency periodic energy in this interval, a lower first formant frequency (F_1) and fundamental frequency (F_0) at the edges of flanking vowels, a shorter VOT into the following vowel, and a longer preceding vowel (Lisker, 1986).[3] These properties apparently integrate into at least two intermediate perceptual properties: the *C(onsonant):V(owel) duration ratio* and *low frequency property*.

Kohler (1979) and Port & Dalby (1982) have shown that the ratio of consonant duration to preceding vowel duration is the principal temporal cue to the intervocalic [voice] distinction, with smaller ratios specifying [+voice] consonants (cf. Massaro & Cohen, 1983). The *low frequency property* was first identified by Stevens & Blumstein (1981), who, on the basis of Lisker & Abramson's (1964) results, suggested that [+voice], but not [–voice], consonants, are characterized by the "presence of low-frequency spectral energy or periodicity over a time interval of 20–30 ms in the vicinity of the acoustic discontinuity that precedes or follows the consonantal constriction interval" (p. 29). As Stevens and Blumstein pointed out, the *low frequency property* can be analyzed into at least three different acoustic properties, voicing during or shortly after the consonant constriction interval, and a low F_0 and F_1 at the edges of vowels next to that interval. Each has been found to cue or enhance the perception of the [+voice] category (Fujimura, 1971; Stevens & Klatt, 1974; Lisker, 1975, 1986). Three non speech-analogue experiments are described next which show how the covarying acoustic properties listed above are integrated into intermediate perceptual properties.

2.3 Experiments

2.3.1 Parker, Diehl & Kluender (1986): The effect of voicing on perceived closure duration

Lisker (1957) showed that variation in closure duration is sufficient to signal the distinction between intervocalic [+voice] and [−voice] consonants. Later (1986), he found that closure voicing yields an increase in [+voice] identification responses, even for very long closure durations. Parker, Diehl & Kluender (1986) combined Lisker's two manipulations, using two /aba/ –/apa/ stimulus series in which consonant closure duration and closure voicing were varied orthogonally. Variation in closure duration proved to be sufficient to cue the /b/–/p/ distinction, and closure voicing shifted the crossover from /b/ to /p/ judgments toward longer closure durations, i.e., more [+voice] responses.

The boundary shift caused by closure voicing is, of course, predicted by its contribution to the *low frequency property* characteristic of [+voice] consonants. However, Parker *et al.* hypothesized that closure voicing has another effect as well; namely, it reduces the perceived closure duration, which, by reducing the *C:V duration ratio*, will make the stimulus appear even more strongly [+voice]. To uncover the origin of this ratio, Parker *et al.* also prepared several paired sets of nonspeech stimuli that mimicked the /aba/–/apa/ stimuli in both the variation in closure duration and closure voicing.

The vowel analogues in the nonspeech stimuli were two square waves, whose envelopes had the same durations and peak amplitudes as the vowels of the /aba/–/apa/ stimuli. Between the square-wave segments were gaps whose duration was varied incrementally from 20 to 120 ms; in one series the gaps were silent, as in the speech stimuli without closure voicing, and in the other, the gaps contained up to 60 ms of the same laryngeal pulsing as the speech stimuli with closure voicing. The F_0 of the square waves was either fixed, C(onstant), fell before and rose after the gap, F(alling) R(ising), or rose before and fell after the gap, R(ising) F(alling). For each of the three nonspeech spectral conditions, listeners identified both the Pulsing and the No Pulsing series according to whether the gap was short or long.

Gap pulsing shifted the boundary significantly in the same direction as for the /aba/ –/apa/ stimuli, but only about one third the magnitude, and only in the FR condition. The relatively larger boundary shift in the /aba/–/apa/ condition can be explained if voicing contributes to the *low frequency property* over and above its enhancement of the *C:V duration ratio* difference by making brief closures seem even shorter. For the square-wave stimuli, gap pulsing only shortens the perceived gap duration, because the nonspeech categories were defined on the basis of gap duration alone and were uncorrelated with the presence or absence of pulsing. That gap pulsing shifted the boundary only in the FR condition may reflect the fact that only this spectral pattern makes the pulsing approximately continuous spectrally with the flanking vowel-like sounds. Spectral continuity might be necessary for gap pulsing to be perceptually integrated with flanking square waves (Bregman & Dannenbring, 1973).

If spectral continuity is also required in speech stimuli for voicing to shorten the perceived duration of a stop closure, then it can be asked whether F_0, F_1, or both create the necessary continuity, because both source and resonance characteristics fall before and rise after closures containing voicing. The following experiments attempted to tease apart and measure the contributions of the F_0 and F_1 contours to spectral continuity between flanking vowels and closure voicing.

2.3.2 Kingston, Diehl, Kluender & Parker (1990): Contributions of F_0 and F_1 to spectral continuity

2.3.2.1 Methods, stimulus parameters, and procedures
Kingston, Diehl, Kluender & Parker's (1990) stimuli were synthesized to mimic a vowel–stop–vowel sequence in the form of two single-formant vowel analogues separated by a gap. Like the square-wave stimuli used by Parker *et al.*, these stimuli also did not sound like speech. Away from the gap, the frequency of F_1 was 500 Hz and F_0 was 125 Hz. Both F_0 and F_1 either remained constant before and after the gap, or they fell or rose linearly (over 55 ms), in mirror image fashion, as illustrated in Figure 2.1. The change in F_1 was 250 Hz up or down, to 750 or 250 Hz, and the change in F_0 was 25 Hz up or down, to 150 or 100 Hz.

The gap between the two single formant sequences was again varied between 20 and 120 ms.[4] The gap contained either silence (NP) or 100 Hz pulsing (P) for up to the first 60 ms of its duration. Each of nine listeners made 12 judgments of whether a given gap duration was short or long in each of the 18 combinations of F_1, F_0, and Pulsing conditions.

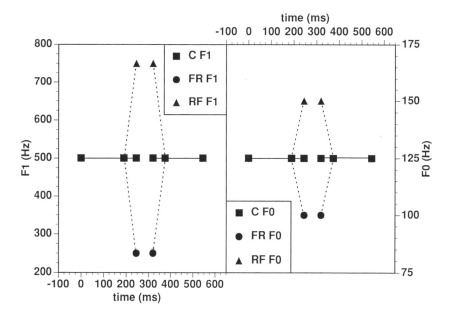

Figure 2.1. Patterns of spectral change in F_1 (a) and F_0 (b) in the one-formant vowel analogues flanking the gap in Kingston *et al.*'s (1990) stimuli. Solid lines represent the Constant F_1 or F_0 stimuli (C), and dashed lines represent Rising–Falling (RF) or Falling–Rising (FR) stimuli.

2.3.2.2 *Results*

Repeated measures analyses of variance were performed on the overall percentage of short gap responses across the entire gap duration continuum.[5] Although more stimuli were judged to have short gaps when pulsing was present than when it was not, this difference was not statistically significant. As Figure 2.2a shows,[6] the effect of pulsing was small, and only present for the shorter closures.

Of the two spectral pattern variables, only F_1 pattern was statistically significant (F (2,16) = 44.84, $p < 0.0001$), reflecting fewer short gap responses (mean = 39%) for FR F_1 than C (45%) or RF (47%) F_1. As Figure 2.2b shows, a FR F_1 induces fewer short gap responses across nearly the entire range of gap durations, while a RF F_1 yields more short gap responses than C F_1 only for longer gaps (> 60 ms). F_0 pattern, on the other hand, did not significantly affect total percent short gap responses; Figure 2.2c shows that F_0 did not affect gap duration judgments at any duration.

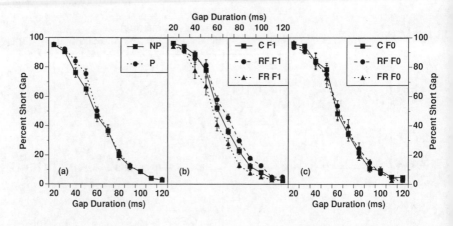

Figure 2.2. (a) Mean (across listeners) identification functions for stimuli with No Pulsing (squares, solid line) vs. Pulsing (circles, dashed line), with standard errors, (b) for stimuli with Constant (squares), Rising–Falling (circles), and Falling–Rising (triangles) F_1 patterns, and (c) for stimuli with Constant (squares), Rising–Falling (circles), and Falling–Rising (triangles) F_0 patterns.

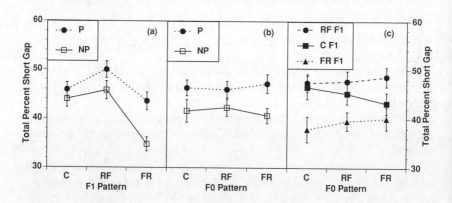

Figure 2.3. (a) Mean total percent short gap judgments with standard errors for Pulsing (circles) vs. No Pulsing (squares) stimuli with Constant, Rising–Falling, and Falling–Rising F_1 patterns; (b) for P vs. NP stimuli with C, RF, and FR F_0 patterns; and (c) for C, RF, and FR F_0 patterns and with RF (circles), C (squares), and FR (triangles) F_1 patterns.

12

More interesting than these main effects for determining whether F_1 or F_0 affects spectral continuity, however, were the interactions between F_1 or F_0 patterns and pulsing. The only interaction that reached significance was that between pulsing and F_1 pattern (F (2,16) = 3.66, $p < 0.05$), reflecting the fact that pulsing had a noticeably larger effect on the percentage of short gap responses with a FR F_1 than either a C or RF F_1. Figure 2.3a shows that the FR F_1 pattern actually had two effects: it induced fewer short gap responses to both Pulsing and No Pulsing stimuli, and it induced a more noticeable difference between Pulsing and No Pulsing stimuli than the other F_1 patterns. No similar interaction was observed between F_0 and Pulsing (Figure 2.3b), nor between F_1 and F_0 (Figure 2.3c).

2.3.2.3 Discussion
We had hypothesized that in Parker *et al.*'s (1986) experiment, pulsing affected perceived gap duration only with FR F_0 in the square-wave vowel analogues because this spectral change made gap pulsing approximately continuous spectrally with the flanking square waves and that spectral continuity is essential if pulsing is to be considered by listeners to be part of the same signal as the flanking square waves. The results with the single-formant stimuli suggest that any analogous spectral continuity effect in speech sounds probably arises from a FR F_1 rather than a FR F_0. This interpretation is compatible with Parker *et al.*'s results if it is spectral change in the square waves' higher harmonics, not their F_0 *per se*, that produced the spectral continuity effect in their stimuli.

The results of these two experiments demonstrate several ways in which acoustic correlates of the [+voice] stops contribute to a single, integrated perceptual property, a *C:V duration ratio* that is perceived as small. Brief closures and long preceding vowels are obviously the primary building blocks of this integrated property, but the presence of closure voicing in the context of a relatively low F_1 at the edges of flanking vowels enhances the perceived shortness of the closure and hence reduces the perceived ratio.

Complementary evidence of an effect of consonant voicing on the perceived *C:V duration ratio* was reported by Javkin (1976). When listeners were asked to vary the duration of a tone to match that of a vowel, the presence of voicing in the following consonant yielded reliably longer adjustments of the tone's duration. Thus, independent of its contribution to the *low frequency property*, voicing further enhances the distinctiveness of [+voice] by reducing the perceived *C:V duration ratio* in two ways: by shortening the apparent duration of the consonant and by lengthening the apparent duration of the vowel.

The persistence of voicing well into [+voice] closures as well as early voice onset after them could also ensure that listeners perceive spectral continuity from flanking vowels into [+voice] closures by preventing F_1 from being canceled by a subglottal antiresonance before the mouth is completely closed.

The resulting FR F_1 flanking [+voice] stops in turn allows closure voicing to be integrated with the rest of the signal, and thereby to reduce the $C:V$ *duration ratio*.

In his commentary, Nearey observes that one of our results undermines our interpretation of a FR F_1's perceptual value: that independent of Pulsing a FR F_1 makes a listener more likely to judge a gap of a given duration as longer than the other F_1 patterns do. He furthermore suggests that the presence of Pulsing "merely undoes the damage to gap duration done by the FR pattern in F_1" by shortening the perceived gap duration as much as do the other F_1 patterns without the aid of Pulsing. However, we do not claim that a FR F_1 will shorten perceived gap duration by itself, but only that it allows the presence of Pulsing to shorten perceived gap duration by making Pulsing in the gap spectrally continuous with flanking vowel analogues. Our experiments were designed to test whether it is necessary that these two properties integrate perceptually for them to affect perceived gap duration in a way that would explain why speakers should find it useful to covary the articulations that produce them. In this, we were successful. The "illusion" which listeners can perceive with a FR F_1 is that Pulsing belongs to the same signal as the flanking vowel analogues, and as such may (partially) fill the gap between them, shortening its perceived duration.

Because the listeners in both Parker *et al.*'s and Kingston *et al.*'s experiments judged gap durations, these experiments could not reveal anything about how F_0, F_1, or Pulsing might contribute to the atemporal *low frequency property*. (For other nonspeech analogue evidence that F_1's frequency contributes to the low frequency property, see Parker, 1988.) The experiments presented in the next section were accordingly designed to draw listeners' attention to spectral rather than temporal stimulus properties.

2.3.3 The integration of F_1 and F_0 with gap pulsing

2.3.3.1 Symmetry in the assessment of perceptual interactions
All the experiments described above use the trading relations paradigm. In this paradigm, identification functions for one dimension are measured for two or more values of another. If the functions shift with respect to the dimension of judgment, the dimensions are said to "trade"; the interpretation usually given is that a single psychological dimension reflects the contributions of each of the two physical variables (see Repp, 1982, 1983, for fuller discussion). There are two difficulties related with the typical use of this paradigm, however.

First, the two stimulus dimensions are usually treated asymmetrically. One dimension is varied incrementally across a range broad enough to cause listeners to hear more than one phonetic category, while the other dimension is varied only enough to shift category boundaries with respect to the incrementally

14

varied dimension. Second, the boundary shifts are only one aspect of how one of the stimulus dimensions may affect the perception of the other; they reflect a change in the listeners' willingness to use one response rather than the other, i.e., a change in response bias. But the secondary dimension could also affect the listeners' ability to detect differences in the primary dimension, i.e., it could change sensitivity independently of bias. Sensitivity changes are occasionally (e.g. by Best, Morrongiello & Robson, 1981, and Best, Studdert-Kennedy, Manuel & Rubin-Spitz, 1989) but too rarely assessed in use of the trading relations paradigm, but such assessments require looking at the slope of identification functions – which requires assumptions about their shapes or taking the additional time to run discrimination as well as identification tasks.

The experiments described in this section avoid these difficulties by using an adaptation (Kingston & Macmillan, submitted) of a paradigm codified by Garner (1974), in which listeners' ability to classify stimuli differing along two dimensions is assessed symmetrically (cf. Wood, 1974; Eimas, Tartter & Miller, 1981; Green & Kuhl, 1991; Kingston, 1991). This paradigm was designed to distinguish between a case where a stimulus's perceptual value on one dimension does not depend on its value on the other (perceptual *separability*) from the case where it does (perceptual *integrality*). So long as accuracy is used as the dependent measure, detection theory methods can be applied directly to results obtained with this paradigm, allowing independent assessment of sensitivity and bias.

Two experiments were run using this paradigm: one examined the perceptual integration of F_0 at the edge of flanking vowel analogues with pulsing in the intervening gap, the other the integration of F_1 with pulsing. As four out of ten listeners performed at chance on many of the classifications in the F_0 by Pulsing experiment, its results will not be discussed further here.

2.3.3.2 The adapted Garner paradigm
In this adapted Garner paradigm, a 2×2 stimulus array was constructed by varying two stimulus dimensions orthogonally, as in Figure 2.4a, and listeners were required to classify stimuli from various two-item subsets of the array.

A single stimulus was presented on each trial, and the listeners chose one of two responses. Examples of the two tasks are illustrated in Figure 2.4c, e.

(1) In *baseline* conditions, the two possible stimuli differed along just one dimension. There were four such tasks: A_0 vs. C_0 and B_0 vs. D_0 for classification by F_1, and A_0 vs. B_0 and C_0 vs. D_0 for classification by Pulsing (see below for discussion of subscripts). Figure 2.4c illustrates a Pulsing classification in which stimulus A_0 (filled square) is to be classified differently from stimulus B_0 (open square).

(2) In *correlated* tasks, listeners were presented with the two stimuli from the opposite corners of the array, B_0 vs. C_0 or A_0 vs. D_0. The values of the stimuli

on the two dimensions were either positively (B_0 vs. C_0) or negatively (A_0 vs. D_0) correlated. Figure 2.4e illustrates the positively correlated task, B_0 (filled square) vs. C_0 (open square).

For each classification task, listeners heard 32 randomized practice trials with feedback, followed by 80 randomized test trials, also with feedback, with each of the two stimuli presented equally often.

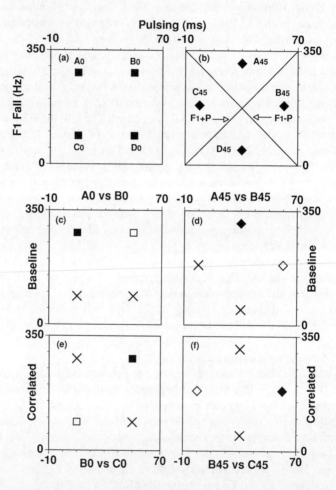

Figure 2.4. The 2 × 2 arrays of stimuli in a space defined by F_1 (vertical axis) and Pulsing (horizontal axis): (a) 0° rotation; (b) 45° rotation. Stimulus and response arrangements for the two classification tasks employed in the Garner paradigm experiments: (c, d) baseline; (e, f) correlated; (c, e) 0° rotation; (d, f) 45° rotations. Filled and open squares (or diamonds) indicate stimuli to which distinct responses must be given; ×s indicate stimuli not used in a particular task.

2.3.3.3 Stimuli

The stimuli in these experiments closely resembled those employed by Kingston *et al.* (1990), in that they consisted of a gap between two single formant vowel analogues, but with one essential difference. The duration of the gap was fixed, at 75 ms, a value slightly longer than the mean identification boundary between short and long judgments obtained by Kingston *et al.*

Each stimulus parameter was varied orthogonally and its two values were chosen so as to be just barely discriminable; Figure 2.4a shows that a substantial interval (B_0 and D_0) vs. the (near) absence (A_0 and C_0) of Pulsing was combined with a contrast between a (nearly) Constant (C_0 and D_0) vs. Falling–Rising (A_0 and B_0) F_1 contour. The positively correlated stimuli B_0 and C_0 thus combine values for the stimulus dimensions as in naturally occurring [+voice] and [−voice] stops, respectively. Accordingly, if the naturally occurring covariation between these dimensions is mutually enhancing, then the positively correlated stimuli should be easier to classify than the negatively correlated stimuli, A_0 and D_0, whose combinations of values are potentially contradictory.

Figure 2.4b shows values for Pulsing duration and the size of the F_1 fall for a 2×2 array obtained by rotating the original array $45°$ in the space defined by the two stimulus dimensions. Stimuli in the rotated array maintain the same Euclidean distances as at $0°$, as well as differing along axes parallel to those at $0°$. Figure 2.4d illustrates a "baseline" task in which A_{45} and B_{45} have to be separately classified, while Figure 2.4f illustrates a "correlated" task in which B_{45} and C_{45} have to be. Note that at $45°$ the stimuli in the correlated tasks no longer display a correlation between dimensions, but differ on just one stimulus dimension, while those in the baseline tasks now differ on both dimensions.

There are two advantages to having listeners classify stimuli at both rotations. First, the stimulus space is systematically sampled more densely. Second, listeners' responses to the $45°$ rotation provide two tests of the models we develop for their responses to the $0°$ rotation.

The first is a consistency test, obtained by interpolating performance between the two rotations. Interpolation is guided by a simple geometric observation: that the correlated stimuli at $45°$ differ along axes parallel to those along which the baseline stimuli at $0°$ differ and vice versa: in Pulsing (P), C_{45} vs. B_{45} parallels A_0 vs. B_0 and C_0 vs. D_0; in F_1 fall (F_1), A_{45} vs. D_{45} parallels A_0 vs. C_0 and B_0 vs. D_0; in the difference between F_1 fall and Pulsing (F_1–P), A_{45} vs. B_{45} and C_{45} vs. D_{45} parallel A_0 vs. D_0; and in the sum of F_1 fall and Pulsing (F_1+P), A_{45} vs. C_{45} and B_{45} vs. D_{45} parallel B_0 vs. C_0. If our listeners use the same decision space for the $45°$ as the $0°$ rotation, it should be possible to predict the classification of the $45°$ stimuli and their geometric arrangement in the decision space from our models of the $0°$ stimuli.

The second test employs a more sophisticated model of our listeners' performance, in which the two-dimensional stimulus space is mapped onto a two-dimensional *decision space*. This model allows us to try to predict quantitatively performance with a rotated array, via bilinear transformation of performance at another, unrotated array, regardless of whether the stimulus dimensions are integral or separable.

This second test also allows us to test whether any stimulus dimensions are perceptually *primary*. Melara & Marks (1990) have recently argued that even if stimulus dimensions are integral, they may nonetheless be detectable in the stimuli and their values used by listeners to classify the stimuli. If F_1 and P are primary dimensions in this sense, then listeners should classify the stimuli more reliably when they are aligned with these dimensions, i.e., at $0°$, than when they are rotated to $45°$. On the other hand, if performance is quantitatively predicted between rotations by the bilinear transformations, then it is unnecessary to assume that any dimensions of the stimuli are perceptually more primary than any others. (For further discussion of the effects of rotation see Kingston & Macmillan, submitted.)

Both the motor and direct realist theories of speech perception predict that acoustic properties of the [voice] contrast which have independent articulatory origins should be perceptually primary. Primacy is neither expected nor necessary in auditory enhancement theory, because the speaker opportunistically combines articulations whose acoustic consequences are similar enough auditorily that they will integrate in the listener's perception of the sounds uttered and thus exaggerate the differences between contrasting sounds. F_1's frequency at the edge of a vowel flanking a stop depends on when vocal fold vibration begins or ends relative to the closing and opening of the mouth: the earlier it begins or the later it ends, the lower F_1 will be. As F_1's onset or offset frequencies have the same articulatory origin as low-frequency periodicity in the transition between vowel and consonant, the motor theory and direct realism both predict that they should be integral and nonprimary during these transitions (see Kluender, 1991, for relevant discussion). However, because the speaker need not maintain the vibration into the closure nor begin it before the release in order to lower F_1 at the edges of flanking vowels, the presence of voicing in the closure itself, rather than the flanking transitions, is articulatorily independent of F_1 onset or offset frequency, and closure voicing and F_1 offset–onset frequencies are therefore predicted by both motor theory and direct realism but not auditory enhancement theory to be perceptually primary.

2.3.3.4 Results
We used recently developed detection theory methods to analyze the effects of manipulating stimulus dimensions and tasks on classification accuracy in classifying them (Kingston & Macmillan, submitted). Detection theory estimates the same performance measure, d', from each of the classification

Table 2.1 Mean ds (standard errors) across listeners for the F_1 by Pulsing experiment by rotation, with summary means for parallel baseline tasks, task types, and rotations.

Task/Stimuli			Rotation		
	Axis	0°	45°	Axis	
Baseline					
A vs. B		0.51 (0.28)	1.44 (0.42)		
C vs. D		0.94 (0.30)	2.82 (0.39)		
	P mean	0.73 (0.29)	2.13 (0.33)	F_1–P mean	
A vs. C		2.68 (0.53)	1.12 (0.38)		
B vs. D		3.22 (0.35)	2.48 (0.51)		
	F_1 mean	2.95 (0.39)	1.80 (0.42)	F_1+P mean	
Baseline mean		1.84 (0.26)	2.30 (0.22)		
Correlated					
B vs. C F_1+P		3.66 (0.39)	0.95 (0.48)	P	
A vs. D F_m–P		2.79 (0.25)	3.48 (0.47)	F_1	
Correlated mean		3.22 (0.25)	2.21 (0.44)		
Rotation mean		2.30 (0.21)	2.27 (0.21)		

tasks of this paradigm and thus allows us to quantify any differences in performance.

Table 2.1 lists mean d's calculated across listeners for each task, axis, and rotation. For the 0° array, the names of the tasks make sense, in that the stimuli's values differ along just one dimension in the baseline tasks and their values are correlated in the correlated task. As the task names do not make similar sense with the 45° rotation, we henceforth refer to the axes along which stimuli differ rather than the task names. Repeated measures analyses of variance revealed a highly significant effect of the axis along which the stimuli differed: P, F_1, F_1+P, and F_1–P correlated, for each rotation (0°: $F(3, 27) = 24.42$, $p < 0.0001$; 45°: $F(3, 27) = 11.65$, $p < 0.0001$). Across rotations, the stimuli differing along the F_1 axis (A_0 vs. C_0, B_0 vs. D_0, A_{45} vs. D_{45}) were markedly easier to classify than those differing along the Pulsing axis (A_0 vs. B_0, C_0 vs. D_0, B_{45} vs. C_{45}).

At 0°, the stimuli differing along the F_1+P axis (B_0 vs. C_0) were much easier to classify than those differing along the F_1–P axis (A_0 vs. D_0), but at 45°, it is

19

the stimuli differing along the F_1–P axis (A_{45} vs. B_{45} and C_{45} vs. D_{45}) that are (slightly) easier to classify.

Our models assume that the observer's decision space, like the stimulus space, has two dimensions. The decision space is partitioned by the observer into regions corresponding to the possible responses, defined by the mean and variance of the perceived location of each stimulus in that space. Reliability in classifying the members of any pair of stimuli depends on the distance d' between the means of the corresponding distributions, i.e., it is expressed in units of their standard deviation. Because various sources of noise produce trial-to-trial variability on both coordinates, stimuli's perceptual values with respect to the two dimensions form bivariate distributions of response likelihood, as shown in Figure 2.5a.

Figure 2.5b provides a two-dimensional, aerial perspective on the decision space of Figure 2.5a. The means of the distributions are represented as points and contours of equal likelihood as circles (the correct shape, for any likelihood value, if the distributions are equal-variance bivariate normal). When, as in this hypothetical case, the means define a rectangle in the decision space, the perceptual value of a stimulus on one dimension does not depend on its value on the other, and the dimensions are separable. In Figure 2.5c, the means of the distributions are no longer arranged orthogonally, and the value of a stimulus on one dimension *does* depend on its value on the other. Following Kingston & Macmillan (submitted), we call this "mean-integrality."

To apply detection theory, we first estimate the spatial arrangement of the four distributions separately from the baseline and correlated tasks. These estimates indicate whether the stimulus dimensions are integral or separable. The extent to which the two estimates predict the same spatial arrangement of the distribution means also serves to test the model. The difference between the estimates is expressed as rms error, and is a measure of what the models do not explain about our listeners' performance.

The choice between the two arrangements in Figure 2.5b, c is determined by whether listeners are equally accurate on the two correlated tasks: if they are, the spatial arrangement of distributions is rectangular and the dimensions are separable; unequal accuracy, on the other hand, suggests a mean-integral arrangement, as in Figure 2.5c. Our measure of mean-integrality is the angle *CAB* (see the inset in Figure 2.5c), henceforth θ, which indicates mean-integrality to the extent that it differs from 90°. The angle θ was determined by fitting a parallelogram whose length is equal to baseline d'(P) and whose height is equal to baseline d'(F_1), and then iteration was used to find the parallelogram whose diagonals best fit the correlated d' values. The extent to which the correlated data fit the baseline-determined parallelogram is a test of the model.

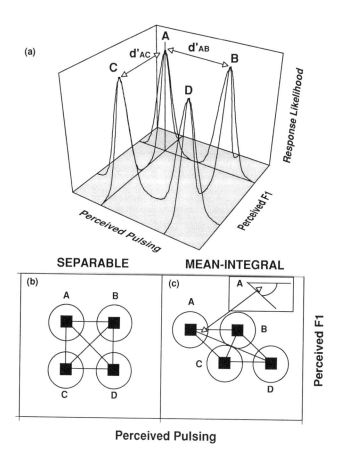

Figure 2.5. (a) Response likelihood distributions for the four stimuli of the 2 × 2 array, arranged in a two-dimensional decision space (the plane of the figure). (b) and (c) Aerial views of the decision space in Figure 2.5a. Points represent the means of the response likelihood distributions, circles equal-likelihood contours: (b) perceptually separable stimuli; (c) mean-integral stimuli. The value of the angle CAB (θ) in the inset Figure 2.5c is the measure of mean-integrality.

Figure 2.6a shows the results of this analysis at $0°$. The θ of $125°$ is noticeably larger than $90°$, because the positively correlated stimuli B_0 and C_0 (F_1+P axis) were classified much more easily than the negatively correlated stimuli A_0 and D_0 ($F_1–P$ axis). This is the result predicted if a FR F_1 and Pulsing in the gap both enhance the perception of the *low frequency property*. The rms error between the two estimates of means of the response likelihood distributions is 0.211, indicating a reasonably good fit.

21

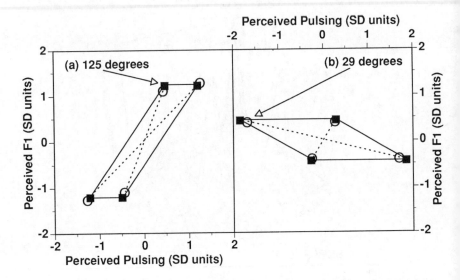

Figure 2.6. Parallelograms modeling relative locations of the means of the response likelihood distributions. The lengths of the sides equal the average of parallel baseline d's. The filled squares represent the means calculated from observed baseline performance; the open circles from observed correlated performance. (a) F_1 by Pulsing, 0°; (b) F_1 by Pulsing, 45°. Values of θ are listed for each rotation.

This figure also shows that stimuli differing in F_1 are more easily classified than stimuli differing in Pulsing. This difference can also be observed in the parallelogram representing listeners' responses to the 45° rotation (Figure 2.6b), where the diagonal representing the perceptual distance between stimuli differing in F_1 (A_{45} vs. D_{45}) is noticeably longer than that representing the perceptual distance between stimuli differing in Pulsing (B_{45} vs. C_{45}). As a result, the θ of 29° obtained at this rotation was markedly smaller than 90°.

There is one clear discrepancy in performance between the two rotations. At 0°, stimuli differing along the F_1+P axis, B_0 vs. C_0, were more easily classified than stimuli differing along the F_1-P axis, A_0 vs. D_0. However, at 45°, this inequality was just barely reversed, with the stimuli differing along the F_1-P axis, (A_{45} and C_{45} vs. B_{45} and D_{45}) classified slightly better than those along the F_1+P axis (A_{45} and B_{45} vs. C_{45} and D_{45}).

Despite this discrepancy, performance on one rotation can largely be predicted from performance on the other, as shown by two methods in the next two sections, interpolation and bilinear transformation.

2.3.3.5 Interpolation

If the stimuli from the two rotations are mapped onto the same decision space, then the classification of any pair of stimuli at one rotation should be interpolatable from the classification of stimuli differing along a parallel axis at the other. By the Pythagorean theorem, the physical difference between the stimuli in any correlated task is $\sqrt{2}$ greater than that between the stimuli in any baseline task, so average parallel baseline performance at $45°$ should equal parallel correlated performance at $0°$ after dividing by $\sqrt{2}$, and vice versa (compare Figure 2.4b with 2.4a). Because the interpolation involves dividing by a constant, these predictions are parameter-free. The discrepancies obtained in predicting baseline performance at one rotation from observed correlated performance (divided by $\sqrt{2}$) at the other were modest: rms error in d' units is 0.47 and in $p(c)_{max}$ units 0.05, though F_1+P performance at $45°$ is noticeably worse than predicted and F_1 performance at $0°$ noticeably better.

2.3.3.6 Bilinear transformation

As noted above, besides testing our models of listeners' performance, rotation also tests whether some stimulus dimensions are perceptually primary. We can use the parallelogram for performance at $0°$ to predict quantitatively what performance at $45°$ should be if neither F_1 and P nor F_1+P and F_1-P are primary dimensions. Primacy can be inferred for the dimensions defining a rotation at which performance is markedly better than these predictions. Because we have demonstrated that F_1 and P are mean-integral rather than separable, we assume that the stimulus-perception transformation is *bilinear*, that is, that each perceptual dimension is a linear function of both stimulus dimensions rather than each perceptual dimension being a function of just one of the stimulus dimensions:

(1) $x_p = ax_s + by_s$
(2) $y_p = cx_s + dy_s$

In these equations, (x_s, y_s) is the location of a point in the stimulus space, and (x_p, y_p) is the corresponding distribution mean in the decision space. Predicted mean baseline d's at $45°$ are reasonably close to observed values: F_1-P, predicted $= 1.84$, and observed $d' = 2.42$; F_1+P, predicted $d' = 2.42$ and observed $d' = 1.80$; rms error $= 0.49$ in d' units or 0.06 in $p(c)_{max}$ units. The predicted θ of $23°$ is also quite close to the observed value of $29°$. The success of this prediction suggests that our listeners did employ the same decision space in classifying stimuli from both rotations, and that neither rotation corresponds to perceptually primary dimensions.

John Kingston and Randy L. Diehl

2.3.3.7 Discussion

The results obtained with this adaptation of the Garner paradigm extend those obtained with the trading relations paradigm by Kingston *et al.* (1990) in three ways. First, they show that F_1's offset frequency contributes to the perception of the *low frequency property* as well as the *C:V duration ratio*. Second, they show that when F_1 and Pulsing covary in the way they do in naturally occurring [+voice] and [−voice] intervocalic stops, the stimuli are more easily classified. That is, a covariation which makes stimuli have high or low values for the *low frequency property* enhances the [voice] contrast. Finally, neither F_1 nor Pulsing appears to be a perceptually primary property of the stimuli, despite their being products of independent articulations.

2.4 Conclusion

The results of Parker *et al.*'s (1986) and Kingston *et al.*'s (1990) trading relations experiments show that closure duration, closure voicing, and F_1 offset frequency all contribute to the perception of the *C:V duration ratio*, but F_0 offset frequency does not. The results of the last pair of experiments show that F_1 offset frequency and gap pulsing also contribute to the low frequency property, but the role of F_0 remains unclear because our listeners had difficulty classifying stimuli differing by the amounts used.

The adapted Garner paradigm is a very strong test of the claim that certain acoustic correlates of a phonological distinction are integrated into perceptual properties that enhance contrasts (Diehl & Kluender, 1989), because it assesses the effects of varying one dimension on listeners' sensitivity to differences along another. Two results, that F_1 and Pulsing are mean-integral in the enhancing direction and that neither acoustic property is perceptually primary, support the hypothesis that acoustic properties are encoded into intermediate perceptual properties in the process whereby the listener determines what value a sound has for a distinctive feature.

Nearey presents results in the following commentary which show that these F_1 and Pulsing each remain accessible to listeners. These results do not conflict with ours, because we showed that two properties were partially rather than completely integral ($\theta = 125°$ not $180°$). We would also not expect any acoustic property to be preempted perceptually by its contribution to an intermediate perceptual property, because acoustic properties may contribute to more than a single perceptual property, as F_1 has been shown to do by the results of the experiments described in this paper.

24

Notes

1 In this respect, our nonspeech analogues differ conspicuously from the sine wave analogues employed by Best, Morrongiello & Robson (1981) and Best, Studdert-Kennedy, Manuel & Rubin-Spitz (1989), which could be heard as speech or nonspeech, depending on the listener or instructions (cf. also, Repp, 1983).

2 Listeners from other species integrate the acoustic properties of speech sounds much like human listeners do, even though nonhuman listeners cannot have evolved specific mechanisms for perceiving speech (Kuhl & Miller, 1978; Kluender, Diehl & Killeen, 1987; Kluender, 1991; Kluender & Lotto, 1994), and must rely on general auditory mechanisms that they already possess. Parsimony demands that we attribute humans' performance, with speech and nonspeech analogues, to similarly general mechanisms (Diehl & Kluender, 1989; Diehl, Walsh & Kluender, 1991; cf. Fowler, 1990, 1991).

3 For precision's sake, low-passed, low-frequency, periodic energy will be referred to below as "voicing" when it occurs in signals which are heard as speech, and as "pulsing" in nonspeech analogues. Similarly, "closure duration" will be used to refer to the duration of the interval of low-passed, attenuated energy in speech signals, and "gap duration" to its counterpart in nonspeech analogues.

4 To keep total stimulus duration constant, each 10 ms increase in gap duration was compensated by a 5 ms decrease of each of the flanking vowel analogues' steady states. We are indebted to Richard Fahey for pointing out that without this compensation, subjects could actually evaluate the stimuli with respect to their total duration rather than the duration of the gap alone.

5 ANOVAs on crossover points yielded the same results as the analyses of total percent short-gap judgments reported here.

6 The identification functions in Figure 2.2 make clear that listeners' gap duration judgments were quite categorical, a more speech-like result than has been obtained by some other experiments using nonspeech analogues (Best *et al.*, 1981, 1989). The slopes of the probit-transformed identification functions were also quite steep.

References

Best, C. T., B. Morrongiello & R. Robson. 1981. Perceptual equivalence of acoustic cues in speech and nonspeech perception. *Perception and Psychophysics* 29: 191–211.

Best, C. T., M. Studdert-Kennedy, S. Manuel & J. Rubin-Spitz. 1989. Discovering phonetic coherence in acoustic patterns. *Perception and Psychophysics* 45: 237–250.

Bregman, A. S. & G. L. Dannenbring. 1973. The effect of continuity on auditory stream segregation. *Perception and Psychophysics* 13: 308–312.

Diehl, R. L. & J. Kingston. 1991. Phonetic covariation as auditory enhancement: the case of the [+ voice]/[– voice] distinction. In O. Engstrand & C. Kylander (eds.), *Current*

John Kingston and Randy L. Diehl

Phonetic Research Paradigms: implications for Speech Motor Control, PERILUS 15. Stockholm: University of Stockholm, 139–143.

Diehl, R. L. & K. R. Kluender. 1989. On the objects of speech perception. *Ecological Psychology* 1: 121–144.

Diehl, R. L., M. A. Walsh & K. R. Kluender. 1991. On the interpretability of speech/nonspeech comparisons: a reply to Fowler. *Journal of the Acoustical Society of America* 89: 2905–2909.

Eimas, P. D., V. C. Tartter & J. L. Miller. 1981. Dependency relations during the processing of speech. In P. D. Eimas & J. L. Miller (eds.), *Perspectives on the Study of Speech*. Hillsdale, NJ: Lawrence Erlbaum Associates, 283–309.

Fowler, C. A. 1990. Sound-producing sources as the objects of perception: rate normalization and nonspeech perception. *Journal of the Acoustical Society of America* 88: 1236–1249.

Fowler, C.A. 1991. Auditory perception is not special: we see the world, we feel the world, we hear the world. *Journal of the Acoustical Society of America* 89: 2910–2915.

Fujimura, O. 1971. Remarks on stop consonants: synthesis experiments and acoustic cues. In L. Hammerich, R. Jakobson & E. Zwirner (eds.), *Form and Substance: Phonetic and Linguistic Papers Presented to Eli Fischer-Jørgensen*. Akademisk Vorlag, 221–232.

Garner, W. R. 1974. *The Processing of Information and Structure*. Hillsdale, NJ: Lawrence Erlbaum Associates.

Green, K. P. & P. K. Kuhl. 1991. Integral processing of visual place and auditory voicing information during phonetic perception. *Journal of Experimental Psychology: Human Perception and Performance* 17: 278–288.

Javkin, H. R. 1976. The perceptual basis of vowel duration differences associated with the voiced/voiceless distinction. *Report of the Phonology Laboratory* 1: 78–92. Berkeley, CA: University of California.

Kingston, J. 1991. Integrating articulations in the perception of vowel height. *Phonetica* 48: 149–179.

Kingston, J. & R. L. Diehl. 1994. Phonetic knowledge. *Language* 70: 419–454.

Kingston, J., R. L. Diehl, K. R. Kluender & E. M. Parker. 1990. Resonance versus source characteristics in perceiving spectral continuity between vowels and consonants. *Journal of the Acoustical Society of America* 88: S54–S55 (Abstract).

Kingston, J. & N. A. Macmillan. Submitted. Integrality of nasalization and F_1 in vowels in isolation and before oral and nasal consonants: a detection-theoretic application of Garner paradigm. *Journal of the Acoustical Society of America*.

Kluender, K. R. 1991. Effects of first formant onset properties on VOT judgments can be explained by auditory processes not specific to humans. *Journal of the Acoustical Society of America* 90: 83–96.

Kluender, K. R., R. L. Diehl & P. Killeen. 1987. Japanese quail can learn phonetic categories. *Science* 237: 1195–1197.

Kluender, K. R. & A. J. Lotto. 1994. Effects of first formant frequency on [voice] judgments result from auditory processes not specific to humans. *Journal of the Acoustical Society of America* 95: 1044–1053.

Kohler, K. 1979. Dimensions in the perception of fortis and lenis plosives. *Phonetica* 36: 332–343.

Kuhl, P. K. & J. D. Miller. 1978. Speech perception by the chinchilla: identification functions for synthetic VOT stimuli. *Journal of the Acoustical Society of America* 63: 905–917.

Lisker, L. 1957. Closure duration and the intervocalic voiced–voiceless distinctions in English. *Language* 33: 42–49.

Lisker, L. 1975. Is it VOT or a first formant transition detector? *Journal of the Acoustical Society of America* 57: 1547–1551.

Lisker, L. 1986. "Voicing" in English: a catalogue of acoustic features signaling /b/ versus /p/ in trochees. *Language and Speech* 29: 3–11.

Lisker, L. & A. S. Abramson. 1964. A cross-linguistic study of voicing in initial stops: acoustical measurements. *Word* 20: 384–422.

Lisker, L. & A. S. Abramson. 1970. The voicing dimension: some experiments on comparative phonetics. *Proceedings of the VIth International Congress of Phonetic Sciences*, Prague, 563–567.

Massaro, D. W. & M. M. Cohen. 1983. Consonant/vowel ratios: an improbable cue in speech. *Perception and Psychophysics* 33: 501–505.

Melara, R. D. & L. E. Marks. 1990. Perceptual primacy of dimensions: support for a model of dimensional interaction. *Journal of Experimental Psychology: Human Perception and Performance* 16: 398–414.

Parker, E. M. 1988. Auditory constraints on the perception of stop voicing: the influence of lower-tone frequency on judgments of tone-onset simultaneity. *Journal of the Acoustical Society of America* 83: 1597–1607.

Parker, E. M., R. L. Diehl & K. R. Kluender. 1986. Trading relations in speech and nonspeech. *Perception and Psychophysics* 39: 129–142.

Port, R. & J. Dalby. 1982. Consonant/vowel ratio as a cue for voicing in English. *Perception and Psychophysics* 32: 141–152.

Repp, B. H. 1982. Phonetic trading relations and context effects: new evidence for a phonetic mode of perception. *Psychological Bulletin* 92: 81–110.

Repp, B. H. 1983. Trading relations among acoustic cues in speech perception are largely a result of phonetic categorization. *Speech Communication* 2: 341–361.

Stevens, K. N. & S. E. Blumstein. 1981. The search for invariant acoustic correlates of phonetic features. In P. D. Eimas & J. L. Miller (eds.), *Perspectives on the Study of Speech*. Hillsdale, NJ: Lawrence Erlbaum Associates, 1–38.

Stevens, K. N. & D. H. Klatt. 1974. Role of formant transitions in the voiced-voiceless distinction for stops. *Journal of the Acoustical Society of America* 55: 653–659.

Wood, C. C. 1974. Parallel processing of auditory and phonetic information in speech discrimination. *Perception and Psychophysics* 15: 501–508.

3

A double-weak view of trading relations: comments on Kingston and Diehl

TERRANCE M. NEAREY*

3.1 Distinctive features and physical properties

Kingston and Diehl (hereafter, K&D) raise the controversial question of the relation of physical properties to phonological categories. I agree with many aspects of K&D's approach. Above all, I agree that categories can generally be specified as functions of acoustic properties *without specific reference to articulatory events* (Nearey, 1980, 1990). However, I have strong reservations about some of the specific claims made in their paper and my discussion will focus on these differences. I will evaluate aspects of K&D's work in light of a range of theoretical frameworks, including my own *double-weak* perspective (Nearey, 1992). While experimental evidence will be brought to bear on some specific issues with the usual technical detail, much of what I have to say is of a more speculative, philosophical character. For the sake of clarity, much of the discussion is relatively informal and incorporates several extended metaphors.

To situate K&D's approach within a range of other theories, consider first Figure 3.1 which is based on Lindau & Ladefoged's (1986) diagram of *"traditional feature theories,"* as exemplified by Stevens & Blumstein (1981). Characteristic of this account is the one-to-one relation of physical properties to distinctive features (hereafter, the term "feature" will be used exclusively to denote distinctive features in the usual sense), where each feature is associated with a *single universal property*. Features occupy *quantal* "sweet spots" in the articulatory-by-auditory space such that well-defined aspects of articulatory gestures map onto stable, distinctive auditory properties. Temporal–spectral discontinuities are critical for alignment but the properties themselves are essentially static. Finally, only a very limited role is admitted (Stevens & Blumstein, 1981: 34) for more temporally distributed contextual cues in speech perception, and much covariation observed in speech is treated as noise.

A double-weak view of trading relations

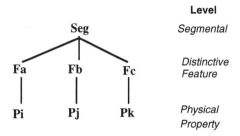

Figure 3.1. Relation of properties to distinctive features in traditional feature systems such as Stevens & Blumstein (1981). After Lindau & Ladefoged (1986).

This contrasts with Lindau & Ladefoged's own view (shown here in Figure 3.2), where relations between physical properties and features are *many-to-one* in both directions. Further, the mapping of properties to features is language-specific and the importance of quantal theory is challenged. In Lindau & Ladefoged's view, *both articulatory and acoustic* properties stand in such many-to-one relations to features. In other theories, the kind of relations between physical properties and features interacts with the nature of the physical properties in question.

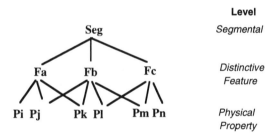

Figure 3.2. Relation of properties to distinctive features in Lindau & Ladefoged's view. After Lindau & Ladefoged (1986).

3.1.1 Strong and weak theories of the relations among domains

There are three domains of interest. One is discrete and *symbolic*, consisting of one or more layers of phonological elements, including features, segments, moras, syllables, etc. Following K&D, I will focus on features. The other two domains are quasi-continuous and physical: *gestural/articulatory* on the one hand and *auditory/acoustic* on the other. There are four distinct theoretical postures involving the relations between these three domains (Nearey, 1991,

29

1992). The first can be called *double strong*, exemplified by Stevens & Blumstein (1981); *strong* here implies a *simple, robust, transparent* relationship among elements. *Double-strong* theory postulates (i) strong relations between symbols and gestures, and (ii) strong relations between symbols and auditory properties.

The *strong gestural* position, exemplified by the motor theory (Liberman & Mattingly, 1985), accepts (i) but not (ii). Strong ties are postulated between symbols and gestures, but links between symbols and auditory properties are complex and indirect.

The *strong auditory* position, exemplified by K&D, postulates the opposite, i.e., (ii) but not (i). There are strong relations between symbols and auditory properties, but only complex and indirect links between symbols and gestures.

The *double-weak* position denies both (i) and (ii). Without constraints, this is too weak to be of interest. What I have proposed (Nearey, 1990, 1991, 1992) is a "fortified" double-weak theory that strives to approach the strong positions as closely as possible. Since even the double weak perspective holds them as philosophically attractive, though probably not empirically tenable, I will concentrate first on the strong positions.

Figure 3.3 illustrates the symmetry between articulation and audition in a double-strong theory (Stevens & Blumstein, 1981). Articulation is chosen so as to produce auditorily distinct output. However, such distinct output is selected only if the articulatory implementation is robust and quantal. The resulting "sweet spots," the universal features, are such that neither the auditory system nor the articulators are required to reach too far. Neither perceptual nor motor gymnastics are required.

By contrast, strong gestural theories claim that phonological entities are directly related to gestural properties, while the relation to acoustic/auditory properties is mediated by complex biophysical factors. The net effect seems aptly characterized by Hockett's (1955, as cited in MacNeilage, 1970: 184) Easter-egg-on-a-conveyer-belt model, where well-defined phonological intentions are grimly smashed by a packing system which includes a clothes-wringer as a key component. As in Hockett's account, strong articulatory theories emphasize cases involving sequences of phonological units, where interactions are most dramatic.

Figure 3.4 is a sketch of a generic motor theory account of a VC sequence. Features map onto gestural properties in a simple way. The gestural-to-acoustic mapping is indirect, involving interactions of overlapping movements of different articulators with aerodynamic and acoustic principles. This account implies that the listeners are very talented. They must be doing perceptual gymnastics to decode this complex web of interactions. But K&D have quite a different story of who has to do the cartwheels.

A double-weak view of trading relations

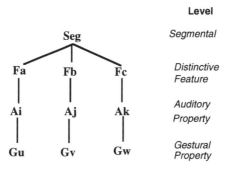

Figure 3.3. Relation of gestural and auditory properties to distinctive features in Stevens & Blumstein's (1981) theory. Note that the bottom two rows could be interchanged.

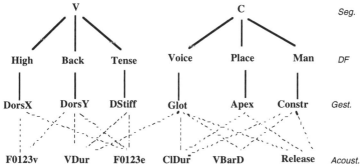

Figure 3.4. Relation of physical properties to symbolic elements in a VC sequence according to a strong gestural theory. The gestural and acoustic properties shown are generic and do not necessarily correspond to critical factors in any real theory. *F0123v* stands for F_0, F_2, F_2, F_3 of the vocoid section of the signal. *F0123e* represents analogous properties at the end of the vocoid. *VDur* is the duration of the vocoid. *VBarD* is duration of voice bar (= K&D's "pulsing"). *ClDur* is the duration of the acoustic correlates of oral closure. *Release* refers to acoustic properties of the consonantal release. *DorsX (DorsY)* is the horizontal (vertical) position of the tongue dorsum. *DStiff* refers to stiffness of the dorsal articulator. *Glot* refers to glottal articulation. Apex refers to activity of the tongue tip. *Constr* to other properties associated with oral constriction.

3.2 Intermediate Perceptual Properties and the strong auditorist position

In K&D's account, acoustic events are crafted by the speaker to produce distinctive auditory events. K&D (see also Kingston, 1992; Diehl & Kluender, 1989) go beyond other auditorists in emphasizing the perceptual integration of acoustically distinct properties with disparate articulatory origins. K&D's approach involves a distinct level of representation, called *intermediate*

31

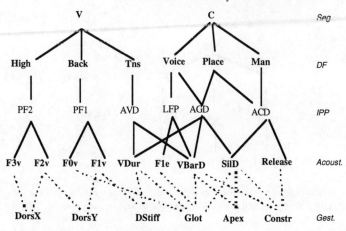

Figure 3.5. Relation of physical properties to symbolic elements in a VC sequence in the strong auditory theory of K&D. The acoustic and gestural properties are as defined in Figure 3.4. *F0v, F1v, F2v, F3v* are F_0, F_1, F_2 and F_3 of the vocoid, and *F1e* represents analogous properties of the vocoid offset. *SilD* is duration of closure silence. *LFP* and *AGD* are the low frequency property and apparent gap duration discussed by K&D. The others are speculations about other kinds of intermediate properties that may be contemplated (*PF1* = perceived F_1, *PF2* = *perceived* F_2, *AVD* = apparent vowel duration, *ACD* = *apparent* constriction duration).

perceptual properties (hereafter, IPPs; see Figure 3.5). IPPs discussed at length by K&D are *apparent gap duration* and the *low frequency property* .[1]

Apparent gap duration is a function of the durations of the pulsing (i.e., closure voicing), of a silent period and, possibly, of the vocoid preceding the closure. In Figure 3.5, the low frequency property presumably depends on pulsing and F1e (the offset F_1 just before the closure) and, possibly, on F_0 patterns. Note that articulation is now one step removed from IPPs and thus twice removed from phonological contrast.

3.3 Trading relations

Much of the disputed territory between K&D and the motor theory centers on trading relations, i.e., covariation in signal properties that is perceptually helpful. Gesturalists attribute such patterns to biophysical interactions or gestural overlap. The resultant acoustic covariation is deemed helpful because it provides evidence about the articulatory source of the signals. Double-strong theorists are generally uncomfortable with trading relations. They sometimes suggest that perceptual context effects represent a marginal phenomenon largely confined to bad synthetic stimuli that do not sound much like real speech. In contrast, K&D accept many of the phenomena represented by trading relation experiments as central facts about speech perception that need to be explained. Their explanation is, however, quite different from that of the gesturalists. Specifically, K&D challenge gesturalist claims that trading relations arise as by-products of articulatory interactions (see their section 2.1, and Kingston, 1992). They counter that many phenomena attributed by the gesturalists to passive coarticulatory effects actually result from *deliberately programmed activity of disparate articulators*. This activity is directed at producing the correct result for listeners in the form of IPPs.

3.4 Criticism of IPPs

Kingston (1992) argues forcefully that many phenomena that are said to "fall out" from natural articulatory interactions have not been shown to do so when actual productions are studied in detail. While much more work is still needed, I take the title of Whalen's (1990) paper very seriously: "Coarticulation is largely planned."   A case can be made that virtually every acoustic property of perceptual import is highly stylized and effectively controlled, at least in careful (hyper) speech (Lindblom, 1990). It is less clear, however, that the acoustics is being controlled with the purpose of specifying IPPs.

My doubts stem from the (tentative) conclusion that the relation between listeners' categorization behavior and raw stimulus properties is highly systematic and *far simpler than should be the case on either motor theory or K&D's account*. Evidence for this comes from models of listeners' categorization in perceptual experiments where several stimulus properties are systematically manipulated (see e.g. Massaro & Oden, 1980; Massaro & Cohen, 1983; Nearey, 1990, 1991, 1992). Such studies have been quite successful at predicting listeners' behavior using little more than linear combinations of simple stimulus effects combined with an elementary choice model. No strongly nonlinear interactions of stimulus properties seem warranted in these experiments. But according to K&D, listeners may not have ready access to the kinds of stimulus information used in these modeling experiments.

3.4.1 *Psychophysical acuity and perceptual threshold effects*

K&D's IPPs can be viewed as *perceptual threshold effects*, a term used by Watson & Kewley-Port (1988) to refer to certain psychophysical phenomena cited by Pastore (1988). These include the peaks in discrimination functions found for VOT-continua near category boundaries. Similar effects have been found for parallel nonspeech stimuli and for nonhuman listeners. However, Watson & Kewley-Port found that these peaks disappeared in a *minimal uncertainty task*, wherein trained listeners respond "same" or "different" to pairs of items consisting of a standard and a highly similar comparison stimulus.

When such a task was applied to a VOT continuum, Watson & Kewley-Port found that, despite its presence for the same stimuli on other tasks, the peak near the /pa–ba/ category boundary vanished. Rather, the observed discrimination shows the monotonic, Weber's law-like trend of classical psychophysics. Using minimum uncertainty tasks, Watson and his colleagues have repeatedly shown that human listeners are more sensitive to small stimulus differences than other methods indicate (see, e.g. Watson, 1973; Watson & Foyle, 1985; Kewley-Port, Watson & Foyle, 1988). The other methods, according to these researchers, involve additional central processing that may obscure the underlying acuity of the auditory system.

This is not to deny the validity of K&D's experiments, nor of the dozens of others that have shown enhanced auditory discrimination of the perceptual threshold variety. Nor is it even to deny that such phenomena may play some role in the choice of phonological categories (see Kuhl & Padden, 1983: 1009 for a thorough discussion of a range of possibilities). The question is whether such IPPs are *preemptive* when it comes to the formation of speech categories. If not, then speech perception may access properties lower than IPPs and, consequently, phenomena studied by K&D, though reflecting interesting psychoacoustic behavior, may not be part of *the necessary front end* of speech perception. Indeed, results from the experiment discussed below suggest that the kind of profound integration suggested by K&D's gap-judgment experiment does not underlie listeners' categorization of VC stimuli which have characteristics relevant to apparent gap duration and the low frequency property.

3.4.2 Additivity of pulsing and F_1 offset

Consider first the results of the gap-labeling experiment shown in K&D's Figure 2.3. K&D emphasize the non-additivity of the F_1 type and pulsing on gap duration judgments: judgments of gap duration are more affected by pulsing when a speech-like F_1 pattern is present.

Their discussion also clearly suggests that pulsing should be an effective cue to voicing of postvocalic stops in English *only when it is connected to a low F_1 offset*, as "happens to happen" in natural speech. This implies that the slope of /t–d/ categorization plotted against pulsing duration should be steeper for stimuli with low F_1 offsets, and shallower for high offsets.

An experiment recently completed in our laboratory shows otherwise. The experiment involved 480 stimuli arrayed in a four-factor, fully crossed design that consisted of /h/-like noise followed by a steady-state vocoid that ranged in duration from 90 to 218 ms in five steps. This was followed by a pulsing (i.e., closure voicing) with duration ranging from 0 to 90 ms in four steps. A nonvoiced alveolar stop burst was always present 90 ms after the offset of the vocoid, with any interval following the voicing offset being silent. The steady-state F_1 ranged from 330 to 730 Hz in eight steps and the separation between F_2 and F_1 of the vocoid ranged from 90 to 700 ms in three steps. The responses were /hVC / syllables with V ranging over the vowels /u, o, ʊ, ɒ, ʌ/ and C ranging over /t/ and /d/.[2] Fifteen Canadian English speakers (with some phonetic training) categorized each stimulus five times, for a total of more than 300,000 responses.

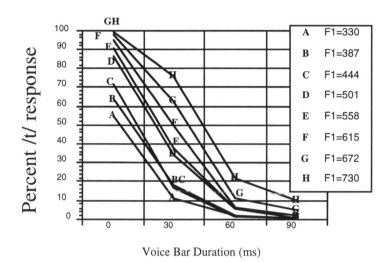

Figure 3.6. Categorization of final stops in experiment described in text (section 3.4.2). Responses are pooled over 15 listeners and over vowel duration and F_2 frequency.

A simple graphic summary of the proportion of /t/ (vs. /d/) judgments shows no evidence of the kind of interaction of F_1 frequency with pulsing that is predicted by K&D's arguments (see Figure 3.6). K&D's results lead us to expect a decreasing slope with higher F_1 offsets. On the contrary, Figure 3.6 shows that pulsing has a powerful effect on voicing response for all F_1 values and the slopes of the ogives at their steepest point are about the same. This is the general kind of pattern that would be expected in a logistic regression model (Nearey, 1990) in which F_1 frequency and pulsing duration have *essentially additive contributions* in the transformed scale.

There is also internal evidence from K&D's gap labeling task suggesting it is not directly relevant to voiced stop perception. Consider again K&D's Figure 2.3. The outlying point is the "no pulsing" stimulus with speech-like (FR) F_1 transitions. Gaps sound significantly *longer* to listeners under this condition. But longer gaps are characteristic of [–voice] stops (despite the fact that experiments with synthetic speech show falling F_1 to enhance [+voice] responses). For

K&D's nonspeech stimuli, the pulsing merely undoes the damage to gap duration done by speech like (FR) F_1 patterns. It is as though a second *illusion* is constructed to counter the effects of the first.

3.5 Discussion

Indeed, apparent gap duration must be viewed as an *illusion*, a distorted perception of the real acoustic world. What possible selective advantage is there to auditory systems that give rise to such (preemptive) illusions, especially given the implications this has for speakers learning to control articulation to produce perceptual effects. If the auditory goals for speech categories involve nearly veridical transductions of physical signal properties (primitive perceptual properties) then the task for speech production may not be trivial, but at least the output of the last stage of production corresponds closely to the first stage of perception. But if the earliest accessible perceptual properties are as abstract as IPPs, more severe difficulties arise. Speakers must be both acrobats and magicians: they must learn to do articulatory cartwheels to produce perceptual illusions.

I have elsewhere admitted to auditorist proclivities (Nearey, 1980, 1990), arguing, for example, that speakers appear to be trying to produce F_1 and F_2 patterns to meet listeners requirements for vowel perception. However, K&D suggest that speakers produce lower F_1 before /d/ not as an end in itself, but in service of apparent gap duration and the low frequency property. They virtually dismiss the fact that closing the vocal tract with voicing switched on automatically leads to low frequency F_1, as any gesturalist would be quick to point out.

But there is a middle ground available in a double-weak framework, illustrated in the following extended example. Suppose, following Stevens & Blumstein (1981: 34), that good articulatory–acoustic "sweet spots" are chosen to serve as seeds for linguistic categories. In attempting to implement such *protofeatures,* there tend to be signature side-effects (available to listeners through primitive perceptual properties) that arise naturally in production, but which are incorporated into perception through "accidental learning" described by Stevens & Blumstein. But suppose further, contrary to Stevens & Blumstein, that these protosecondary cues are nearly as effective as the protofeatures themselves. Suppose further that some listeners, in acquiring the sound patterns of the ambient environment (Kuhl, 1992), incorporate some of the covarying primitive perceptual properties into the primary definition of the contrast. These listeners might then work actively to enhance these former byproducts in their own speech.

Thus, in the case of stop voicing, assume that the protofeature is the classic property of voicing during closure. This has a fairly simple acoustic correlate and a well-defined (though aerodynamically challenging) articulatory implementation. An unavoidable side-effect of continuing voicing into closure is a falling F_1. Conversely, while making sure to shut off voicing during closure for voiceless stops, voicing may be shut off too early (via preaspiration or glottalization), resulting in a higher F_1 offset frequency, and a shorter audible vocoid. If we perceived gestures directly, such automatic covariance would be opaque to the listener–acquirer. But if we can "hear out" the acoustic consequences of the natural interaction, the *magnitude* and *extent* of covariation may be enhanced, as active control is asserted over what might have started out as an incidental covariate.[3]

Rather than managing illusions, as in K&D's account, speakers may manipulate acoustic cues that relate more directly to specific aspects of production. Vocoid duration, closure duration, pulsing durations, and rate of F_1 change all result from relatively well-defined actions of the articulators. Producing all the acoustic properties in the right mix requires coordination of disparate articulators to a common perceptual goal. But rather than the fixed, preemptive intermediate properties of K&D's account, the goal may be the result of auditory perceptual learning (Watson & Foyle, 1985) of patterns that were spawned in an articulatory pool. While some light articulatory gymnastics may be involved to achieve such goals, the biosocial conditions of their evolution keep them within the range of the average speaker's psychomotor capabilities.

The issue of what is accessible to listeners is crucial. It is reasonable to assume, as K&D do, that mature listeners are typically aware of events nearer to the symbolic level. But Watson and his colleagues show that listeners are often capable of hearing much more detail than they are able to report. My account requires no more than that the immediate psychophysical correlates be available to the category formation process during learning. Given some variation as to which cues speakers implement in production, the weights assigned in different languages to different cues (or, possibly, the location of prototypes along specific stimulus dimensions; see Kuhl, 1992) might be expected to vary in roughly the way described by Lindau & Ladefoged (1986) for production or by Kohler (1981) for perception.

This account has a major theoretical downside in that the phonetic basis of phonological universals is called into question (see Blumstein, 1986). This is a serious matter, since the quest for explanatory universals is an important one. But reliable, quantifiable differences among languages must not be ignored in the zeal to generalize, whether to auditorist, gesturalist or double-strong positions.

One alternative is to continue examining patterns in production and perception carefully, proposing theoretical constraints along the way with a degree of conviction proportional to the degree that they are supported by well-tested empirical generalizations. Strong theories (and especially the double-strong theory) represent scientifically appealing asymptotes that no researcher in phonetics can safely ignore. However, viewing such asymptotes from below, with a fuller appreciation of *what might be* and fewer postulates about *what must be*, may lead to a theory of phonological contrast that more closely resembles *what is*.

Notes

* I would like to thank Bernard Rochet and Radecka Apiah-Padi for useful discussions on issues related to the work presented here. This work was supported by a grant from SSHRC.

1 Although K&D's low frequency property stems from suggestions of Stevens & Blumstein (1981), for K&D disparate articulatory sources may underlie a single IPP and more than one IPP may be directly integrated into a single distinctive feature. Arguably, Stevens & Keyser's (1989) "enhancement features" are a little closer to IPPs.
2 The F_1 offset frequency is the same as the steady state. A weak thump can be heard in some stimuli with high F_1 values. This discontinuity with pulsing is actually an advantage for evaluating K&D's hypothesis.
3 This is basically a continuous, subphonemic version of Ohala's (1986) *hypercorrection*. Phenomena like tonogenesis seem much more plausible under this type of account than under those of Stevens and Blumstein or of K&D. For K&D, F_0 has to escape from both the low frequency property and [±voice]. Under my account, the weight of additive cues can tilt in favor of the F_0 difference, which becomes enhanced in production, allowing other cues to the opposition to weaken. If the other cues become weak enough, new speakers may fail to realize there is a connection between the F_0 pattern and a consonantal opposition, and interpret the F_0 pattern prosodically.

References

Blumstein, S. 1986. Comment on Lindau and Ladefoged. In J. S. Perkell & D. H. Klatt (eds.), *Invariance and Variability in Speech Processes*. Hillsdale NJ: Lawrence Erlbaum, 465–478.
Diehl, R. L., & K. R. Kluender. 1989. On the objects of speech perception. *Ecological Psychology* 1: 121–144.
Hockett, C. G. 1955. *A Manual of Phonology*. (*International Journal of American Linguistics, Memoir II.*) Baltimore: Waverly Press.
Kewley-Port, D., C. Watson & D. Foyle. 1988. Auditory temporal acuity in relation to category boundaries: speech and non speech stimuli. *Journal of the Acoustical Society of America* 83: 1133–1145.

38

Kingston, J. 1992. The phonetics and phonology of perceptually motivated articulatory covariation. *Language and Speech* 35: 99–113.

Kohler, K. J. 1981. Contrastive phonology and the acquisition of phonetic skills. *Phonetica* 38: 213–226.

Kuhl, P. 1992. Infants' perception and representation of speech: development of a new theory. *Proceedings of the 1992 International Congress of Spoken Language Processing*, Banff, 1: 449–455.

Kuhl, P. K. & D. M. Padden. 1983. Enhanced discriminability at the phonetic boundaries for the place feature in macaques. *Journal of the Acoustical Society of America* 73: 1003–1010.

Liberman, A. M. & I. G. Mattingly. 1985. The motor theory of speech perception revised. *Cognition* 21: 1–36.

Lindau, M. & P. Ladefoged. 1986. Variability of feature specifications. In J. S. Perkell & D. H. Klatt (eds.), *Invariance and Variability in Speech Processes*. Hillsdale NJ: Lawrence Erlbaum, 465–478.

Lindblom, B. 1990. Explaining phonetic variation: a sketch of the H&H theory. In W. J. Hardcastle & A. Marchal (eds.), *Speech Production and Speech Modelling*. Amsterdam: Kluwer, 403–439.

MacNeilage, P. 1970. Motor control of the serial ordering of speech. *Psychological Review* 77: 182–196.

Massaro, D. & M. Cohen. 1983. Phonological context in speech perception. *Perception and Psychophysics* 34: 338–348.

Massaro, D. & G. Oden. 1980. Evaluation and integration of acoustic features in speech perception. *Journal of the Acoustical Society of America* 67: 996–1013.

Nearey, T. M. 1980. On the physical interpretation of vowel quality: cinefluorographic and acoustic evidence. *Journal of Phonetics* 8: 213–241.

Nearey, T. M. 1990. The segment as a unit of speech perception. *Journal of Phonetics* 18: 347–373.

Nearey, T. M. 1991. Perception: Automatic and cognitive processes. *Proceedings of the XIIth International Congress of Phonetic Sciences,* Aix-en-Provence, 1: 40–49.

Nearey, T. M. 1992. Context effects in a double-weak theory of speech perception. *Language and Speech* 35: 153–172.

Ohala, J. J. 1986. Against the direct realist view of speech perception. *Journal of Phonetics* 14: 75–82.

Pastore, R. E. 1988. Burying strawmen in imaginary graves: a reply to Kewley-Port, Watson and Foyle (1988). *Journal of the Acoustical Society of America* 84: 2262–2265.

Stevens, K. N. & S. Blumstein. 1981. The search for invariant acoustic correlates of phonetic features. In P. D. Eimas & J. L. Miller (eds.), *Perspectives on the Study of Speech*. Hillsdale, NJ: Lawrence Erlbaum, 1–38.

Stevens, K. N. & S. J. Keyser. 1989. Primary features and their enhancement in consonants. *Language* 65: 81–106.

Watson, C. S. 1973. Psychophysics. In B. B. Wolman (ed.), *Handbook of General Psychology*. Englewood Cliffs, NJ: Prentice-Hall, 275–306.

Watson, C. S. & D. C. Foyle. 1985. Central factors in the discrimination and identification of complex sounds. *Journal of the Acoustical Society of America* 78: 375–379.

Watson, C. S. & D. Kewley-Port. 1988. Some remarks on Pastore (1988). *Journal of the Acoustical Society of America* 84: 2266–2270.

Whalen, D. H. 1990. Coarticulation is largely planned. *Journal of Phonetics* 18: 3–35.

4

Speech perception and lexical representation: the role of vowel nasalization in Hindi and English

JOHN J. OHALA and MANJARI OHALA*

4.1 Introduction

The theory of underspecification of lexical representation maintains that the stored form of words omits any predictable or nondistinctive information (Archangeli, 1988). As a data compression technique, there is no dispute that lexical storage can be minimized via underspecification. However, this leaves open the question of whether underspecification corresponds to how words are represented in speakers' mental lexicons. There have been various attempts to gather empirical evidence on the issue (Davidsen-Neilsen, 1975; Keating, 1988; Cohn, 1990; Choi, 1992; Stemberger, 1991, 1992). A recent attempt of this sort was made by Lahiri & Marslen-Wilson (1991, 1992; henceforth L&MW) and Lahiri (1991) who looked to speech perception as a domain where underspecification might be validated. In this paper we summarize their experiment and report our attempt to replicate it.

L&MW suggested that the underlying lexical representations posited by phonologists "correspond, in some significant way, to the listener's mental representation of lexical forms . . . and that these representations have direct consequences for the way . . . the listener interprets the incoming acoustic-phonetic information" (1992: 229). Lahiri (1991: 385) argued specifically that "the surface structures derived after postlexical spreading do not play a distinctive role in perception; rather, a more abstract underspecified representation determines the interpretation of a phonetic cue."

L&MW investigated Bengali and English listeners' identification of syllables in their respective languages which had had varying amounts of their terminal portions gated out. Of interest was their reaction to the presence or absence of nasalization on the vowels heard without the following consonant. To understand L&MW's predictions, it is convenient to refer to Figure 4.1 (corresponding to Figure 9.1 in L&MW, 1992).

41

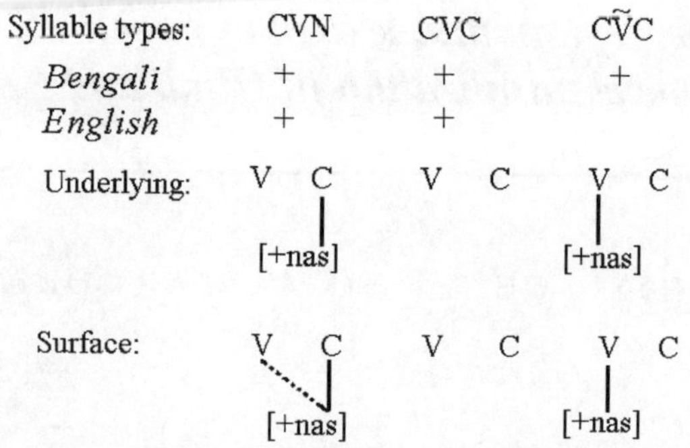

Syllable types: CVN   CVC   CṼC

Bengali   +   +   +

English   +   +

Underlying: V C   V C   V C

            [+nas]   [+nas]

Surface: V C   V C   V C

            [+nas]   [+nas]

Figure 4.1. Schematic illustration of the representation of VC portion of CVN, CVC, and CṼC syllables in the mental lexicon ("underlying"), and as they appear in speech ("surface"), according to underspecification theory. Pluses ("+") opposite *Bengali* and *English* indicate whether the given syllable type occurs in the language. Vowel nasalization due to postlexical spreading of [+nasal] from a nasal consonant (N) is indicated by the dashed line.

As shown in Figure 4.1, insofar as vowel nasalization is concerned, Bengali has three syllabletypes phonologically: CVC, CVN and CṼC. In the CVC syllable the vowel is regarded as *unspecified* for [nasal] at the underlying (phonological) level and is oral at the surface (phonetic) level. In the CṼC syllable the vowel is [+nasal] at both levels. In the CVN the vowel is said to be unspecified for nasal at the underlying level, but is nasal at the surface due to posited postlexical rules spreading the nasalization from the following consonant onto the vowel (represented by the dashed line in Figure 4.1). What this implies is that although the vowel is uttered with nasalization, this nasalization is non-distinctive. English has only the CVC and CVN syllable types, to the vowels of which the same pattern of vowel nasalization applies as in Bengali.

If the final consonant were spliced off of such syllables and listeners required to guess which word (or type of word) they were excised from, L&MW make different predictions depending on whether the listeners compared the stimuli with the underlying underspecified representation (UR) or with the fully specified surface representation (SR). Table 4.1 summarizes their predictions according to the two competing hypotheses, UR and SR. CV(C), CV(N), CṼ(C) refer to the stimuli having the canonical shapes CVC, CVN, and CṼC with the final consonant spliced off; Beng3, Beng2, Engl2 etc. refer to conditions where the possible responses were any of these three syllable types or just two of them (CVC and CVN). A prediction that a given stimulus would be ambiguous is indicated by listing all possible response types. For example, according to the UR hypothesis, stimulus CV(C) would be ambiguous between CVC and CVN.

Of the seven possible conditions, the UR and SR hypotheses make identical predictions about one, Engl2 CV(N). They make different predictions about the remaining six, Beng3 CV(N), Beng3 CV(C), Beng3 Cṽ(C), Beng2 CV(N), Beng2 CV(C), Engl2 CV(C).

Table 4.1. L&MW's predictions of responses to end-truncated stimuli according to two competing hypotheses, UR and SR.

STIMULUS → LISTENERS' ACCESS ↓	CV(N)	CV(C)	Cṽ+(C)
UR	*Beng3*: CⱽC *Beng2*: CVC/CVN -------------------- *Engl2*: CVN	*Beng3*: CVC/CVN *Beng2*: CVC/CVN -------------------- *Engl2*: CVC/CVN	*Beng3*: CⱽC
SR	*Beng3*.: CVN/CṽC *Beng2*: CVN -------------------- *Engl2*: CVN	*Beng3*.: CVC *Beng2*.: CVC -------------------- *Engl2*: CVC	*Beng3*: CⱽC/CVN

4.2 L&MW's experiment

L&MW (1991, 1992) employed a gating paradigm (Cohen & 't Hart, 1964; Grosjean, 1980) in which listeners were presented with a syllable with its final consonant and most of the vowel preceding it gated out, and on subsequent trials with progressively more of the syllable included until finally the entire intact syllable was presented. At each trial listeners were asked to guess what the word was. Subjects were not constrained in their choice of possible guesses except that it was supposed to be a complete word. Up to 11 gates were placed at 40 ms intervals, with some variation to ensure that one gate coincided with the vowel offset, i.e., the onset of the syllable-final consonant. Of interest were the listeners' reactions to those stimuli that did not include any portion of the final consonant, the hypothesis being that when they heard this consonant the character of the syllable would be perceptually evident and their responses would no longer help to differentiate between the competing hypotheses.

L&MW ran three separate conditions as a function of the type of stimuli used: (a) Bengali triplets, in which all three syllable types (CVC, CṼC, CVN) appeared; e.g. /bad/ "difference", /bãd/ "dam", /bãn/ "flood"; (b) Bengali doublets, in which, given the initial CV, the only existing Bengali words would have been CVC or CVN (i.e., where subjects would not have the option of giving CṼC responses); e.g. /lop/, /lom/, */lõC-/; and (c) English doublets involving CVC and CVN syllables; e.g. /dʌb/ *dub*, /dʌm/ *dumb*. Conditions (b) and (c) were designed to permit partial comparison between the Bengali and English results.

L&MW obtained results in the six relevant conditions which they interpret as supporting the UR hypothesis. In the Beng3 CV(C), Beng2 CV(C), and Engl2 CV(C) conditions, they predicted responses split between CVN and CVC. This did occur although the percentages of CVN responses were low (13.4%, 14.7%, and 16.6%, respectively). L&MW characterize these percentages as "relatively high" (1991: 271) and equal to the proportion of the CVN syllable type in the total set of monosyllables of each language. In other words, when hearing the truncated CV(C) stimuli subjects were in effect guessing whether the word was CVC or CVN, and the incidence of guesses matched approximately the incidence of those syllable types in the language.

As predicted by the UR hypothesis, the majority of responses to the Beng3 CV(N) stimuli were CṼC (63%), and the majority of responses to the Beng3 CṼ(C) stimuli were CṼC (56.8%), i.e., the responses in these conditions were not split equally between CṼC and CVN, as would be predicted by the SR hypothesis. In the Beng2 CV(N) condition, the majority of responses were CVC, while some subjects gave CṼC responses (17%), even though the condition was designed to eliminate CṼC as a possible response. On the other hand, the "correct" CVN response was the minority response. L&MW (1992: 244 ff.) remark: "this difficulty in producing a CVN response follows directly from the [UR] hypothesis, where nasalization on the surface is interpreted as a cue to an underlyingly nasal vowel."

In sum, L&MW find multiple points of support for the UR hypothesis in their results.

4.3 A replication

We attempted to replicate L&MW's study (with some modifications) using English and Hindi stimuli and subjects. As far as oral and nasal vowel patterns are concerned, Hindi is virtually identical to Bengali (as described by L&MW).[1]

4.3.1 Method

Some aspects of our experiment differed from that of L&MW. First, our word lists, given in Tables 4.2–4.4, were much shorter than theirs. The Hindi triplet condition contained five near-minimal triplets (L&MW had 21), the Hindi doublet condition four (L&MW had 20), and the English doublet condition eight minimal pairs (L&MW had 20).

Table 4.2. Hindi minimal triplets used in the Hindi triplet condition.

sas	"mother-in-law"	sãs	"breath"	san	"to mix (e.g. flour)"
k^has	"main"	k^hãs	"cough"	k^han	"mine (for ore)"
bas	"bad smell"	bãs	"bamboo"	ban	(type of rope)
b^huk²	"hunger"	b^hūk	"bark (of dog)"	b^hun	"roast" (v.)
baʈ	"path"	bãʈ	"distribution"	ban	(type of rope)

Table 4.3. Hindi minimal pairs used in the Hindi doublet condition.

ʧeʈ	"a month"	ʧɛn	"peace"
ʈis	"thirty"	ʈin	"three"
ḍuḍʰ	"milk" (n.)	ḍun	"twice something; name of a train"
ḍekʰ	"see"	ḍen	"gift"

Second, instead of the open response set used by L&MW, we used a closed response set. The problem with an open response set is that it does not permit any statistical analysis of the results. L&MW suggested that the approximately 15% rate at which CVN responses were given to CV(C) stimuli mirrored the incidence of CVN words in the lexicon. But it is not clear how relevant this figure is; according to the cohort model (Marslen-Wilson, 1984),when listeners are looking for candidate words to match the incoming truncated signal to, they are not searching the *entire* lexicon, but only that subpart of the lexiconthat has the same initial CV sequence. Since in L&MW's experiment subjects were apparently allowed to give polysyllabic words as responses, the possible matches would not have been confined to monosyllables, so it is very difficult to assess what the proportion of CVN syllables was out of the total cohort.

45

Table 4.4. English minimal pairs used in the English doublet condition.

rube	room
lewd	loon
seed	seen
raze	rain
lead [lid]	lean
ride	Rhine
laud	lawn
seize	seen

The open response set presents other difficulties as well. As noted by L&MW (1991, footnote 9) some of their subjects' responses on the early, more severely gated stimuli could not be scored according to their criteria, and thus approximately 3–5% of the responses had to be discarded. Furthermore, in the Beng2 CV(N) condition, a full 17% of the responses were CṼC, although CṼC was not supposed to be a possible response. Finally, an open response set does not guarantee that in the triplet condition, all three syllable types were always available in each subject's mental lexicon.

For these reasons, we restricted our subjects' answers to each stimulus just to the target triplet or pair. This enabled us to analyze the results statistically. We do not think this modification of the technique used by L&MW materially changed the comparability of the experiments. L&MW endorse Marslen-Wilson's "cohort" model, which characterizes the act of word recognition as an ongoing reduction in the number of possible matches an incoming speech signal has to items in the lexicon. At some point in the identification of words the cohort set must also be reduced to two or three possibilities even in the L&MW experiment. In our experiment *we* provided listeners with that reduced cohort set. In addition we believe that by providing subjects with a restricted response set we avoided the thorny problem of trying to find words which would be of equal frequency.

Third, we modified the way the stimuli were gated. L&MW gated their stimuli into silence. But a relatively abrupt attenuation of the signal could in itself be a potent segmental cue for a voiceless stop, and might lead listeners to interpret, for example, a gated [sã(n)] as /sãp/. To avoid this effect, we gated into wide-band white noise which was 1 dB less in intensity that the peak intensity of the word itself. Furthermore, to avoid transients the amplitude of the speech was attenuated from full scale to zero over 5 ms and the noise increased from zero to full scale in 5 ms. These two ramps overlapped such that the start of the attenuating speech ramp coincided with the start of the increasing noise ramp. In this way listeners were not presented with a spurious segmental cue and could imagine that the latter part of the signal was simply obscured (Pols & Schouten, 1978).

Fourth, we also had only five gate points (as opposed to L&MW's 11): one coincided with the vowel offset and three others were spaced at 60 ms intervals before that. Vowel offset was determined as that point where there was an abrupt discontinuity in the amplitude and/or spectrum of the vowel. The fifth gate included the whole word.

Fifth, we gathered subjects' responses in a way to avoid a possible "hysteresis effect." As discussed in J. Ohala (1992a), by presenting first the most severely gated version of a word and then in immediate succession the progressively longer versions until the whole word was heard, L&MW's subjects' responses may have been contaminated by a kind of "hysteresis effect," i.e., their judgments on any given stimulus may have been partly influenced by their judgments on an earlier version. In other words, once having made a judgment, subjects may be reluctant to change it (see Fredricksen, 1967). Insofar as vowel nasalization is concerned, the early portions of a vowel in a CVN syllable would be less nasalized than later portions, and so this effect could suppress CVN or CṼC judgments. Evidence that the relatively low number of CVN judgments L&MW obtained with the CV(N) stimuli in the case of the English doublets may be due to hysteresis comes from Ali, Gallagher, Goldstein & Daniloff's (1971) results, which showed that English listeners *could* differentiate between CV(C) and CVN syllables that had had the last one third of the vowel and the final consonant removed. The Engl2 CV(N) condition is not one that L&MW consider capable of differentiating between the UR and SR hypothesis, but a hysteresis effect could have had an influence on the other conditions as well. L&MW (1992: 237) state that previous studies show that such an effect would be negligible. But these cited studies do not give separate results for words of the type that we focus on here, i.e., words differing only in presence or absence of nasalization on the vowel.

Although this methodological issue is not completely resolved, we divided our subjects and our stimuli into five groups such that no group heard more than one gated version of a word type, with the following exception: if a given group heard the most severely gated version of a word, then four tokens later they were presented with the whole (ungated) word. We counted on there being minimal influence from their judgment on the earlier gate on their judgment of the whole ungated word. In any case, the only responses of interest, and those treated statistically, were of those stimuli with gates up to and including the vowel offset.

The speech samples were recorded under high quality conditions, the second author providing the Hindi words and the first author, the English words. They were digitized at 16 kHz after being low-pass filtered at 7 kHz, and gated with

John J. Ohala and Manjari Ohala

added noise using both commercial speech analysis software (CSRE) and custom-made software.

The stimuli were presented to the subjects over headphones via a high quality portable tape recorder. The Hindi subjects (N = 39) were students at the Jawaharlal Nehru University, Delhi, and listened to the stimuli in a quiet room. The English subjects (N = 44) were students at the University of Alberta and listened to the stimuli in a sound-attenuated booth. All subjects were paid for their participation. Although we differentiate between the Hindi triplet and doublet conditions (following L&MW), stimuli from both sets were intermixed and differentiated for the subjects only by virtue of having three or two possible answers, respectively, on the answer sheet. Each group's answer sheets had a randomized order of the possible responses to a given stimulus. Subjects were presented with the answer sheet (in Devanagari, the Hindi script, and English, for Hindi and English subjects respectively), and were told that they would hear some words some of which had been interrupted by noise. They were told to attempt to identify the words from among the choices given on the answer sheet, guessing if necessary.

4.3.2 Results and discussion

Overall results are presented in Tables 4.5–4.7; results for each gate in all conditions (with L&MW's results superimposed) are presented in Figures 4.2 to 4.8.

The one part of the experiment in which the UR and SR hypotheses would, according to L&MW, give identical predictions is the Engl2 CV(N) condition, to which the responses should all be CVN. Curiously, in L&MW's results, CVN was the minority response, but they do not view this as undermining their predictions. In our data the CVN judgments to Engl2 CV(N) stimuli were overwhelmingly correct (see Table 4.7), and as is evident from Figure 4.8, this judgment was largely correct from the earliest truncation point. Our results are congruent with the earlier study by Ali *et al.* (1971). We surmise that this higher rate of correct responses may result from our efforts at reducing a possible hysteresis effect, as discussed above.

The results for the Hind3 CV(N) condition are similar to those of L&MW, in that the majority response was $C\tilde{v}C$ ($\chi^2 = 35.8$ (2 df), $p < 0.001$). However, among the minority responses, we had a higher rate for CVN than did L&MW (24.4% as opposed to their 7.9%), and this was comparable to the CVC responses (19.9%). In the Hind2 CV(N) condition we found no significant difference between the CVN and CVC responses ($\chi^2 = 0.4$ (1 df), n.s.) although the trend is in the same direction found by L&MW. Neither result provides support for the SR hypothesis, and are rather in accord with the predictions of the UR as formulated by L&MW.

48

Table 4.5. Results for the Hindi triplet condition: raw numbers (in bold), and percentages (in italics) of response type to stimulus type, up to vowel offset. χ^2 probability levels for each set of responses are shown in parentheses after the stimulus label. For comparison, L&MW's results (presented as percentages) for their Bengali triplet condition are given in square brackets.

| | | RESPONSE | | |
		CVC	CṼC	CVN
STIMULUS	CV(C) (*p* < 0.001)	**140** (*71.8*) [80.3]	**38** (*19.5*) [0.7]	**17** (*8.7*) [13.4]
	CṼ(C) (*p* < 0.001)	**28** (*14.4*) [33.2]	**139** (*71.3*) [56.8]	**28** (*14.4*) [5.2]
	CV(N) (*p* < 0.001)	**31** (*19.9*) [23.5]	**87** (*55.8*) [63.0]	**38** (*24.4*) [7.9]

In the three cases where CV(C) stimuli were involved (see Tables 4.5, 4.6 and 4.7) the majority responses were the correct CVC, a result which was highly significant in all cases (χ^2 = 133 (2 df), χ^2 = 35.1 (1 df), χ^2 = 109 (1 df), for Hindi triplets, Hindi doublets and English doublets respectively; *p* < 0.001 in all cases). Clearly, the subjects did *not* find the stimuli ambiguous between CVC and CVN. L&MW state that according to the SR hypothesis there should be *no* CVN responses to CV(C) stimuli. But this is an unreasonable claim; although it can be granted that the unelaborated SR theory would not predict CVN responses, in real life when such perceptual experiments are done one always encounters "noise" in the data due either to unanticipated defects in the stimuli, subjects' inattention, or defects in the theory (because it does not cover all events in the domain to which it pertains). Rather than zero CVN responses, all that can be expected is that there be a statistically significant "tilt" in the incidence of the responses. This is what we have shown.

In the discussion of their results for the Beng3 CV(C) condition, L&MW draw attention to the higher rate of (incorrect) CVN over CṼC responses. In our results, this was reversed: there were 19.5% CṼC responses to 8.7% CVN responses. We have no explanation for this, and do not attach any importance to it since both responses were overwhelmingly in the minority.

Table 4.6. Results for the Hindi doublet condition: raw numbers (in bold), and percentages (in italics) of response type to stimulus type, up to vowel offset. χ^2 probability levels for each set of responses are shown in parentheses after the stimulus label. For comparison, L&MW's results (presented as percentages) for their Bengali doublet condition are given in square brackets. (Note that CṼC responses have no entries for our results, since we obtained forced-choice responses.)

		RESPONSE	
		CVC	CṼC	CVN
STIMULUS	CV(C) ($p < 0.001$)	**115** *(73.7)* [82.6]	[0.0]	**41** *(26.3)* [14.7]
	CV(N) (n.s.)	**82** *(52.6)* [64.7]	[17.0]	**74** *(47.4)* [15.6]

Table 4.7. Results for the English doublet condition: raw numbers (in bold), and percentages (in italics) of response type to stimulus type, up to vowel offset. χ^2 probability levels for each set of responses are shown in parentheses after the stimulus label. For comparison, L&MW's results (presented as percentages) for their English doublet condition are given in square brackets.

		RESPONSE	
		CVC	CVN	
STIMULUS	CV(C) ($p < 0.001$)	**278** *(79.0)* [83.4]	**74** *(21.0)* [16.6]	
	CV(N) ($p < 0.001$)	**55** *(17.9)* [59.3]	**253** *(82.1)* [40.7]	

50

In the Hind3 Cṽ(C) condition, our results were again quite similar to those of L&MW, in that the majority response was CṼC (χ^2 = 126 (2 df), p < 0.001). The only difference is that the minority responses were evenly split between CVC and CVN, as opposed to the greater preponderance of CVC responses in L&MW's experiment. We attach no importance to the even split between the minority responses.

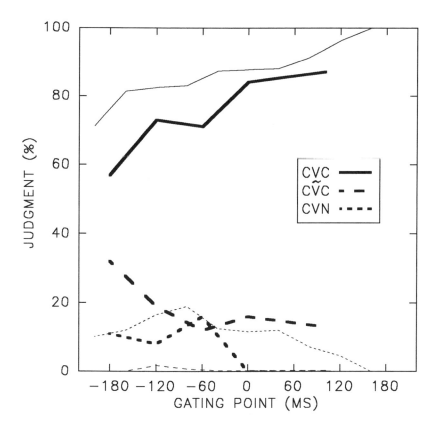

Figure 4.2. Superimposed results from the Hind3 CVC condition (thick lines) and L&MW's Beng3 CVC condition (thin lines). Horizontal axis: gating points (in ms), with respect to vowel offset (= 0 ms); vertical axis: percent judgments in indicated category. Parameters: solid line = CVC responses, medium broken line = CṼC responses, short broken line = CVN responses.

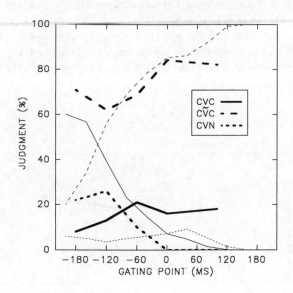

Figure 4.3. Superimposed results from the Hind3 CṼC condition (thick lines) and L&MW's Beng3 CṼC condition (thin lines). Other details as in Figure 4.2.

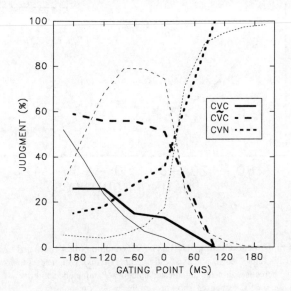

Figure 4.4. Superimposed results from the Hind3 CVN condition (thick lines) and L&MW's Beng3 CVN condition (thin lines). Other details as in Figure 4.2.

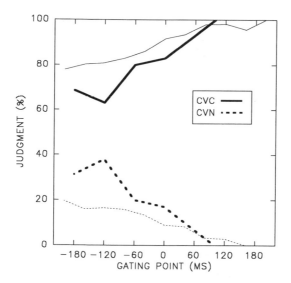

Figure 4.5. Superimposed results from the Hind2 CVC condition (thick lines) and L&MW's Beng2 CVC condition (thin lines). Other details as in Figure 4.2.

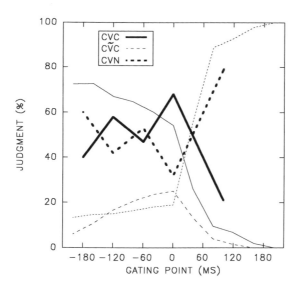

Figure 4.6. Superimposed results from the Hind2 CVN condition (thick lines) and L&MW's Beng2 CVN condition (thin lines). Other details as in Figure 4.2.

53

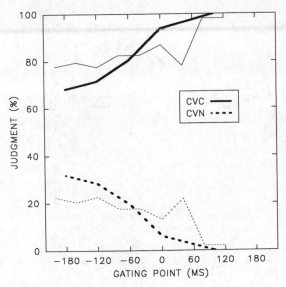

Figure 4.7. Superimposed results from the Engl2 CVC condition (thick lines) and L&MW's Engl2 CVC condition (thin lines). Other details as in Figure 4.2.

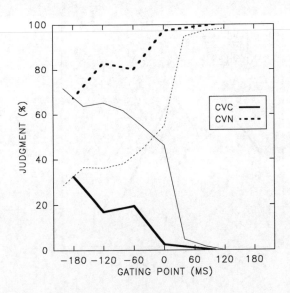

Figure 4.8. Superimposed results from the Engl2 CVN condition (thick lines) and L&MW's Engl2 CVN condition (thin lines). Other details as in Figure 4.2.

4.4 General discussion and conclusion

Of the seven parts of the experiment, one, Engl2 CV(N), was stated to be unable to differentiate between the UR and SR hypotheses. Of the remaining six, our results support the SR hypothesis in three (Hind3 CV(C), Hind2 CV(C), Engl2 CV(C)), and the UR hypothesis in the other three (Hind3 CV(N), Hind3 C ṽ(C), and Hind2 CV(N)). However we do not accept L&MW's characterization of the different predictions these two hypotheses would make.

We disagree first with their contention that the results of the Engl2 CV(N) condition would be the same according to the two hypotheses. In spite of the explicit claim, quoted above, that "the surface structures derived after postlexical spreading do not play a distinctive role in perception" L&MW, while still advocating the UR hypothesis, allow the postlexical spreading of nasalization from a tautosyllabic nasal to the preceding vowel to be accessible to the listener in identifying word fragments. This is inconsistent. To counter this criticism (made also in J. Ohala, 1992a) they point out that the nasalization tells the listener about the *consonant* that will follow the vowel, not the vowel itself (L&MW, 1992: 238). But virtually all the processes commonly labeled "postlexical spreading" have this characteristic. By allowing the listener to access a form exhibiting postlexical spreading they have endorsed the SR hypothesis. Therefore, we consider that our results with the Engl2 CV(N) condition also support the SR not the UR hypothesis. This impacts on the results from the various CV(C) conditions: L&MW throughout their papers refer to the vowels in the CVC and CVN syllables as underlyingly "oral", but according to the UR hypothesis this is not strictly accurate. Rather they are *unspecified* for the feature [nasal]; they are neither [+nasal] nor [−nasal]. As suggested by Keating (1989) and Cohn (1990), segments unspecified for a certain feature value have, on the surface phonetic level, an interpolation of the values of adjacent segments which are specified for that feature. Thus the surface oral vowel in CVC syllables could be regarded as the product of postlexical spreading of orality, just as the nasalization on the vowels in CVN syllables is regarded as postlexical spreading of nasality. Thus the results of four of our experimental conditions are consistent with the SR hypothesis.

Two of the remaining three conditions, Hind3 CV(N) and Hind3 C ṽ(C), involve the confusion of CVN (phonetically [C ṽN]) with C ṽC, and the lack of any confusion of C ṽC with CVN; in other words they involve giving C ṽC responses to what are phonetically [C ṽ] fragments. This is not too difficult to explain under what we think is a more reasonable SR hypothesis, namely one which includes the cues a listener requires to make phonemic and lexical decisions. There are two parts to our argument.

First, distinctive speech sounds, as they are manifested phonetically, are not time-invariant. They have a dynamic structure which changes over time. This has always been recognized for diphthongs, affricates, pre- and postnasalized stops, etc. Equally, an important cue for a stop is a release found only at the end of the period of reduced amplitude. M. Ohala (1979, 1983) assigned the feature [distinctive release] to Hindi voiceless aspirated and voiced aspirated stops, as well as affricates to account for certain sound patterns they have in common, in contrast to simple unaspirated stops (see also Steriade, 1993). Similarly, it is well known that the *perceptual cues* for some aspects of segments lie in the "transitions" at their onset and offset. This can have surprising manifestations: Maturi (1991) showed that by cross splicing the final vowels of the Italian words *strada* "street" and *strana* "strange", the results are perceived by listeners as most like *strana* and *strada*, respectively: only the vowels were interchanged but this caused most listeners to hear different consonants! Evidently the presence or absence of what might be considered "non-distinctive" nasalization on the preceding vowel *is* part of what makes a consonant a nasal or an oral segment. We believe that part of what makes a vowel non-distinctively nasal (in Bengali and Hindi) is the presence of a following nasal consonant. This might be regarded as a truism but has important perceptual consequences that bear on the interpretation of the experimental results reported above. And this is the second point in our argument. We illustrate it by an analogy.

Consider the task of identifying capital letters of the Roman alphabet when parts of those letters have been erased. In Figure 4.9, erasure of one side of a letter corresponds to the temporal truncation of part of a speech sound. On the left is a letter whose right side has been erased. Is it "underlyingly" a *C*, *O*, *Q*, or a *G*? Likewise, for the fragment of the letter in the third column: is it "underlyingly" an *F*, *P*, or a *R*? From a strictly logical point of view, we cannot say, of course, but from a perceptual and practical point of view the viewer's inclination is to associate it with that underlying letter to which it bears the greatest *surface* resemblance. In these cases, that means *C* and *F*, respectively. Except under special circumstances, the default strategy in perception is the inverse of WYSIWYG: WYGIWYS ("What You Get Is What You See"). Apparently, in perception, the default strategy is to pay most attention to what is present rather than what is absent but might have been present. (See also McQueen's commentary to this paper; however, see as well Ohala & Shriberg, 1990 and Shriberg, 1992 for special circumstances where the default strategy does not apply and the perceiver "fills in" missing parts of the stimulus array.)

The relevance of these two points to both L&MW's and our studies is this: if the release of a nasal vowel into a nasal consonant is crucial to the differentiation of CṼC and CVN syllables, just as the release of an affricate is essential to differentiate it from a simple stop, then when listeners hear [CṼ] stimuli, whether these come from CṼC or CVN words, it is not surprising that they associate them with CṼC words. This is equivalent to identifying a *G* with its right half missing as a *C*. (It should be noted that perception of Ṽ, i.e., of a

Figure 4.9. Partially erased and fully-specified letter shapes. See text for explanation.

distinctively nasalized vowel, in Bengali and Hindi would presumably not rely as much on the following segment since Ṽ can occur in open syllables.)

To sum up our argument, we do not believe that our results or those of L&MW's regarding listeners' judgments on [CṼ] stimuli necessarily support the UR hypothesis; at best they are compatible with both the UR and SR hypotheses. Obviously more research on this issue would be desirable.

There remains the Hind2 CV(N) condition, where we found no significant difference between the CVC and CVN judgments. This does not support any version of an SR hypothesis that we are aware of. Our expectation was that CVN responses should have predominated; they did not. These stimuli were ambiguous to listeners as L&MW predicted according the UR hypothesis.

By our count, then, of the seven experimental conditions, four support the SR hypothesis, one, the UR hypothesis, and two are a draw.

4.5 Summary

The phonological theory of underspecification maintains that the lexical representation of words in the mental lexicon does not include predictable phonetic details. Lahiri & Marslen-Wilson (1991, 1992) and Lahiri (1991) offer experimental results showing that when accessing words during speech perception listeners attempt to match the incoming signal with such an underspecified representation. We present a replication of their experiment and a re-interpretation of their results which do not fully support their claim.

McQueen, in his commentary to this paper, notes that there are really two hypotheses proposed by L&MW: (a) that the underlying representation is underspecified and (b) that the incoming speech signal is compared with this underspecified form. He notes that our results disproved only hypothesis (b). Hypothesis (a) remains untested and could still be true if a fully specified form was derived from a lexically underspecified form and the incoming signal compared with that. Logically he is correct, but we regard this as an extravagant hypothesis which begs to be pared by Occam's razor. The principal arguments in favor of underspecification are that it is simpler; but "simpler" at what cost?

Counting features in the grammar cannot be the only measure of "cost" (J. Ohala, 1992b). In addition, it is generally assumed in psycholinguistic studies that although the incoming speech stream may itself be transformed in some way, what it is compared to ultimately for perception is the underlying (lexical) representation (Cutler, 1986). Intuitively, the mental representation of things we perceive and recognize seem to include predictable details: in our conception of the shape of the letter *G*, do we omit the entirely predictable left side? Our intuitions tell us "no"; the reader can follow his or her own intuitions, but whatever they are, these intuitions should apply to speech perception as well as letter shapes.

Notes

* We thank Terry Nearey for the use of his laboratory facilities at the University of Alberta, Edmonton, and Anvita Abbi for facilitating the recruiting of subjects at Jawarharlal Nehru University, Delhi. We are also grateful to Aditi Lahiri for sending us the Bengali word list used in hers and William Marslen-Wilson's experiment. In addition, we thank John Ingram, Elisabeth Shriberg, James McQueen, Sarah Hawkins, and Amalia Arvaniti for helpful comments on earlier drafts of the paper. Finally, our thanks to all our subjects both in Delhi and Edmonton.

1 A potential difference that may exist between Bengali and Hindi involves constraints on the types of stops that can appear after long nasalized vowels. As documented by M. Ohala (1983), given the Hindi sequence ṽ: + STOP, the stop can only be voiceless. Where historically there has been a voiced stop, today there is a sequence of (homorganic) nasal followed by the stop, e.g. Old Hindi [ʧãːda] > Mod. Hindi [ʧã̃nd]. This point has gone unnoticed by those working on the phonology of Hindi because the orthography fails to reflect it. We do not know whether Bengali has the same constraint or not. The list of Bengali words used by L&MW contains some 20–25% words with final voiced stops among those with distinctively nasal vowels (Aditi Lahiri, personal communication).

2 This word is spelt with a final /kʰ/ but in pronunciation the aspiration is neutralized. The word is pronounced as given here.

References

Ali, H. L., T. Gallagher, J. Goldstein & R. G. Daniloff. 1971. Perception of coarticulated nasality. *Journal of the Acoustical Society of America* 49: 538–540.

Archangeli, D. 1988. Aspects of underspecification theory. *Phonology* 5: 183–207.

Speech perception and lexical representation

Choi, J. D. 1992. Phonetic underspecification and target interpolation: An acoustic study of Marshallese vowel allophony. *UCLA Working Papers in Phonetics* 82.

Cohen, A. & J. 't Hart. 1964. Gating techniques as an aid in speech analysis. *Language and Speech* 7: 22–39.

Cohn, A. C. 1990. Phonetic and phonological rules of nasalization. *UCLA Working Papers in Phonetics* 76.

Cutler, A. 1986. Phonological structure in speech recognition. *Phonology Yearbook* 3: 161–178.

Davidsen-Nielsen, N. 1975. A phonological analysis of English *sp, st, sk* with special reference to speech error evidence. *Journal of the International Phonetic Association* 5: 3–25.

Fredricksen, J. R. 1967. Cognitive factors in the recognition of ambiguous auditory and visual stimuli. (Monograph.) *Journal of Personality and Social Psychology* 7.

Grosjean, F. 1980. Spoken word recognition processes and the gating paradigm. *Perception & Psychophysics* 28: 267–283.

Keating, P. A. 1988. Underspecification in phonetics. *Phonology* 5: 275–292.

Keating, P. A. 1989. The window model of coarticulation: articulatory evidence. In J. Kingston & M. E. Beckman (eds.), *Papers in Laboratory Phonology I: Between the Grammar and Physics of Speech*. Cambridge: Cambridge *University Press*, 281–302.

Lahiri, A. 1991. Anteriority in sibilants. *Proceedings of the XIIth International Congress of Phonetic Sciences,* Aix-en-Provence, 1: 384–388.

Lahiri, A. & W. D. Marslen-Wilson. 1991. The mental representation of lexical form: A phonological approach to the recognition lexicon. *Cognition,* 38: 245–294.

Lahiri, A. & W. Marslen-Wilson. 1992. Lexical processing and phonological representation. In G. J. Docherty & D. R. Ladd (eds.), *Papers in Laboratory Phonology II: Gesture, Segment, Prosody.* Cambridge: Cambridge University Press, 229–254.

Marslen-Wilson, W. D. 1984. Function and process in spoken word recognition. In H. Bouma & D. G. Bouwhuis, (eds.), *Attention and Performance X: Control of Language Processes.* Hillsdale, NJ: Erlbaum, 125–150.

Maturi, P. 1991. The perception of consonantal nasality in Italian: conditioning factors. *Proceedings of the XIIth International Congress of Phonetic Sciences,* Aix-en-Provence, 5: 50–53.

Ohala, J. J. 1992a. Comments on chapter 9 [Discussion of paper by Lahiri and Marslen-Wilson]. In G. J. Docherty & D. R. Ladd (eds.), *Papers in Laboratory Phonology II: Gesture, Segment, Prosody.* Cambridge: Cambridge University Press, 255–257.

Ohala, J. J. 1992b. The costs and benefits of phonological analysis. In P. Downing, S. D. Lima, & M. Noonan (eds.), *The Linguistics of Literacy.* Amsterdam, Philadelphia: J. Benjamins 211–237.

Ohala, J. J. & E. E. Shriberg 1990. Hyper-correction in speech perception. *Proceedings of the 1990 International Conference on Spoken Language Processing,* Kobe, 1: 405–408.

Ohala, M. 1979. Phonological features of Hindi stops. *South Asian Languages Analysis* 1: 79–88.

Ohala, M. 1983. *Aspects of Hindi Phonology.* Delhi: Motilal Banarsidass.

John J. Ohala and Manjari Ohala

John J. Ohala and Manjari Ohala

John J. Ohala and Manjari Ohala

John J. Ohala and Manjari Ohala

Pols, L. C. W. & M. E. H. Schouten. 1978. Identification of deleted consonants. *Journal of the Acoustical Society of America* 64: 1333–1337.

Shriberg, E. E. 1992. Perceptual restoration of filtered vowels with added noise. *Language & Speech* 35: 127–136.

Stemberger, J. P. 1991. Apparent anti-frequency effects in language production – the addition bias and phonological underspecification. *Journal of Memory and Language* 30: 161–185.

Stemberger J. P. 1992. Vocalic underspecification in English language production. *Language* 68: 492–524.

Steriade, D. 1993. Closure, release, and nasal contours. In M. K. Huffman & R. A. Krakow (eds.), *Nasals, Nasalization, and the Velum*. Orlando, FL: Academic Press, 401–470.

5

Processing versus representation: comments on Ohala and Ohala

JAMES M. McQUEEN*

5.1 Introduction

The data reported by Ohala & Ohala, and by Lahiri & Marslen-Wilson (1991, 1992) can be explained by a processing model in which surface acoustic-phonetic information is used to constrain perceptual decisions. Nevertheless, this interpretation is perfectly consistent with the underspecification hypothesis. Like Ohala & Ohala (henceforth O&O), I have a good deal of sympathy with the theoretical concept of an underspecified mental lexicon, as proposed by Lahiri & Marslen-Wilson (henceforth L&MW), but I do not believe that the data presented by them, or by O&O, give us any direct insight into the nature of lexical representations. My main point, therefore, is that it is inappropriate to find a unified *representational* explanation of these data in terms of stored forms which either match surface phonetics or are underspecified. An appropriate explanation is one based on the *processing* of information given in the speech signal.

The interpretation I will give has five principal features. First, I make the assumption that listeners *do* use surface phonetic information in perception: they do not depend solely upon underspecified representations, as argued by L&MW. On this point, I am in agreement with O&O.

Second, I assume that listeners base their decisions primarily on the information available in the input, rather than primarily on stored representations onto which the input has been mapped. Again, this seems to be a view with which O&O are in agreement (but which they fail to describe explicitly), and is counter to the position held by L&MW.

Third, in line with O&O, I assume that there is some form of bias operating in the gating task. This is a general processing bias: where possible, subjects prefer to perceive all the parts of an input signal as belonging together, rather than to treat some of this information as a cue to another perceptual object which is otherwise absent. In the present case, this means that speakers of languages with nasal and oral vowels prefer to attribute nasalization in a Cṽ sequence to the vowel rather than to a possible following nasal consonant.

Fourth, the acoustic-phonetic information available to a listener changes over time. In the context of the gating task, this means that information changes over successive gates. The fact that the pattern of performance changed over gates in both O&O's and in L&MW's experiments is a clear indication that the listeners were responding to changes in acoustic-phonetic detail (see O&O's Figures 4.2 – 4.8).

Finally, and most importantly, we must analyze the task: what is the listener being asked to do? The gating task requires that the listener provide a possible completion of a speech fragment. If there is sufficient information in the fragment, listeners may hear it as a particular word. If, however, there is insufficient information to uniquely specify a word, the fragment will partially match a number of lexical hypotheses, and listeners will be forced to guess from among this set of alternatives. In gating experiments, confidence ratings normally give an indication of whether or not there is enough of the fragment for word recognition to have taken place. They are not reported in either experiment, so it is impossible to ascertain whether responses at a given gate reflect confident identification or not. Under these circumstances, we can only assume that the subjects' responses for gates within the vowels were guesses, since the materials did not become unique until their final consonants. In most cases it is unlikely that there was sufficient information in the fragments for subjects to unambiguously identify them as particular words. For gates within the vowels, the subjects' task was therefore to match a fragment against a set of lexical candidates, and ascertain which word the fragment was most like. To do this, subjects made use of the acoustic-phonetic information available in the fragment.

5.2 The data revisited

Most of the results of both O&O and L&MW can be explained in terms of this process of matching the acoustic-phonetic information against lexical candidates. This account predicts that listeners will respond to the changing phonetic information in the signal. As more nasalization is heard, nasal responses increase and oral responses decrease; as more of an oral vowel is heard, oral responses increase and nasal responses decrease. Since the data are complex, I will briefly describe the results again (the reader is referred to Figures 4.2–4.8 and Tables 4.5, 4.6 and 4.7 in O&O). Consider first the general data pattern. In all the CVC conditions, there is a gradual increase in the proportion of CVC responses, and a gradual reduction in the number of nasalized vowel (CṼC and CVN) responses (see Figures 4.2 , 4.5 and 4.7). In the CVN doublet condition, as more of the word is heard, that is, as the evidence for nasalization builds up, more CVN responses and fewer CVC responses are made (see Figure 4.6).

There are a few minor exceptions to these general trends. In the Hindi CVC triplet condition, even when the listeners could hear the whole word, there were over 10% CṼC responses (see Figure 4.2). Similarly, in the Hindi CVN doublet condition, even when the whole word was heard, there were still 20% CVC responses (see Figure 4 .6). Furthermore, in this condition, the performance for gates before word offset appears to be random fluctuation around chance (50%). The patterns of performance in both the Hindi CVC triplets and the Hindi CVN doublets indicate some overall phonetic ambiguity in the materials.

A third exception to the general trends is the temporary increase in nasal responses just after the offset of the vowel in the English CVCs reported by L&MW (see Figure 4.7). Their explanation is that the vocal murmur after the offset of the vowel is consistent with a following nasal. (The murmur is likely to have been much weaker in the Ohalas' experiment.) L&MW (1991: 277) also make an important point about the use of negative information, i.e., the absence of a cue: "The possibility that the final consonant is nasal is only conclusively banished by the information in Gate +2, containing an oral rather than a nasal release." In other words, in the absence of mismatching information, subjects quite rightly continue to consider hypotheses that are consistent with the input. Similarly, it is difficult to ascertain that vowel nasalization is absent from a vowel; until the end of the vowel, it is always possible that nasalization has not yet begun. This reasoning suggests that there should be nasalized vowel responses to CVCs, particularly near vowel onset; indeed, such responses were found in both studies. This explanation of the presence of nasal responses to CVCs is completely consistent with both representational hypotheses, contrary to the claim that L&MW make about the surface representation hypothesis. According to them, this hypothesis predicts that there should be no nasalized vowel responses to CVCs (because the stored surface representations with nasalized vowels mismatch the oral vowel in the input). But if subjects do not rule out lexical hypotheses unless they have contradictory evidence in the input, words with nasalized vowels (either CVN or CṼC) should be available as possible responses whether they are stored as surface or underlying forms.

There is also a difference between the L&MW and the O&O English CVN results. This is presumably due partially to the closed response set (thus counteracting the statistical fact that there are more possible CVC than CVN responses), and partially to the extent of nasalization in the items. This difference, however, is unlikely to be due to hysteresis, as O&O argue. Cotton & Grosjean (1984) demonstrated that results in the gating task are not confounded by repeated presentation of items, showing that there were very similar results for repeated and nonrepeated presentation formats. The overall similarity between the two sets of results in most of the other conditions of the present experiments also suggests that there are no significant hysteresis effects in these data.

The interesting results, however, are the responses made to Bengali and Hindi nasalized vowels in a context where there are possible CṼC words, namely the Bengali/Hindi CVN/ CṼC triplets (see Table 4.5). The L&MW subjects gave many CṼC responses to the CṼs from CVNs, but very few CVN responses. Why? One reason is that these fragments were confidently recognized as CṼCs: "the subjects' consistent report was that . . . they interpreted this as a nasal vowel followed by an oral consonant" (L&MW, 1991: 273). So for these items, it appears that there was sufficient information in the signal to result in word identification. This is very likely to have been a confound due to the editing procedure, where gates were spliced into silence. As O&O note, this abrupt offset is likely to have cued an obstruent. Gating into noise may reduce this confound. As O&O show, there is indeed a reduction in the size of the preference (in Hindi now) for CṼC responses over CVN responses, given CṼ (stimuli) from CVNs, but the preference is not completely removed. Clearly, a CṼ is considered to be more likely to have come from a CṼC than from a CVN. This is the only challenging result in either experiment, and is best interpreted as a bias in the matching process.

In the Bengali/Hindi triplets, it should be noted that to the extent to which the nasalization in vowels from CVNs and CṼCs is equivalent, we should predict identical performance on CṼs from either context. Until the offset of the vowel, this is true for the Bengali data (see Figures 4.3 and 4.4): there was a gradual increase in the proportion of CṼC responses, a consistently low number of CVN responses, and a gradual reduction in the proportion of CVC responses to these items. As evidence of nasalization accrues, CVC responses were ruled out, and CṼC responses became more popular. For the Hindi items, there was a similar pattern, except that the CṼC bias was less extreme, and that for the CṼC stimuli there were still 20% CVC responses when the listeners could hear the whole word (at the final gate). This degree of overall ambiguity explains why CVC responses did not drop out over gates within the vowel.

5.3 A processing bias

O&O provide an explanation for the CṼC bias to CṼ fragments. They point out that an important perceptual cue for the discrimination of CṼC and CVN words is the release of the vowel into the consonant. Thus, in the absence of a release into a nasal consonant, they argue, listeners prefer to interpret CṼ fragments (taken from both CṼCs and CVNs) as coming from words that do not have nasal consonants, that is, CṼC words. This explanation focuses on how subjects deal with the absence of a perceptual cue. I have already argued, however, that listeners appear not to use negative information: they continue to consider different alternatives until the arrival of positive information which is consistent with some alternatives but not others. But this in turn suggests that both C ṽC and CVN responses should have been made to the C ṽ fragments. I would like to suggest that the C ṽC preference is due to a simple processing bias: listeners prefer to attribute the nasalization they hear to a segment which is present (the vowel) rather than to a segment which is absent (a possible following nasal consonant). This is likely to be a general perceptual bias, rather than something specific to vowel nasalization.

A bias of some kind seems necessary in any account of these data. One is even included in L&MW's account. Since the vowels in the CVN representations are considered to be unspecified for nasality (they are neither oral nor nasal), they match the vowel in a C ṽ fragment. Thus the C ṽC preference does not follow directly from the underspecification hypothesis: it is necessary to postulate an additional bias to account for the data. L&MW (1991: 263) argue that C ṽC words "provide the best match with the speech input, and will therefore be preferred as responses." In other words, they consider that an explicit match of input to stored representation (between C ṽ and C ṽC) is more complete than an implicit match (between C ṽ and CVN, where the vowel in the CVN is not specified for nasality).

There appear to be no direct analogues of the C ṽC bias in the experimental literature. Our intuitions about how such experiments would turn out, however, seem clear, as O&O have demonstrated with the example of the partially erased letters (see Figure 4.9). But in that situation, the reason subjects are likely to respond with a C or an F is simply because the partially erased letter looks most like a C or an F. In the gating task however, the bias seems to be that of attributing a separate cue (nasalization) to other information already present, rather than to something which is absent (though possible in a continuation). A closer analogy to the gating task would therefore be a task where readers are presented with a written word fragment, such as *lar*, and asked to complete the string to form a monosyllabic word. It is likely that readers would come up with completions such as *larch, lard, large,* and *lark;* that is, they would attribute the *r* to the vowel (if they were speakers of nonrhotic dialects of English). But an *r* (depending on font) is also the beginning of an *n*, giving possible completions such as *lance, land, lane,* and *lank.* It is unlikely that readers would attribute the *r* to a following *n* (or *m*).

As far as I can tell, this bias has not been shown experimentally. Other biases, however, have been found in the gating task. Tyler (1984) presented listeners with a range of different materials including bisyllabic words, presented in isolation, with gates every 50 ms. Over the first five gates (that is, up to 250 ms into the word), 60.8% of responses to these fragments were monosyllabic. Even at the fifth gate, 56% of responses were still monosyllables. One can estimate that listeners were hearing approximately half of the complete word at the fifth gate, that is, approximately the first syllable. Listeners appear to prefer to give monosyllabic responses when they are presented with a single syllable, even though the fragments were consistent with longer words. A single syllable thus tends to be interpreted as such, not as evidence for a bisyllable whose second syllable is absent. Furthermore, over the entire experiment, Tyler (1984) found that for the first two gates, 63% of responses were words which occur frequently in the language. Listeners appear to be biased to give the most plausible response. These data do not provide an exact analogy to the CṼC bias, but they clearly show not only that there are biases in the gating task, but that the biases are towards what is most plausible given the available input. It seems likely that another example of this type of bias is what has been shown for CṼ fragments: that listeners prefer to form a unified percept of the information they are presented with rather than to associate part of the information they have already received with an absent continuation.

5.4 Summary

O&O argue that their results are generally consistent with a surface representation hypothesis. What I have attempted to do in this response is take their line of argument further forward. First, I have argued that these data are best explained in the context of a model of the processing which takes place during the presentation of word fragments in a gating task. Subjects compare the fragments to lexical hypotheses with which they are consistent, and display a marked sensitivity over successive gates to the changing acoustic-phonetic information in the input. Second, I have shown that the CṼC bias is compatible with this model. The tendency for speakers of languages which contrast nasal and oral vowels to identify CṼ fragments as coming from CṼC rather than CVN words can be accounted for by a bias: listeners prefer not to associate available acoustic-phonetic information with a segment that is absent.

The processing account I have discussed may seem to be more consistent with the surface representation hypothesis than with the underspecification hypothesis. But it is important to stress that it is in fact neutral with regard to lexical representations, which could either contain surface phonetic details or be radically underspecified. Obviously, listeners must perform the matching required in the gating task by referring to stored lexical entries. But it is unlikely that they consult the representations themselves. Instead, they compare the fragment with what is available as output from the lexicon. If the lexicon consisted of surface representations, words with surface detail could be output directly for comparison. If the lexicon consisted of underspecified representations, the input could again be matched against the output of lexical lookup. This output would not be an underspecified form, since this would not provide the necessary information for a comparison with the surface phonetic detail available in the input. It would be a structure on which postlexical rules have operated. This is my most fundamental disagreement with L&MW. Even if forms are stored in an underspecified way, when it comes to comparing these forms against the input fragments, postlexical rules are likely to be applied. The structure that is then available for comparison is a surface form. The gating task is therefore not an appropriate tool with which to study the form of representations in the mental lexicon.

Note

* Preparation of this paper was supported by the Joint Councils Initiative in Cognitive Science and HCI, grant no. E304/148. I thank Dennis Norris and Anne Cutler for their comments.

References

Cotton, S. & F. Grosjean. 1984. The gating paradigm: A comparison of successive and individual presentation formats. *Perception & Psychophysics*, 35(1): 41–48.

Lahiri, A. & W. Marslen-Wilson. 1991. The mental representation of lexical form: a phonological approach to the recognition lexicon. *Cognition,* 38: 245–294.

Lahiri, A. & W. Marslen-Wilson. 1992. Lexical processing and phonological representation. In G. J. Docherty & D. R. Ladd (eds.), *Papers in Laboratory Phonology II: Gesture, Segment, Prosody.* Cambridge: Cambridge University Press, 229–254.

Tyler, L. K. 1984. The structure of the initial cohort: Evidence from gating. *Perception & Psychophysics,* 36(5): 417–427.

6

On the status of redundant features:
the case of backing and rounding in American English

KENNETH DE JONG*

6.1 Introduction: enhancement features

Stevens, Keyser, & Kawasaki (1986) lay out a theory of phonological features in which languages employ features from a universal set in two different ways. Each language employs some features from this set to minimally distinguish lexical items; this is a distinctive use of the feature. Cases often arise in which a particular feature is never employed all by itself to contrast lexical items, but rather, it always occurs in conjunction with another, distinctive, feature. For reasons of compactness of description, various linguists, e.g. Halle (1958, 1964), have proposed that, at some level of the linguistic grammar, only one of the features needs to be specified. The other of the two features is redundant, and can thus be filled in by rule.

While the phonological literature on redundancy of featural specifications is quite large, there has been relatively little consideration of these phonologically based distinctions in feature usage from a phonetic standpoint. Stevens *et al.* add the phonetic property of variability to the phonological, informationally based diagnostic of redundant and distinctive features. They state that, while distinctive features serve directly to convey lexical distinctions, redundant features serve to enhance the salience of the distinctive features. Thus, an alternative term for redundant features is enhancement features. As a corollary to this claim, they suggest that distinctive features are invariantly present in speech, while enhancement features are more variable, being employed especially in situations where the distinctive feature may be obscured by some attribute of the context in which the feature appears.

The present paper reports on aspects of some American English speakers' production of back vowels and semi-vowels which shed light on the relationship between distinctive and redundant features. Stevens *et al.*'s theory of enhancement features has four aspects which are important for the present study.

68

First, enhancement features phonetically increase the salience of the distinctive features to which they are redundantly specified. The presence of an enhancement feature makes activity associated with a distinctive feature more effective in producing an acoustic contrast. Second, enhancement features may, over time, take over the role of the distinctive feature to which they are redundantly specified. Enhancement features may become distinctive features, and conversely, distinctive features may take on an enhancement capacity, or simply disappear. Third, enhancement features can be identified for a particular language by the fact that they are informationally unnecessary. All lexical contrasts can be communicated by the specification of other distinctive features, and enhancement features, then, can be filled in by rule in the phonological grammar. Fourth, enhancement features also differ from distinctive features in that they are more variable. According to Stevens *et al.*, distinctive features will always occur in the phonetic expression of a particular lexical item; enhancement features will occur especially in conditions where the distinctive contrast might be obscured by context. This paper examines how these four aspects of this version of enhancement theory apply to the case of rounding and backing in American English.

6.2 An example: tongue backing and lip rounding in American English

The first example of an enhancement feature/distinctive feature pair considered by Stevens *et al.* is that of [back] and [round]. Articulatorily, [back] refers to a retracting of the tongue body, and [round] to the protrusion of the lips. Stevens *et al.* show that rounding is a reasonable example of an enhancement feature for backing, by showing that the acoustic correlates of backing and rounding are complementary. Backing, especially with the tongue body raised toward an oral constriction, has the effect of lowering the second formant (F_2). Rounding, the protrusion of the lips, has a similar depressing effect on F_2. They point out that, by rounding the lips, the F_2 lowering will be increased enough for the first formant (F_1) and F_2 to closely approximate, thus increasing the salience of the general lowering of the vowel's timbre. In a similar vein, they argue that another feature, labiality, the approximation of the lips, may have an enhancing relationship with backing, at least for high vowels. Again, the approximation of the lips, like backing and rounding, lowers F_2. This relationship is readily apparent in the electronic analogue modeling of vocal tract acoustics reported in Stevens *et al.*, just as it is in other more general works, such as Stevens & House (1955), Fant (1960), and Maeda (1990).

Considering the case of American English in particular, the second aspect of enhancement theory, mentioned above, is also evident. The roles of backing and rounding seem to be in a process of change. Northern midwestern dialects, such

Kenneth de Jong

as those which will be examined in more detail below, have both rounding and backing in non-low back vowels. However, other dialects are well on their way towards either eliminating the redundant rounding specification, or switching the contrast to one of rounding and eliminating the newly redundant backing specification. A dialect typical of Anglo southern California exhibits little or no rounding of back non-low vowels. Thus, here the redundant rounding feature is being eliminated. In contrast, some speakers of the southern midwest seem to be losing the backing contrast. Figure 6.1 shows tongue movement trajectories taken from an X-ray microbeam database, such as that analyzed below. The speaker in this case is from St. Louis. Shown here are the movement trajectories of one token of the nonsense sequences, "keek" (above) and "kook" (below). As can readily be seen, the tongue pellet movement trajectories lie in identical horizontal locations within the oral cavity. This indicates that the horizontal tongue positioning in the sagittal plane for the two sequences is nearly identical, and thus there is no retraction distinction between the two vowels. A retraction distinction would show up as a shift to the left in the lower panel of Figure 6.1. The difference between the two sequences lies in the protrusion of the lips – shown to the right in the figure. The lips during the vowel in "kook" are more anterior, indicating an increased rounding of the vowel. Thus, the distinction between these two sequences is more accurately described as between [kik] and [kyk], not between [kik] and [kuk], as in the northern midwestern dialects, and not between [kik] and [kɯk], as in the Anglo southern California dialects.

Considering again the case of the northern midwestern dialects, which have both phonetic rounding and tongue backing, the question arises as to which feature, [back] or [round], is redundant. To answer this question, consider the featural specifications given in Table 6.1. The specifications are reflective of claims made in Chomsky & Halle (1968); many more recent phonological works assume these or their equivalent autosegmental representations. This description is, however, overspecified, and thus some of the specifications are not necessary to contrast each vowel. There are several possible ways of compacting the representation, so some criterion must be used to determine which analysis should be assumed. Usually, the optimal compaction is determined as that which needs the smallest number of specifications over the whole set of vowels (as argued for in Halle, 1958). Stevens et al., however, describe the process as limiting the number of features which must be used, rather than the number of specifications. In the case of general midwestern American English, it is not possible to eliminate either the rounding or the backing specifications, since the mid, lax vowels contrast minimally in both features: [ɛ] and [ʌ] contrast minimally in the feature [back], and [ʌ] and [ɔ] contrast minimally in the feature [round]. However, the specifications of the vowel [ɔ] are debatable in the general American case, and more important, the vowel [ɔ] has merged with the vowel [ɑ] in most of the western and western

70

midwestern dialects of American English. Thus, in these dialects it is possible to compact the underlying feature set by eliminating the feature [round], filling in the values with the rules given in (1)–(5). For this dialect of American English, backing and rounding are a distinctive and enhancing feature, respectively.

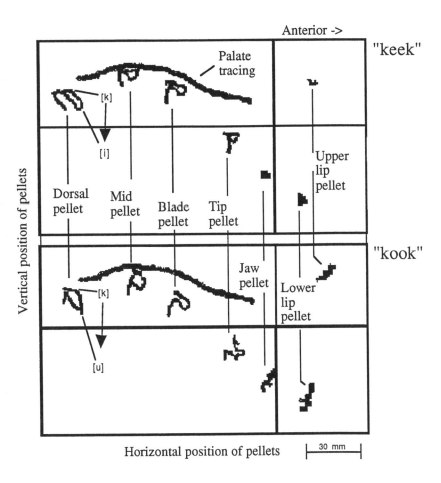

Figure 6.1. Pellet movement trajectories for the utterance, "keek" (top panel), and "kook" (bottom panel), produced by a speaker of a southern midwest dialect of American English (St. Louis). The horizontal location of the tongue pellets for the two utterances is very similar, while the horizontal position of the lip pellets differs.

71

Table 6.1. Feature specifications for American English vowels.

	High	Low	Back	Round	Tense
i	+	–	–	–	+
e	–	–	–	–	+
ɑ	–	+	+	–	+
o	–	–	+	+	+
u	+	–	+	+	+
ɪ	+	–	–	–	–
æ	–	+	–	–	–
ɛ	–	–	–	–	–
ʌ	–	–	+	–	–
ɔ	–	–	+	+	–
ʊ	+	–	+	+	–

(1) [+high, +back] → [+round]
(2) [–high, +back, –low, +tense] → [+round]
(3) [–back] → [–round]
(4) [+low] → [–round]
(5) [–high, tense] → [–round]

6.3 An experiment: the articulation of [ow]

Given that rounding and backing conform well to three of the four aspects of Stevens *et al.*'s theory mentioned above, their theory predicts that the articulation of the backing specification by the tongue body should be invariant, while the articulation of the rounding and labiality features should be more variable. Following, I shall present aspects of an analysis of articulatory records of some western northern American English speakers which suggest that redundant specification of a contrast makes that contrast more robust. Other aspects of the theory should be refined, however, especially the claim that distinctive features are invariantly present in speaker behavior.

The corpus of X-ray microbeam data was gathered at the University of Wisconsin (Nadler, Abbs, & Fujimura, 1987). X-ray microbeam systems use a narrow beam of X-rays to record the movement in the sagittal plane of metal pellets attached to speakers' articulators. The corpus which I discuss consists of the x- (horizontal) and y- (vertical) positions of seven pellets, three located on the tongue, one each on the upper and lower lip, and two indexing the movement of the jaw. Of interest in the present study are pellets placed midsagittally on the vermilion border of the upper and lower lip, and the rear-most of the tongue pellets, placed approximately 40 mm from the apex of the tongue as measured with the tongue extended. The lip pellets should index the actions associated with rounding and labiality. The rearmost tongue pellet indexes movement of the tongue dorsum as it is used to make velar constrictions for high back vowels. In addition, a time-aligned digital acoustic record of each utterance was recorded.

The speakers recorded in this corpus were all speakers of some northern midwestern dialect of American English, and, thus, had diphthongs whose nuclear component was fairly far back – as opposed to more southern dialects of midwestern American English where the nuclear component in this diphthong is much more centralized. To assess the variability in the production of this vowel, it appeared in varied segmental environments as well as with different amounts of stress. The speakers were cued to recite one of eight target words in the frame sentence, *I said, "Put the _____ on the table."* The target words were *toe, toes, toast, toasts, tote, totes, toad,* and *toads*. To vary the amount of stress on the target words, the subjects were given miniature discourse conditions in which they were to respond to someone mishearing the sentence. For example, to elicit a rendition of the sentence with nuclear (sentence) accent on *put*, the subjects were given the following dialogue:

Did you say, "Throw the toes on the table"?
I said, "ᴘᴜᴛ the toes on the table."

There were three accentual conditions. Speakers placed nuclear accent on the target word, before the target word (precluding accents on the target word), and after the target word. In the last condition, the speakers consistently placed a prenuclear accent on the target word; thus, the target word appears with three levels of stress: nuclear accented, prenuclear accented and postnuclear (unaccented).

6.4 Redundant features and coarticulatory robustness

The top of Figure 6.2 plots the movement of the rear-most tongue pellet during a nuclear accented rendition of the target word. (In this figure, as in other ones in this paper, anterior is to the right.) The motion displayed here for the vowel is what one would expect, if one assumes that the vertical motion of the tongue dorsum is roughly correlated with the height of F_1 and the horizontal motion of the dorsum is correlated with the height of F_2. As is illustrated schematically in the lower part of the figure, one expects a lowering of the dorsum for the relatively high F_1 in [o], followed by a raising of the dorsum for the lower F_1 in

Kenneth de Jong

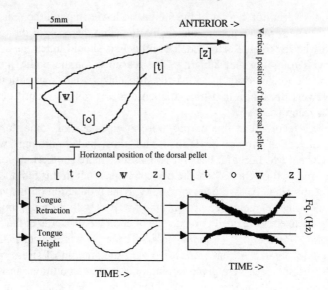

Figure 6.2. A tongue dorsum movement trajectory for an utterance of the word *toes* by speaker MB (upper panel). Below is an schematic illustration of the expected formant movement patterns associated with such a dorsal motion.

the offglide (hereafter transcribed as [w]). In addition, one expects a retraction motion of the dorsum for the F_2 lowering in [w]. This retraction should occur after the lowering motion, yielding the circular motion exhibited in the top of Figure 6.2.

However, this motion was not always present in this speaker's utterances of the target word. Figure 6.3 represents the dorsal motion for three other repetitions of the same word by the same speaker. The top panel shows one of many cases in the corpus in which there is no apparent raising and retraction of the dorsum for velar constriction in [w]. There simply is no velar constriction motion corresponding to the off-glide. It is tempting at this point to simply say that the [w] has been deleted in these cases. However, there are two arguments against this approach. The first is evident in the lower two panels of Figure 6.3 which show two more tokens of the same word by the same speaker. These tokens show that the disappearance of the velar constriction motion is a gradient effect – here are two tokens with less and less raising and retraction of the dorsum. Deleting the offglide would yield a categorical distinction, rather than a gradient one. The movement patterns in this corpus show that the velar off-glide is apparent in the dorsal movement to a variable degree.

74

ANTERIOR ->

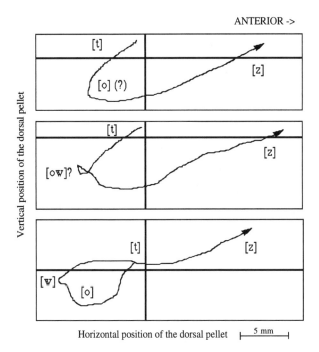

Figure 6.3. Tongue dorsum movement trajectories for three utterances of the word *toes* by speaker MB. Scale is as in Figure 6.2.

The second argument against positing a deletion of the [w] is even more revealing and shows another way in which the notion of enhancement is useful. The top panel in Figure 6.4 is a spectral representation of the utterance shown in the top panel of Figure 6.3. The bottom panel in Figure 6.4 is of the utterance shown in the top panel of Figure 6.2. Especially of interest here is the fall in F_2 for the offglide, even though there was no apparent velar constriction motion for the offglide in this token. Thus, even though articulatory tongue backing was not present in all of the tokens, the primary acoustic correlate of phonological backing was present.

To more carefully assess the relationship between the observed motion of the dorsal pellet and the height of F_2, the timing of various acoustic events was measured and correlated with the timing of the tongue dorsum retraction. From spectral displays, such as Figure 6.4, the value and timing of the highest point in the F_1 trace, and the lowest point in the F_2 trace were estimated. The location of the F_1 maximum and F_2 minimum were confirmed by consulting LPC time slices, calculated with a window size of 20 ms. Maximum values of F_1 and minimum values of F_2 were measured as peaks in the LPC time slices. In all of

75

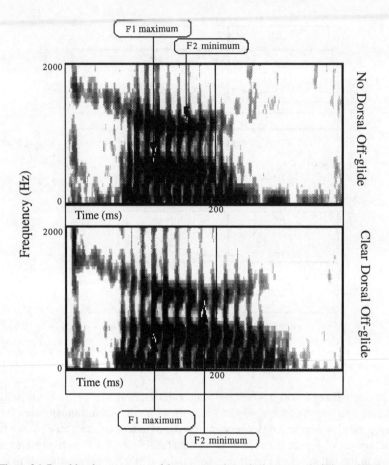

Figure 6.4. Broad-band spectrograms of the utterance shown in the top panel of Figure 6.3 (above) and the top panel of Figure 6.2 (below). Also shown here are timing marks for the two acoustic events discussed in this paper, the F_1 maximum and the F_2 minimum.

the cases and for each of the speakers the F_2 minimum came later in time than the F_1 maximum. This was the case even though many of the dorsal motion trajectories, such as that shown in the top panel of Figure 6.3, had a retraction maximum which preceded the time of maximum lowering.

Figure 6.5 plots the timing of the F_2 minima relative to the timing of a dorsal index of the occurrence of the offglide, usually the timing of maximum dorsal retraction.[1] Both events are relative to the timing of a dorsal index of the [o], usually the timing of maximum dorsal lowering. The speaker is the same as that shown in Figures 6.2 and 6.3. Tokens with simultaneous dorsal retraction and F_2 lowering would appear along the diagonal line, which indicates the function, x = y. Tokens above the line indicate an F_2 lowering occurring after the dorsal retraction; tokens below the line indicate F_2 lowering occurring before the dorsal retraction. In many of the cases, the F_2 minimum corresponds closely in time with the dorsal retraction, as is evident in the clustering of points around the x = y diagonal. However, there are cases in which the F_2 minimum comes considerably later in time than the dorsal retraction, as is evident in points lying above the diagonal. Many of these are cases such as that in the top of Figure 6.3, in which there was no apparent dorsal motion for the [w] offglide.

Figure 6.6 suggests that the F_2 lowering in these cases is due to labial activity. Figure 6.6 plots for the same speaker the deviation of the time of F_2 lowering from the time of dorsal retraction against the deviation of the time of the maximum lip protrusion from the time of dorsal retraction. There is a fairly strong correlation between the timing of the two events. When the F_2 lowering occurs much later than the dorsal retraction, the labial protrusion maximum occurs later as well.

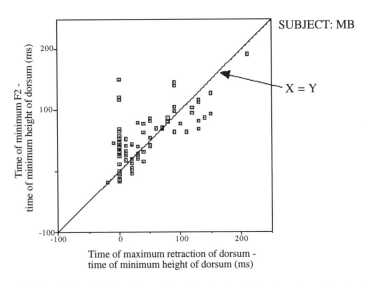

Figure 6.5. The timing of the F_2 minimum plotted against the timing of maximum dorsal retraction. If the F_2 minimum were synchronous with the maximum dorsal retraction (as would be the case if dorsal retraction were uniquely and directly causing the F_2 lowering), all tokens would lie on the x = y function.

77

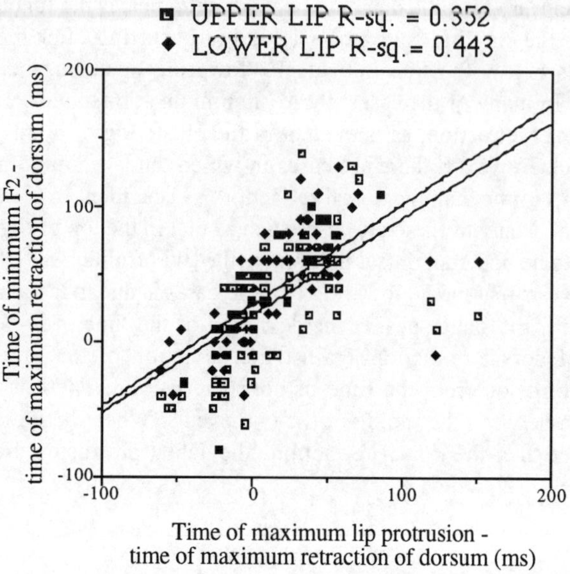

Figure 6.6. The temporal deviation of the F_2 minimum from the time of maximum dorsal retraction plotted against the temporal deviation of the time of maximum upper lip protrusion from the time of maximum dorsal retraction.

A reasonable interpretation of these results is that there are many cases in which demands of the neighboring alveolar consonants on the positioning of the tongue body, when weighed against the demands of the velar offglide, result in a more advanced positioning of the tongue dorsum. Hence the offglide is gradiently being obscured according to the temporal proximity and strength of the neighboring alveolar consonants. In these cases in which the velar motion is obscured, however, the distinctive fall in F_2 remains, because there is a redundant specification of labial rounding which remains relatively unperturbed by the alveolar consonants. This is because alveolar consonants do not make demands on the placement of the lips (with the possible exception of [s]).

These data suggest that redundantly specifying a contrast not only increases the acoustic salience of the contrast, but also makes the contrast more robust to coarticulatory influences. In the present case, the redundant specification of lingual and labial activity gives the speaker more options in maintaining the contrast in the face of the conflicting motor demands of neighboring consonants.

6.5 A phonetic relationship between rounding and backing

These results present a problem for the analysis of rounding and backing as an enhancement/distinctive feature pair in that the articulatory correlate of backing specifications is not invariantly present in speakers' lingual activity, even though [back] should be the distinctive specification. One possible explanation for this aspect of the results is that the rounding specification is the invariant, distinctive feature, while the backing specification is the optional enhancement feature. Perhaps the unit being studied here should be treated as a consonant, and therefore the redundancy analysis above may not be appropriate for the present case.

Switching the redundant and enhancement roles of backing and rounding does not alleviate the problem, since the rounding is not invariant either. What is more, the variation in rounding is related to the variation in dorsal retraction. Figure 6.7 plots the most protruded position of the lips against horizontal position of the tongue dorsum for two of the three speakers. Speaker MB exhibits a negative correlation between tongue retraction and lip protrusion. Speaker SD exhibits a positive correlation between retraction and protrusion. The third speaker shows the same pattern as speaker SD.

Theories of phonetic variability, such as Lindblom's Hyper- and Hypoarticulation (H&H) theory (Lindblom, 1983, 1990), would predict this positive correlation between retraction and protrusion. Lindblom posits a continuum between hyper- and hypo-articulate speech. Hyperarticulate speech – found in more formal settings, and in noisy conditions – is characterized by increased speaker activity in producing distinctions. In the present case, this would mean more tongue retraction and simultaneously more lip protrusion. Indeed, Stevens *et al.* (1986) allow for this kind of variability in redundant features, when they note that redundant features may be particularly called upon when there is contextual danger to the communication of the distinction, conditions which Lindblom would expect to give rise to hyperarticulate speech. The bottom plot of Figure 6.7 (speaker SD) shows this positive relationship between lip protrusion and dorsal retraction. When the tongue body is further retracted (evident in a more negative, posterior position), the lips are further protruded (evident in a more positive, anterior position). This is also the result one expects due to variation associated with stress – stress in English acts to increase the movement of articulators toward distinctively specified positions (de Jong, Beckman & Edwards, 1993). Due to this stress-related effect on the overall amount of retraction and protrusion, separate regressions were calculated for each stress category. For this speaker, the positive relationship also holds within each stress category. This effect can be interpreted as a result of background variation along Lindblom's H&H scale occurring even within stress categories.

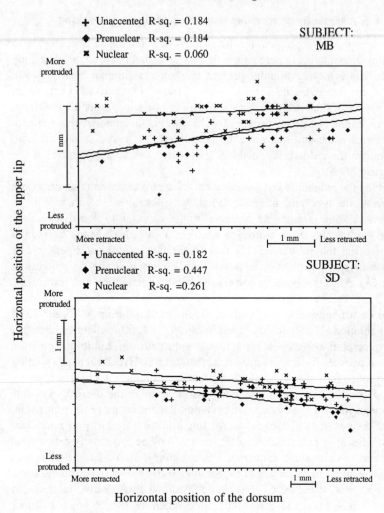

Figure 6.7. The horizontal position of the upper lip plotted against the horizontal position of the tongue dorsum for two of the speakers. All position values are with respect to a consistent reference point.

The top plot (subject MB), however, shows a different and more interesting relationship. Here, there is a negative relationship between lip protrusion and tongue advancement – the less tongue retraction (evident in a more positive, anterior location of the tongue pellet), the more protrusion (evident in a more positive, anterior location of the lip pellets). This speaker shows a tendency to increase rounding in those situations where retraction has been reduced. This relationship can be interpreted as indicating a compensatory relationship between labial protrusion and dorsal retraction; that is perturbations of the movement of one articulator are being counter-balanced by activity in another articulator. Similar results are evident in analyses of this speaker's renditions of the word *put* as well as in speakers analyzed by Perkell, Matthies, Svirsky & Jordan (1993). This raises problems for enhancement theory as Stevens *et al.* (1986) describe it. Neither feature, round nor back, is invariantly present at the level of articulation. Both features vary. Thus, it is not clear that there is any phonetic distinction between enhancement and distinctive features.

6.6 Labial–dorsal compensation and featural specifications

Compensatory relationships between articulatory positions, such as those shown here, have also been demonstrated for articulatory sub-components of an articulatory complex, such as the jaw and lower lip, or the upper and lower lip for labial closures (e.g. as shown in Abbs, Gracco & Cole, 1984, and Shaiman, 1989) or the tongue blade and the jaw in coronal articulations (e.g. in Kelso, Tuller, Vatikiotis-Bateson & Fowler, 1984). These kinds of complementary relationships have provided a basis for recent theories of speech production, such as Task Dynamics (Saltzman & Munhall, 1990), which treat the various speech articulators as being yoked together around the attainment of articulatory goals. Both the jaw and the lip contribute to the approximation of the lips; both the jaw and the tongue blade contribute to the attainment of alveolar closures.

However, labial–dorsal compensation differs from these earlier cases. Each of these earlier examples indicates a yoking of articulators centered around the articulation of a particular feature – [labial] for jaw and lip, [coronal] for jaw and tongue blade. The labial and the dorsal activity studied here, however, are thought to be behaviors associated with two separate features, [round] and [back]. Labial–dorsal compensation suggests that activities associated with different features may be phonetically yoked in the same fashion as articulatory structures are yoked together for the production of a single feature.

In Stevens *et al.*'s (1986) theory, as well as that presented more generally in a later paper, Halle & Stevens (1990), the phonology presents to the phonetics an abstract structure which includes both underlying and redundantly specified features. Many recent phonological theories (e.g. Clements, 1985; Sagey, 1986; Halle & Stevens, 1990) group features hierarchically, based primarily on the types of phonological processes, especially assimilations, apparent in a sampling of the world's languages. Thus a final representation to be interpreted phonetically for the segment [w] would be as shown in (6) or (7). In general, it is not difficult to see how such structures can be mapped onto phonetic goals. Terminal features under one articulator node can be interpreted as giving the location and various attributes of a vocal tract constriction to be implemented.

Information about the degree and time course of the execution of the constriction is to be taken from major class specifications found on or around the root node, as well as from information about the position of the features in the prosodic structure of the utterance (as is discussed in de Jong, Beckman & Edwards, 1993). Such prosodic information is usually graphically described as residing above the root node in the form of labeled metrical trees (see, e.g. Pierrehumbert & Beckman, 1988).

The present case of rounding and backing presents a problem for this general model of the relationship between phonetics and phonology. There are two separate feature complexes – one labial-dependent, one dorsal-dependent – which are said to represent the labial and dorsal movements observed in the speech of the present speakers. The phonological representations given here, however, are missing one crucial piece of information for mapping features onto phonetic goals: that labiality and backing are subparts of a single phonetic unit, a contrast.

(6) (7)

Halle & Stevens (1990): Sagey (1986):

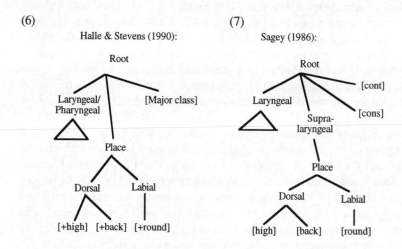

There are two types of approaches to remedy the problem. The first general approach is to reconsider the relationship between phonological features and phonetic goals. Specifically, one could propose that what is phonetically important in phonological representations are not the featural primes used in expressing phonological operations, but rather the meaningful lexical contrasts. Speakers in the process of acquiring and fine tuning their production systems are presented with the problem of producing acceptable lexical contrasts. Their solution to this problem may involve any of a number of articulatory strategies, including in the present case different amounts of rounding and tongue backing. Speakers acquiring a motor system for producing the front–back distinction may come up with rather different techniques for producing the distinction – using the tongue dorsum, using the lips, or using some combination of the two. Variation in the solution to this problem, then, provides the seeds for diachronic variation, such as that exhibited in American English, as aspects of the particular articulatory strategies become part of the formulation of what is considered an acceptable contrast.

Stating this general approach in terms of a difference in phonetically and phonologically important information entails that phonological representations do not directly dictate phonetic behavior. One might say that phonological descriptions tell us about the informational structure that speakers use in organizing their lexicons and their morphological systems, but they do not tell us directly about the physical behavior of a particular speaker. While this view may allow for a simple approach to the present problem, insulating the phonetics from the phonology complicates the understanding of the phonetics and of the phonology. It is difficult to imagine how to approach the study of the phonetics of languages with particularly rich morphological structure – ones in which the structure of the lexicon is not clear from rudimentary phonemic analysis – without having a clear analysis of the phonological system. Similarly, it is difficult to imagine how to approach the phonological study of (postlexical) prosodic systems (whose construction is not primarily posited on the basis of lexical contrasts) without assuming a fairly immediate relationship between phonetic behavior and surface phonological structure.

The second general approach is to change the posited phonological structure. For example, one could modify the phonological inventory with an eye toward providing more acoustically isomorphic phonological groupings. In this case, adding the feature [grave] (Jakobson, Fant & Halle, 1963) would be one possible solution. This is essentially the structure argued for by Odden (1991), using the same kinds of argumentation from phonological processes used to support the feature hierarchies posited by Sagey (1986), and Halle & Stevens (1990). A part of the featural representation for [w] is shown in (8). The feature node *Back–Round* combines the features back and round into a single constituent, and it is in the articulation of this constituent that (at least) subject MB's labial and dorsal activity is focused. The labial–dorsal yoking under the feature [grave], then would be exactly parallel to the jaw-lip yoking for the feature [labial].

This solution is not entirely without problems, however. For example, the lip–jaw yoking and the labial–dorsal yoking are not entirely parallel with respect to the posited phonological structure. While there are no phonological features representing the jaw and the lip separately under labial, there remain the features [round] and [back]. Are these to be considered separate phonetic goals from that represented by the parent [grave]? Or should the [round] and [back] features

Kenneth de Jong

simply be eliminated? This would leave the [grave] feature as a terminal node to be interpreted by some unspecified means, labial or dorsal.

(8)

Odden (1991):

Place
Dorsal   Coronal   Labial   Vowel Place
Height   Back-Round
                [+back]   [+round]

Another potential problem with changing the feature inventory to match up with phonetic goals, might also become apparent in examining other cases of redundancy. Keating (1985) suggested several cases which she construed as cases in which several phonetic parameters are yoked together under one feature, such as the case of vowel lengthening before voiced obstruents in English. Vowel lengthening acts as a redundant cue to voicing distinctions. A parallel case to that found above for rounding and backing would be evident in a compensatory relationship between amount of voicing and amount of lengthening in the preceding vowel. Another case would be that of consonant-induced high tone in Chonnam Korean (Jun, 1990). Here, initial high tones appear on initial syllables after aspirated and fortis obstruents, while low tones appear after lenis obstruents. A parallel to the case above would be a compensatory relationship between F_0 raising and the sharpness of the attack for the fortis consonant. If such cases often show the same kind of mutual compensation as that shown here for backing and rounding, the feature inventory might become prohibitively large.

A second way of changing the phonological structure, without modifying the inventory of features, is to add some sort of linking mechanism, which would effectively unify previously disparate features on a language specific basis (though the linking mechanism might be governed by universal principles). Stevens et al. (1986) talk of such linking in terms of transformational redundancy rules. Similar is another suggestion of theirs, that distinctive features may be subsumed under "cover-features". (See the similar treatment of the feature [flat] by Jakobson et al., 1963.) Whatever the formal shape of the mechanism, it should have the effect of allowing one to express a contrast as a phonological entity comprised of several features.

Of these solutions, modifying the feature hierarchy is most in line with current generative phonological theory. Pursuing this line of explanation,

84

researchers into the structure of featural representations should pay attention to more than just the expression of phonological processes; they should also account for the apparent phonetic goals of the speakers of the languages being analyzed. Thus, though issues in feature geometry might not be decided by *a priori* considerations of vocal tract anatomy or other phonetic facts (as is pointed out by Clements, 1985), they should be amenable to explaining the phonetic behavior of particular speakers of a particular language. In line with this goal, the present study shows that the investigation of feature structure will be especially illuminated by careful phonetic research on the variation found in the production and perception of similar redundantly specified contrasts in a broad range of languages.

Notes

researchers into the structure of featural representations should pay attention to more than just the expression of phonological processes; they should also account for the apparent phonetic goals of the speakers of the languages being analyzed. Thus, though issues in feature geometry might not be decided by *a priori* considerations of vocal tract anatomy or other phonetic facts (as is pointed out by Clements, 1985), they should be amenable to explaining the phonetic behavior of particular speakers of a particular language. In line with this goal, the present study shows that the investigation of feature structure will be especially illuminated by careful phonetic research on the variation found in the production and perception of similar redundantly specified contrasts in a broad range of languages.

Notes

* Work supported by the NSF under grant number IRI-8617852 and by the NIDCD under grant number T32 DC00029. I also especially thank Mary Beckman, Lisa Zsiga and two anonymous reviewers for helpful comments on an earlier version of this paper.

1 In cases in which maximum retraction was reached before maximum lowering, such as in the upper and lower trajectories in Figure 6.3, the dorsal event for both [o] and [w] was a forty five degree combination of retraction and lowering. Thus, all of the points in Figure 6.5 with x approximately equal to zero had the trajectory shape of the upper and lower ones in Figure 6.3.

References

Abbs, J. H., V. L. Gracco & K. J. Cole. 1984. Sensorimotor actions in the control of multimovement speech gestures. *Trends in Neuroscience* 6: 391–395.

Chomsky, N. & M. Halle. 1968. *The Sound Pattern of English.* New York: Harper and Row.

Clements, G. N. 1985. The geometry of phonological features. *Phonology Yearbook* 2: 225–252.

de Jong, K. J., M. E. Beckman & J. R. Edwards. 1993. The interplay between prosodic structure and coarticulation. *Language and Speech* 36: 197–212.

Fant, G. 1960. *The Acoustic Theory of Speech Production.* The Hague: Mouton.

Halle, M. 1958. Questions of linguistics. *Il Nuovo Cimento* (suppl.) 13, Series X: 494–517.

Halle, M. 1964. On the bases of phonology. In J. A. Fodor & J. J. Katz (eds.), *The Structure of Language: Readings in the Philosophy of Language.* Englewood Cliffs, NJ: Prentice-Hall, 324–333.

Halle, M. & K. N. Stevens. 1991. Knowledge of language and the sounds of speech. In J. Sundberg, L. Nord & R. Carlson (eds.), *Music, Language, Speech, and Brain:*

Kenneth de Jong

Wenner-Gren Center International Symposium Series, Vol. 59. Basingstoke, Hampshire: MacMillan Press, 1–19.

Jakobson, R., G. Fant & M. Halle. 1963. *Preliminaries to Speech Analysis.* Cambridge, MA: MIT Press.

Jun, S.-A. 1990. The accentual pattern and prosody of the Chonnam dialect of Korean. *Ohio State University Working Papers in Linguistics* 38: 121–140.

Keating, P. A. 1985. The phonology-phonetics interface. *UCLA Working Papers in Phonetics* 62: 14–33.

Kelso, J. A. S., B. Tuller, E. Vatikiotis-Bateson & C. A. Fowler. 1984. Functionally specific articulatory cooperation following perturbations during speech: evidence for coordinative structures. *Journal of Experimental Psychology: Human Perceptions and Performance* 10: 812–832.

Lindblom, B. E. F. 1983. Economy of speech gestures. In P. F. MacNeilage (ed.), *Speech Production.* New York: Springer Verlag, 217–245.

Lindblom, B. E. F. 1990. Explaining phonetic variation: a sketch of the H&H theory. In H. J. Hardcastle & A. Marchal (eds.), *Speech Production and Speech Modelling: NATO ASI Series D: Behavioural and Social Sciences*, Vol. 55. Dordrecht: Kluwer A.P., 403–439.

Maeda, S. 1990. Compensatory articulation during speech: evidence from the analysis and synthesis of vocal-tract shapes using an articulatory model. In H. J. Hardcastle & A. Marchal (eds.), *Speech Production and Speech Modelling*, NATO ASI Series D: Behavioural and Social Sciences, Vol. 55. Dordrecht: Kluwer A. P., 130–150.

Nadler, R. D., J. H. Abbs & O. Fujimura. 1987. Speech movement research using the new X-ray microbeam system. *Proceedings of the XIth International Congress of Phonetic Sciences,* Tallinn, 1: 221–224.

Odden, D. 1991. Vowel geometry. *Phonology* 8: 261–289.

Perkell, J. S., M. L. Matthies, M. A. Svirsky & M. I. Jordan. 1993. Trading relations between tongue-body raising and lip rounding in production of the vowel /u/: a pilot 'motor equivalence' study. *Journal of the Acoustical Society of America* 93: 2948–2961.

Pierrehumbert, J. B. & M. E. Beckman. 1988. *Japanese Tone Structure.* Cambridge, MA: MIT Press.

Sagey, E. C. 1986. The Representation of Features and Relations in Non-linear Phonology. Ph.D. dissertation, MIT.

Saltzman, E. L. & K. G. Munhall. 1990. A dynamical approach to gestural patterning in speech production. *Ecological Psychology* 1: 333–392.

Shaiman, S. 1989. Kinematic and electromyographic responses to perturbation of the jaw. *Journal of the Acoustical Society of America* 86: 78–88.

Stevens, K. N. & A. S. House. 1955. Development of a quantitative description of vowel articulation. *Journal of the Acoustical Society of America* 27: 484–493.

Stevens, K. N. & S. J. Keyser. 1989. Primary features and their enhancement in consonants. *Language* 65: 81–106.

Stevens, K.N., S.J. Keyser & H. Kawasaki. 1986. Toward a phonetic and phonological theory of redundant features. In J. S. Perkell & D. H. Klatt (eds.), *Invariance and Variability in Speech Processes.* Hillsdale, NJ: Lawrence Erlbaum Associates, 426–449.

7

The perceptual basis of some sound patterns

JOHN J. OHALA

By invitation of the editors, the following is a summary of remarks I offered at the Fourth Conference in Laboratory Phonology on the subject of language change and its causes. They were stimulated principally by observations by Tore Janson.

7.1 Features: positive and/or negative correlates?

Janson stated that "a credible model for perceptual retrieval should contain only such features that can be detected in the auditory signal. This excludes features . . . that have no positive phonetic correlates at all." There are many cases where this is undoubtedly a sensible principle, but I would discourage an interpretation that denies the distinctive character of absence of a phonetic event in cases where two (or more) speech sounds are similar except for presence vs. absence of the phonetic event as a typical *co-occurring* feature. For example, [t, k] usually have prominent bursts but [p] does not since it has no downstream resonator. An [i] is similar to an [u] in F_1 and F_3 but only the former has a very high F_2.

An experiment by Ohala & Shriberg (1990) provides evidence for this. The experiment involved listeners' perception of filtered vowels. Simplifying somewhat, their study had listeners identify 11 short (85 ms) American English vowels that had been excised from the speech of four male speakers. Each vowel was presented after a short precursor sentence *I will now say the word . . .* by the same speaker who produced the vowel. Both precursor sentence and stimulus vowel could be separately or together low-pass filtered (at 1000 Hz) (LP), or presented full-band (approximately 50 Hz-20 kHz) (hi-fi). Briefly, those experiments showed the following:

John. J. Ohala

(a)   When both precursor and vowel were hi-fi, the rate of correct identification was 83%. Most errors were due to the elimination of temporal cues to long-short pairs such as [ʌ] vs. [ɑ] and [ɛ] vs. [æ].

(b)   When the precursor sentence was hi-fi but the vowels LP, the rate of correct identification fell to 33%. In addition to other errors, there were many where front vowels, now with their high F_2 filtered out, were confused with corresponding back vowels.

(c)   When both precursor and vowel were LP, the correct identifications rose to 51%. The gain (over condition (b)) was a dramatic reduction in the number of front to back confusions.

The only difference between conditions (b) and (c) is that in the latter the precursor sentence had the same filtering as the vowel stimuli. Thus the increase in intelligibility from condition (b) to (c) cannot be attributed to any change in the information content in the vowels themselves. Rather what condition (c) provides listeners with is useful "meta-information", namely that the vowels are filtered just like the precursor sentence (which, being highly redundant, does not itself suffer in intelligibility from the filtering), and therefore that one cannot rely on the absence of a signal above 1 kHz as being informative. Shriberg (1992) reports a variation on this experiment where instead of a precursor sentence the vowel stimuli were presented to listeners either with or without 1 kHz high-pass noise added, i.e., in the portion of the spectrum complementary to the filtered speech. Much the same results were obtained, in that when noise was added the overall recognition rate increased *vis-à-vis* the condition when just the plain LP filtered vowels were presented. Here the noise provided listeners with the meta-information: "Don't rely on the *absence of spectrum above 1 kHz* as a cue." What both of these studies suggest, which is also my main point, is this: in condition (b), where listeners are apparently unaware that the signal is filtered (or at least have impoverished information about the characteristics of the filtering), they interpret the vowels as they hear them, and it is the *absence* of formant structure above 1 kHz that serves as a cue that the stimuli are not front vowels.

7.2 On feature hierarchies

Feature hierarchies are much in vogue these days (cf. McCarthy, 1989). It may be useful to recall that this is not a new concern. As I noted in Ohala (1991: 4):

[Amman 1694: 66-67] establish[es] an elementary binary, hierarchical classification of phonetic features which incorporates certain notions that might well be considered seriously by modern phonologists, e.g., that manner features dominate place of articulation features. He considered his system as a 'natural' hierarchical taxonomy and comments that substitutions of sounds (e.g., in pathological speech) involve similar

88

sounds at the lowest strata of the hierarchy, not the highest, i.e., a dental 'semi-vowel' like ḻ is substituted for another, ṛ, or one nasal for another, i.e., we don't see substitutions of vowels for consonants, etc.

In a similar vein, Janson promoted the notion of a hierarchy of phonological-phonetic features for two reasons. He suggested that the relevance of a given feature may depend on another feature; for example, in Swedish [± round] is distinctive only for front vowels (those with high or mid F_2–F_1). In addition, he noted that these dependent features, such as rounding on vowels or retroflexion on consonants, may not be as perceptually salient as independent features, and this in turn will determine the probability of their being used in languages.

There is additional suggestive evidence in support of Janson's claim: Stevens (1980), and Stevens & Keyser (1989) have made an empirically based distinction between robust and weak features. The robust ones are manifested in a very short time window (within a few cs) and include features such as [± voice], [± nasal], [± continuant], [± grave] (or [± coronal]), [± compact]). The auditory system is said to detect these first and only afterwards scan remaining portions of the speech signal for the slower, weaker features such as palatalization, pharyngealization, and the like. This distinction correlates quite well with the way languages' segment inventories are constructed: those with a small number of phonemes use the robust features almost exclusively; those with many phonemes use the same robust features but also exploit weaker, slower features (see also Maddieson, 1984, esp. 13ff.).

This characterization of certain features or, the term I prefer to use, "cues", as more or less robust as a function of how much time they require for their detection has implications for other phonological behavior. In various papers I have presented an account of sound change in which listeners' perceptual errors are the main source of phonological change. I give here a brief summary: imagine a speaker attempting to produce a string of phonetic units, *A, B, C* (see Figure 7.1). Some units, e.g. *A* in the figure, may give rise to two or more phonetic events, a_1, a_2, which are distributed over time and the frequency spectrum. For example, the cues for velarized lateral might include both the abrupt amplitude and spectral discontinuities at its onset and offset, as well as the long transitions leading into it. Normally the listener parses these events together and correctly deduces the speaker's intended pronunciation. A correct parsing of this phonetic string is shown at the bottom of Figure 7.1a. It may happen, however, that the listener mis-parses the signal and the distinct phonetic events a_1, a_2 may be parsed separately, i.e., associated with the phonological units A_1, A_2. Something close to this may underlie sound changes commonly called "l-vocalization", where the [u]-like on-glide to the *l* replaced the *l* itself; e.g. Latin *alterum* > French *autre, alba* > *aube*. This can be called a "dissociation" parsing error; two events that should have been associated were not. The signal may also be mis-parsed if two phonetic events, *B, C*, that should

89

be parsed separately are parsed together. This can be designated as a "false association" parsing error. These two types of parsing errors are represented schematically in Figure 7.1b. I have proposed that cases of dissimilation arise from false association parsing errors, e.g. the dissimilatory change from Latin *quinquĕ* [kwiŋkwe] to Italian *cinque* [tʃiŋkwe] (loss of the first [w] under the influence of the second [w]) involved parsing the separate [w]s as one phonological entity – based on the expectation that the lip rounding associated with [w] could spread some distance through the word. It follows from this that dissimilations will be most likely when segments share a feature whose cues are temporarily spread out. From phonetic studies we know that this is true of labialization, palatalization, pharyngealization, aspiration, glottalization, etc., but is not true of such manner distinctions as stop and affricate. In general, the historical phonological data bear this out. These lists of features likely to dissimilate and those not, are parallel to Stevens' hierarchic distinction between robust and weak features.

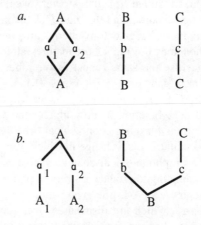

Figure 7.1. Schematic representation of two possible outcomes of listeners' parsing of the events in the speech signal. Top line: hypothetical units, *A, B, C,* the speaker intends to convey; middle line: the speech signal with phonetics $a_1, a_2, b, c,$ corresponding to the units intended by the speaker; bottom line: the string of units, $A, A_1,$ etc., that the listener extracts from the speech signal by parsing it. (a) The listener parses the signal correctly; (b) the listener mis-parses the signal.

7.3 Perceptual processes active in the spread of sound change

Janson noted that facultative perception rules have "a potential for enlargement of scope" and that this may be how "sound changes tend to spread in such a way that the first instances occur in a very restricted context, but . . . with time . . . more and more forms in the language are affected by the change." I think this is

a very important observation and would like to support it by elaborating a bit on it.
The pioneering work of Rask, Grimm, and others in the nineteenth century give the impression that most sound changes are like Grimm's Law, where whole classes of speech sounds change into other classes; e.g. Indo-European /p t k/ (as preserved in Greek and Latin) changed in Germanic to /f θ x/. But these are surely special cases; most sound changes affect individual phonemes; e.g. in Dutch the change /ɡ/ > /χ/, which did not affect /b d/, or in Japanese the change /p/ > /h/ (probably via the intermediate stage /ɸ/), which did not affect /t k/. In many cases a plausible phonetic reason can be given for changes of this latter type (Ohala, 1983). Janson suggested how a change in an individual phoneme can spread to a whole class of phonemes. Through the application of a facultative rule the listener establishes the functional equivalence of two variant pronunciations, say, a [p] and a [ɸ] (the innovative variant possibly having arisen through some other listener's mis-parsing and misapprehension). This would allow the listener to learn the cues differentiating these variants, i.e., the cues to frication and continuancy at the same place of articulation. From this the listener's ears would be "sensitive" to the same variation at other places of articulation. If the same type of variation exists phonetically at these other places of articulation, this sets the stage for (though does not actually cause) the spread of the sound change to other places of articulation.

7.4 Areal phonetic features

I think a variant of the above sketch of a mechanism for spread of a sound change may also underlie areal phonetic phenomena. Areal phonetic features are those shared phonetic characteristics of languages which have different genetic background but exist in close geographical proximity. Often the shared features are felt to be unusual or statistically uncommon, such that their existence in two or more adjacent linguistic communities could not have arisen by chance. Examples are: the clicks in the languages of South Africa, both Bantu and Khoisan; retroflexes in the languages of South Asia, both Indo-Aryan and Dravidian; glottalization in the languages of North America, including Athabascan, Mayan, Uto-Aztecan; front rounded vowels in the languages of Eurasia; contour tones in the languages of Southeast and East Asia. Borrowing is, of course, one way that features could spread, but in the case of retroflexes in Indo-Aryan there is good evidence that they arose first in native Indo-Aryan words, not in Dravidian loanwords (Turner, 1924). A speaker of language A, who is exposed to novel lexical contrasts in language B, essentially enhances his auditory sensitivity to the phonetic cues supporting the new contrast. For example, an English speaker learning Hindi adds the dental vs. retroflex contrast to his auditory repertory. This allows him to "hear" English with increased

John. J. Ohala

sensitivity: variation in English pronunciation that may have been sporadic or contextually conditioned, e.g. the dental /d/ in *width* or the retroflex flap in *arty*, can be differentiated from the normally alveolar manifestation of the /d/ and /t/ phonemes. This sets the stage for (though does not directly cause) some listeners' re-interpretation of these contextual variants as purposeful, i.e., phonological entities distinct from the alveolar versions.

I hope the above remarks illustrate some of the conceptual, methodological, and theoretical advances that phonology can expect by integrating its concerns with phonetics and psychology.

References

Amman, J. C. 1694. *The Talking Deaf Man: or, a Method Proposed Whereby He Who is Born Deaf May Learn to Speak.* London: Tho. Hawkins.

Maddieson, I. 1984. *Patterns of Sounds*. Cambridge: Cambridge University Press.

McCarthy, J. J. 1989. Feature geometry and dependency: a review. *Phonetica* 45: 84–108.

Ohala, J. J. 1983. The origin of sound patterns in vocal tract constraints. In P. F. MacNeilage (ed.), *The Production of Speech*. New York: Springer-Verlag, 189–216.

Ohala, J. J. 1991. The integration of phonetics and phonology. *Proceedings of the XIIth International Congress of Phonetic Sciences*, Aix-en-Provence, 1: 1–16.

Ohala, J. J. & E. E. Shriberg 1990. Hyper-correction in speech perception. *Proceedings of the 1990 International Conference on Spoken Language Processing*, Kobe, 1: 405–408.

Shriberg, E. E. 1992. Perceptual restoration of filtered vowels with added noise. *Language and Speech* 35: 127–136.

Stevens, K. N. 1980. Discussion. *Proceedings of the IXth International Congress of Phonetic Sciences*, Copenhagen, 3: 185–186.

Stevens, K. N. & S. J. Keyser 1989. Primary features and their enhancement in consonants. *Language* 65: 81–106.

Turner, R. L. 1924. Cerebralization in Sindhi. *Journal of the Royal Asiatic Society*, 555–584.

Part II
Prosody

8
Stress shift: do speakers do it or do listeners hear it?

ESTHER GRABE and PAUL WARREN*

8.1 Introduction

Metrical Phonology has given considerable attention to stress shift of the "thirteen men" type. This phenomenon is said to apply when a word such as *thirtéen*, with two full vowels and the strongest prominence on the last stressable syllable in citation form, is closely followed by a further strong syllable such as *men*. In such cases, the stresses "clash", and the prominence pattern of *thirtéen* is reversed, producing the sequence *thírteen mén*.

This paper presents an experimental investigation of stress shift sequences[1] in Southern British English, focusing on three aspects of our research. First, we test predictions derived from standard assumptions made by Metrical Phonology (e.g. Hogg & McCully, 1987) concerning the application of stress shift in read connected speech. Second, we investigate acoustic and perceptual evidence for stress shift. Finally, we discuss an alternative account of stress shift which does not involve stress clashes.

8.1.1 Background

In providing accounts for various rhythmical structures in continuous speech, Metrical Phonology has given considerable attention to stress shift (Liberman & Prince, 1977; Kiparsky, 1979; Selkirk, 1981, 1984; Hayes, 1984; Giegerich, 1985; Nespor & Vogel, 1989; Hogg & McCully, 1987; Gussenhoven, 1991). One notion that has been used in the description of stress shift in English phonology is *eurhythmy* (e.g. Selkirk, 1984; Prince, 1983), i.e., a general tendency towards a particular spacing of stressed syllables so that utterances exhibit a preferred periodicity. In English, this preference is reflected in a tendency for stressed and unstressed syllables to alternate. Disruptions of this periodicity trigger processes such as stress shift, hence the stress shift's designation also as a "rhythm rule". The metrical environment that induces the shift is described as a "stress clash", i.e., the presence of two immediately abutting strong prominences which disrupt the preferred strong–weak alternation.[2] Stress shift is described as an optional process which restores the alternating pattern, by moving the first of the adjacent prominences onto an earlier full-vowel syllable within the same lexical item, thereby reversing the prominence distribution within the stress shift item (e.g. Giegerich, 1985; Hogg & McCully, 1987).

Stress clashes have often been described in terms of metrical grids; these are representations of rhythm in which the strength of syllables is represented by grid marks on different grid levels. Elements in the grid "clash" if they and their counterparts one level down are on adjacent tiers and there is no intervening element one level down. Mostly, we find no reference as to whether the marks in metrical grids refer to units of speech production, perception or both; and the acoustic correlates of strong and weak prominences are rarely specified explicitly. At best, we find reference to durational differences (Liberman & Prince, 1977), or to a "strengthening" or "weakening" of the prominences involved in the phenomenon (Nespor & Vogel, 1989).[3] A further shortcoming of most descriptions is that examples consist of two-word sequences which appear to be concatenations of words with citation form prominence patterns. We rarely find surrounding context, and matters of intonational phrasing such as nucleus placement tend to be implied rather than overtly incorporated into the account.[4] Exceptions are found in Liberman & Prince (1977), who state that stress shift does not apply if the stress shift word is the designated terminal element of an intonational phrase, and in Nespor & Vogel (1989), who suggest that the domain of stress shift is the phonological phrase and that stress shift does not apply across phonological phrase boundaries.

A number of researchers have attempted to provide empirical evidence for the application of stress shift. Cooper & Eady (1986) fail to find support either for Selkirk's (1984) claim that speakers use compensatory lengthening and pausing to avoid stress clashes, or for Hayes' (1984) claim of metrical grid euphony. Horne (1990) provides experimental evidence for Gussenhoven's (1988) phonological analysis of the rhythm rule as a pitch accent deletion phenomenon. Van Heuven (1991) tests claims made for postnuclear stress shift to the right in Dutch compounds. He excised from their surrounding context tokens perceived as shifted and found that the excised items were no longer perceived as shifted. Shattuck-Hufnagel (1988) proposes a production account of stress shift in which speakers have the option to place a pre-nuclear pitch accent on a full-vowel syllable earlier in the word than the lexically stressed syllable. She suggests that speakers make use of this option especially when the word carries the first pitch accent of its phrase. In an extended analysis of a corpus of radio news stories,

Shattuck-Hufnagel, Ostendorf & Ross (1992) suggest that speakers shift stress either when the first syllable of the following word also bears a prominence, or when the stress shift item carries the first prominence of the prosodic phrase (onset marking). Horne (1993) found some evidence for stress shift creating a phrase-initial prominence in post-focal position. Finally, Beckman, Swora, Rauschenberg & de Jong (1990) provide evidence for Liberman & Prince's (1977) proposition that stress shift does not apply if the stress shift word carries the nuclear accent of an intonational phrase, and show that a full account of stress shift must include the link between intonation and rhythm.

As comprehensive production data for stress shift are scarce, we will firstly present the results of a production study with auditory and acoustic analysis. Our detailed acoustic analysis sheds light on the relationship between the claims of Metrical Phonology, the phonetics of stress shift, the metrical grid, and to some extent, the interaction of stress shift with intonational phrasing.

8.2 Incidence of stress shift in connected speech

Our materials were chosen to provide evidence for the following claims:

(i) In a sequence consisting of a stress shift item and an immediately following word with an early, potentially strong full-vowel syllable, stress shift will apply.

(ii) If a stress shift word is the designated terminal element of an intonational phrase, stress shift will not apply.

8.2.1 Method

The materials consisted of 42 locally ambiguous sentence pairs with stress shift sequences, such as in (1a) and (1b) below.

(1) a. When my father watches TV soaps, they're his favorite.
     b. When my father watches TV, soaps are his favorite.

If we ignore any prosodic distinctions and equivalent punctuation in the written form, the sentences in (1a) and (1b) are identical until after the potential stress clash site, in this case the word *soaps*. We will refer to words in this position as the stress shift "trigger." In the (a) version, a clause boundary follows the trigger, and the sequence of stress shift item plus trigger is referred to as a "–CB sequence," since it does not contain a clause boundary. In the (b) version, the clause boundary falls between the stress shift item and the trigger – we refer to this as the "+CB sequence."

In our materials, all potential stress shift items were nouns, adjectives or nominal/adjectival compounds, with two stressable syllables. Test sentences were embedded in random order in a large set of fillers in two lists, each list containing only one member of each sentence pair

Recordings were made in a sound treated room. Subjects read the sentences in two sessions, approximately one week apart. They were encouraged to take some time to read each sentence silently before reading it out aloud. Some sentences were repeated at the end of a session if they had been read hesitantly or with errors.

Four female and eight male subjects read each list. Their age range was 20–30 and they were all native speakers of Southern British English. A trained phonetician performed an auditory analysis on all the materials elicited from a subset of four female and four male speakers (668 sentences). Another two trained phoneticians analyzed the materials (334 sentences) produced by four of those eight speakers (two male, two female). All three phoneticians listened to complete stress shift sequences excised from context, and agreed on whether stress had been shifted in 84% of the cases. The tokens on which no initial agreement was reached were later discussed, and a majority decision was taken in the subsequent labeling of items as shifted or otherwise.

8.2.2 Predictions

The prediction deriving from the claims of Metrical Phonology was that stress clashes between the stress shift item and trigger would be avoided by the application of stress shift. In our test material, stress shift items occurred in two conditions, as part of a –CB sequence or in a +CB sequence. This allowed us to investigate our prediction (i) in a prosodic environment in which stress shift should apply, since the stress shift word was followed by a strong syllable and was unlikely to carry nuclear stress, and (ii) in an environment in which stress should not shift, because the stress shift word was likely to be nuclear, and not followed by a further strong syllable in the same clause.

8.2.3 Results

The results of the auditory study are summarized in Figure 8.1. In –CB sequences, 84% of items were transcribed as shifted. This supports Metrical Phonology's account of stress shift. Intonational analysis of shifted sequences showed that in each case, the following strong word was nuclear. In a further 12% of the data, intonational analysis showed that the stress shift item was in nuclear position; since the following word was postnuclear and therefore not pitch prominent, the result is a weak–strong–weak sequence which does not contain abutting strong prominences, i.e., there is no stress clash. Genuine stress clashes turned out to be rare (4% of the total data set).

98

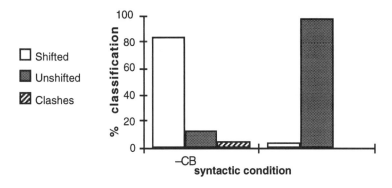

Figure 8.1. Distribution of items in shifted, unshifted and clashing categories in –CB and +CB conditions.

In +CB sequences, 97% of test items were perceived as unshifted. Intonational analysis showed that these unshifted items were in nuclear position; hence the results clearly support the prediction that stress shift will not apply if the word is the designated terminal element of an intonational phrase.

A very small percentage of items exhibited a strong–weak (i.e., shifted) stress pattern, despite being in nuclear position. This was restricted to a number of stress shift items which carry default stress on the first syllable for some speakers of British English (e.g. *Héathrow*). Other items, especially when morphologically complex (e.g. *navy-blue, home-grown*) may have been stressed contrastively on the first syllable.

In summary, stress shift is heard if the stress shift word is in prenuclear position and the following trigger is nuclear. The phenomenon does not apply when the stress shift word is in nuclear position.

8.3 Acoustic correlates of stress shift

The auditory analysis shows clear evidence for stress shift being heard in our materials. What, then, are the acoustic correlates for stress shift?

8.3.1 Method

Acoustic analysis was carried out on shifted tokens in –CB sequences and the corresponding unshifted tokens from +CB sequences. The relevant recordings were digitized at 16 kHz after low-pass filtering at 7.5 kHz. Forty-two pairs of tokens from each of four of our speakers (two female, two male) were analyzed. This is the same group of speakers for which auditory analysis was carried out by all three listeners above. Duration, amplitude and fundamental frequency measurements were taken for the potential stress shift item and the trigger. Since the material contains a mixture of vowel lengths and qualities, and as this clearly affects the parameters of duration, amplitude and F_0, we analyzed separately a subset of the data, from all 12 speakers, in which the two relevant syllables of the stress shift item have the same rhyme (e.g. *Hong Kong*). This subset will be referred to as the "controlled subset", although it should be noted that even here the structure of the two stressable syllables is not completely identical, and such differences may have affected the results, albeit to a small extent. In the main analysis, statistical tests were carried out on 111 sentence pairs, distributed over the four speakers, for which there were both a shifted –CB sequence and a corresponding unshifted +CB sequence. The controlled subset produced a set of 22 sentence pairs over the 12 speakers.

Durations for all syllable nuclei within a stress shift sequence were obtained from wide-band spectrograms. The nucleus included the voiced part of the vowel and also any syllable-final sonorants that could not be reliably separated from the vowel.

Two amplitude measurements were obtained, following Beckman (1986). Beckman uses a "total amplitude" value as an approximation to amplitude integral. We used a somewhat differently defined amplitude integral (AI) measure, namely the square root of the sum of squared amplitude values across the syllable nucleus. This measure attempts to capture the phenomenon of temporal summation of loudness (i.e., the fact that when holding amplitude constant, a vowel nucleus of longer duration sounds "louder" than one of shorter duration). The second measure, replacing Beckman's "average amplitude", is the root mean square (RMS) of the amplitude values across the nucleus, i.e., the sum of squared amplitude values is divided by the number of sample points, and the square root taken of the result. These measures were derived automatically within the Audlab package on a Masscomp workstation.

Three F_0 measurements were obtained from F_0 traces (also provided by Audlab). First, values were obtained for highest and lowest points of F_0 excursion within each syllable nucleus. Second, "average F_0" was calculated by averaging the F_0 values obtained for the highest and lowest points of F_0 excursion within each nucleus. Third, "F_0 range", defined as the largest displacement of F_0 over the syllable nucleus (i.e., from highest to lowest point) was calculated, without taking account of the direction of F_0 movement.

As some of the proponents of Metrical Phonology (e.g. Giegerich, 1985, Hogg & McCully, 1987) predict that stress shift involves a shift of prominence from the second syllable of a stress shift item onto the first, one might expect the first syllable (S1*) of a shifted token to exhibit greater acoustic prominence than the second (S2*); for instance, one might expect the first syllable of shifted tokens to be relatively longer than the second, and to have greater amplitude and a larger F_0 inflection. This pattern would not be expected for the unshifted counterparts, since not only should unshifted tokens have acoustically "stronger" second syllables, but also in the +CB context they immediately precede a major syntactic and prosodic boundary, which should result in final lengthening, greater F_0 inflection, etc. To test these predictions, we conducted Analyses of Variance (ANOVAs) on the acoustic data for all cases of items for which there were both shifted –CB sequences and unshifted +CB sequences. Because the data were not equally distributed across the four subjects (since not all subjects shifted the same –CB items), we included Subject as a group variable in our analysis, along with Context (±CB) and Syllable (S1* or S2*) as within-items variables.[5] The same analyses for the controlled subset did not include Subject as a variable, since there were very few items per speaker. Although our analyses compare items from the two contexts, it should be clear that our main interest is in whether the shifted items show acoustic marking of a stronger first syllable. Where appropriate, the following presentation partitions interactions into their component effects to investigate this issue.

8.3.2 Results

The analysis of syllable durations shows a significant main effect for Speaker (F (3, 107) = 3.80, $p < 0.02$), due to one speaker having considerably longer durations than the others. However, Speaker does not interact with either of the other variables, and so can be ignored for present purposes. There is a significant interaction of Context and Syllable (F (1, 107) = 21.73, $p < 0.01$), which reflects the fact that S2* is longer than S1* in the unshifted instances (196 ms vs. 122 ms; F (1, 110) = 39.24, $p < 0.01$), but also reveals that S1* and S2* do not differ in the shifted cases (115 ms vs. 123 ms). The controlled subset of items shows the same pattern of results, with a significant interaction of Context and Syllable (F (1, 21) = 34.86, $p < 0.01$) reflecting a significant durational difference between the two syllables for the unshifted –CB items (F (1, 21) = 69.4, $p < 0.01$), but not for the shifted +CB tokens.

The Amplitude Integral measure again shows a main effect of Speaker, which does not interact with the other factors and can be ignored. Again there is a significant interaction of Context and Syllable (F (1, 107) = 15.44, $p < 0.01$), which in this case reflects greater AI in S2* in the unshifted case and in S1* in the shifted case. While this suggests greater prominence in the first syllable under stress shift, it is also clear that the ratio between the two syllables is much smaller here (at 1.08) than the S2*/S1* ratio in the unshifted tokens (1.36). The RMS values also show a Speaker main effect, but Speaker also interacts with the other variables, including a three-way interaction (F (3, 107) = 5.24, $p < 0.01$). An exploration of this interaction reveals inconsistency between speakers; two show the predicted differences between shifted and unshifted tokens, while the other two have the same pattern for all tokens, regardless of whether they are shifted. The controlled subset of items confirms the pattern for AI, with a significant interaction of Context and Syllable (F (1, 21) = 10.32, p < 0.01) resulting from a significant difference for the unshifted items (S2* has greater AI value than S1*, F (1, 21) = 12.39, p < 0.01), but no such difference for the shifted items. This subset produces no significant effects whatsoever for the RMS measure, confirming the variability of this index in the data.

The analysis of the F_0 data again shows a Speaker effect, for both average F_0 (F (3, 102) = 1032.08, p < 0.01) and F_0 range (F (3.102) = 20.07, p < 0.01).[6] The Speaker variable interacts with the other factors, but here it is a question of degree rather than direction: the basic pattern of results holds for all four speakers (and is confirmed in separate ANOVAs not reported here), but differs in extent because of speaker characteristics, not least the use of two male and two female voices. The average F_0 data show a significant interaction of Context and Syllable (F (1, 102) = 4.47, p < 0.05), reflecting a greater difference between the two syllables for unshifted than for shifted tokens (11 Hz vs. 6 Hz, in both cases S1* has a higher average F_0). This difference in average F_0 is not independent of the other F_0 measure, the F_0 range, since the unshifted tokens show a much greater F_0 range on the second syllable than on the first (33 Hz vs. 13 Hz, F (1, 108) = 92.86, p < 0.01), while the shifted tokens have no difference between the syllables (both 13 Hz). This greater range on S2* in the unshifted case reflects a lower finishing value, which in part results from the following boundary, and which also produces a lower average F_0. For the controlled subset, we find significant main effects for average F_0 for both the Context (F (1, 19) = 5.64, p < 0.03) and Syllable effects (F (1, 19) = 9.93, p < 0.01), but no interaction. In other words, for this subset, S1* has a higher average F_0 than S2*, regardless of whether the stress is shifted, and the –CB context has both these syllables at a higher F_0 than the corresponding syllables in the +CB context, where they immediately precede a clause boundary. The F_0 range data for this subset show a significant interaction between the two variables (F (1, 19) = 9.19, p < 0.01); again there is no difference in F_0 range for the two syllables in the unshifted items, but a significant difference for the shifted items (the range of S1* was 15 Hz, while that of S2* was 27 Hz, F (1, 20) = 10.04, p < 0.01).

Finally we compared the first syllables of shifted and unshifted tokens within the controlled subset. Again there were no significant differences between the two syllables in any of the relevant parameters, supporting Shattuck-Hufnagel's (1991) results.

In summary, these data fail to provide strong evidence for an acoustic strong–weak pattern in the items classified as "shifted": in these items the two syllables have equal duration and equal F_0 range; the first syllable has higher average F_0, but it does so also in the unshifted cases, where the difference between S1* and

S2* is actually greater; and while the first syllable has greater RMS amplitude and AI values in the shifted case, the differences are not consistent across subjects (for RMS at least), are not present in the controlled subset (and can presumably be attributed, at least in part, to inherent differences between vowels in the larger set of data), and are less marked than the S2*/S1* difference in the unshifted tokens. However, further analyses not reported in detail here confirm that both the stressable syllables in the –CB sequences differ from neighboring unstressable syllables, which exhibit considerably shorter duration, lower amplitude, lower average F_0 and smaller F_0 range. Furthermore, in both –CB and +CB sequences, syllables carrying a nuclear accent are distinguished from preceding syllables by a larger F_0 range, and pre-boundary lengthening. These effects are relevant to our discussion below.

8.4 Contextual effects on the perception of stress shift

As the preceding analysis suggests, stress shift items appear to be characterized by similar values for all acoustic parameters that could show prominence in the two stressable syllables. As there is no acoustic evidence of a strong–weak stress pattern, one might conclude that the stress shift effect is purely perceptual, i.e., the perceived stress pattern of a potential stress shift item might be conditioned by context: the precursor may build up a rhythmic expectancy, and the following trigger may be responsible for perceptual prominence assignment. If this is the case, then a stress shift item may no longer be judged as shifted if separated from the trigger. If separated from the precursor as well, it may lack any framework in which it is possible to determine relative prominence reliably. These are the manipulations carried out in a further set of auditory analyses.

8.4.1 Method

The materials consisted of the –CB sequences in the controlled subset. All stress shift items had previously been judged as shifted by all three trained listeners in the auditory analysis described in section 8.2; therefore, the comparisons below are with a baseline of 100% shifted judgments for these materials. To test the effect of the *following* context, precursor and stress shift item were separated from the trigger and played to the same three listeners. To test the influence of the *preceding* context, stress shift items were excised from preceding and following context and played to the same three listeners.[7] In each case, the judges could respond "shifted," "unshifted" and "unsure."

8.4.2 Results

The effect of context on the perception of stress shift is shown in Table 8.1. Clearly, the absence of the trigger has a noticeable effect on judgments: the 100% "shifted" judgments have now become 67% shifted, 13% unshifted, and 20% unsure. The results confirm our hypothesis that a stress shift item needs to be heard in a stress shift context to be consistently perceived as shifted.

Table 8.1 also shows the effect of the preceding context on the perception of stress shift. When presented with stress shift items with no surrounding context, judgments were made with less confidence, with the stronger prominence heard on either of the stressable syllables for a large number of tokens (42% "unsure"), with 38% "shifted" and 20% "unshifted" judgments. This represents a noticeable increase in "unsure" judgments compared with when just the trigger was removed, and a small increase in "unshifted" judgments. We conclude that the precursor might build up a rhythmic expectancy which enhances the stress shift effect. Further, more detailed, testing is clearly necessary.

Table 8.1. Effect of following and preceding context on the perception of stress shift.

	Shifted	Unshifted	Unsure
Complete sequence	100%	0%	0%
Without trigger e.g. *When John watches TV* . . .	67%	13%	20%
Without any context e.g. . . .*TV*	38%	20%	42%

8.5 Discussion and conclusion

In Metrical Phonology, stress shift has frequently been portrayed as a process which is motivated by a stress clash and which reverses the prominence pattern of certain lexical items, i.e., of words with two full vowels and strongest prominence on the last stressable syllable in citation form.

Our experimental investigation of stress shift suggests the following:

(i) In complete stress shift sequences, stress shift is perceived regularly; the citation form weak-strong pattern of stress shift items is reversed unless the stress shift item carries the nucleus of the intonational phrase.

104

(ii) There is no convincing acoustic evidence for a strong–weak stress pattern in tokens perceived as shifted; acoustically, the citation form stress pattern is not reversed. A paradigmatic comparison of the first syllable of shifted items with the first syllable of unshifted items shows that no part of the prominence of the second syllable has been shifted onto the first.[8]

(iii) When stress shift items are excised from stress shift contexts, their prominence patterns are unlikely to be judged reliably. The perception of a strong–weak pattern in shifted items depends on the following and to some extent on the preceding context.

Some proponents of Metrical Phonology claim that stress clashes in the metrical grid trigger stress shift, and that stress shift involves a reversal of the citation form prominence pattern of stress shift items. The above summary of our findings shows that stress clashes do not motivate a reversal of prominence at the acoustic level, and that a perceived reversal of prominence in shifted items is motivated not only by the following but also (to some extent) by the preceding context. In the following section, we will relate these findings to the notion of stress clash in the metrical grid.

8.5.1 Stress clashes in the metrical grid: from lexical to metrical prosody

In the metrical grid, before grid operations apply, a stress shift sequence such as *ideal partners* is assumed to contain clashing prominences. *Ideal* has stress on the second syllable and the first syllable of the following word *partners* is also strong. The assumption that *ideal* is stressed on the second syllable is based on a weak–strong lexical prosodic[9] or citation form, i.e., on how it is produced as a separate tone unit. Phonetically, in citation form, we find the acoustic correlates of nuclear stress on the second syllable of *ideal*, since this is the one normally specified for nuclear stress assignment. From this we must conclude that before grid operations apply, any sequence in the metrical grid represents a concatenation of words in citation form. The task of grid operations is then to change these citation form patterns to produce a well-formed grid representing appropriate metrical prosodic patterns. This implies, for instance, that we need rules to change the metrical strength of words such as *the* and *a*, which are realized with full vowels in citation form, and with reduced vowels in non-nuclear positions in connected speech.[10] Consideration of this and of our data for stress shift leads us to suggest that an account of metrical prosody which involves changing a string of citation forms into a metrical string may involve more processes than strictly necessary.

It appears that there are just two contexts in which the acoustic correlates of prominence on the two syllables of a word like *ideal* differ significantly: (i) in postnuclear phrase-final position,[11] where phrase-final lengthening assigns greater duration to the second syllable relative to the first, and (ii) in nuclear position, where we are likely to find citation form stress patterns, and where the second syllable differs from the first at least in F_0 range. In all other positions, the two stressable syllables are acoustically "equal", and rhythmic context may assign more perceptual prominence to either of them. Thus, instead of describing a stress shift word such as *ideal* as having "default" stress on the second syllable, we say it has two full vowels and context-determinable stress. It then follows that stress shift sequences do not contain "underlying" stress clashes: the potential stress shift item is neither in phrase-final nor in nuclear position and does not exhibit the acoustic correlates of a strong prominence which might clash with a following strong prominence. Thus, recognizing that prominence patterns in connected speech are not necessarily like citation form prominence patterns allows us to formulate a more straightforward account of stress shift, which does not involve a rule that changes a lexical prosodic pattern into a metrical prosodic pattern.

Clearly, further research is needed to establish where exactly the perceived strong–weak pattern of shifted sequences comes from, i.e., which acoustic parameters need to apply to create a percept of stress shift. For instance, Beckman & Edwards (1994) and Shattuck-Hufnagel (1992, this volume) explain stress shift in terms of a potential for prenuclear accent placement. Specifically, Beckman & Edwards suggest that if a stress shift word carries an accent on both stressable syllables, an upstep in F_0 from a preceding syllable is responsible for the percept of stress shift. Our results provide some support for this view. However, we have shown that stress shift is also perceived reliably in stress shift sequences in the absence of preceding context. Furthermore, since our data have shown that stress shift applies reliably if the stress shift item is prenuclear and the following word nuclear, we may require a more constrained account of stress shift. If we define stress shift items as words exhibiting a certain potential, it is not yet clear how we can account for the high regularity with which the phenomenon applies.

Appendix

The following stimuli were presented to subjects in random order embedded in a large set of fillers; there were no line-breaks. (1)–(42) show all –CB sequences; (43)–(45) exemplify the corresponding +CB sequences.

–CB sequences

(1) Even if they're not <u>home-grown bay leaves</u>, they're full of flavor.

(2) Whenever parliament discusses <u>Hong Kong problems</u>, they are solved instantly.

(3) If they're advertised as <u>infrared video-cameras</u>, they'll be expensive.

Stress shift: do speakers do it or do listeners hear it?

(4)   The local youths are rather messy when they meet outside; whenever you want to sit on the <u>Village Green benches</u>, they are covered with empty bottles and crisp bags.

(5)   Whenever Sky News contacts the <u>UN envoys</u>, they're out for lunch.

(6)   As John had not practiced his <u>Chinese cooking</u>, they had a pizza.

(7)   After gossiping about the old and <u>insane patients</u>, the doctor proceeded to other matters.

(8)   I get moderately entertained by all sorts of programs, but when my father watches <u>TV soaps</u>, he is happy.

(9)   Although they seem to be rather <u>snap-happy photographers</u>, they have to be like that.

(10)   Whatever you may have heard about the <u>East End riots</u>, nothing really ever happens there.

(11)   As there are countless restaurants around the <u>West End streets</u>, we eat somewhere different every day.

(12)   There are lots of different forms of language in Japan, so that when linguists discuss <u>Japanese dialects</u>, they never agree.

(13)   When the media stops focusing on <u>BR prices</u>, the situation may calm down.

(14)   We can only go on holiday in July and at that time, whenever we get near the <u>North Sea resorts</u>, it rains the whole time.

(15)   After the contestant had eaten more than <u>sixteen cakes</u>, he announced defeat.

(16)   When several refugees wished to become <u>European citizens</u>, there was protest.

(17)   If the management tries to dress me in <u>pea-green overalls</u>, I'll quit this job.

(18)   As biased barristers are bound to be <u>unfair judges</u>, they should not be allowed to hold that position.

(19)   While the police searched <u>Heathrow terminals</u>, air traffic was severely disrupted.

(20)   Whenever the BBC shows a documentary about <u>Bangkok cuisine</u>, Sally has to watch it.

(21)   As most Irish archaeological finds are <u>neolithic settlements</u>, our research group travels to Ireland fairly often.

(22)   As they are <u>academic questions</u>, they are a waste of time.

(23)   Japanese companies pay high wages in Britain, but whenever the boss visits the <u>UK factories</u>, workers are dissatisfied.

(24)   Although Mary and Emma were <u>OK players</u>, they lost the match.

(25)   Whenever he asks for <u>first class tickets</u>, they are unavailable.

(26)   Whenever he thinks of <u>Hyde Park concerts</u>, he remembers the Pavarotti one in 1991.

(27)   Although the most interesting items of archaeological interest may be <u>megalithic tombs</u>, younger remains tell us just as much about life in the past.

(28)   When Britain refused to support the <u>US officials</u>, the operation was canceled.

(29)   The talks on Croatia were proceeding smoothly, but when a Serbian advisor criticized the position of the <u>EC members</u>, they were not amused.

(30) As the experiment requires the light source to be <u>ultraviolet bulbs</u>, it is going to be very expensive.

(31) When the nurse does the daily <u>routine checkups</u>, more patients turn up.

(32) After Sue Lawley had talked to the <u>prime-minister's secretaries</u>, they asked her to leave quietly.

(33) Although everything Jane ever cooks is <u>ready-made soup</u>, meals at her house are never boring.

(34) When journalists interviewed <u>BA co-pilots</u>, the airline complained.

(35) Even though they're <u>home-made fruit-scones</u>, they just don't appeal to me.

(36) Funding for GPs is still OK, but as many people depend on the <u>NHS hospitals</u>, they ought to be better funded.

(37) As scientists are worried about the <u>North Pole controversy</u>, they will go public.

(38) After they had decided that the food for the party didn't have to be <u>home-baked pizza</u>, they bought some at the supermarket.

(39) Although Emma hates wearing <u>navy-blue uniforms</u>, they suit her quite well.

(40) When journalists approached <u>Bombay officials</u>, all knowledge of the incident was denied.

(41) Whether the nurse looks after the visitors or the <u>infirm patients</u>, she is always charming.

(42) As they will never find their <u>ideal partners</u>, they must learn to compromise.

sample +CB sequences

(43) Even if they're not <u>home-grown</u>, <u>bay leaves</u> are always full of flavor.

(44) The local youths are rather messy when they meet outside; whenever you want to sit on the <u>Village Green</u>, <u>benches</u> are covered with empty bottles and crisp bags.

(45) Whenever Sky News contacts the <u>UN</u>, <u>envoys</u> are out for lunch.

Notes

* We would like to thank Francis Nolan, April McMahon and two anonymous reviewers for many helpful comments. The work reported in this paper has been funded by the Joint Research Councils' HCI initiative under grant SPG 9030657 to P. Warren, F. Nolan and E. Briscoe, and by SERC Fellowship B/ITF/226 to P. Warren.

1 In our materials, a "stress shift sequence" consists of a stress shift item (a word with two stressable full-vowel syllables in a "canonical" weak-strong pattern) and an immediately following word with an early strong syllable.

2 Selkirk (1984) suggests that strong and weak–syllables differ in their behavior as far as alternation is concerned. Two adjacent strong but three adjacent weak syllables are said to be avoided.

3 Nespor & Vogel (1989) do not explain stress shift as a movement of prominence from the late onto the early stressable syllable of a stress shift word, but account for the phenomenon via two separate rules, Beat Deletion and Beat Insertion.

4 As the second word in a stress shift sequence is presented as metrically stronger, some kind of intonational phrase is clearly assumed. Each word within this phrase, however, appears to be presented with a citation form stress pattern before grid operations apply.

5 It should be noted that we also conducted ANOVAs for a subset of 13 items for which there were relevant data for all four subjects. The results do not differ in their pattern from those reported for the larger set here.

6 Note that fewer data points are included in the F_0 analyses. A total of five measurements were not possible for tokens with creaky voice.

7 It is not clear whether this task should be replicated by experiments with naive listeners. Metrical prominence distinctions are made by a variety of acoustic cues in connected speech, depending on the level a word occupies in the prosodic hierarchy (Beckman & Edwards, 1994). Linguistically naive listeners are unlikely to be aware of this and when asked to judge the stress pattern of a word, are likely to compare the word's pattern with that of its citation form (nuclear) pattern. But clearly, prominence patterns in connected speech are not necessarily realized in the same way as they are in citation form. As a result, almost any word with two full vowels that does not resemble the citation form pattern might be judged as shifted.

8 These results agree to some extent with Nespor & Vogel's (1989) and Gussenhoven's (1991) predictions for stress shift, and with those of Vogel, Bunnel & Hoskins (this volume).

9 Cutler (1989) distinguishes between lexical and metrical prosody: lexical prosody is defined on the basis of citation form pronunciations of words and involves more than two levels of prominence, whereas metrical prosody refers to the rhythmic patterns of longer stretches of speech and allows only two levels: strong and weak. She states that lexical prominence patterns may differ from prominence patterns in connected speech just as canonical pronunciations may not always be fully realized.

10 Nespor & Vogel (1989) propose to arbitrarily label such function words as weak.

11 We assume a model of intonation similar to the one presented in Ladd (1986) which distinguishes between two levels of phrasing. "Major Phrases" are delimited by rhythmic breaks and boundary tones; "Tone Groups" are the domain of a nucleus and do not need to be separated from each other by any kind of rhythmic break. In this spirit, "phrase-final position" refers to the boundary of a full intonational phrase where we can expect some degree of phrase-final lengthening.

References

Beckman, M. E. 1986. *Stress and Non-stress Accent.* Dordrecht: Foris.

Beckman, M. E., M. G. Swora, J. Rauschenberg, & K. de Jong. 1990. Stress shift, stress clash and polysyllabic shortening in a prosodically annotated discourse. *Proceedings of the 1990 International Conference on Spoken Language Processing,* Kobe, 1: 5–8.

Beckman M. E. & J. Edwards. 1994. Articulatory evidence for differentiating stress categories. In P. A. Keating (ed.), *Phonological Structure and Phonetic Form: Papers in Laboratory Phonology III*. Cambridge: Cambridge University Press, 7–33.

Cooper, W. E. & S. J. Eady. 1986. Metrical phonology in speech production. *Journal of Memory and Language* 25: 369–384.

Cutler, A. 1989. Auditory lexical access: where do we start? In W. Marslen-Wilson (ed.), *Lexical Representation and Process*. Cambridge, MA: MIT Press, 342–356.

Giegerich, H. 1985. *Metrical Phonology and Phonological Structure*. Cambridge: Cambridge University Press.

Gussenhoven, C. 1988. Lexical accent rules in English. Unpublished manuscript, Instituut Engels-Amerikaans, Nijmegen University.

Gussenhoven, C. 1991. The English rhythm rule as an accent deletion rule. *Phonology* 8: 1–35.

Hayes, B. 1983. A grid-based theory of English meter. *Linguistic Inquiry* 14: 357–393.

Hayes, B. 1984. The phonology of rhythm in English. *Linguistic Inquiry* 15: 33–74.

Heuven, V. van. 1991. Stress clash avoidance in Dutch: inversion of stress patterns in complex nouns? *Proceedings of the XIIth International Congress of Phonetic Sciences*, Aix-en-Provence, 3: 226–229.

Hogg, R. & C. B. McCully. 1987. *Metrical Phonology*. Cambridge: Cambridge University Press.

Horne, M. 1990. Empirical evidence for a deletion formulation of the rhythm rule in English. *Linguistics* 28: 959–981.

Horne, M. 1993. The phonetics and phonology of the rhythm rule in post-focal position: data from English. *Phonum* 2: 69–77.

Kiparsky, P. 1979. Metrical structure assignment is cyclic. *Linguistic Inquiry* 10: 421–442.

Ladd, D. R. 1986. Intonational phrasing: the case for recursive prosodic structure. *Phonology Yearbook* 3: 311–340.

Lehiste, I. 1977. *Suprasegmentals*. Cambridge, MA: MIT Press.

Lehiste, I. 1977. Isochrony revisited. *Journal of Phonetics* 5: 253–264.

Liberman, M. & A. Prince. 1977. On stress and linguistic rhythm. *Linguistic Inquiry* 8: 249–336.

Nespor, M. & I. Vogel. 1989. On clashes and lapses. *Phonology* 6, 69–116.

Prince, A. 1983. Relating to the grid. *Linguistic Inquiry* 14: 19–100.

Selkirk, E. O. 1984. *Phonology and Syntax: the Relation between Sound and Structure*. Cambridge, MA: MIT Press.

Shattuck-Hufnagel, S. 1988. Acoustic phonetic correlates of stress shift. *Journal of the Acoustical Society of America* 84: S98.

Shattuck-Hufnagel, S. 1991. Acoustic correlates of stress shift. *Proceedings of the XIIth International Congress of Phonetic Sciences*, Aix-en-Provence, 4: 266–269.

Shattuck-Hufnagel, S., M. Ostendorf, & K. Ross. 1992. Pitch accent placement within words. *Proceedings of the IRCS Workshop on Prosody in Natural Speech*, University of Pennsylvania, Philadelphia, 181–191.

9
The phonology and phonetics of the Rhythm Rule

IRENE VOGEL, H. TIMOTHY BUNNELL, and STEVEN
HOSKINS*

9.1 Introduction

The Rhythm Rule, the phenomenon responsible for the perceived rhythmic
adjustment of adjacent stresses in such items as *thirtéen* and *Tennessée* vs.
thírteen wómen and *Ténnessee législature*, has received much attention in recent
years from both the phonological and phonetic points of view. In this paper, we
address issues relating to both the phonology and phonetics of the Rhythm Rule,
and in particular, the relation between the two. Our investigation shows how the
phonetic analysis of a phonological rule can provide insight where phonological
analysis by itself is inconclusive. Finally, in our phonetic analysis, we not only
investigate production data, but also data relative to the perception of our speech
samples in order to determine how particular acoustic correlates of the Rhythm
Rule are interpreted by listeners.

9.2 Background and issues addressed

9.2.1 Phonology

Of primary concern here are two treatments of the Rhythm Rule (RR) that have
received broad acceptance, and which we will refer to as the Reversal Analysis
(RA) and the Deletion Analysis (DA). According to the Reversal Analysis,
when a clash arises between adjacent word stresses, the RR applies to alleviate
this clash by shifting the primary stress of the first word from the final syllable
to an earlier syllable in the word (e.g. Liberman, 1975; Liberman & Prince,

111

1977; Hayes, 1984), as illustrated in (1), where the level 3 grid marks indicate primary stress.

(1) Reversal Analysis

```
    x   x           x       x
  x x   x         x x       x
  x x   x x       x x     x x
thirteen women   →   thirteen women
```

The Deletion Analysis only requires that the stress on the final syllable of the first word be reduced, as shown in (2). No claim is made about a concomitant change in any other syllable, although independent processes may lead to strengthening of other syllables to yield a more "eurhythmic" effect (e.g. Prince, 1983; Selkirk, 1984; Nespor & Vogel, 1989).

(2) Deletion Analysis

```
    x   x                   x
  x x   x         x x       x
  x x   x x       x x     x x
thirteen women   →   thirteen women
```

In favor of the RA is the common perception of a strengthening of the stress on the first syllable of *thirteen* in a phrase such as *thirteen women*, in addition to a weakening of the final syllable, as compared with the pronunciation of the word in isolation. On the other hand, there are many cases in which a clash arises and there is no place to move the offending stress, for example, when the word involved is a monosyllable, or when it does not contain a "stressable" syllable (i.e., one which itself bears some degree of stress), as illustrated in (3a) and (3b), respectively.

```
(3) a. ?  ←    x   x        b. ?  ←  x       x
              x   x                   x     x
              x   x x               x x   x   x
           ten women              serene children
```

The DA, however, only predicts weakening of the final stress of the word in question, relieving the clash without raising other rhythmic problems.

Horne (1990) argues for the DA on acoustic grounds; however, her measurements confounded sentence position effects with clash effects since she compared target words in sentence final (no clash) and sentence internal (clash) positions. It is thus unclear to what extent the shortening of the final syllable of the target observed in the latter context is due to the clash, as opposed to its sentence internal position, where it is not subject to the same degree of final lengthening as in the former context.

Another issue that arises in relation to the RR is how it interacts with the overall rhythmic structure of a sentence. We therefore also consider here the effect of the environment preceding the words potentially involved in a clash. In particular, we compare (a) the absence of any material in this position, (b) the presence of a weak syllable, and (c) the presence of a strong syllable, as is discussed further in section 9.3.1.2.

9.2.2 Phonetics

Although it is generally agreed that the main acoustic correlates of stress are duration, pitch and amplitude, it has not been consistently demonstrated that any of these factors can be reliably used in examining the RR. Cooper & Eady (1986), in fact, argue on the basis of duration and F_0 measurements of the first syllable of words in clash vs. nonclash contexts that there is no such phenomenon as the RR, since they found no significant difference in the two contexts. It has been subsequently argued, however, that this study is too restricted in its analysis and thus misses other types of evidence including intonation and the relative durations of the syllables in question to the whole word (cf. Beckman, 1986; Beckman, de Jong, & Edwards, 1987; Beckman, Swora, Rauschenberg & de Jong, 1990; Beckman & Edwards, 1994).

In work by Beckman and colleagues, as in work by Shattuck-Hufnagel (1991), it is also reported that there do not appear to be significant effects of clash on the duration of the first syllable of the target. One potential problem here, as in Cooper & Eady's study, arises from the theoretical position assumed by all of these researchers, namely that the correct view of the RR is the RA, as opposed to the DA. The effect of clash on the duration of the final syllable was not investigated, and thus a crucial element of the analysis is missing. This problem is corrected in the present study.

Additionally, Beckman and her colleagues found that F_0 is not a reliable cue to stress in English. They argue that the widely accepted view that F_0 is a cue to stress derives from an erroneous interpretation of intonation patterns. However, Shattuck-Hufnagel (1991) finds consistent F_0 effects in relation to the application vs. nonapplication of the RR.

Where all the studies seem to agree, however, is in the variable nature of the RR itself. It is not an obligatory rule, and speakers seem to vary in the extent to which they use it. There also seems to be considerable variation in the way listeners perceive stress, and the strategies they use in determining whether one syllable bears more stress than another. In this regard, the small sizes of the data sets examined may cause more general patterns to be obscured by the variability inherent in the data. In this study, we therefore base our analysis on a relatively large number of subjects, sentences and repetitions.

In addition to determining the primary acoustic correlates of the RR, it is important to determine which of these listeners make most use of. Given the lack of clarity in the production studies cited above, the task of relating the perception of stress to the different correlates is not straightforward. Furthermore, it has been observed (e.g. Beckman *et al.*, 1987; Beckman *et al.*, 1990; Beckman & Edwards, 1994; Shattuck-Hufnagel, 1991, 1992) that stress is perceived on the first syllable of words such as *Chinese* and *thirteen* more frequently than on the second syllable, independently of the stress pattern of the following word, leading to the conclusion that factors other than rhythm may affect perception.

Since considerable variation has been reported in the perception of stress in relation to the RR (e.g. Beckman *et al.*, 1987; Beckman *et al.*, 1990), it is possible that some of the more surprising results are again due to the relatively small samples involved in the studies. We thus use large numbers of targets and responses to allow us to abstract away from some of the variation that potentially obscures the results in smaller studies. Since our perception stimuli are the same as those used in the production experiment, we again have relatively large numbers of observations to base our analysis on. Crucially, too, we use the same sentences uttered for the production study to ensure that the subjects in the perception study are responding to precisely those acoustic traits on which the conclusions about production are based.

9.3 Methods

9.3.1 Experiment 1: production

In the production study, the major questions related to clash are whether the presence of a clashing stress affects the preceding word and if so, in what ways. In addition, we were interested in whether the context preceding the clash has an effect on the stress pattern. We thus measured the duration of different portions of the words involved as well as the F_0 and amplitude of the rhyme portions of these words. We are interested here not only in what acoustic correlates of stress are involved, but also in where the changes occur so as to evaluate the different theoretical positions regarding the RR (i.e., RA vs. DA).

9.3.1.1 Subjects
Ten talkers ranging from 19 to 25 years in age read the stimulus sentences. All the talkers were from the northeastern portion of the United States

9.3.1.2 Stimuli

The four target words (*thirteen, seventeen, Chinese, Japanese*) have final stress when uttered in isolation and secondary stress on the first syllable, making it "stressable". The targets (W1) were followed by a two syllable noun (W2) with stress either on the first syllable (*clients, colleagues*) or on the second syllable (*canoes, cadets*), the clash vs. nonclash contexts, respectively. The crucial sequence thus formed a Phonological Phrase, the postlexical prosodic domain within which the RR uncontroversially applies (cf. Selkirk, 1978; Nespor & Vogel, 1986). These sequences, along with any preceding material, constituted the subject NP of a sentence. The structure of the VP was kept as constant as possible, consisting of a monosyllabic verb and a PP or NP in which the preposition or article was monosyllabic and the following noun stressed on the first syllable. The context preceding the targets was varied to permit comparison of three rhythmic possibilities: no preceding material, a preceding weak syllable (*the*), and a preceding strong syllable (*Jack's*). The structure of the stimuli is shown in Table 9.1. (See Appendix for a complete list of the target sentences.)

The 24 experimental sentences (four targets by three preceding and two following contexts) were supplemented by 24 distractor sentences which had the same degree of consistency across sentences but different structures and stress patterns.

Table 9.1. Overview of sentence structures

Prior Context	W1	W2
null	two-syllable (*thirteen, Chinese*)	Clash
weak (*the*)	three-syllable (*seventeen, Japanese*)	No Clash
strong (*Jack's*)		

9.3.1.3 Procedure

The 10 talkers read the 48 (target + distractor) sentences 10 times each. Each set of 48 sentences was randomized and the target and distractor sentences appeared alternately. The talkers were instructed to read the sentences as naturally as possible. All productions were recorded in a sound dampened booth.

9.3.1.4 Data analysis

The recorded sentences were digitized at an 8 kHz sampling rate with appropriate prefiltering. Following the first occurrence of each sentence, which we discarded, the next six acceptable repetitions were excised for measurement.

Occasionally a repetition was rejected if the talker produced (a) a lexical error, (b) a hesitation or other dysfluency, or (c) an atypical intonation pattern.

Four segments within each target were marked for subsequent acoustic analysis: the onsets of the first and last syllables (O1 and O2, respectively), and the rhymes of the first and last syllables (R1 and R2, respectively).

From the marked segments, we obtained the duration, pitch, and amplitude measurements listed in (4). F_0 and amplitude measurements were estimated for 10 ms analysis frames throughout the two rhyme segments of each target. Average values of F_0 and amplitude were then computed over the frames of each segment. The F_0 data were screened for outliers to capture probable errors, and those errors were corrected by hand. The results discussed below are based on the analysis of the five talkers for whom acoustic analyses are presently complete.

(4)   Acoustic measurements
       a. Duration measures (ms): O1D, O2D, R1D, R2D
       b. Pitch measures (Log Hz): R1P, R2P
       c. Amplitude measures (dB RMS): R1A, R2A

9.3.2 Experiment 2: perception

The aim of this experiment was to determine whether the acoustic measurements made in Experiment 1 were able to predict listeners' perception of stress in the target items. While acoustic measurements alone provide insight into how speakers produce the stress patterns under consideration here, it is ultimately crucial to know how the different physical properties of these utterances are interpreted by listeners.

9.3.2.1 Subjects

The 20 listeners were students at the University of Delaware. All were from the eastern U.S. and ranged in age from 18 to 25.

9.3.2.2 Stimuli

The six good repetitions of the 24 target sentences produced by each of the 10 listeners in the production experiment were used in the perception experiment. Each talker's sentences were randomized differently.

9.3.2.3 Procedure

Listeners were seated at a CRT terminal in a sound dampened booth. On each trial, the CRT first displayed the text of the sentence the listener was about to hear, along with two response alternatives for which stress was indicated by capitalization (e.g. *CHInese* and *chiNESE* indicated first and last syllable prominence, respectively). Each response was associated with a key to press when responding. The audio presentation of the sentence was given binaurally over headphones after the printed sentence was displayed. Following the audio presentation, the system waited for a response and then proceeded with the next trial. If the subject did not respond within 10 seconds, a new trial was begun without collecting a response.

At the start of a session, the experimenter read instructions which illustrated different stress patterns and described how stress can shift from one to another syllable of some words. The sentences were then presented, blocked by talker. The test sentences for each of the 10 talkers were preceded by 10 practice sentences to familiarize the listener with the new voice.

9.3.2.4 Data analysis

To provide perceptual measurements which parallel the acoustic measurements for each sentence, the number of last syllable stress responses per sentence was tallied. With 20 listeners, this measure of final syllable stress (FSS) ranged from 0 to 20. The Analysis of Variance (ANOVA) using FSS examined the effects of TALKER (1-10), WORD (*Chinese, Japanese, thirteen, seventeen*), CONTEXT (null, weak, strong), and CLASH (no, yes) using sentence token as the observational unit. In addition to this "by token" analysis, a more conservative repeated measures ANOVA was carried out using listeners as the observational unit. This analysis was considerably less powerful statistically since it was based on a number of 20 (listeners) as opposed to 1440 (sentences).

9.3.3 Regression analysis

In addition, the 720 sentences for which both perceptual and acoustic measurements were obtained formed the data set for regression analyses. In these analyses, the acoustic measures described above were supplemented by the addition of two variables: an offset, in ms, from the beginning of the sentence waveform to the beginning of O1 (hereafter O1S), and a categorical variable that coded CONTEXT condition (Null = 0, Weak = 1, Strong = 2) for each sentence (hereafter CX).

9.4 Results

9.4.1 Production data

Separate analyses of variance were run for each of the measurements listed in (4), as summarized in Table 9.2. Two variables, O1D and O2D, were not

Table 9.2. ANOVA summary. T = TALKER; W = WORD; Cn = CONTEXT; Cl = CLASH; $* - p < 0.05$; $** = p < 0.01$.

Effect	R1D	R2D	R1P	R2P	R1A	R2A
T	**	**	**	**	**	**
W	**	**	**	**	**	**
T.W	**	**	*	*	**	**
Cn	**	*	*	**	**	**
T.Cn	**		**	**		**
W.Cn	**		**	*		*
T.W.Cn	*					
Cl		**		*		
T.Cl		**				
W.Cl		**				
T.W.Cn.Cl	**					

analyzed due to measurement difficulties stemming from the nature of the stimulus sentences themselves.

The effects due to TALKER and WORD, and their interaction, were significant for all acoustic measures. While this was to be expected given differences in the way individuals speak, and the inherent acoustic properties of different words, the overall consistency among talkers was striking as illustrated in Figure 9.1.

Given the substantial consistency seen here, we base our analyses on the means taken across talkers and across words.

Table 9.3 presents means for each acoustic measure in each CONTEXT condition, averaged over all other factors. In addition, the results of Tukey HSD *post hoc* tests on the differences among the means for each measure are indicated. When two labels are grouped together, their means are not statistically different (alpha = 0.05). In Table 9.3 and subsequent tables, mean pitch values have been converted to linear Hz units.

For pitch and amplitude measurements, it is most instructive to examine the changes between the first and second rhymes. Despite differences in the absolute values across words, the direction of change in pitch was consistent within each context. That is, there was an increase when the target was at the beginning of the sentence and when it followed a weak syllable, but a decrease was observed when the target followed a strong syllable.

The comparison of R1A and R2A also revealed a highly consistent pattern across contexts. In all cases, the amplitude was lower on the final rhyme. The presence of a strong preceding syllable, furthermore, had the most marked lowering effect on both rhymes.

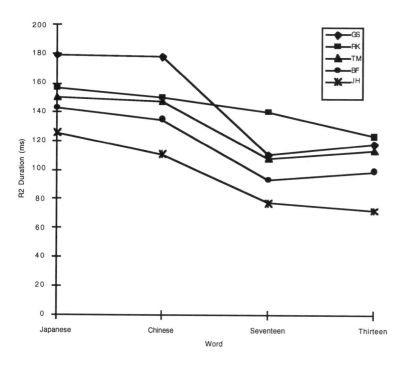

Figure 9.1. Average final rhyme (R2) duration for each target word shown separately for each talker.

Table 9.3. Means in each CONTEXT condition for each measure.

Measure	Context			
	N(ull)	W(eak)	S(trong)	
R1D	90.1	101.2	96.9	W > S > N
R2D	129.0	126.0	125.0	NW > WS
R1P	126.1	126.5	125.0	NW > S
R2P	128.9	128.5	120.5	NW > S
R1A	81.4	81.5	80.7	NW > S
R2A	76.0	75.9	74.5	NW > S

Table 9.4 presents the effects of CLASH. Here again, the means averaged across talkers and words are presented. The only significant effects of CLASH were on R2D and R2P, indicating a decrease in both duration and F_0 of the final rhyme when a clash was present.

Table 9.4. Means in each CLASH condition for each measure.

Measure	Clash		
	No	Yes	
R1D	97.1	97.7	NY
R2D	130.4	122.9	N > Y
R1P	126.0	125.7	NY
R2P	126.6	125.2	N > Y
R1A	81.2	81.2	NY
R2A	75.5	75.5	NY

9.4.2 Perception data

A conservative repeated measures ANOVA using the 20 listeners as sampling units revealed significant main effects of WORD (F (3, 57) = 13.42, $p < 0.01$) and CONTEXT (F (2, 38) = 12.39, $p < 0.01$). The main effect of CLASH in this analysis was marginal (F (1, 19) = 3.95, $p = 0.061$), and there were no significant interactions.

For our primary ANOVA, each of the 1440 sentences was assigned a Final Syllable Stress score (FSS = percentage of final stress responses for the target word). Thus, if a target word was heard as stressed on its final syllable by every listener, an FSS score of 100 would be assigned to that sentence; if half the listeners labeled the target word as final syllable stressed, an FSS score of 50 would be assigned. Overall, listeners identified words as FSS only 21.79% of the time.

The analysis revealed significant main effects of TALKER (F (9, 1200) = 11.22, $p < 0.01$), WORD (F (3, 1200) = 165.24, $p < 0.01$), and the interaction of these two effects (F (27, 1200) = 2.99, $p < 0.01$). While differences due to TALKER and WORD provide information about the variability of the Rhythm Rule itself, they do not provide insight into effects of the linguistic parameters under investigation here (i.e., preceding context and clash). We therefore focus our attention here only on these linguistic parameters.

The ANOVA revealed two additional significant main effects. The effect of CONTEXT was significant (F (2, 1200) = 69.84, $p < 0.01$) with mean FSS of 17.7, 20.4, and 24.0 for Null, Weak, and Strong CONTEXTs respectively. The effect of CLASH was also significant (F (1, 1200) = 14.49, $p < 0.01$) with FSS higher in the nonclash condition (mean FSS = 21.6 and 20.0, for nonclash and clash respectively).

9.4.3 Regression analyses

Generally, greater stress is associated with greater syllable duration, marked F_0 (either high or low), and greater amplitude. Indeed, it was seen above that for the clash context, where reduced stress was expected, there was a shortening of the final rhyme of the targets, as well as a decrease in the FSS score. When the effect of preceding context is considered, however, the picture is more complex. While context had significant effects on the duration of both the first and last rhymes, as well as significant consequences for the perceived stress pattern, the correlation was not direct, as it was in the case of clash. That is, while a strong preceding context resulted in the shortest final rhymes, it also resulted in the greatest perception of final stress (i.e., highest FSS scores).

Bearing in mind that the presence of parallel significant effects in the perception and production data does not necessarily imply a strict correlation between the sentence-by-sentence variation in specific acoustic measures and the perception data, we used regression analyses to examine the relation between these two types of data. FSS served as the dependent variable and acoustic measures as predictor variables. The acoustic measures are those used in the production study (i.e., rhyme duration, F_0 and amplitude) plus two additional variables: (a) O1S, the location of the start of the target word in the sentence (i.e., an offset, in ms, from the beginning of the sentence waveform to the beginning of O1), and (b) CX, a categorical variable that coded CONTEXT condition (Null = 0, Weak = 1, Strong = 2) for each sentence. The prediction was that if the actual durations were perceptually important, O1S would yield significantly better regression models than those containing CX.

In addition to the foregoing considerations, since WORD was a highly significant effect in the ANOVA of the perceptual data, accounting for almost 22% of the variance in the FSS scores, separate regression models were fitted for each WORD.

The results of the regression modeling are summarized in Table 9.5, which presents parameter estimates for each variable and word. Since the coded context variable CX yielded slightly better fitting models than O1S, the models presented here use CX. Asterisks indicate that the contribution of a variable to the model is significant by t-test (* = $p < 0.05$; ** = $p < 0.01$). The variable B is a constant intercept term.

Table 9.5. Regression analysis summary.

Variable	Word			
	Chinese	*Japanese*	*thirteen*	*seventeen*
B	** 17.70	5.90	4.60	2.80
CX	** 0.65	** 1.07	** 0.97	** 0.59
R1D	0.01	* –0.02	** –0.03	* –0.04
R2D	** 0.02	** 0.02	* 0.02	0.02
R1P	–4.18	–0.68	–1.34	* 6.73
R2P	0.35	0.63	1.13	* –7.31
R1A	* –1.62	** –2.53	–0.79	0.30
R2A	** 1.65	** 2.28	0.78	0.25
Rsq	0.29 (0.26)	0.26 (0.23)	0.21 (0.17)	0.19 (0.15)

The models represented here can be interpreted as equations which weight the direction and extent of influence of the acoustic variables in predicting the FSS scores. For example, the equation in (5) indicates that the FSS scores for *Japanese* are predicted from positively weighted values of B, CX, R2D, R2P, R2A and negatively weighted values of R1D, R1P and R1A:

(5) FSS(Japanese) = 5.95 + 1.07*CX – 0.02*R1D + 0.02*R2D – 0.68*R1P + 0.63*R2P – 2.53*R1A + 2.28*R2A

Further examination of Table 9.5 reveals, however, that only CX, R1D, R2D, R1A, and R2A contributed significantly to the Japanese model. Generally, the models displayed complementarity between the first and last rhyme measures, with one tending to be negatively weighted if the other was positively weighted. Thus, in most cases R1D contributed negatively to FSS scores while R2D contributed positively. In other words, the perception of final stress increased as R1D decreased and R2D increased.

All the models represented in Table 9.5 account for a significant proportion of the FSS score variance (ranging from 19% to 29%). There nevertheless remains a substantial amount of variance that is not accounted for, and which must be attributed either to error or to factors that are not captured by the acoustic measures and code variable, a point we address briefly in the next section.

9.5 Discussion

In this section we discuss the results of the various experiments in relation to the theoretical issues raised in section 9.2 above. The phonological issues relating to the nature of the Rhythm Rule and its conditioning factors are discussed along with the phonetic issues relating to the acoustic correlates of the rule since the two matters are intimately connected. We also address two other issues that were briefly mentioned in section 9.2, and which, although they did not form the basis for the present study, nevertheless turn out to be important in the present findings. These are the surprisingly high rate of perception of first syllable stress in the targets and the variability in production across talkers.

9.5.1. Clash

Since the central theoretical assumption behind the present investigation is the existence of a particular phonological phenomenon of English, the Rhythm Rule, we consider first evidence for this rule from the present results.

Our results on both the production and perception studies leave no doubt that the Rhythm Rule is a systematic component of English phonology, at least in the northeastern US variety examined here. In the production data, there was a strong effect of clash, the phonological pattern that is claimed to give rise to the RR. More specifically, we found that the presence of a clash led to physical reduction of the final rhyme (R2) of the target word in two respects: it caused a shortening in the duration of this element (R2D) and a lowering of its pitch (R2P) relative to the nonclash context. No effect of clash was observed on the amplitude values. It is also noteworthy that the effect of the clash was not observed beyond the adjacent rhyme. That is, no effect on either the duration or pitch of the first rhyme was found.

We noted above that, contrary to our findings, earlier studies failed to find consistent acoustic effects of the RR. We suspect there are several reasons for this. First, previous studies used relatively small stimulus sets. Given the degree of variability in the RR observed in the present and previous studies, it is not surprising that a large number of observations (e.g. the 144 sentences × five talkers = 720 observations used here) is needed to reveal consistent patterns.

Another, more interesting, factor is that most previous studies examined only the first syllable of the word, assuming a Reversal Analysis of the RR. The most notable exception is Horne (1990) (cf. section 9.2.1 above). Our results, in fact, confirm the absence of an effect of clash on the first syllable (or rhyme in this case), while showing significant effects on the final rhyme. This pattern supports the Deletion Analysis of the RR, and demonstrates that acoustically there is no evidence for the Reversal Analysis.

In addition to the effects of clash on speech production, we found evidence of significant effects on perception. Listeners perceived stress on the final syllable of the targets less frequently in clash conditions. Thus, even though there is no acoustic evidence for the Reversal Analysis of the RR, weakening the final rhyme nevertheless leads to the perception of stronger stress on the first syllable. This is not surprising given the relative nature of stress, and is perhaps the primary source of the earlier, erroneous view of the RR as actually involving a physical shift of stress from the final syllable onto an earlier one in the word.

In regression models of the relation between the acoustic correlates of the RR and the perception of initial stress, we saw that the duration and pitch of the final rhyme contributed significantly to which syllable was perceived as having stronger stress. There are, nevertheless, other factors involved that lead to a surprisingly strong preference for perceived stress on the first syllable, in the absence of clash, and in the absence of the reduced duration and pitch of the final syllable associated with the RR. We return to this issue in section 9.5.4.

9.5.2 Context

While the context preceding the target had a highly significant effect on the duration of the first rhyme, it had only a marginal effect on the duration of the last rhyme. Its effect is thus somewhat analogous to that of clash, in that each contextual factor affects the rhyme in the target that is adjacent to it. The fact that no significant interaction between clash and context was observed is thus not surprising, since these two linguistic parameters primarily affect different portions of a word.

As seen in Table 9.3, the effect of context on the duration of the first rhyme is to produce the longest duration when a weak syllable precedes the target and the shortest when nothing precedes the target; the duration following a strong syllable falls in between the other two values. One possible account is that if the duration of R1 following a strong syllable were too great, this would be perceived as a clashing effect. Given the general principle of eurhythmy mentioned in section 9.2.1, it would seem that some degree of lengthening on R1 to indicate the beginning of the word is acceptable, as long as the overall alternating pattern begun by the preceding strong syllable is not contravened.

All the other acoustic measures except R2D showed a significant decrease following a strong syllable with respect to both the null and weak contexts, which were statistically not distinct. In the case of R2D, the strong context was distinct from the null context, but the weak context was not distinct from either of these. This suggests that in general the entire target word following a strong context syllable is suppressed in both loudness and pitch relative to other contexts.

Despite our finding in the production data that prior context leads to an increase in the duration of R1, listeners in the perception study reported increased stress for the final syllable of the target words in the presence of weak or strong prior context. Moreover, the lower pitch and amplitude measurements following a strong syllable coincide with the highest scores for stress perceived on the last syllable. Thus, the production data show an overall weakening or de-emphasis of both the first and last syllables of the target word following a preceding strong syllable, and the perception data for this context indicate a resultant shift in perceived stress toward the final syllable. This may be an indication that the default pattern following a strong context is the final stress form found in isolation. More generally, however, other factors, for example, a shift in the location of the pitch accent, may play a role in perceived stress location.

9.5.3 Relating production and perception

Regression analyses were used to systematically probe the relationships between perceptual and acoustic properties of the stimuli. Across the four target words, we find generally that R2D and the coded preceding context variable, CX, are the most important in predicting the perceptual data from the acoustic measures. As R2D increases and CX becomes stronger, the perception of final stress increases. While the amplitude of the final rhyme also contributes positively to the regression models in general, its effect is weaker than those of CX and R2D. These findings are consistent with the above observations regarding the effects of clash and context on the RR. Since the strongest acoustic indication of a clash is the shortening of R2D, it follows that R2D will be directly related to our measure of final syllable stress. It was also seen that the strong preceding context tended to push listeners to perceive stress on the final syllable independently of the acoustic properties of the items involved. However, what is surprising here is that the regression models do not account for more of the observed pattern of stress perception. Indeed, the best model accounted for only 29% of the observed variance.

9.5.4 Additional considerations

As observed above and in the literature on the RR, speakers of English exhibit a strong tendency to indicate stress on the first syllable of words which, like our targets, have a stressable syllable in that position. This preference appears to be stronger than is predicted either by the structural (i.e., clash) or the acoustic properties of the items in question.

This overwhelming preference for initial stress in our data might in part reflect a task artifact. Each listener had to provide judgments for 1440 sentences, a task that took about two and a half hours. Despite the break in the middle, the task may have been so demanding that instead of concentrating on what they heard each time, the subjects may have resorted to judgments based on their beliefs about their own pronunciations of the words in question, especially in cases where the differences were subtle. Although it appears that our experiment may not have always tapped the perceptual faculties we were hoping to tap, the alternative strategy we observed is in accord with the results of Beckman *et al.* (1987), and Beckman *et al.* (1990). Thus, alternative patterns associated with different types of words will need to be taken into consideration in order for the picture to be complete. How such factors can be included in a regression analysis is not obvious, however, since they are not easily quantifiable. This means that either the extent of the match we arrived at is essentially all we can expect, or that some other way of evaluating the relation between the production and perception of the Rhythm Rule may be more appropriate.

Appendix

Target sentences

1. Thirteen clients called at noon.
2. Chinese colleagues work the most.
3. The thirteen clients paid their bills.
4. The Chinese colleagues came on Monday.
5. Jack's thirteen clients rode their bicycles.
6. Jack's Chinese colleagues speak with accents.
7. Thirteen cadets passed their finals.
8. Chinese canoes sink in storms.
9. The thirteen cadets left at midnight.
10. The Chinese canoes won the race.
11. Jack's thirteen cadets sleep in class.
12. Jack's Chinese canoes brought more people.
13. Seventeen clients called at noon.
14. Japanese colleagues work the most.
15. The seventeen clients paid their bills.
16. The Japanese colleagues came on Monday.
17. Jack's seventeen clients rode their bicycles.
18. Jack's Japanese colleagues speak with accents.
19. Seventeen cadets passed their finals.
20. Japanese canoes sink in storms.
21. The seventeen cadets left at midnight.
22. The Japanese canoes won the race.
23. Jack's seventeen cadets sleep in class.
24. Jack's Japanese canoes brought more people.

Note

* The research reported here was funded partly by NSF Grant No. HRD9255940 to the first author, with additional support from the Nemours Foundation to the second author. We would like to thank Michael Kelly for his helpful comments on the design of our experiments.

References

Beckman, M. E. 1986. *Stress and Non-Stress Accent*. Dordrecht: Foris.
Beckman, M. E., K. de Jong & J. Edwards. 1987. The surface phonology of stress clash in English. Paper presented at the Annual LSA Meeting.
Beckman, M. E. & J. Edwards. 1994. Articulatory evidence for differentiating stress categories. In P. A. Keating (ed.), *Phonological Structure and Phonetic Form: Papers in Laboratory Phonology III*. Cambridge: Cambridge University Press, 7–33.
Beckman, M. E., M. Swora, J. Rauschenberg & K. de Jong. 1990. Stress shift, stress clash, and polysyllabic shortening in a prosodically annotated discourse. *Proceedings of the 1990 International Conference on Spoken Language Processing*, Kobe, 1: 5–8.
Cooper, W. & S. Eady. 1986. Metrical phonology in speech production. *Journal of Memory and Language* 25: 369–384.
Hayes, B. 1984. The phonology of rhythm. *Linguistic Inquiry* 15: 33–74.
Horne, M. 1990. Empirical evidence for a deletion formulation of the rhythm rule in English. *Linguistics* 28: 959–981.
Liberman, M. 1975. The Intonational Structure of English. Ph.D. dissertation, MIT.
Liberman, M. & A. Prince. 1977. On stress and linguistic rhythm. *Linguistic Inquiry* 8: 249–336.
Nespor, M. & I. Vogel. 1986. *Prosodic Phonology*. Dordrecht: Foris.
Nespor, M. & I. Vogel. 1989. On clashes and lapses. *Phonology* 6: 69–116.
Prince, A. 1983. Relating to the grid. *Linguistic Inquiry* 14: 19–100.
Selkirk, E. O. 1978. On prosodic structure and its relation to syntactic structure. Distributed by Indiana University Linguistics Club, 1980.
Selkirk, E. O. 1984. *Phonology and Syntax*. Cambridge, MA: MIT Press.
Shattuck-Hufnagel, S. 1991. Acoustic correlates of stress shift. *Proceedings of the XIIth International Congress of Phonetic Sciences*, Aix-en-Provence, 4: 266–269.
Shattuck-Hufnagel, S. 1992. Stress shift as pitch accent placement: within-word early accent placement in American English. *Proceedings of the 1992 International Conference on Spoken Language Processing*, Banff, 2: 747–750.

10

The importance of phonological transcription in empirical approaches to "stress shift" versus "early accent": comments on Grabe and Warren, and Vogel, Bunnell and Hoskins

STEFANIE SHATTUCK-HUFNAGEL

10.1 Introduction

The titles used by Grabe & Warren and Vogel, Bunnell & Hoskins indicate agreement on a central point about the study of "stress shift" (or perceived early prominence in the word): it is critical to investigate this phenomenon from several different points of view at the same time. Although the authors differ in their methods, findings, and conclusions about early prominence, they share the conviction that an adequate test of early prominence theories requires several different kinds of data. These include perceptual judgments and acoustic measurements of the test utterances, which should contain a number of different target words in a number of different contexts, produced by more than a single speaker and judged by more than one listener. It will be argued here that a key addition to this list of requirements is a phonological transcription of the prosodic structure of the utterances as they are actually produced.

This information is critical to the interpretation of all other data, because speakers have a number of options for the prosodic structure of a given sentence, and their choice is not always predictable from the text alone. A prosodic transcription allows us to evaluate two different kinds of predictions: predictions about the contexts in which early prominence will occur, and proposals about the acoustic cues that signal early prominence when it does occur. The requisite phonological transcription includes both the prosodic constituent structure and the distribution of phrase-level prosodic prominences (pitch accents) in each utterance. The location of these boundaries and prominences is important because an alternative to the rhythmic stress account of early prominence, the Early Pitch Accent Placement account, based on the intermediate intonational phrase (see section 10.4), has been shown to provide a concise description of the early prominence phenomenon in at least one large speech database.

In this commentary, we will review some of the points of agreement and disagreement between the two papers in their tests of the theory of rhythmic stress shift (section 10.2), describe an alternative approach based on pitch accent placement (section 10.3), and then revisit the empirical findings with this alternative approach in mind (section 10.4). Finally, we will note some of the important new points and productive research issues that are highlighted by the investigations described in the two papers (section 10.5), before summarizing our conclusions (section 10.6).

10.2 Two empirical investigations of the metrical theory of rhythmic stress shift

10.2.1 Perceptual judgments

Both Grabe & Warren (G&W) and Vogel, Bunnell & Hoskins (VB&H) set out to test the metrical theory of rhythmic stress shift, which predicts that speakers will move the greatest prominence in a late-main-stress word like *Japanese* to an earlier stressable syllable, when the word occurs in contexts where there is a rhythmic stress clash with the following material in the same phrase, as in *JApanese FOOD*. (Prominent syllables are represented here in upper case.) The theory describes both stress clash and stress shift in terms of a metrical grid, which defines the relative rhythmic prominence of the syllables of an utterance as the relative number of grid marks in the column of grid marks erected over each syllable. In the experiments, listeners heard spoken utterances that contained stress-shiftable words (i.e., words with late main stress and an earlier strong syllable) either in stress-clash contexts or in nonclash contexts, and reported perceptual judgments of prominence location within the target words.

For clash contexts, the results were clear: listeners reliably report early prominence in target words like *Japanese* and *neolithic*, when they occur in contexts like *JApanese COLleagues* or *NEolithic SETtlements*, just as the metrical theory of rhythmic stress predicts. The results for the nonclash conditions were more mixed, and seemed to depend on the type of manipulation used to eliminate the clash. G&W used an intervening syntactic clause boundary (presumably with a corresponding prosodic phrase boundary) to eliminate clash; e.g. nonclashing . . . *TV, soaps* . . . vs. clashing . . . *TV soaps*). They report almost no judgments of early prominence in the nonclash condition, just as the theory predicts. In contrast, VB&H used a reduced initial syllable in the following word to block clash (e.g. nonclashing *Chinese canoes* vs. clashing *Chinese colleagues*), without an intervening phrase boundary. Stress clash theory also predicts a much lesser likelihood of shift in the contexts which have no rhythmic stress clash. Yet, listeners often reported early prominence in the nonclash stimuli. VB&H report a Final Stress Score (FSS), reflecting main-stress prominence, of only about 20% for both their clash and nonclash stimuli. The difference in FSS between clash and nonclash contexts was significant (19.98 vs. 21.60), but the size of the difference hardly accords with the claim that speakers shift stress leftward primarily to avoid rhythmic stress clash. Instead, it appears that speakers produce target words with early prominence in both clash and nonclash contexts.

Overall, then, the perceptual results of these two experiments confirm the prediction that early prominence is perceived in clash conditions, as the metrical theory of rhythmic stress shift predicts, but the significance of this observation is somewhat clouded by the fact that early prominence is also perceived in nonclash conditions in one of the experiments. Thus the question arises, under what nonclash conditions is early prominence perceived?

VB&H also varied the prominence of the syllable preceding the target word, contrasting three contexts: no preceding syllable, a weak preceding syllable (a reducible function word), and a strong preceding syllable (an unreducible monosyllabic content word). Listeners reported final stress on the shiftable target word decreasingly often (i.e., reported early prominence increasingly often) as the preceding context changed from a strong syllable to a weak syllable to no syllable. This demonstration of the effect of preceding context on the judgment of prominence location in the word is the first empirical evidence of its kind. The finding that a strong monosyllable in the immediate left context reduces judgments of early prominence in the target word raises the question, under what circumstances does the preceding context have an effect?

10.2.2 Acoustic measures

Besides gathering perceptual judgments of prominence location within the word, both G&W and VB&H also made acoustic measurements of the utterances in order to determine the acoustic correlates of perceived early prominence. G&W compared the early and main-stress syllables for target words in the clash context utterances that actually elicited judgments of early prominence; this is a substantial advance over simply assuming that early prominence has occurred. They compared the duration of syllabic nuclei, amplitude integral (an approximation to the integral of amplitude over time), average amplitude of the nuclei (amplitude integral divided by the duration), average F_0 of the nuclei (essentially by averaging the initial and final F_0 measures), and F_0 range over the nuclei. None of these measures (with the possible exception of amplitude integral) indicated a greater acoustic prominence on the earlier syllable than on the main-stress syllable when the earlier syllable was perceived as more prominent. This was true even for a subset of target words where the early and main-stress nuclei were phonologically similar, which made direct acoustic comparisons more reliable. G&W conclude that stress does not actually shift to the earlier syllable, because none of the generally accepted acoustic correlates of stress have more extreme values for that syllable. They then go on to test the possibility that the perception of early prominence is determined by the rhythmic expectations induced by stress alternations in the preceding portion of the utterance.

VB&H focus on the rhymes rather than the nuclei of the target syllables, measuring the duration of the rhymes of the early and main-stress syllables, computing the average F_0 from estimates at 10 ms analysis frames through the rhymes (expressed in Log Hz), and similarly the average amplitude through the rhymes (expressed in Log RMS amplitude). They note that the preceding context affects the duration of the *early* syllable's rhyme, while the following clash affects the duration of the later *main-stress* syllable's rhyme. In addition, F_0 and amplitude are lower in both of the stressable syllables of the target word when the preceding monosyllable is strong.

In sum, the two sets of experiments confirm that early prominence can be heard in the target words in stress clash conditions; they provide conflicting results about what happens in two different types of nonclash conditions; and they fail to find convincing evidence that the early syllable that is heard as more prominent has more extreme values for the commonly-accepted acoustic correlates of stress than the later main-stress syllable does. Perhaps the most puzzling aspect of these results, from the point of view of metrical theories of rhythmic stress shift, is VB&H's finding that perceived early prominence is common even when the target words appear in nonclash contexts. This finding suggests that the occurrence of major perceptual prominence on the main-stress syllable of a target word is not as pervasive as might have been supposed. As we shall see, this observation fits well with the results of other empirical studies of early perceptual prominence within the word, and accords with the predictions of an alternative account of early prominence which is based on pitch accent placement. This theory is described in the following section. An additional puzzling result is the failure to find consistent acoustic correlates of the early prominence which is so reliably perceived by listeners. This observation is also consistent with the pitch accent account.

10.3 Pitch-accent-based views of early prominence

Metrical theories of rhythmic stress shift emerged in the 1970s and 1980s from a tradition that regards rhythmic stress in spoken utterances as a parameter which can take many values; some syllables of an utterance have little of it, others have more, others have still more, but this variation occurs along a single dimension. Metrical theories often admit candidly that the acoustic and articulatory correlates of these variations in rhythmic prominence are not well understood. A separate tradition in the literature, brought into the spotlight by Bolinger (1958, 1965), makes more specific claims about the acoustic correlates of perceived prominence. This tradition takes a very different view of what constitutes perceptual prominence in spoken utterances, and thus of what underlies the early prominence in the word that is perceived in some contexts. Bolinger proposed that prominence at the phrase or sentence level was a matter of pitch accents, or prominence-lending F_0 markers, and that perceived early prominence in the word results from a pitch accent on an early syllable.

This intonation-based account of early prominence reflects Bolinger's general view that there are only two kinds of contrast in prosodic prominence: reduced vs. unreduced syllables (i.e., lexical stress) and pitch-accented vs. non-pitch-accented syllables (i.e., phrasal prominence). A pitch accent can occur only on an unreduced syllable, i.e., a syllable with full-vowel quality. But once this criterion is met, just about any full-vowel syllable can be pitch accented, as long as it does not occur after the main-stress syllable of the word. Thus either or both of the two full-vowel syllables of a word like *Japanese* can be a candidate for pitch accent location. Additionally, Bolinger suggests that speakers prefer to place the first pitch accent of an intonational phrase as early as possible, and the last accent as late as possible. These two factors combined could result in the accent pattern *JApanese FOOD*, i.e., an apparent stress shift in *Japanese*. In contrast to the metrical view, this early prominence might equally well occur without a stress clash, e.g. in *JApanese rePLY*. But it will not occur when the word contains the nuclear or final accent of a phrase, because speakers prefer to place the final accent of a phrase as late as possible. As a result, the nuclear accent of a phrase will always appear on the main-stress syllable of its word. For example, when a word like *Massachusetts* is produced in citation form in isolation, the main-stress syllable will invariably carry a pitch accent as the nuclear pitch accent of the phrase; if the word has an earlier full-vowel syllable, that syllable may or may not carry a prenuclear pitch accent.

A notable fact about this view is that it postulates different acoustic cues to different types or levels of prominence: e.g. spectral or quality cues to the contrast between lexically stressed vs. reduced syllables, and F_0 cues to phrasal prominence. Vanderslice & Ladefoged (1972) expanded on this notion, proposing a three-way contrast between four levels of prominence: reduced-vowel syllables, full-vowel syllables, accented syllables, and those with nuclear

"Stress shift" versus "early accent"

accent (see also Ladefoged, 1975). Beckman & Edwards (1991, 1994) relate these distinctions to the prosodic hierarchy, suggesting that the head of each type of constituent in the hierarchy may be characterized by a different dominant acoustic cue. Although distinct in many ways, these approaches share three characteristics that are relevant here: (1) lexical stress *per se* is not cued by F_0 variation, but rather by some combination of duration, vowel quality and perhaps amplitude; prominence-lending F_0 markers are phrase-level pitch accents rather than correlates of lexical stress; (2) lexical stress serves as a roadmap to pitch accent location, and different types of lexical stress impose different constraints on accent placement; prenuclear pitch accents can occur on early full-vowel syllables of their words (sometimes described as having secondary or even tertiary stress), but the nuclear pitch accent of a phrase must occur on the main-stress syllable of its word; and (3) perceived early prominence in the word is often a matter of early pitch accent location, at least for the first accent in a phrase.

Bolinger's initial formulation of the intonation-based theory of early prominence, and other early versions were limited to the first accent in a phrase. These versions of the theory envisioned no role for rhythmic constraints on the placement of other prenuclear pitch accents. However, the intuitions behind metrical theory suggest a powerful tendency toward regularization of the alternation between greater and lesser phrase-level prominence in the successive syllables of an utterance. Bolinger's (1981) formulation of his intonation-based theory integrated this rhythmic tendency with the early and late placement of pitch accents, claiming that speakers tend towards a regular alternation between pitch-accented and unaccented syllables when other factors permit it. In other words, Bolinger's (1981) integrated theory suggests that speakers avoid pitch accent clash as well as marking intonation phrases with early and late accents. Gussenhoven's (1991) theory, based on the deletion of alternate accents leftward from the nuclear accent of a phrase (under constraints imposed by structure), with non-deletion of both nuclear (phrase-final) and phrase-initial accents, achieves some of the same results within the framework of the prosodic hierarchy and relying on pitch accent deletion rather than pitch accent placement.

Integrated pitch-accent-based accounts of early prominence in the word ("stress shift") emerge from a theory of the nature of prosodic structure and prominence that differs broadly from that adopted by metrical theories of rhythmic stress. Thus it is critical to determine the extent to which each type of theory can provide a parsimonious explanation of the within-word prosodic patterns observed in actual utterances, as part of a more general evaluation of their explanatory power. An overview of some empirical studies that address this question, including the two studies under consideration here, is provided in the next section.

133

Stefanie Shattuck-Hufnagel

10.4 Intonation-based interpretation of empirical investigations of early prominence

The two most striking observations to emerge from early experimental investigations of apparent stress shift were that (a) it was difficult to find any acoustic correlate of the early prominence that was predicted to occur in stress shiftable words when they occur in clash contexts (Cooper & Eady, 1986), and (b) perception of early prominence was regularly and reliably reported in conditions of no rhythmic stress clash, where metrical theory does not predict it will occur (Beckman, Swora, Rauschenberg & de Jong, 1990; Shattuck-Hufnagel, 1991). The first observation was not a direct problem for the theory, since it was generally noted that the acoustic correlates of rhythmic stress prominence were poorly understood, but it left the status of early prominence somewhat undefined. The second observation was more problematic, especially given its pervasiveness.

However, both observations are consistent with an integrated pitch accent account of early prominence. For example, many of the utterances that were analyzed in these early investigations placed the target stress-shiftable word in phrase-initial position in both the clash and nonclash contexts, e.g. *the Chinese dresser* vs. *the Chinese antique* (Beckman *et al.*, 1990), *the Massachusetts miracle* vs. *the Massachusetts marauder* (Shattuck-Hufnagel, 1991), *the Pennsylvania legislature* vs. *the Pennsylvania legislation* (Cooper & Eady, 1986). The pitch accent account suggests that the first strong syllable in the target word may carry a pitch accent in both contexts, because it is the first accentable syllable in a new phrase. Since this syllable is likely to be pitch accented in both conditions, it is not surprising to find that listeners perceive early accent in both conditions, or that it has proved difficult to find an acoustic difference in the early syllable. A similar possibility can be invoked for VB&H's stimuli, e.g. *the thirteen clients* vs. *the thirteen cadets*. For G&W's nonclash condition, we cannot generalize because we do not know the prosodic constituent structure of the utterances as actually produced, so we do not know if the early syllable of the target word is the first accentable syllable of a new phrase or not. As experimenters are finding out, ensuring that speakers produce stimulus sentences with the expected or desired placement of prosodic constituent boundaries and prominences is a challenging task, particularly since speakers prefer to vary the prosody of successive utterances rather than keeping it constant. Prosodic transcription of the utterances would reveal (a) whether or not the perceived early prominence corresponds to a pitch accent, and (b) whether or not it occurs in the first accented word in a new intonational phrase. Without this information, the meaning of results is hard to interpret, particularly with respect to whether an account of early prominence in terms of the shift of rhythmic stress is necessary.

134

The integrated theory also provides a plausible account for the behavior of the main-stress syllable of the target word in these two sets of experiments. For this syllable, the integrated theory makes different predictions depending on which kind of nonclash context is selected. If clash is eliminated by placing the target word in phrase-final position, as in . . . *TV, soaps* . . . , then the target word is likely to carry the nuclear pitch accent of the phrase, which must occur on the main-stress syllable of its word. Such utterances are unlikely to be judged to have early accent, just as G&W found. In contrast, if clash is eliminated by providing a following word in the same phrase with an initial unstressed syllable, as VB&H did in, for example, *the Japanese canoe*, then the main-stress syllable of the target word is likely to be produced without a pitch accent, in order to avoid pitch accent clash. As a result, the pattern *the JApanese caNOE* may be produced, and perceived, with an early and a late pitch accent in the phrase. Finally, in contexts where a strong monosyllable precedes the target word, as in VB&H's *Jack's Japanese canoe*, the initial pitch accent may fall on the first stressable syllable, *Jack's*, and the nuclear pitch accent on the main-stress syllable of the final constituent, *canoe*. The entire intervening word, *Japanese*, may be unaccented, since it carries neither the first accent nor the nuclear accent of the phase. The resulting pattern of *JACK'S Japanese caNOE* would be consistent with VB&H's finding that F_0 values were lower for the target word *Japanese* in this context.

Some empirical support for the hypothesis that pitch accent placement patterns within the word can account for many instances of apparent stress shift comes from the work of Horne (1990). She tested Gussenhoven's claim that the middle of three potential accents will be deleted in phrases like *Dundee marmalade*, by measuring the F_0 excursion on the late main-stress syllable *-dee* and comparable syllables in other target words in clash vs. nonclash contexts. Her results for at least some candidate words are compatible with the claim that the pitch accent on syllables like *-dee* is deleted in clash contexts.

We have presented some conjectures about how the integrated theory of pitch accent placement might account for some of the more puzzling results of both G&W's and VB&H's experiments, and shown that they fit well with some of the details of the experimental results. But these speculations cannot be tested fully in the absence of a phonological transcription of (a) the location of pitch accents within words and (b) the location of prosodic phrase boundaries, for the utterances that were analyzed acoustically. However, an indication of the plausibility of this account is provided by a different speech database for which such phonological transcriptions are available. Ross, Ostendorf & Shattuck-Hufnagel (1992), and Shattuck-Hufnagel, Ostendorf & Ross (forthcoming) describe the patterns of perceived early prominence in "stress shiftable" words in the Boston University Corpus of FM radio news speech (Ostendorf, Price & Shattuck-Hufnagel, in preparation). The utterances in this corpus have been labeled perceptually with pitch-accented vs. non-accented syllables, and with the boundaries of intermediate intonational phrases and other prosodic constituents. More than 400 word tokens in this database that were candidates for early prominence were analyzed in terms of the position of the accent both within the word (early, main-stress or double accent) and within the intermediate intonational phrase (a prosodic constituent proposed by Beckman & Pierrehumbert (1986), defined by a perceptually coherent F_0 contour with at least one pitch accent, and a phrase tone which controls the F_0 contour from the final (nuclear) pitch accent to the final syllable). The prominence patterns in these word tokens could be largely accounted for by a combination of three principles: early accent placement in the phrase (i.e., speakers place the first accent of a new intermediate intonational phrase as early as possible in its word), avoidance of pitch accent clash, and placement of nuclear pitch accent on the main-stress syllable of its word. In addition, there were many examples of double accent within a single word, particularly in cases where the early syllable carried the initial accent of the phrase, and the main-stress syllable carried the nuclear accent. (If double accenting occurred in G&W's or VB&H's utterances, then the listener's task of reporting which of the two stressable syllables of the target words is more prominent might be particularly difficult. A more accurate measure of the listener's perception might be obtained if additional responses were permitted, i.e., "both syllables prominent", for double-accented words, and "neither syllable prominent" for deaccented words.)

Exceptions to these regularities in the BU corpus occurred primarily in words with adjacent stressed syllables, such as *illicit* and *downtown*, where adjacent pitch-accentable syllables may cause special problems for a system which prefers alternation of prominence. We note that many of the "stress shiftable" target words employed in the two investigations discussed here, as well as in the previous literature on apparent stress shift, are adjacent-stress lexical items, like *thirteen* and *ideal*. In view of the differences in prosodic behavior between these words and alternating-stress words like *Massachusetts* and *University* in the BU FM Radio News Corpus, we suggest that it might be useful to analyze the results for the two classes of words separately.

In summary, as for earlier empirical results in the literature, some of the aspects of G&W's and VB&H's experiments which are especially puzzling under the view of rhythmic stress clash and shift might be more simply accounted for by the integrated theory of pitch accent placement. While these conjectures must remain speculative in the absence of phonological labeling of the utterances themselves, the plausibility of this claim is increased by the demonstrated ability of the integrated theory to account for within-word prominence patterns in a speech database (described in more detail elsewhere) that has been labeled for pitch accent and prosodic phrase boundary location.

The two investigations discussed here raise some valuable additional points and questions, to which we turn in the final section.

10.5 Additional observations and questions

The results of G&W's and VB&H's empirical investigations of early prominence in the word highlight several important new findings and raise some important questions in newly specific and concrete form. As we have already noted, VB&H's demonstration of the effect of left context on the judgment of prominence location in target words that are candidates for early prominence is a significant new finding. The fact that this finding can be interpreted in terms of pitch accent placement adds further plausibility to the integrated intonational view.

G&W's finding that excision of the following clashing context from the utterance makes listeners less sure of the prominence pattern of the target word, and excision of the preceding context makes them even less sure, may reflect the necessity of hearing an intact intonational constituent in order to determine the relative prominence of its component syllables. Or, as they suggest, this finding may reflect the fact that context can set up a rhythmic expectation that influences perceived prominence in non-pitch-accented words, as reported by Huss (1978) for English and van Heuven (1991) for Dutch. Transcription of the location of pitch accents in the utterances as the speakers choose to produce them might allow a clearer understanding of how and when the surrounding context influences reports of perceptual prominence within the word.

G&W also raise the question of whether the prominence of the right-hand element in a clash must be stronger than the prominence of the left-hand member, in order to elicit early prominence. This highlights the fact that most of the examples of apparent stress shift cited in the literature involve the first accent of the phrase on the left-hand word, and the nuclear accent of the phrase on the following word, as in *the thirteen men* and *the Mississippi legislature*. The empirical facts about the distribution of perceptual prominence within words that are phrase-medial and carry neither the initial nor the final accent of a phrase, and about the necessity for an asymmetry in the two clashing prominences, remain to be discovered. In fact, the questions of what principles govern the placement of phrase-medial pitch accents and whether early prominence is perceived in stretches of non-pitch-accented speech offer rich possibilities for experimental investigation.

10.6 Conclusions

There are several important lessons to be drawn from this brief review of empirical investigations of competing theories of early prominence in the word.

137

The first is that adequate phonological transcription of the prosodic constituents and prominences that are actually produced by speakers of the test utterances is a useful, perhaps even necessary, part of the analysis. Without this transcription, i.e., without knowing the location of intonational phrase boundaries and of syllables that have pitch accents, we cannot evaluate the claim that the first accent in a new phrase may occur on the early syllable of its word, the nuclear accent on the main stress syllable, and double accents on words with both the initial and nuclear accents of a phrase. In other words, we need to know which of the possible options the speaker has chosen for constituent boundary placement and pitch accent placement, in the particular utterances of the sentences that have been analyzed. In fact, an even more detailed phonological transcription may be required. For example, acoustic comparisons are difficult to evaluate unless means are taken across similar elements. Since some pitch accents may involve a high F_0 while others involve a low one, only a detailed phonological transcription of, for example, the particular pitch accent type can ensure that comparisons are made for classes of similar elements. Moreover, simple measures of F_0 values or ranges, or of duration, may not be the most appropriate measures to take, since the F_0 markers that indicate pitch accents are not always simple rises or falls; they may consist of failure to fall where expected, etc. All of these difficulties suggest that a phonological transcription of prosodic prominence locations and types, as well as of constituent boundary locations, can provide useful insight into the factors that govern perceived early prominence in the word.

One barrier that has prevented widespread phonological transcription of prosodic boundaries and prominences is the time-consuming nature of the transcription task; a related problem has been the inability to share labeled data across sites because of variability in transcription systems. A recent proposal to address both of these problems, by adopting a transcription system (ToBI, for Tones and Break Indices) that captures the basic facts about phrase-level prominence and prosodic constituent structure, is described in Silverman, Beckman, Pitrelli, Ostendorf, Wightman, Price, Pierrehumbert & Hirschberg (1992). Other efforts to develop a generally accepted transcription system are underway within the international community. The motivation for these developments is the hope that they will lead to the general availability of large corpora of speech which is prosodically labeled in a widely accepted format. This resource will provide the opportunity to test the predictions of the integrated theory of pitch accent placement and the metrical theory of rhythmic stress in even greater detail.

References

Beckman, M. E. & J. Edwards. 1991. Lengthenings and shortenings and the nature of prosodic constituency. In J. Kingston & M. E. Beckman (eds.), *Papers in Laboratory Phonology I: Between the Grammar and Physics of Speech*. Cambridge: Cambridge University Press, 152–178.

Beckman, M. E. & J. Edwards. 1994. Articulatory evidence for differentiating stress categories. In P. A. Keating (ed.), *Phonological Structure and Phonetic Form: Papers in Laboratory Phonology III*. Cambridge: Cambridge University Press, 7–33.

Beckman, M. E. & J. Pierrehumbert. 1986. Intonational structure in English and Japanese. *Phonology Yearbook* 3: 255–309.

Beckman, M. E., M. G. Swora, J. Rauschenberg & K. de Jong. 1990. Stress shift, stress clash and polysyllabic shortening in a prosodically annotated discourse. *Proceedings of the 1990 International Conference on Spoken Language Processing*, Kobe, 1: 5–8.

Bolinger, D. 1958. A theory of pitch accent in English. *Word* 14: 109–149.

Bolinger, D. 1965. Pitch accent and sentence rhythm. In D. Bolinger (ed.), *Forms of English*. Cambridge, MA: Harvard University Press, 139–180.

Bolinger, D. 1981. *Two Kinds of Vowels, Two Kinds of Rhythm*. Distributed by the Indiana University Linguistics Club.

Cooper, W. E. & S. J. Eady. 1986. Metrical theory in speech production. *Journal of Memory and Language* 25: 369–384.

Gussenhoven, C. 1991. The English rhythm rule as an accent deletion rule. *Phonology* 8: 1–35.

Heuven, V. van. 1991. Stress clash avoidance in Dutch: inversion of stress patterns in complex nouns? *Proceedings of the XIIth International Congress of Phonetic Sciences*, Aix-en-Provence, 3: 226–229.

Horne, M. 1990. Empirical evidence for a deletion formulation of the rhythm rule in English. *Linguistics* 28: 959–981.

Huss, V. 1978. English word stress in the post-nuclear position. *Phonetica* 35: 86–105.

Ladefoged, P. 1975. *A Course in Phonetics*. New York: Harcourt Brace Jovanovich.

Ostendorf, M., P. Price & S. Shattuck-Hufnagel. In preparation. The BU FM Radio News Speech Corpus.

Ross, K., M. Ostendorf & S. Shattuck-Hufnagel. 1992. Factors affecting pitch accent placement. *Proceedings of the 1992 International Conference on Spoken Language Processing*, Banff, 1: 365–368.

Shattuck-Hufnagel, S. 1991. Acoustic correlates of stress shift. *Proceedings of the XIIth International Congress of Phonetic Sciences*, Aix-en-Provence, 4: 266–269.

Shattuck-Hufnagel, S., M. Ostendorf & K. Ross. Forthcoming. Pitch accent placement within words in American English. *Journal of Phonetics*.

Silverman, K., M. Beckman, J. Pitrelli, M. Ostendorf, C. Wightman, P. Price, J. Pierrehumbert & J. Hirschberg. 1992. TOBI: a standard for labeling English prosody. *Proceedings of the 1992 International Conference on Spoken Language Processing*, Banff, 2: 867–870.

Vanderslice, R. & P. Ladefoged. 1972. Binary suprasegmental features and transformational word accentuation rules. *Language* 48: 819–836.

11
Perceptual evidence for the mora in Japanese

HARUO KUBOZONO*

11.1 Introduction

The past decade or so has seen an increasing interest in developing universal models of phonological structure and representation. Research in this area has produced several theoretical concepts that seem to be universally relevant. One such concept is the mora, which is now claimed to play a crucial role not only in "mora-timed" languages, such as Japanese, but also in the phonological description of English and other languages, e.g. in accounting for stress patterns and compensatory lengthening (Hyman, 1985; Hayes, 1989). Despite this popularity, one can point out several crucial differences in the role played by the mora in Japanese and in other languages (for a review, see Kubozono, 1992, 1993).

However, the mora's role in Japanese has been studied largely from the viewpoint of speech production, through analysis of speech timing, speech errors, accent assignment rules, morphological patterns, etc., while little is known about its relevance to speech perception. With this background, this paper explores the role of the mora in speech perception in Japanese, by examining the ways in which auditory stimuli are segmented by native speakers of the language.

I shall first report the results of a series of experiments involving word blends, which demonstrate that the strategy used by native speakers of Japanese in segmenting monosyllabic words is crucially different from that used by native speakers of English. I shall argue that this striking difference can best be explained if the mora is assumed to be a basic phonological unit in Japanese. The second half of the paper considers the implications of the experimental evidence, with special reference to the relation between speech perception and phonological structure.

11.2 The mora in speech production

Various blend experiments carried out over the past ten years, typically those by Treiman (e.g. Treiman, 1986), show that native speakers of English tend to segment monosyllabic words before the nuclear vowel, as illustrated in (1a), and not after the vowel, as illustrated in (1b).

(1) a. D(ick) / (f)og → dog
     b. Di(ck) / (fo)g → dig

This segmentation pattern accords with a number of speech production data, including the patterns observed in spontaneous speech errors such as those in (2) (cf. Fromkin, 1973):[1]

(2) a. cl(ose) / (n)ear → clear
     b. *Ch*omsky and *H*alle → *H*omsky and *Ch*alle

Phonologists have attributed the segmentation pattern in (1a) and (2) to the syllable structure illustrated in (3), where the nuclear vowel and the following consonant(s) form a constituent called *rhyme* (or *rime*) as opposed to the pre-vocalic consonant(s).

(3)

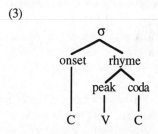

While this right-branching syllable structure is widely accepted in the literature (see, for example, Fudge, 1987, and the references cited therein), evidence from Japanese suggests that it does not apply to the Japanese data. Kubozono (1985, 1989) has shown this through analysis of spontaneous speech errors. In the blend errors in (4a), for example, the first syllable of the words *nyanko*, *doosite*, and *nande* splits into two parts, *nya* and *n*, *do* and *o*, and *na* and *n*, respectively. The transposition (i.e., metathesis) error in (4b) involves the splitting of the disyllabic word *noren* into *nore* and *n*, with the first part subsequently replaced by the bimoraic sequence *ude*. Similarly, the substitution errors in (4c) show the interaction of postvocalic consonants with the second half of long vowels or diphthongs.

142

(4) a.   ne.(ko) "cat" / (nya)n.ko "kitten" → nen.ko
do(o.si.te) "why" / (na)n.de "how come" → donde

    b.   *no.re*n ni *u.de*.o.si "pushing a curtain" → *u.de*n ni *no.re*.o.si

    c.   zyuu.go pa*a.se*n.to "fifteen percent" → zyuu.go pa*n*.sen.to
su.te*i*.syo*n* "station" → su.te*n*.syon

What is important about these errors is that the quite un-Germanic segmentation patterns are not marked patterns in speech errors in Japanese. On the contrary, the pattern in (4a) is the most common pattern of blending in Japanese, where one finds only one instance out of some one hundred blend errors which unambiguously shows the English-type segmentation pattern presented in (1a) and (2a). Based on this observation, I have proposed that Japanese has the syllable structure shown in (5), where the nuclear vowel is combined with the preceding consonant to form a constituent called "mora" (μ), while the postvocalic consonant or a postnuclear vowel (i.e., the second half of a long vowel or a diphthong) forms another mora (Kubozono, 1985, 1989, 1990, 1992).

(5)

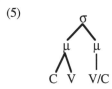

Interestingly, research on speech timing has produced several pieces of evidence that support both the syllable model in (3) and that in (5). As is well known, temporal compensation effects are observed between the nuclear vowel and the following consonant in a number of languages, including English. For example, vowels tend to be phonetically shorter in closed syllables than in open syllables: cf. *feed* vs. *fee* (Maddieson, 1985). Likewise, vowels tend to be shorter when followed by voiceless consonants, e.g. *feet*, than when followed by voiced consonants, e.g. *feed*, which are, other things being equal, intrinsically shorter than their voiceless counterparts. These tendencies may be linked to the syllable structure described in (3), i.e., vowels may lengthen (or shorten) to minimize differences in the combined duration of the vowel and the following consonant(s).[2]

While the temporal effects in English seem to support the syllable model in (3), analogous phenomena in Japanese support the model in (5). First, in Japanese vowels in closed syllables do not tend to be phonetically shorter than those in open syllables (Homma, 1981), which suggests that little or no temporal compensation occurs between the vowel and the following consonant in this language. Second, Campbell and Sagisaka's (1991) analysis of a large corpus of speech data demonstrates that a noticeable effect of temporal compensation occurs between the onset consonant and the nuclear vowel in Japanese. Thus vowel duration varies in inverse proportion to the intrinsic duration of the preceding consonant, and the onset consonant tends to be shorter when preceding an intrinsically long vowel such as /a/ than when preceding an intrinsically shorter vowel such as /i/ or /u/.

Both Homma's (1981) and Campbell and Sagisaka's (1991) data can be interpreted in a principled manner if the syllable structure in (5) is adopted, that is, if it is assumed that the nuclear vowel forms a constituent with the onset rather than the coda in Japanese. Given this second type of syllable structure, however, one may ask why and how syllable structure varies from one language to another. Putting aside this interesting question for the moment (but see the discussion in section 11.4 below), it is worth emphasizing that by assuming the two different syllable models, (3) and (5), one can generalize that various processes of speech production (including speech errors) are subject to the internal structure of the syllable in both types of languages.

11.3 Blend experiments

I carried out a series of experiments to see if the segmentation pattern modeled in (5) is also observed in speech perception. These experiments involved a task similar to that employed by Treiman in her series of experiments (e.g. Treiman, 1986): subjects were given auditory stimuli consisting of a pair of monosyllabic words and were asked to blend them into a monosyllabic form. Treiman's experiments have shown that native speakers of English tend to segment the auditory stimuli at the onset–rhyme boundary, i.e., they prefer the segmentation pattern in (1a) to the pattern in (1b) at a statistically significant rate.

If native speakers of Japanese employ the same strategy as English speakers in speech perception, they will show the segmentation pattern in (1a) rather than that in (1b). If, on the other hand, Japanese speakers rely on a different strategy from English speakers, as they do in various processes of speech production, they will segment the stimuli at the peak–coda boundary, i.e., choose the segmentation pattern in (1b).

Experiment 1 employed native speakers of English as subjects with a view to confirming Treiman's experimental results. A second experiment (Experiment 2) was then carried out in the same way as Experiment 1 except for employing native speakers of Japanese as subjects. A third experiment (Experiment 3) was designed to see if the results of Experiment 2 could be reproduced with another group of native speakers of Japanese and with a different set of auditory stimuli.

144

11.3.1 Experiment 1

11.3.1.1 Method

The materials used in this and the following experiments were similar to those used in Treiman's (1986) experiments: 20 pairs of real English words, all of which were monosyllabic words of the structure CVC, were used as stimuli. As the examples in (6) show, there were only two possible blends, one in which the two stimuli are split before the vowels, and one in which they are split after the vowels. The stimuli of each pair were carefully selected so that blending them would produce meaningful English words irrespective of the switch point.

(6)		C/VC	CV/C
	a. cup / mitt →	kit	cut
	b. pen / fat →	pat	pet

Real English words were chosen as stimuli for several reasons. First, it seemed desirable to make a direct comparison of prospective data with the data reported in the literature. Second, English words were used instead of Japanese words because the use of Japanese words could have involved an unnecessary factor by inducing the subjects to rely on their knowledge of orthography (or the system of *kana* letters), which is largely a CV-based system. This factor had to be removed because orthographic knowledge seemed to have an undesirable effect in a pilot experiment in which Japanese words were used as stimuli. Third, real English words were chosen instead of nonsense words because the former were more familiar to the subjects (especially the Japanese subjects), and thus were easier to recognize than nonsense stimuli.

Nine native speakers of English, who were studying at a university in Nagoya, Central Japan, served as subjects. They were originally from the USA, Britain, Australia, and New Zealand. They were paid for their participation.

The following instructions were given in English prior to the experiment. The subjects were told that they would hear two English words produced by a native speaker of English (a male native speaker of British English, in this first experiment). They were asked to repeat the two words and then make a third word by combining the initial part of the first word they heard with the end part of the second word. They were told to make a short (monosyllabic) word and repeat it twice in each trial. Any misperception of the stimuli was corrected. When the subjects produced a disyllabic word, they were requested to make a shorter word. The 20 stimulus pairs were ordered at random, but the order was not changed from one subject to another.

At the beginning of the experiment, the pair in (7a) was given as a test trial in order to help the subjects understand the task. Since both words involve the same vowel, the two segmentation patterns illustrated in (6) would yield one and the same blend form, i.e., *dam*. A subject who had understood the instructions was expected to make the response in (7b) in this test trial. The experimenters made sure that each subject had given this response before they started the 20 pairs.

(7) a. dad / mam
     b. dad, mam, dad, mam . . . dam, dam

At the end of the experiment, the experimenters gave the subjects a written questionnaire asking which of the two possible blend forms for each pair was more familiar to them. This questionnaire was designed to test whether (and to what extent) the subjects' familiarity with the words influenced their choice in the blend experiment.

11.3.1.2 Results
A total of 180 responses were obtained from the nine subjects and the 20 pairs of stimulus words. These responses were classified in three categories: C/VC blends, CV/C blends and "other." The results are summarized in Table 11.1.

Table 11.1. Results of Experiment 1.

Pattern	C/VC	CV/C	other	Total
Frequency	155 (86%)	23 (13%)	2 (1%)	180 (100%)

The results in Table 11.1 demonstrate that the subjects preferred to segment the stimuli at the onset–rhyme boundary rather than at the peak–coda boundary: the difference between the two patterns was statistically significant both for subjects ($t = 6.31$, $p < 0.001$) and for items ($t = 2.73$, $p < 0.02$). This confirms the claim made by Treiman for the syllable structure model described in (3).[3] The responses summarized in Table 11.1 were subsequently compared with the responses obtained in the written questionnaire. This comparison showed that the subjects had chosen a more familiar word for 10.2 pairs (out of 20) on average (*s.d.* = 1.31). This suggests that the subjects' familiarity with the stimuli did not influence their choice of a blend form.

11.3.2 Experiment 2

11.3.2.1 Method
The same 20 pairs of stimuli used in Experiment 1 were used in Experiment 2. The subjects were 20 university students studying at a university in Nagoya, Central Japan. They were all native speakers of Japanese, and most of them came from Central Japan (i.e., they spoke Japanese more or less similar to Tokyo Japanese). Half of them were English majors, while the other half were economics majors. All the subjects were paid for their participation.

The experiment was carried out in the same way as Experiment 1 from the test trial to the final pair of stimuli. The only difference was that the instructions were given in Japanese instead of English. For the reasons already explained, real English words were used as stimuli for the Japanese subjects too. As in many of the stimuli word-final stops (but not nasals) were released, these stops could have been perceived as entire syllables in Japanese (Janet Pierrehumbert, personal communication). Although these and some other stimuli are not phonotactically well formed in Japanese, the subjects were familiar with English and its phonotactic rules.

11.3.2.2 Results
A total of 400 responses were obtained from the 20 subjects and the 20 stimulus pairs. The results are summarized in Table 11.2.

Table 11.2. Results of Experiment 2.

Pattern	C/VC	CV/C	other	Total
Frequency	55 (14%)	317 (79%)	28 (7%)	400 (100%)

The results in Table 11.2 are markedly different from those in Table 11.1. Namely, native speakers of Japanese preferred to segment the stimuli at the peak–coda boundary rather than the onset–rhyme boundary: the difference between the two switching patterns was statistically significant both for subjects ($t = -3.46$, $p < 0.01$) and for items ($t = -19.18$, $p < 0.001$). A closer examination of the data summarized in Table 11.2 revealed that 40 out of the 55 instances showing the English-type segmentation pattern came from three subjects, all of whom were English majors. However, there was no overall significant difference between the two groups of subjects (English majors and economics

147

majors) with respect to the degree to which they favored the peak–coda division ($t = -1.398, p > 0.10$).

The responses obtained in the experiment were then compared with the responses which the subjects gave in the post-experimental questionnaire. This comparison showed that the subjects' choice of a particular blend form was not influenced by their previous familiarity with the possible blend forms.

11.3.3 Experiment 3

11.3.3.1 Method
This experiment was a slightly revised version of Experiment 2. A new set of 20 pairs of real English words, which would also produce real English words as blend forms, were chosen as stimuli. The 20 pairs fell into four types depending on the length (or weight) of the vowels involved: (a) short (or lax)–short, (b) short–long (or tense), (c) long–short, and (d) long–long. These types are illustrated in (8), along with the two possible blend forms.

(8)

			C/VC	CV/C
a.	fan / put	→	foot	fat
b.	lot / take	→	lake	lock
c.	team / such	→	touch	teach
d.	five / sheet	→	feet	fight

These four combinations were included in order to see if there is an effect of vowel length (or, equivalently, syllable weight) on the choice of blend forms.

Twenty five university students volunteered to serve as subjects. They were all native speakers of Japanese. Most of them were from the western half of Japan, with about half of them coming from the Osaka area.

The 20 pairs of test words were presented in the same way as in the previous experiments. The only difference was that the stimuli were read by a native speaker of American English.

11.3.3.2 Results
A total of 500 blend forms were obtained from the 25 subjects and the 20 pairs of test words. The results, summarized in Table 11.3, again show a clear asymmetry whereby the subjects favor peak–coda divisions over onset–peak divisions ($t = -12.31, p < 0.001$ for subjects; $t = -17.62, p < 0.001$ for items). The results for the English-type or C/VC segmentation pattern in Table 11.3 are largely due to six out of the 25 subjects, whose data account for 52 instances out of the 61 showing the onset-peak division. The reason for this inter-subject difference remains unclear.

Perceptual evidence for the mora

Table 11.3. Results of Experiment 3.

Pattern	C/VC	CV/C	other	Total
Frequency	61 (12%)	401 (80%)	38 (8%)	500 (100%)

The four combinations of vowel length presented in (8) show a slight difference in the choice of blend patterns, as summarized in Table 11.4. Specifically, although CV/C responses predominated for all four combinations, C/VC responses were more frequent in types (8b) and (8d), i.e., in those cases where the second stimulus contained a long vowel (or a diphthong): the difference between (8a, c) and (8b, d) is statistically significant ($t = 4.669$, $p < 0.001$). Equally interesting is the fact that the two combinations in question yielded a substantially larger number of "other" patterns, including *mitt/house* → [mɪʊs]; *pope/mail* → [poɪl].

Table 11.4. Vowel length and segmentation pattern.

Pattern	C/VC	CV/C	other	Total
(8a)	22 (8%)	237 (86%)	16 (6%)	275
(8b)	21 (28%)	44 (59%)	10 (13%)	75
(8c)	7 (9%)	66 (88%)	2 (3%)	75
(8d)	11 (15%)	54 (72%)	10 (13%)	75
Total	61	401	38	500

While the length of the vowels involved had a slight effect on the preferred segmentation pattern, the fact remains that CV/C blends were much more common than C/VC blends in all vowel length types, which suggests that vowel length causes only a secondary effect.

11.4 Discussion

The experimental data presented in the preceding section show that native speakers of English and those of Japanese exhibit a remarkable difference in the preferred pattern of perceptual segmentation: English speakers prefer to break CVC sequences into the onset and the rhyme while Japanese speakers,

149

irrespective of differences in their accent, predominantly choose to segment such sequences at the peak–coda boundary, which corresponds to the mora boundary in Japanese.

In connection with this, it is worthwhile to refer to some experiments in which reaction times (RT) were measured. Hayashi & Kakehi (1990), for example, measured RTs to CVs and syllable-initial Cs, and report that Japanese listeners exhibit substantially shorter RTs to mora-sized units than to mora-initial consonants. These results contrast sharply with the opposite tendency shown by native speakers of English (Norris & Cutler, 1988). In addition, there is recent experimental evidence that Japanese listeners make a mora-based segmentation rather than a syllable-based segmentation (Otake, Hatano, Cutler & Mehler, 1993). Both Hayashi & Kakeshi's results and those of Otake *et al.* agree with the evidence from the word blend experiments described above, confirming the view that the mora, rather than the phoneme or the syllable, serves as a perceptual unit in Japanese.

Given these different sources of evidence for the mora in Japanese and the inter-language differences in the manner of segmentation, one can go further and ask why speakers of different languages employ different strategies for the segmentation of speech (or the word or the syllable). Specifically, it is interesting to ask why native speakers of Japanese show the CV-based segmentation pattern at all – or, equally, why and how they acquire 'mora' as a segmentation unit.

11.4.1 Influence of orthography

There seem to be at least two explanations of the seemingly peculiar pattern shown by Japanese speakers. The first is that in speech segmentation Japanese speakers rely on their knowledge of the writing system. This is possible because two of the three writing systems used in Japanese, *hiragana* and *katakana*, are largely CV-based (the third being syllable-based Chinese characters). There are two versions of this explanation: one is to assume that orthography influences the segmentation process in a rather direct manner, while the other is to suppose that orthography exerts an indirect influence.

The first version holds that in the experiments the subjects converted the auditory stimuli into strings of *kana* letters and then made a blend on the basis of these *kana* strings. This account cannot be supported for several reasons, however. First, the stimuli were existing English words, and most of the Japanese subjects commented after the experiment that they did not think of *kana* letters during the experiment. Second, as already noted, the segmentation pattern observed in the blend experiments is also observed in various processes of speech production. Since it is difficult to suppose that all these processes (especially speech errors) are directly induced by the speakers' knowledge of orthography, it seems safe to assume that the segmentation pattern observed in speech perception stems from a given structure of the language which is part of the speakers' linguistic competence.

A second, and more plausible, version of the orthography-based account is that orthographic knowledge is integrated into the speakers' linguistic competence. Under this analysis, even if orthography does not directly determine the pattern of speech segmentation, it may exert an indirect, secondary influence on the phonological patterning of the language, which, in turn, may determine the ways in which certain stimuli are segmented. In the case of Japanese, this means that native speakers of Japanese have "acquired" the habit of making a mora-based segmentation of speech under the influence of, or exposure to, the CV-based *kana* syllabary; in other words, the basic structure of the writing system has somehow been "integrated" into the phonological competence of Japanese speakers.

This orthography-based analysis cannot, however, explain why English speakers favor the VC-based segmentation: since the alphabetic writing system can be assumed to be basically neutral to segmentation, it should not influence the way in which monosyllabic words are to be segmented by native speakers of English. However, the analysis in question is supported, at least in part, by evidence from Korean, a language which has a writing system similar to the Japanese *kana* syllabary. The native orthography of Korean, called *hankul* (or *hangul*), is a syllable-based system but includes letters which imply a CV/C segmentation. In these letters the onset consonant and the nuclear vowel are written on the upper half (with the consonant at the top left, and the vowel at the top right), while the coda consonant is written on the lower half, thus implying a division between the peak and the coda. According to Derwing, Yoon, and Cho (1993), who carried out word blend experiments similar to those which are described in this paper, native speakers of Korean prefer the Japanese-type segmentation pattern, and not the English-type pattern: they prefer to break CVC words into CV and C. Although the difference they found between the two segmentation types is not as large as the difference we saw for Japanese speakers, it is a statistically significant one. This experimental evidence may hint that speakers' knowledge of orthography plays a crucial role in determining the pattern of speech segmentation (see Derwing, 1992, for a review of orthographic influences on phonology).

11.4.2 Syllable structure

The other possible explanation for the segmentation patter observed in Japanese is to assume that the CV-based segmentation pattern characteristic of Japanese is directly determined by a certain feature of its syllable structure. For example, Japanese is a typical open-syllable language, where open syllables account for over 90 percent of all syllables occurring in running speech (Kubozono, 1992), in clear contrast with the relatively low frequency of the same syllable type in English (about 40 percent, according to Dauer, 1983).

Under this hypothesis, native speakers of Japanese learn to segment on a CV basis because of their exposure to linguistic data where open syllables predominate. Like the first hypothesis sketched above, this second hypothesis cannot explain why the VC-based segmentation predominates in languages like English, where most syllables do have an onset. Yet, it has the advantage of providing a satisfactory account of the relation between speech segmentation and lexical access, since the CV-based segmentation seems to be the most effective way of detecting word boundaries in languages like Japanese where most words end with a vowel.

One effective way of testing this hypothesis is to see how native speakers of other open-syllable languages behave in the same kind of experiments. With this in mind, I conducted a preliminary word blend experiment in which I examined how native speakers of Italian and Spanish blend the total of 40 pairs of stimuli used in the three experiments described in the preceding sections. These pairs were presented in the same way as in the preceding experiments. Table 11.5 gives the average number of responses for each segmentation pattern with the standard deviation given in parentheses. Although the results in this table should be interpreted with caution, given their preliminary nature, they clearly show a substantial asymmetry similar to the Japanese cases, indicating that native speakers of Italian and Spanish also tend to prefer the CV-based pattern when segmenting monosyllabic words.

Table 11.5. Results of a preliminary blend experiment for Italian and Spanish speakers; Italian (2 subjects), Spanish (9 subjects, Mexicans).

Pattern → Subject ↓	C/VC	CV/C	Other	Total
Italian	1.5 (1.5)	38.0 (1.0)	0.5 (0.5)	40
Spanish	7.4 (12.1)	25.1 (12.2)	7.4 (6.4)	40

11.4.3 Summary

The data presented in the preceding section put us into a difficult situation by providing evidence of seemingly contradictory nature, as summarized in Table 11.6.

Table 11.6. Comparison of predictions and experimental data.

	Japanese	English	Korean	Italian / Spanish
a. CV-based orthography	Yes	No	Yes	No
b. Open syllables predominate	Yes	No	No	Yes
Obtained segmentation pattern	CV/C	C/VC	CV/C (?)	CV/C (?)

The Korean evidence, on the one hand, suggests that it may be orthography that determines the preferred segmentation pattern. On the other hand, the evidence from Italian and Spanish suggests that it may be the frequency of open vs. closed syllables that plays the primary role.[4] All together, the above data suggest that probably more than one factor is responsible for determining the segmentation pattern in a given language.

In connection with this, it is worth adding that the CV-based segmentation pattern characteristic of Japanese speakers may have to do with the fact that Japanese does not generally permit a consonant cluster in the onset position while English permits rather complex sequences of consonants in this position. Supposing that speakers attempt to recognize words from the beginning of the word to its end, phonological information about the beginning of the word will be more directly relevant to the task of lexical access than information about the rest of the word. If this is the case, Japanese speakers cannot probably identify a word simply by knowing the structure of the onset of the initial syllable (which generally consists of a single consonant) and, as a consequence, require information about the nuclear vowel that follows. In English, on the other hand, it will be relatively easy to identify a word simply by referring to the consonant cluster because of the complexity of the onset structure. Although this hypothesis cannot account for all the facts summarized in Table 11.6, it can account for the differences between English and Japanese quite well. Details of this interpretation as well as other possibilities remain to be explored.

11.5 Concluding remarks

In this paper I reported the results of several blend experiments conducted in the same way as Treiman's (1986) experiments except for using as subjects native speakers of Japanese as well as English. The results of these experiments show that Japanese speakers tend to segment words in a different way from English speakers, by blending two source words between the peak (nucleus) and the coda: e.g. *Di*(*ck*)/(*fo*)*g* → *dig*, **dog*. This striking difference between Japanese

Haruo Kubozono

and English speakers can best be explained if the mora is posited as a basic phonological unit in Japanese, that is, if it is assumed that Japanese speakers segment words at mora boundaries. In this respect the present study has provided yet another piece of evidence for the theoretical notion of the mora whose relevance in speech production has hitherto been confirmed from various viewpoints. The same finding also demonstrates the extent to which perceptual strategies can vary from one language to another.

In the second half of the paper I considered the implications of the experimental evidence, with emphasis on the question of why native speakers of Japanese prefer the CV-based (or mora-based) segmentation. Two characteristics of Japanese were put forward as possible explanations of this seemingly peculiar tendency: indirect influence of the CV-based orthography, and the dominance of open syllables as opposed to closed syllables in this language.

I would like to emphasize that the present work raises as many questions as it has answered. The most interesting question that remains is why Japanese speakers differ from English speakers in the preferred pattern of perceptual segmentation, and, for that matter, how native speakers of other languages segment the same stimuli. Secondly, it also remains largely unanswered as to how bilingual speakers segment the auditory stimuli. Do they show a monolingual pattern of segmentation as proposed by Cutler, Mehler, Norris & Segui (1992), or do they use more than one strategy? Finally, it may also be interesting to ask whether (and to what extent) speakers utilize the segmentation patterns reported here in segmenting natural connected speech. The present study was limited to the analysis of monosyllabic words, but do people really employ the strategy reported here (i.e., CV-based segmentation in the case of Japanese speakers, and VC-based segmentation in the case of English speakers) in segmenting a continuous speech signal into discontinuous strings of words (whether morphological or phonological)? All these questions seem to be closely related to the fundamental issues of speech research such as the general strategies of speech segmentation and the relation between speech segmentation (or speech processing, in more general terms) and the phonological structure assumed in theoretical phonology.

Notes

* This paper is based in part upon work supported by The Nissan Science Foundation and the Japanese Ministry of Education, Science and Culture under Grant Nos. 04207104, 04207106, 04710248, 05301104, and 05710290.

154

1 It should be noted, however, that the switch point in the blend errors in Fromkin (1973) can be quite variable; as Pierrehumbert (1993) points out "approximately half the blends were consistent with postulation of a switch point at head position".
2 A reviewer has pointed out that much recent work in phonological theory would place the word-final consonants in question in a word-level appendix rather than within the rhyme; according to this view, the timing information described here cannot be used as evidence for phonological constituency.
3 A closer look at the 23 instances showing the second pattern in Table 10.1 reveals that one subject was responsible for 14 instances out of 23. It remains unclear why this particular subject preferred the second pattern to the first one.
4 An analysis of basic Italian words suggests that the lexical frequency of open syllables in Italian is about 80 percent. Dauer (1983) reports similar statistics for Spanish concerning the frequency of open syllables in running speech. In Korean, by contrast, a similar analysis of lexical frequency reveals that open syllables account for only 40 percent, a rate similar to that of English.

References

Campbell, W. N. & Y. Sagisaka. 1991. Moraic and syllable-level effects on speech timing. (In Japanese.) *IEICE Technical Report* SP90–106: 35–40.
Cutler, A., J. Mehler, D. G. Norris & J. Segui. 1992. The monolingual nature of speech segmentation by bilinguals. *Cognitive Psychology* 24: 381–410.
Dauer, R. M. 1983. Stress-timing and syllable-timing reanalyzed. *Journal of Phonetics* 11: 51–62.
Derwing, B. L. 1992. Orthographic aspects of linguistic competence. In P. Downing, S. D. Lima & M. Noonan (eds.), *The Linguistics of Literacy*. Amsterdam: John Benjamins, 193–211.
Derwing, B. L., Y. B. Yoon & S. W. Cho. 1993. The organization of the Korean syllable: experimental evidence. *Japanese/Korean Linguistics* 2: 223–238.
Fromkin, V. 1973. *Speech Errors as Linguistic Evidence*. The Hague: Mouton.
Fudge, E. 1987. Branching structure within the syllable. *Journal of Linguistics* 23: 359–377.
Hayashi, M. & K. Kakehi. 1990. An experimental study on basic perceptual units of speech based on reaction time. Paper presented at the Spring Meeting of the Acoustical Society of Japan.
Hayes, B. 1989. Compensatory lengthening in moraic phonology. *Linguistic Inquiry* 20: 253–306.
Homma, Y. 1981. Durational relationships between Japanese stops and vowels. *Journal of Phonetics* 9: 273–281.
Hyman, L. M. 1985. *A Theory of Phonological Weight*. Dordrecht: Foris.
Kubozono, H. 1985. Speech errors and syllable structure. *Linguistics and Philology* 6: 220–243.
Kubozono, H. 1989. The mora and syllable structure in Japanese: evidence from speech errors. *Language and Speech* 32: 249–278.

Kubozono, H. 1990. Phonological constraints on blending in English as a case for phonology–morphology interface. *Yearbook of Morphology* 3: 1–20.

Kubozono, H. 1992. Japanese mora: its roles and characters. (in Japanese) In S. Haraguchi (ed.), *Studies in the Mora and Syllable Structure in Japanese*, 1: 48–61.

Kubozono, H. 1993. The syllable in Japanese. ms. Osaka University of Foreign Studies.

Maddieson, I. 1985. Phonetic cues to syllabification. In V. Fromkin (ed.), *Phonetic Linguistics*. Orlando: Academic Press, 203–221.

Norris, D. G. & A. Cutler. 1988. The relative accessibility of phonemes and syllables. *Perception and Psychophysics* 45: 485–93.

Otake, T., G. Hatano, A. Cutler & J. Mehler. 1993. Mora or syllable? Speech segmentation in Japanese. *Journal of Memory and Language* 32: 258–278.

Pierrehumbert, J. B. 1993. Alignment and prosodic heads. Paper presented at the 10th Eastern States Conference on Linguistics, Ohio State University.

Treiman, R. 1986. The division between onsets and rimes in English syllables. *Journal of Memory and Language* 25: 476–491.

12
On blending and the mora: comments on Kubozono

MARY E. BECKMAN*

12.1 Introduction

In his paper, Kubozono nicely summarizes the literature on the mora as a salient unit in speech production in Japanese, and then describes new results which he takes as evidence for the mora as a comparably salient unit in speech perception. His experiments presented pairs of English CVC monosyllables, such as *hill* and *top*, to which subjects responded with a third word blending the two stimulus words. Responses differed for different subject groups; English speakers combined the onset of the first word with the rhyme of the second (*hill + top = hop*), whereas Japanese speakers usually took both the onset and the nucleus from the first word and only the coda consonant from the second (*hill + top = hip*). Pilot results for two Italian and nine Spanish speakers also showed the Japanese pattern.

Kubozono interprets these results as indicating a difference in syllable-internal prosodic structure among the languages, illustrated in (1a) for English and (1b) for the other three. (1c) is Derwing, Yoon & Cho's (1993) alternative interpretation of the Japanese pattern of responses, which their Korean subjects also showed in a similar word-blend experiment. The difference between hypotheses (1b) and (1c) should not obscure the premise in common: Kubozono, like Derwing *et al.* (1993), takes the pattern of blends as evidence that speakers parse syllables exhaustively into some set of syllable-internal prosodic constituents which can differ from language to language.

157

Mary E. Beckman

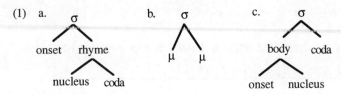

(1) a. σ
     onset   rhyme
             nucleus   coda

     b. σ
         μ   μ

     c. σ
         body   coda
         onset   nucleus

In this commentary, I will question this basic premise, and suggest another interpretation of the blending task that does not require positing onset and rhyme as syllable-internal constituents in English. Before motivating the alternative account, however, I will first argue for another point that Kubozono makes in his concluding section.

12.2 Orthographic and phonological knowledge

Kubozono considers several possible explanations for the Japanese versus English results, including one that invokes the different writing systems used for the two languages. The Japanese system intermingles logographic *kanji* with phonographic *kana* symbols. Except for the digraphs used to write moras with palatalized onsets, each kana corresponds to a mora, and even a digraph is distinguished from a two-mora sequence by subscripting its second symbol. This regular correspondence must induce a phonological awareness of moras in a literate Japanese speaker, which is then available when the speaker is faced with a task that requires choosing some syllable-internal cutting point.

Such an account might seem difficult to reconcile with Kubozono's Japanese-like results for the Italian and Spanish speakers, but it accords with other results for native speakers of Korean (Derwing *et al.*, 1993) and of Taiwanese (Wang & Derwing, forthcoming). The Koreans preferred the body–coda cut, whereas the Taiwanese preferred the onset–rhyme cut. Korean *hangul* is a *nagari* type alphabet which groups phoneme symbols into syllable-sized units, and arranges the letters for the onset consonant and nucleus vowel closely together above the letter for the coda consonant to write a closed syllable. Taiwanese is not usually a written language. However, Taiwanese speakers are literate in Mandarin, which they learn first using *bo-po-mo-fo*, an onset–rhyme based phonographic system, which is used alone in first grade texts and as an interlinear trot after the logographic *hanzi* system is introduced in the second grade. Thus, an account that posits orthographically induced awareness of CV/C or C/VC segmentation accords with the results of the blending experiments.

There is strong evidence that this sort of experiment taps phonological awareness of a kind associated with knowing a phonographic writing system. The classic study is Read, Zhang, Nie & Ding (1986), which tested two groups of Beijing Mandarin speakers using a paradigm that earlier had demonstrated phonological awareness of subsyllabic units in literate but not illiterate Portuguese speakers (Morais, Cary, Alegria & Bertelson, 1979). The task was to remove a constant onset consonant from a set of consonant-initial syllables, or to prefix a given consonant to a set of vowel-initial syllables. Unlike the literate versus illiterate Portuguese speakers in the earlier study, the Chinese groups were matched for education level and for literacy in the hanzi logographic system. The only difference was that the slightly older group had learned to read before the *pinyin* alphabetic system was introduced in Beijing elementary schools, although none in the younger group could read pinyin easily. The pinyin group behaved like literate Portuguese speakers (the majority got at least 90% correct), but those who had learned only hanzi behaved like illiterate Portuguese speakers (only two got even 50% correct). Since this task involved removing or adding an onset, these results might be interpreted as evidence that metalinguistic awareness of onsets and rhymes is linked to learning to read an alphabetic writing system.

On the other hand, the subjects were not asked to choose between an onset–rhyme and a body–coda response. In Kubozono's experiments, speakers of English preferred a C/VC division, but speakers of two other languages written with the same roman alphabet preferred a CV/C cut. We cannot know whether Beijing Mandarin speakers who learned pinyin in first grade would choose the same C/VC segmentation in a word-blend experiment as did the Taiwanese Mandarin speakers who learned bo-po-mo-fo. However, my guess is that they would. In general, I think the cross-language differences in the word-blend experiments reflect real prosodic differences among the languages, and that literacy merely brings these differences to the fore, either directly, by transmitting an older generation's analysis of prosodic structure (as in hangul and bo-po-mo-fo), or indirectly, by enhancing metalinguistic phonological awareness in general. Thus, I agree with Kubozono that his results reflect a prosodic difference between Japanese and English, although I do not agree that the difference involves the syllable-internal structures in (1).

12.3 Morphological productivity and phonetic salience

At higher levels of the prosodic hierarchy, phonologists generally posit a strict layering of homogenous units. Major intonational phrases are parsed exhaustively into minor ones, minor phrases into prosodic words, and so on. Proposals to relax this principle offer only minor adjustments, by allowing recursion at some levels (e.g. Ladd, 1986; Kubozono, 1992), or by allowing nodes at one level to dominate not just nodes at the next lower level, but also the occasional extrametrical node from the level below that (e.g. Pierrehumbert & Beckman, 1988; Itô & Mester, 1992). By contrast, the analysis in (1a) is a radical departure: it groups under the syllable node a terminal element of one type (the onset) and a non-terminal node (rhyme) that dominates one or two terminal elements of types different from the onset (the nucleus and optional coda). A more conservative hypothesis is that if a language has subsyllabic prosodic structure, the terminal nodes must be homogeneous, as in (1b), and that if languages differ at this level of prosody, they differ in whether moras or syllables are the terminal elements (cf. Hubbard, this volume).

There is evidence for moras as the terminal element in some English morphological processes. For example, in deriving nicknames, one common pattern differentiates names such as *Joseph* and *Louisa*, which are clipped after their tense (or "long") first vowels, from names such as *Alvin* and *Mary*, which take a coda consonant, as if to fill a second mora slot. Similarly in assimilating loanwords from Japanese, English speakers tend to assign stress as if they were using the quantity-sensitive Latin rule. They differentiate the surname *Wakíta*, where the penultimate syllable can be analyzed as a tense ("long") /i/, from the brand name *Súbaru*, where the penult is a lax ("short") /a/ (see Hayes, 1994, for more examples supporting the role of the mora in English stress assignment). Such behavior argues that English shares with Japanese the subsyllabic prosodic structure in (1b).

Having different structures is not the only way in which two languages can differ prosodically, if we accept that the same phonological structure can be interpreted differently in different contexts or by different speakers (see, e.g. Pierrehumbert, 1991). In Japanese, the mora is consistently and unambiguously interpreted as a unit of phonetic length. A bimoraic word, such as [baː], [baɴ], or [bagu], is longer than a monomoraic word, such as [ba], by a fairly constant amount that is independent of syllable count (Port, Dalby & O'Dell, 1987). In English, by contrast, the length difference between monomoraic *tin* and bimoraic *teen* is redundant to the vowel quality difference, and the phonetically longest vowel in the language is the monomoraic [æ] of *tan*. If we imagine a scale of phonetic salience, then the mora in Japanese and the mora in English fall at opposite ends. In Japanese, knowledge of the mora is encoded in moraic rhythms which shape every act of producing a fluent utterance in the language, whereas in English, phonological knowledge of the mora is only implicit in productive derivational processes such as nickname formation.

Higher in the prosodic hierarchy, on the other hand, we find the opposite situation. In English, the foot is phonetically salient. The rhythmic structure of the language requires that speakers parse an utterance into some conventional alternation between stressed and unstressed syllables. This fact about English is something that children become aware of well before they learn to speak (see, e.g. Jusczyk, Cutler & Redanz, 1993), and it has profound effects on their first speech productions (e.g. Echols & Newport, 1992; Gerken, in press). By contrast, the foot in Japanese is supported only in such derivational processes as nickname formation (Poser, 1990) or loanword clipping (Itô, 1990). In short, the fundamental prosodic difference between the two languages at these levels seems to be not one of structure *per se*, but in which levels of the hierarchy are most salient in our day-to-day phonetic awareness of prosody.

This difference is particularly evident in tasks that require an online perceptual segmentation for pattern matching or lexical access. Experiments summarized in Otake, Hatano, Cutler & Mehler (1993) suggest that Japanese speakers parse the speech signal mora by mora. Given a visually presented CVC target, such as *TAN*, and a series of auditorily presented stimulus words, they generally do not recognize the target in forms such as *tanisi*, where the match would split a CV mora. But with a CV target, such as *TA*, they respond equally quickly whether the target matches only the first mora of a syllable, as in *tansi*, or an entire monomoraic syllable, as in *tanisi*. This is different from the pattern shown by French speakers, who match *TA* more quickly to *tanisi*, as if parsing the signal syllable by syllable (Mehler, Dommergues, Frauenfelder & Segui, 1981). It is also different from the pattern for English speakers, who show neither the mora effect (Otake *et al.*, 1993) nor the syllable effect (Cutler, Mehler, Norris & Segui, 1986), and instead parse stress foot by stress foot, detecting real monosyllabic words embedded in nonsense words more quickly when the target is contained entirely within a single stress foot – e.g. *mint* is recognized sooner in monopedal *mintef* [mɪn.təf] than in bipedal *mintayf* [mɪn.tef] (Cutler & Norris, 1988). Thus this experimental literature, which demonstrates the perceptual salience of the mora for Japanese speakers, shows no evidence of onsets and rhymes for English speakers, who readily match targets to segment sequences across syllable-internal and even syllable-external constituent boundaries, and only fail to match across stress foot boundaries. How can we reconcile these results with the English speakers' responses on the word-blend task?

12.4 Generalized alignment

A first step is to recognize that the word-blend results cannot be used to argue for any of the structures in (1). We can show the fallacy in this argument by examining its syntactic analogue in such processes as topicalization. Given the input *Robin likes black cats*, English speakers can partition between the verb and the object to make the corresponding sentence *It's black cats that Robin likes*. However, this constitutes evidence only that *black cats* is a constituent, not that *Robin likes* is also a constituent. By the same token, the result that a monosyllabic English word can be divided between its onset and the nucleus vowel might be used to argue for either the onset or the rhyme as a constituent. It cannot be used to argue that both are necessarily constituents. The word-blend task is about partitioning the input. It is not about parsing the input into complete constituents on either side of the partition.

A phonological interpretation of the word-blend results thus involves finding a formal account for this notion of partitioning. Recent work in prosodic morphology develops such a formalism in order to describe the processes of infixation, reduplication, and truncation found in the languages of the world (see, e.g. McCarthy & Prince, 1990, and the many references cited there). The key idea is that a morphological process may partition a base form into two parts by identifying a phonological constituent at an edge. For example, an infix might be placed after the first syllable in the base, or the base form may be clipped after the first bimoraic foot, as in the Japanese nickname in (2a). Prince & Smolensky (1992) and McCarthy & Prince (1993) extend this idea to allow division points which are located near but not necessarily at an edge in order to make the result of the morphological process conform as well as it can to independent phonological constraints. As a result of such optimization of the output, the partition of the base form may have non-constituents on both sides of the division point, as in (2b), where the base is partitioned after the first syllable plus the onset consonant of the second syllable, to make the [t] into the coda of a closed (bimoraic) syllable in the output. (The relevant phonological constraint is that obstruent consonants in coda position must be identical to the following onset, so that *sa.ti.ko* → *sat* can be the first bimoraic foot because of the shape of the hypocoristic suffix - *tyan*.)

(2) a. hi.sa.ko + tyan → hi.sa.tyan
     b. sa.ti.ko + tyan → sat.tyan

Pierrehumbert (1993) shows that two further extensions are necessary in order to apply such an account to the case of blends. First, she adds the prosodic head to the set of primitive locations to which reference can be made. (In the other works just cited, the left and right edges are the only privileged phonological locations.) Second, she extends the theory to support the simultaneous evaluation of several lexical strings. With these modifications, she can describe rhyming in poetry as the production of two lexical strings subject to the constraint that they match from the start of the prosodic head (the vowel of the nuclear stressed syllable of the last phrase) to the end of the line. This is better than any characterization using the structure in (1a), because it captures feminine (i.e., multisyllabic) rhymes as well as masculine (i.e., monosyllabic) ones. (Pierrehumbert shows that the many feminine rhymes in Canto XIV of Byron's *Don Juan* behave exactly like the masculine rhymes under this characterization, giving the same proportion of exact versus partial matches at each point past the head vowel.)

The description of blend-like speech errors is similarly straightforward: "The plan to execute one lexical item is interrupted by the plan for another at a prosodically comparable position." That is, align and switch. This is

Kubozono's own account (cf. Kubozono, 1990) with the added provision that the alignment need not partition a syllable into its immediate constituents. Thus in Kubozono's examples in (3) below, the Japanese blend error aligns disyllabic words at mora boundaries and the English error aligns them at prosodic heads – i.e., at the vowels of the stressed syllables. (Note that in neither case does the partition yield immediate constituents for the utterance; [noreɴ] is not [nore]+[ɴ], and *Chomsky* is not [tʃ]+[ɑmski].)

(3) a. noreɴ ni udeosi → udeɴ ni noreosi
     b. Chomsky and Halle → [h'ɑ mski] and [tʃ'ælə]

Kubozono's experimental task is the same except that the blend is not by accident. Under this account, the difference between English and Japanese blending strategies is directly related to the differences described in section 12.3. In English, the stress foot is a more salient unit than the syllable, and English speakers tend to align and switch at the prosodic heads of these monosyllabic feet, yielding a C/VC partition. In Japanese, by contrast, the mora is a more salient unit, and Japanese speakers seem to align and switch at the beginning of the second mora, yielding a CV/C partition.

Note that this describes the Japanese responses for the stimuli with short vowels (e.g. *fan* + *put* = *fat*), but an extra stipulation is required for it to capture the CV/C responses for pairs in which the second stimulus had a long vowel (e.g. *talk* + *sale* = *tall*). In these pairs, cutting after the first mora yields the "other" response of a diphthong (*talk* + *sale* = [tɔel]), and not the strictly CV/C response which predominated. In these cases, the prosodically optimal partition between the two moras conflicts with a segmentally optimal one, dividing prosodic constituents with the same feature specification. That is, the two moras in *sale* share a single vowel gesture, and erecting a partition there would break the gesture in two, as in (4a), violating "geminate inalterability" (Hayes, 1986). When a bimoraic stimulus is a diphthong, on the other hand, the prosodically optimal partition does not conflict with geminate inalterability, and the speaker can choose a strictly mora-based "other" response, as in (4b). This analysis explains the otherwise puzzling result that the Japanese speakers had many more such "other" responses than did the English speakers. It also accords with Derwing's (1992) findings for a "pause-break" syllabification task with illiterate Arabic speakers. When the input CVCCVC had a medial cluster, the preferred pattern was to pause during the cluster (e.g. [akbar] → [ak] ... [bar]), whereas with a medial geminate consonant, the preferred pausing often was before the consonant (e.g. [zak.kar] → [za] ... [kkar]), although this means breaking before the end of the first syllable. (Interestingly, the literate subjects preferred the pattern, [zak] ... [kar], supporting the idea that literacy promotes metalinguistic awareness of prosodic and other phonological structure.)

Mary E. Beckman

(4)   a. geminate inalterability wins over optimal mora-based cut

talk [tɔk] + *sale* [sel]   → *tall*   [tɔl] (preferred to [tɔel])

   | ∧   ∧ ||
   μ   μ μ   μ μ   μμ

   b. optimal mora-based cut does not split geminate
   mitt [mɪt] + *house*   [haʊs]   → [mɪʊs]

   | || ||
   μ   μ μ   μμ

However, there is an alternative explanation for the CV/C response. As Kubozono points out, closed syllables are relatively rare in Modern Japanese. In Old Japanese, they were nonexistent; all syllables were open and light. Furthermore, all syllables had onset consonants except for a few at the beginning of words such as [ame] "rain", with vowel coalescence or epenthetic consonants remedying VV sequences when such words occurred in compounds (e.g. [haru] "spring" + [ame] "rain" → [harusame] "drizzle"). Historically, long syllables arose in the native vocabulary with the deletion of word-medial consonants, such as [ɸ], and subsequent monophthongization of the resulting VV sequence (e.g. [kinoɸu] "yesterday" → [kinou] → [kinoː]). Thus word-medial syllables in Modern Japanese are still predominantly CV or CVV, and the consonant-initial open syllable is still the most frequent type. Suppose then, that in the word-blend task, Japanese speakers aligned the stimuli not at the beginning of the second mora, but at the beginning of the next optimal syllable. This account accords better with Kubozono's results for Italian and Spanish speakers and with Derwing *et al.*'s results for Korean speakers, where the purely mora-based account is less tenable. It also can explain the preference for the CV/C response to pairs such as *talk* + *sale* and *mitt* + *house*, although it then cannot explain the many "other" responses to these same input pairs. On the other hand, by either this or the mora account, the Japanese strategy differs from the English one in referring to the beginning of a prosodic unit rather than its head.

12.5 Head-driven versus edge-driven alignment

Thus, another way to summarize the different alignment strategies is to say that English prosody emphasizes the heads of constituents whereas Japanese prosody emphasizes their left edges. This description accords with the evidence for perceptual segmentation strategies reviewed in section 12.3. In general, English speech rhythms tend to be defined by the alternation between strong head

164

syllables and their weaker sister syllables. Japanese speech rhythms, on the other hand, tend to be defined by the consonants marking the left edges of most syllables and, at a higher level, by the tones marking the left edges of accentual phrases (cf. Pierrehumbert & Beckman, 1988).

These tendencies appear again and again in comparing the two languages. For example, compare poetic conventions: English poetry counts stress feet and often aligns heads of adjacent lines in rhyming, whereas Japanese poetry counts moras and aligns the beginnings of lines with accentual phrase boundaries. Or, compare the prosodic mechanisms for directing attentional focus. In English, a word (or a strong syllable within a word) can be placed in narrow focus by making it the head of its own intermediate phrase – i.e., by assigning it the nuclear pitch accent and deaccenting everything that follows. The analogous mechanism in Japanese is to place the focused element at the left edge of a new intermediate phrase, dephrasing or downstepping everything that follows. In English, if the focused element is a preposition, article, or auxiliary verb, the mechanism easily defies the default footing patterns, which tend otherwise to make such function words weak sisters to neighboring content words. Similarly, in Japanese, if the focused element is a postpositional case particle, the mechanism easily defies the default accentual phrasing, which would phrase the case particle together with the preceding noun (Venditti, Jun & Beckman, in press).

This description of English versus Japanese mirrors the difference between Taiwanese and Korean. Just as in English, rhyme is an important component of Chinese poetic meter, whereas Korean is similar to Japanese in counting syllables and beginning lines at accentual phrase boundaries. The stress foot is an important concept for understanding tone sandhi patterns in many Chinese languages, including Taiwanese (cf. Hsiao, 1990), whereas Korean shows a strong typological similarity to Japanese at these higher levels of the prosodic hierarchy (cf. Jun, 1993). It is not surprising, then, that the Taiwanese speakers in Wang & Derwing (forthcoming) behaved similarly to Kubozono's English speakers, whereas the Korean speakers in Derwing *et al.* (1993) behaved similarly to Kubozono's Japanese speakers. In summary, it seems that the salient places for cutting strings of segments apart is at least as important an aspect of the rhythmic structure of a language as are the salient units for grouping them together.

Note

* The preparation of this paper was supported in part by the NSF under grant IRI-8858109. I also thank Janet Pierrehumbert for her help in understanding the phonological literature.

References

Cutler, A. & D. G. Norris. 1988. The role of strong syllables in segmentation for lexical access. *Journal of Experimental Psychology: Human Perception and Performance* 14: 113–121.

Cutler, A., J. Mehler, D. G. Norris & J. Segui. 1986. The syllable's differing role in the segmentation of French and English. *Journal of Memory and Language* 25: 385–400.

Derwing, B. 1992. A "pause-break" task for eliciting syllable boundary judgments from literate and illiterate speakers: preliminary results for five diverse languages. *Language and Speech* 1–2: 219–235.

Derwing, B., Y. B. Yoon & S. W. Cho. 1993. The organization of the Korean syllable: experimental evidence. *Japanese and Korean Linguistics* 2: 223–238.

Echols, C. H. & E. N. Newport. 1992. The role of stress and position in determining first words. *Language Acquisition* 2: 189–220.

Gerken, L. A. In press. Sentential processes in early child language: evidence from the perception and production of function morphemes. In H. C. Nusbaum & J. C. Goodman (eds.), *The Transition from Speech Sounds to Spoken Words*. Cambridge, MA: MIT Press.

Hayes, B. 1986. Inalterability in CV phonology. *Language* 62: 321–351.

Hayes, B. 1994. *Metrical Stress Theory: Principles and Case Studies*. Chicago, IL: University of Chicago Press.

Hsiao, Y. E. 1990. The Bermuda triangle of syntax, rhythm and tone. In Y. No & M. Libucha (eds.), *Proceedings of the 7th Eastern States Conference on Linguistics*. Columbus, OH: Ohio State University, 112–123.

Itô, J. 1990. Prosodic minimality in Japanese. In K. Deaton, M. Noske & M. Ziolkowski (eds.), *CLS 26–II: Papers from the Parasession on the Syllable in Phonetics and Phonology*. Chicago: Chicago Linguistics Society, 213–239.

Itô, J. & R. A. Mester. 1992. Weak layering and word binarity. *Technical report* LRC–92–09. Santa Cruz: Linguistics Research Center.

Jun, S.-A. 1993. The phonetics and phonology of Korean prosody. Ph.D. dissertation, Ohio State University.

Jusczyk, P. W., A. Cutler & N. Redanz. 1993. Infants' preference for the predominant word stress patterns of English words. *Child Development* 64: 675–687.

Kubozono, H. 1990. Phonological constraints on blending in English as a case for phonology-morphology interface. *Yearbook of Morphology* 3: 1–20.

Kubozono, H. 1992. Modeling syntactic effects on downstep in Japanese. In G. J. Docherty & D. R. Ladd (eds.), *Papers in Laboratory Phonology II: Gesture, Segment, Prosody*. Cambridge: Cambridge University Press, 368–387.

Ladd, D. R. 1986. Intonational phrasing: the case for recursive prosodic structure. *Phonology Yearbook* 3: 311–340.

McCarthy, J. & A. Prince. 1990. Foot and word in prosodic morphology: the Arabic broken plurals. *Natural Language and Linguistic Theory* 8: 209–283.

McCarthy, J. & A. Prince. 1993. Generalized Alignment. Yearbook of Morphology 6: 79–153.

Mehler, J., J.-Y. Dommergues, U. Frauenfelder & J. Segui. 1981. The syllable's role in speech segmentation. *Journal of Verbal Learning and Verbal Behavior* 20: 298–305.

Morais, J., L. Cary, J. Alegria & P. Bertelson. 1979. Does awareness of speech as a sequence of phones arise spontaneously? *Cognition* 7: 322–331.

Otake, T., G. Hatano, A. Cutler & J. Mehler. 1993. Mora or syllable? Speech segmentation in Japanese. *Journal of Memory and Language* 32: 258–278.

Pierrehumbert, J. 1991. Phonological and phonetic representation. *Journal of Phonetics* 18: 375–394.

Pierrehumbert, J. 1993. Alignment and prosodic heads. Paper presented at the 10th Eastern States Conference on Linguistics, Ohio State University.

Pierrehumbert, J. B. & M. E. Beckman. 1988. *Japanese Tone Structure*. Cambridge, MA: MIT Press.

Port, R. F., J. Dalby & M. O'Dell. 1987. Evidence for mora timing in Japanese. *Journal of the Acoustical Society of America* 81: 1574–1585.

Poser, W. J. 1990. Evidence for foot structure in Japanese. *Language* 66: 78–105.

Prince, A. & P. Smolensky. 1992. Optimality: constraint interaction in generative grammar. Paper presented at the 12th West Coast Conference on Formal Linguistics, Los Angeles.

Read, C., Y. Zhang, H. Nie & B. Ding. 1986. The ability to manipulate speech sounds depends on knowing alphabetic writing. *Cognition* 24: 31–44.

Venditti, J. J., S.-A. Jun & M. E. Beckman. In press. Prosodic cues to syntactic and other linguistic structures in Japanese, Korean, & English. In J. Morgan and K. Demuth (eds.), *Signal to Syntax: Bootstrapping from Speech to Grammar in Early Acquisition*. Hillsdale, NJ: Lawrence Erlbaum.

Wang, H. S. & B. L. Derwing. Forthcoming. Is Taiwanese a "body" language? Submitted to *Toronto Working Papers in Linguistics*.

13

Toward a theory of phonological and phonetic timing: evidence from Bantu

KATHLEEN HUBBARD*

13.1 Introduction

Duration is at the same time one of the easiest and one of the most difficult aspects of speech to analyze: while it is relatively simple to *measure* duration (as compared to pitch or formant structure, for instance), sorting out what part of duration is linguistically determined – rather than mechanically driven, or put to affective use – is a much more complicated matter (Lehiste, 1970). But much has been said about linguistic timing in the phonological literature, with respect to quantity of vowels and consonants, compensatory lengthening, and the like, so it is appropriate to try to examine phonetic timing in the light of these phonological claims. The goal of this paper is to explore the relation between phonological structure and phonetic output, and the mapping between the two, focusing on the mora as a unit of timing in non-stress languages.

13.1.1 The mora

The importance of phonological timing came to the fore with the development of the autosegmental CV or X tier, which assigns one timing unit to each segment and represents the fact that either the segmental melody or the timing tier may be separately affected by phonological rules (Clements and Keyser, 1983; Levin, 1985). The evolution of this notion into mora or weight-tier theory reflects the insight that phonological timing revolves around weight-bearing elements – syllable nuclei, and sometimes consonants in the rhyme, but never onset consonants; thus on the timing tier, timing units are assigned only to weight-bearers, not to every segment (Hyman, 1984, 1985; Hayes, 1989). In all of these phonological models, however, it is explicitly stated that the

168

representations do not necessarily translate to *phonetic* timing: all other things being equal, a melodic element linked to two timing units should be longer than an element linked to just one – but since many factors other than phonological structure may influence phonetic timing, no specific claims about output are made.

So is the mora strictly a unit of abstract representation, or is it also relevant for surface timing? Certainly it is a robust phonological element: as far back as Trubetzkoy (1969) and Jakobson (1971), the mora was recognized as a unit of syllable weight in stress assignment (a heavy syllable has two moras, a light syllable one). Phonological evidence for the mora is also found in the lexicon, where it serves to distinguish long from short segments, and can be the basis for minimal word size; evidence for the mora is also found in several phonological rules, such as compensatory lengthening, tone assignment, and morphological processes of reduplication and truncation.

Japanese, for example, makes reference to a bimoraic foot in the formation of nicknames: the portion of the name that precedes the hypocoristic suffix must be either one or two bimoraic units (Poser, 1984). A number of Bantu languages make use of the mora in morphological processes of affixation or reduplication; e.g. verb stem reduplication in Luganda, which adjusts a subminimal stem so that it reduplicates as a bimoraic unit, and Runyambo suffixal allomorphy, which adjusts the vowel length of a verb suffix based on the mora count of the preceding syllable (Hyman, 1993). Tonal rules also target the mora in many Bantu languages: a Cibemba rule spreads High tone one mora to the right (Hyman, 1993), and in several other languages (including Runyambo) certain verb tenses assign a High tone to the second mora of a stem. Finally, evidence from phonological writing systems around the world shows that the mora is a robust phonological constituent: Poser (1992) demonstrates that most systems that have been called syllabic are actually based on the mora, or on onset and rhyme (including Japanese *kana*, Moose Cree, Ojibwa, and Hieroglyphic Luwian).

While the phonological importance of the mora is well established, it also has a history as a phonetic element. Bloch (1950) identifies it as the roughly constant timing unit reported in Japanese, where a CV sequence is supposed to take about the same time to utter as a moraic nasal (N) or the first part of a geminate consonant (Q). The mora, in this conception, is supposed to be a durational constant. But it is a phonetic fact that not all segments are timed in the same way: inherent durations of different segments vary widely (high vowels are shorter than low vowels, voiceless consonants are longer than voiced, etc.), and segment duration is altered to signal boundaries (syntactic "boundary lengthening") and to express affect (emphasis, surprise, etc.). These non-phonological influences on duration present a problem for the phonetic notion of the mora. So can the two be reconciled?

Beckman (1982) answered this question in the negative: her data showed that phonologically equivalent sequences in Japanese (CV, CV with devoiced vowel, N, Q) do not have the same phonetic duration. Port, Dalby and O'Dell (1987), however, come to a different conclusion for Japanese: their data suggest that mora timing is maintained not at the level of the individual mora, but at the level of the word. That is, if stretches longer than a single mora are examined, they display a regular correspondence of mora count and duration – and compensatory effects can be seen in these longer stretches for the varying inherent durations of segments. Port *et al.*'s experimental model serves as a starting point for Nagano-Madsen (1992), in which comparable results were obtained for Eskimo and Yoruba.[1]

In the present study, I build on this model as I look to see whether Bantu languages – well known for their phonological use of the mora – behave similarly. Bantu languages, with their wealth of prosodic phenomena such as vowel and consonant length, compensatory lengthening, tone assignment, and morphological alternations, are a logical choice for the study of moras and duration. In what follows, I give three types of acoustic evidence for a systematic mapping of phonological timing to surface duration in Bantu languages, and then I explore the ways in which this mapping appears to be implemented.

13.2 Evidence for regular mapping in Bantu

13.2.1 Mora maintenance

In Experiment 1, word durations in Runyambo (a language of northwestern Tanzania) and Luganda (spoken in Uganda) were measured to test the hypothesis that mora maintenance occurs at the word level (as claimed in Port *et al.*, 1987). The hypothesis has two parts: (1) if a sequence of segments is extended by units that are phonologically one mora at a time, the duration of the word should increase by roughly constant increments, and (2) all phonologically *n*-mora words should fall into the same range of duration, regardless of syllable structure or segmental content.

The Runyambo corpus in this experiment included minimal sets of varying shapes (CVC, CVVC, CVNC, CVCVC), as well as roots with varying numbers of prefixes and suffixes. (Bantu verb affixes provide a natural way to extend a sound sequence by one mora or syllable at a time.) The corpus was constructed such that mora count and syllable count matched in some cases and not in others. The Luganda corpus (which was elicited by another researcher for a different study) was not as well balanced, but still contained useful minimal sets.

Toward a theory of phonological and phonetic timing

The word lists were read by one speaker of each language (for Runyambo each token was recorded three times in a frame sentence in randomized order, for Luganda each token was read twice in isolation in the same order). In (1) and (2), representative samples of the corpora are shown (acute accent marks High tone, grave accent Low tone, while unmarked vowels are toneless; roots are in bold face):

(1) Runyambo

roots + affixes

ku-**nógoor**-a	"to mold"	ku-**kóm**-a	"to tie"
ku-**nógoor**-er-a	"to mold for/at"	ku-**kóm**-er-a	"to tie for/at"
ku-ji-**nógoor**-a	"to mold it for/at"	ku-**jeend**-a	"to go"
ku-ji-tu-**nógoor**-er-a	"to mold it for us"	ku-**jeend**-er-a	"to go to"

roots of minimally different shape

ku **gob** a	"reach, arrive"	ku-**sib**-a	"to imprison"
ku-**goob**-a	"bend"	ku-**siib**-a	"pass time at"
ku-**gomb**-a	"desire"	ku-**simb**-a	"erect something"

(2) Luganda

bá-**lim**-a	"they are cultivating"
bá-mù-**lim**-a	"they are cultivating it"
bá-**lim**-ir-a	"they are cultivating for/at"
bá-mù-**lim**-ir-a	"they are cultivating it for him"
bá-**lim**-aa-**lim**-a	"they are cultivating here and there"
bá-mù-**lim**-aa-**lim**-a	"they are cultivating it here and there"
bá-**lim**-ir-a-**lim**-ir-a	"they are cultivating for/at here and there"
bá-mù-**lim**-ir-a-**lim**-ir-a	"they are cultivating for him here and there"

Tokens were digitized (here as for all four experiments reported in this paper) at 10 kHz with 16-bit quantization, and durations were measured from waveforms and broad-band spectrograms. Segmentation criteria were for the most part conventional, as in, for example, Peterson and Lehiste (1960); VOT was excluded from vowel duration. Mean values for each lexical item are given in Tables 13.1 and 13.2; means for word duration by number of moras are shown in Table 13.3.

Table 13.1. Mora and syllable count, and mean durations (in ms) of Runyambo tokens.

Word	Moras	Sylls	Dur	Word	Moras	Sylls	Dur
kusona	3	3	476	kugomba	4	3	549
kukuba	3	3	488	kutaana	4	3	528
kubona	3	3	469	kusiiba	4	3	528
kugoba	3	3	464	kusimba	4	3	546
kutana	3	3	468	kutanga	4	3	561
kusiba	3	3	448	kukomera	4	4	581
kukoma	3	3	484	kugurucira	5	5	677
kuguruka	4	4	572	kunogoora	5	4	675
kusaaga	4	3	548	kujeendera	5	4	621
kusanga	4	3	562	kucigurucira	6	6	807
kusonda	4	3	549	kujinogoora	6	5	779
kukuuba	4	3	562	kunogoorera	6	5	772
kugooba	4	3	529	kucitugurucira	7	7	874
kujeenda	4	3	513	kujinogoorera	7	6	849
kukumba	4	3	575	kujitunogoorera	8	7	957

Table 13.2. Mora and syllable count, and mean durations (in ms) of selected Luganda tokens.

Word	Moras	Syllables	Duration
balima	3	3	426
bamulima	4	4	553
balimira	4	4	538
bamulimira	5	5	599
bagulirira	5	5	610
balimaalima	6	5	769
baagulirira	6	5	852
bamulimaalima	7	6	869
balimiralimira	7	7	817
baamugulirira	7	6	914
bamulimiralimira	8	8	901

Table 13.3. Mean word duration (in ms) by number of moras for Runyambo on the left (mean diff. = 96 ms), and Luganda on the right (mean diff. = 95 ms).

Moras	Duration	Moras	Duration
3	476	3	426
4	550	4	545
5	658	5	604
6	786	6	810
7	859	7	867
8	957	8	901

Analysis of variance demonstrates that the effect of mora count is more important than syllable count (for Runyambo: F (5, 79) = 452.81 for mora count, and F (4, 80) = 185.25 for syllable count; for Luganda: F (5, 97) = 45.64 for mora count, and F (5, 105) = 12.36 for syllable count; $p < 0.0001$ in all cases); other *post hoc* statistical tests confirm this for both languages.

In Runyambo, for example, a four-syllable word containing a long vowel, such as *kunogoora* (675 ms), is much closer in duration to a five-syllable word with all short vowels, such as *kugurucira* (677 ms), than to a four-syllable all-short vowels word, such as *kuguruka* (572 ms). Likewise, *kukumba* (575 ms) is much closer in duration to words like *kukomera* (581 ms) than to words like *kusona* (476 ms). This relationship holds throughout the data set.

As with Beckman's (1982) results for Japanese, it is not the case that every phonologically moraic sequence has the same duration: for example, in Runyambo, one mora /ku/ is 194 ms, while one mora /go/ is 136 ms; similarly, two mora sequences /tana/ and /gom(b)/ are 351 ms and 300 ms respectively. However, it *is* the case that words with the same mora count have very comparable durations. From these patterns it is possible to conclude that these languages employ timing compensation that is sufficient to override large inherent durational differences between segment types and roughly maintain a moraic constant.

13.2.2 Correspondence of a phonological and a phonetic difference

Experiment 2 involves compensatory lengthening (CL) and tone assignment. Many Bantu languages have a synchronic CL process by which vowels preceding a nasal + consonant sequence become longer; this is said to be because the nasal gives up its timing unit to the preceding vowel when it joins

Kathleen Hubbard

with a following consonant to form a prenasalized segment (as in e.g. Clements, 1986, here represented with moras).

(3) Prenasalization and compensatory lengthening in Luganda

  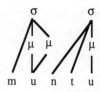

underlying representation   Prenasalization   Compensatory Lengthening

This phonological process does not operate in exactly the same way across Bantu languages. One difference between Luganda and Runyambo is in the tonal result of a CVNC sequence. In a morphological environment where High tone is assigned to the second mora of the verb stem, the nasal in a VNC sequence counts as a tone-bearing unit in Luganda, but not in Runyambo.

(4)   *Luganda*   a-bíng-a[2]   (3sg-chase-FV)   "he who chases"
        Runyambo   a-bing-á   (3sg-chase-FV)   "he chased"

To see whether this phonological difference corresponds to a difference in surface timing, I recorded extensive word lists in Runyambo and Luganda; these contained three non-randomized tokens for each type without a frame sentence and were read by three speakers of Runyambo, and one speaker of Luganda respectively. I measured segment durations in the same way as in Experiment 1. The results show that the timing of VNC sequences is indeed different in the two languages; namely, vowels in the lengthening environment are not lengthened as much in Runyambo as they are in Luganda (Maddieson, 1993, found that Sukuma is like Runyambo in this regard).[3]

Table 13.4. Vowel durations (in ms) and ratios to short V for Runyambo and Luganda.

| | Vowel durations | | | Ratios (to short V) | |
	Short	Pre-NC	Long	Pre-NC	Long
Runyambo	110	168	215	1.5	1.9
Luganda	98	192	240	2	2.5

174

These durational facts suggest that in Runyambo, the nasal does not "give up" all of its moraic status to the preceding vowel; rather the mora is shared between the two segments.

(5) a.
Luganda:

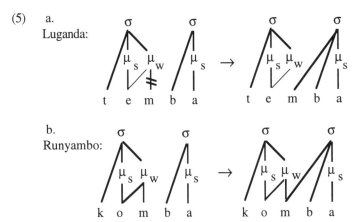

b.
Runyambo:

If we assume this kind of moraic structure, then the account we can give for the tone assignment difference is that a weak mora dominating a nonvocalic segment may not bear tone, and so second-mora High tone docks in different places in Luganda and Runyambo. The point is that a phonological difference that depends on abstract moraic structure – the assignment of tone in the compensatory lengthening environment – correlates with a durational difference in the surface timing of two languages.

13.2.3 Correspondence of a phonetic and a phonological difference

Experiment 3 addresses the same issue as Experiment 2, from the opposite angle: does an observed phonetic difference between languages correlate with a phonological difference that is not immediately apparent? This experiment is a comparison of three Bantu languages with different known quantity characteristics: KiNdendeule (a language of Tanzania) has no lexical vowel length contrast; CiYao (spoken in Mozambique) has lexical length distinctions and no vowel sequences or hiatus; and CiTonga (a language of Zambia) has lexical length and also vowel sequences (au, ai). The aim of the experiment was to compare maximally similar corpora, elicited in identical contexts (word lists as similar as lexically possible, three tokens per type, with a frame sentence, randomized). There was one speaker per language. Durations were measured and analyzed statistically as before (all reported category differences are significant to at least 95% by *post hoc* tests).

175

Table 13.5. Vowel durations (in ms) for KiNdendeule (difference not significant), CiYao (short vs. long is significant, long vs. pre-NC is not), and CiTonga (long vs. short is significant, short vs. pre-NC is not).

	KiNdendeule		CiYao		CiTonga	
	Mean	*s.d.*	Mean	*s.d.*	Mean	*s.d.*
CVC	147.9	*(33.7)*	60.8	*(22.8)*	100.3	*(28.3)*
CVNC	145.5	*(26.6)*	130.4	*(15.7)*	101.4	*(22.4)*
CVVC			131.5	*(18.7)*	240.6	*(39.7)*

The results show that in KiNdendeule (which has no lexical vowel length), vowels before NC have the same duration as in other environments – that is, there is no compensatory lengthening. This accords with the common claim that phonemic vowel length is a prerequisite of CL (de Chene & Anderson, 1979; Hayes, 1989).

In CiYao, which does have lexical vowel length, vowels before NC are just over twice as long as short vowels, and are the same length as lexically long vowels – in other words, the usual compensatory lengthening takes place (of the sort found in Luganda).

CiTonga also has lexical vowel length, but the duration of vowels before NC is the same as that of lexically *short* vowels – i.e., there is no compensatory lengthening.

Why is there this asymmetry among the three languages? The explanation is found in the lexicon of CiTonga: unlike CiYao (or Luganda or many other languages), CiTonga does not retain long vowels in any of the Proto-Bantu long roots (Meeussen, 1980); in those roots it has short vowels. All of the long vowels seen in CiTonga can be shown to have arisen from consonant loss between vowels, or from concatenation of vowels (often not immediately obvious). Also recall that CiTonga has vowel hiatus, of a sort not typically found in languages that preserve Proto-Bantu length (*a.i, a.u*, etc.): these sequences in fact have the same duration as monophthongal long vowels (/ai/ 245 ms, /au/ 213 ms). Thus, the long vowels of CiTonga are arguably bisyllabic – and if there are no vowels linked to two moras, there is no structure available for compensatory lengthening.

176

(6) Available prosodic structures:

   a   KiNdendeule

   b. CiYao

   c. CiTonga

In this instance, a surface phonetic fact points toward a difference in the underlying phonological structures of different languages.

13.2.4 Provisional conclusions

From the kinds of evidence presented here, it is possible to take the following as a working premise: moraic structure, in languages of this type, is reflected in surface duration – not by a direct linear mapping, but nonetheless systematically. If this is true, then it must be the case that segmental adjustment around inherent durational differences is taking place (*contra* Nagano-Madsen, 1992). The next reasonable step is to determine where and how this compensation occurs.

13.3 Segmental adjustment for mora maintenance

The study of compensation can be problematic: for one thing, measurement error can introduce falsely negative correlations between adjacent measurements (Ohala and Lyberg, 1976); thus, a claim of timing compensation based on such negative correlations may be unjustified. For this reason, I took a different approach to segmental adjustment: I used analysis of variance to determine what factors affect the duration of a given segment or segment type, and how those

177

factors are ranked with respect to each other. Another problem is coarticulation: if a difference in duration of a particular segment is observed in various environments, it is difficult to know how much of the difference results from intentional manipulation of overlapping gestures to maintain a higher-order timing scheme, and how much is accidental or automatic. I have little to say about this issue, since my data are acoustic and not articulatory, but it seems clear that cross-linguistic data will help resolve the question, which I set aside for the moment. With these cautions in mind, I move on to Experiment 4.

The goal of this experiment was to determine where segmental adjustment for mora maintenance takes place: is it only in vowels, or also in consonants? Only within syllables, or also across syllable boundaries? To answer these questions, existing corpora from earlier work on Luganda and Runyambo, digitized and measured as in Experiments 1, 2 and 3, were examined statistically with analysis of variance and *post hoc* tests of significance to see which factors correlate most strongly with segment duration.

13.3.1 Luganda

In the Luganda corpus, initial and medial vowels were analyzed separately, because while medial vowels contrast in all five vowel qualities and both length categories, initial vowels do not: only /e/, /a/, and /o/ appear initially, and they do not contrast in quantity. Final vowels had to be excluded from consideration because measurements were unreliable in this data set.

ANOVAs for medial vowels show, unsurprisingly, that the strongest effect is that of length category (F (2, 284) = 1310.266, $p < 0.0001$), which is much greater than that of vowel identity (F (4, 282) = 71.463, $p < 0.0001$). Other factors are much less important; the only noticeable ones are identity of preceding consonant and identity of following consonant (in that order). No other factors tested, such as grammatical category of the word, were significant.

Table 13.6. Luganda medial vowel durations (in ms).

	Short	s.d.	Pre-NC	s.d.	Long	s.d.
a	122	*(20.0)*	218	*(14.3)*	270	*(24.0)*
e	110	*(13.6)*	210	*(16.3)*	242	*(17.9)*
i	79	*(14.1)*	161	*(18.0)*	225	*(25.6)*
o	108	*(17.0)*	198	*(17.1)*	247	*(19.6)*
u	87	*(17.0)*	172	*(17.0)*	217	*(25.4)*
mean	98	*(22.9)*	192	*(27.6)*	240	*(31.2)*

Table 13.7. Luganda initial vowel (IV) durations (in ms).

	Mean	*s.d.*
a	152	*(57.5)*
e	112	*(45.8)*
o	85	*(151)*

As for initial vowels (which were more difficult to measure, so the results are presented more tentatively), it has often been claimed that in Luganda these are always long, except before geminate consonants where this length is said to have a demarcative function (Katamba, 1985). In the present data set, however, initial vowels (IVs) are not consistent in duration: often they are shorter than their medial counterparts, sometimes longer, while the variance is large in most cases. However, initial vowels are never as long as medial phonologically long vowels.

Recall that there is no phonological length distinction in this position (comparison of items where there should be a morphological contrast showed that quantity is neutralized: initial /a/ in *a-gul-a* "he buys" is 156 ms, in *a-a-gul-a* "the one who buys" it is 158 ms), so quantity is not a factor. However, grammatical category does play a role: in verbs, IVs are significantly longer than in nouns (F (2, 136) = 26.783, $p < 0.0001$).

This may be because of the difference in morphological function: in the verbs in question (finite forms), the initial vowel is the subject marker, while in nouns it is a pre-prefix redundantly determined by the noun class prefix. In any case, grammatical category is a much greater influence on IV duration than vowel identity. The next most important determinant is, as expected, the quantity of the following consonant: vowels are shorter before a geminate than a single consonant (F (1, 81) = 51.223, $p < 0.0001$).

For Luganda consonants, there is a statistically significant durational difference between root-initial and root-medial position. This may be partly an artifact of the corpus: most of the items were verbs with an infinitive prefix, thus the contrastive part of each word began at the root-initial consonant. (But the same effect has appeared in other data sets, so it may be a general phenomenon.) In any case, when root-initial (C1) and root-medial (C2) consonant durations are analyzed separately, the ranking of factors is different for the two sets. For both types of consonant, the most significant determinants of duration are of course quantity (single vs. geminate) (F (1, 465) = 1781.817, $p < 0.0001$) and identity (F (9, 697) = 77.625, $p < 0.0001$).

179

Table 13.8. Luganda IV durations (in ms) by grammatical category (left) and following C quantity (right).

	Mean	s.d.		Mean	s.d.
noun	105	(38.7)	single	136	(41.8)
verb	167	(53.3)	geminate	77	(18.6)

Table 13.9. Luganda consonant durations (in ms).

	Single	s.d.	Geminate	s.d.
t	98	(13.2)	194	(26.1)
k	86	(15.2)	214	(29.7)
b	51	(9.0)	193	(10.7)
d	84	(7.3)	214	(12.2)
g	79	(14.3)	192	(16.3)
m*	93	(12.8)		
n	68	(9.3)	173	(20.1)
s	170	(18.6)		
mean	81	(19.9)	195	(21.5)

*Values for /m/ and /n/ here are for intervocalic position.

For C1, there is a small effect of preceding vowel identity, and an even smaller effect of following vowel identity. C2, on the other hand, is affected somewhat by the identity of the preceding vowel, but more so by the identity of the preceding *consonant*; that is, C1 has an effect on the duration of the onset of the next syllable. Voicing of C1 has the greatest impact on C2, followed by a slight influence of place of articulation; manner is not significant. The effect does not occur in the reverse direction: none of these distinctions in C2 affects the duration of C1 (cf. Port *et al.*, 1987, where voicing of C2 affects C1 in Japanese). It was not possible to determine the effect of following vowel identity on C2 duration in this data set, since the final vowel in verb infinitives is invariably /a/ , so that question is postponed for future study.

13.3.2 Runyambo

In the Runyambo data set, it was possible to measure final vowels securely, but there was no contrast among initial vowels in the corpus, so results are reported only for medial and final vowels. Results for vowels are similar to those in Luganda: the most important factor for medial vowels is length category (F $(1, 27) = 167.014$, $p < 0.0001$), followed by preceding consonant identity (F $(3, 23) = 60.324$, $p < 0.0001$), and then vowel identity (F $(2, 14) = 9.216$, $p < 0.0028$). Unlike Luganda, the effect of following consonant identity is not significant. Of final vowels, which do not contrast in quantity, the only one present in this data set (for morphological reasons) was /a/; its duration was affected most by preceding consonant identity (F $(3, 24) = 21.63$, $p < 0.0001$), and then by preceding vowel identity (F $(2, 25) = 11.009$, $p < 0.0004$) – again a trans-syllable effect, as seen in Luganda consonants.

As for consonants, the chief difference from Luganda is that Runyambo has no geminate consonants. Thus, the primary determinant of consonant duration in both positions is segment identity. Beyond this, root-initial consonants are affected only by following vowel identity (F $(2, 25) = 19.505$, $p < 0.0001$). As in Luganda, C1 is not significantly affected by C2 identity. C2 duration *is* affected by C1 identity, then by preceding vowel identity, and somewhat by preceding vowel quantity (which is not a factor in Luganda). Also different from Luganda is the ranking of effects of C1 on C2: in Runyambo, as in Luganda, the greatest factor in this component is voicing of C1; but the next factor is C1 *manner* (which is not significant in Luganda), while C1 *place* is not significant (but it is in Luganda).

13.3.3 Comparisons of Luganda and Runyambo

Compensation results for the two languages are summarized in Table 13.10.

Evidence for compensation can be seen in Figures 13.1, 13.2, and 13.3. Each figure shows mean durations for the three utterances of each word; lines represent vowel-preceding consonants, boxes represent VOT and vowels, and narrow boxes represent nasals in the VNC environment. Since final vowel measurements in Luganda were unreliable, only the stem portion of those words is given.

Figure 13.1 shows minimal pairs in which vowel and consonant duration can be seen to adjust around different consonants; /o/ is shorter after /s/ than after /t/, /u/ is shorter before /m/ than /b/, etc.

Kathleen Hubbard

Table 13.10. Influences on segment duration for Luganda (top) and Runyambo (bottom).

Luganda

VOWELS		CONSONANTS	
V(med)	quantity (S, L, pre-NC) identity preceding C identity following C identity	C(rt-init)	quantity identity w/asp: preceding V i.d. following V i.d.
V(init)	grammatical category identity following C quantity	C(rt-med)	quantity identity C1 identity (voice > place) w/asp: preceding V i.d.

Runyambo

VOWELS		CONSONANTS	
V(med)	quantity (S, L, pre-NC) identity preceding C identity	C(rt-init)	identity following V identity following V quantity
V(fin)	preceding C identity preceding V identity	C(rt-med)	identity C1 i.d. (voice > manner) preceding V identity

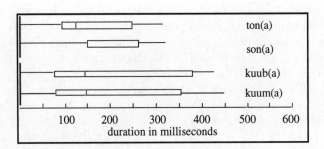

Figure 13.1. Luganda comparisons.

182

Toward a theory of phonological and phonetic timing

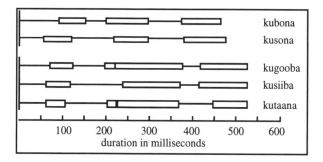

Figure 13.2. Runyambo comparisons.

In Figure 13.2, where whole words are given, the first pair shows adjustment around a minimal contrast (*kubona/kusona*); the next three show that even with widely different segmental content (*kugooba/kusiiba/kutaana*), the total duration of four-mora words is quite constant.

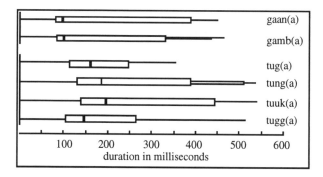

Figure 13.3. Luganda comparisons.

Finally, the Luganda set in Figure 13.3 shows comparisons with lengthened vowels and geminate consonants. Note that mora maintenance is not exact; for instance, *tugg(a)*, with a geminate consonant, is shorter than its CVNC and CVVC counterparts, *tung(a)* and *tuuk(a)* respectively. This was true throughout the data set, though no satisfactory explanation can be given at present. Nonetheless, adjustment does appear to be taking place such that a general moraic constant is sustained.

183

13.4 A theory of mapping

With information such as I obtained in Experiment 4 about how and where segmental compensation for timing maintenance takes place, we can begin to imagine an algorithm for mapping underlying timing to surface timing. Crucial to this enterprise is a model of grammar in which a language-specific phonetic component affects utterances after the end of the phonological derivation (this schema is taken from Cohn, 1990).

(7) From underlying representation to surface (after Cohn, 1990)

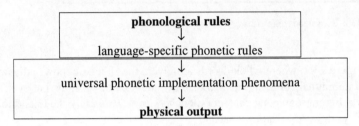

In this model, there would be a point at the output of the phonological component where duration is assigned. For the languages examined in this paper, the highest priority at this stage will be to assign a minimum target duration to segments dominated by a mora – these are the ones that determine distinctive quantity, and thus must maintain a durational contrast, while the duration specification of other segments may be determined mostly by other factors (for instance place and manner features). In a language like English, on the other hand, the greatest priority at this point will be to assign greater duration to stressed syllables. This contrasts with the usual assumption about the computation of timing (e.g. in Klatt, 1979), namely that assigning target *segment* durations is the first step, and that these durations are then adjusted for location of stress and other factors. But the model proposed here has some support from research in speech synthesis: Campbell & Isard (1991), working on a timing algorithm for synthesized speech, examined natural speech in British English and concluded that the syllable was the most relevant unit of programming for duration (rather than the segment, or anything else). In their algorithm, several factors (e.g. number of segments in the syllable, position of the syllable in the foot, stress, content vs. function status of the word, etc.) are considered in calculating a target duration for the syllable as a whole, after which appropriate durations for individual segments are computed within the syllable span.

Based on the measurements of Luganda and Runyambo reported here, it would be possible to conclude that a similar process is taking place, based on the mora rather than on the syllable and the stress foot.[4] So far this is suggested only by acoustic and statistical evidence; without synthesis or perception experiments, there can be no strong claim about how timing computation actually occurs in these languages. Even if synthesis work were to show that a mora-based algorithm produces natural-sounding speech (including successful maintenance of phonological contrasts), we would still know nothing about the real-time processing mechanisms of natural language. But an algorithm of this type *is* a logical possibility, given the measurement results reported here. It would vary in its details from one language to another (recall the different ranking of factors in Luganda and Runyambo), and might be vastly different, or not relevant at all, for languages of other structural types.

But as a first step in charting the link between phonological structure and durational output, these experiments may serve as a model for investigating timing in Bantu and other languages. What is needed to achieve a better understanding of speech timing is more baseline acoustic data from typologically different languages, so that we can determine which durational effects are universal and which are not. Acoustic information can then be compared with articulatory and perceptual data, to find out how timing is realized and what counts as successful output. With careful attention to which elements of timing are universal and which are language-specific, it should be possible to construct a richer model of the mapping between phonological and phonetic structure. As we learn more about how speech is timed, both underlyingly and on the surface, we will have a clearer picture of the rule-governed and the mechanical aspects of speech, and of the important relationship between the two.

Notes

* The work on Luganda in this paper was supported in part by National Science Foundation Grant BNS91-09234.

1 At least for word-level mora maintenance (segmental compensation results were inconclusive).
2 A High tone assigned to the second mora of a long vowel or vowel-nasal syllable is realized on the whole syllable (there are no rising tones in the language, so LH on one syllable is simplified to H). This fact does not bear on the analysis here.
3 Durational results were the same for all three speakers; measurements here are aggregated.
4 As an anonymous reviewer has correctly pointed out, it is not necessary to think of rules in such an algorithm applying in ordered fashion; they could well be unordered rules that produce a "compromise" among different requirements. I would then say

185

that the moraic imperative is *weighted* more heavily than feature specifications in these languages.

References

Beckman, M. E. 1982. Segment duration and the "mora" in Japanese. *Phonetica* 39: 113–135.

Bloch, B. 1950. Studies in colloquial Japanese IV: phonemics. *Language* 26: 86–125.

Campbell, W. N. & S. D. Isard. 1991. Segment durations in a syllable frame. *Journal of Phonetics* 19: 37–47.

Clements, G. N. 1986. Compensatory lengthening and consonant gemination in LuGanda. In L. Wetzels & E. Sezer (eds.), *Studies in Compensatory Lengthening*. Dordrecht: Foris, 37–77.

Clements, G. N. & S. J. Keyser. 1983. *CV Phonology*. Cambridge, MA: MIT Press.

Cohn, A. C. 1990. Phonetic and phonological rules of nasalization. Ph.D. dissertation, UCLA (*UCLA Working Papers in Phonetics* 76).

de Chene, B., & S. R. Anderson. 1979. Compensatory lengthening. *Language* 55: 505–535.

Hayes, B. 1989. Compensatory lengthening in moraic phonology. *Linguistic Inquiry* 20: 253–306.

Hyman, L. M. 1984. On the weightlessness of syllable onsets. *BLS* (*Berkeley Linguistic Society*) 10: 1–14.

Hyman, L. M. 1985. *A Theory of Phonological Weight*. Dordrecht: Foris.

Hyman, L. M. 1993. Moraic mismatches in Bantu. *Phonology* 9: 255–265.

Jakobson, R. 1971. Die Betonung und ihre Rolle in der Wort- und Syntagmaphonologie. In *Selected Writings*. The Hague: Mouton, 117–136.

Katamba, F. 1985. A non–linear account of the syllable in Luganda. In D. L. Goyvaerts (ed.), *African Linguistics: Essays in Memory of M. W. K. Semikenke*. Amsterdam: Benjamins, 267–283.

Klatt, D. 1979. Synthesis by rule of segmental durations in English sentences. *Proceedings of the IXth International Congress of Phonetic Sciences*, Copenhagen, 2: 290–297.

Lehiste, I. 1970. *Suprasegmentals*. Cambridge, MA: MIT Press.

Levin, J. 1985. A metrical theory of syllabicity. Ph.D. dissertation, MIT.

Maddieson, I. 1993. Splitting the mora. *UCLA Working Papers in Phonetics* 83: 9–18.

Meeussen, A. E. 1980. *Bantu lexical reconstructions*. Archief voor antropologie, nr. 27. Tervuren: Koninklijk Museum voor Midden-Afrika.

Nagano-Madsen, Y. 1992. *Mora and Prosodic Coordination: a Phonetic Study of Japanese, Eskimo and Yoruba*. Lund: Lund University Press.

Ohala, J. J. & B. Lyberg. 1976. Comments on "Temporal interactions within a phrase and sentence context". *Journal of the Acoustical Society of America* 59: 990–992.

Peterson, G. E. & I. Lehiste. 1960. Duration of Syllable Nuclei in English. *Journal of the Acoustical Society of America* 32: 693–703.

Port, R. F., J. Dalby & M. O'Dell. 1987. Evidence for mora timing in Japanese. *Journal of the Acoustical Society of America* 81: 1574–1585.

Poser, W. J. 1984. Hypocoristic formation in Japanese. *WCCFL* (*West Coast Conference on Formal Linguistics*) 3: 218–229.

Poser, W. J. 1992. The structural typology of phonological writing. Paper presented at the Annual Meeting of the Linguistic Society of America.

Trubetzkoy, N. S. 1969. *Principles of Phonology*. Translated by C. Baltaxe. Berkeley: University of California Press.

14

On phonetic evidence for the phonological mora: comments on Hubbard

BERNARD TRANEL*

14.1 Introduction

Recent studies in phonological theory have conferred upon the mora a truly essential role, to the exclusion of other theoretical constructs such as labeled syllable constituents (onset, rime, nucleus, coda) or segmental slots (C/V or X-slots) (cf. work on Moraic Theory by Hyman, 1985, McCarthy & Prince, 1986, Zec, 1988, Hayes, 1989, and Steriade, 1990, among others). Hubbard's paper can be viewed as falling within this research paradigm, but on the phonetic side of linguistic investigation. With her proposal that the phonological mora plays a primordial role in the phonology/phonetics interface in Bantu languages, Hubbard draws attention to a new type of evidence for Moraic Theory; she adds phonetic timing to the phonological and morphological arguments traditionally given in support of the mora.

14.2 Summary of Hubbard's main points

Hubbard provides two related sources of evidence for the existence of a correlation between the phonological mora and phonetic timing (section 13.2). First, her measurements and statistical tests indicate that "the effect of mora count [on the total duration of a word in Runyambo and Luganda] is more important than syllable count". Thus, as illustrated in Table 14.1 with Runyambo data (taken from Hubbard's Table 13.1), "words with the same mora count have very comparable duration", even if they differ in syllable count, while words with the same syllable count have significantly different durations when they differ in mora count.

188

Table 14.1. Correlation between word duration (in ms) and mora count vs. syllable count in Runyambo.

Word	Duration	Mora count	Syllable count
kusona	476	3	3
kukumba	575	4	3
kuguruka	572	4	4
kunogoora	675	5	4
kugurucira	677	5	5
kunogoorera	772	6	5

Second, Hubbard observes that for identical segment sequences in distinct Bantu languages, there is a systematic correspondence between, on the one hand, different abstract moraic structures justified on phonological grounds, and on the other, phonetic differences in the timing of these sequences. For example, on the basis of phonological regularities regarding High tone assignment in verbs, Hubbard argues in favor of different moraic structures for bimoraic VNC sequences in Luganda and Runyambo.

(1)   phonological structures   phonetic timing

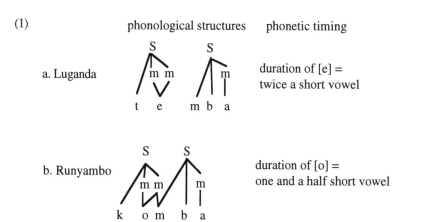

a. Luganda   duration of [e] = twice a short vowel

b. Runyambo   duration of [o] = one and a half short vowel

As (1) shows, the nasal consonant ends up nonmoraic in Luganda and the preceding vowel melody fully occupies the two available moras (as a result of Vowel Spread and Nasal Delinking; see Hyman, 1992: 256), whereas in Runyambo, the vowel melody shares the second mora with the nasal consonant

189

(as a result of Vowel Spread without Nasal Delinking). Correspondingly, as Hubbard observes, at the phonetic level, a pre-NC vowel is comparatively longer in Luganda than in Runyambo (twice vs. one and a half time as long as a short vowel). In sum, what is phonologically motivated in terms of moraic structure is directly reflected here in the phonetics of timing (Maddieson, 1993, makes the same proposal in order to distinguish pre-NC vowels in Luganda and Sukuma).

In the remainder of her paper (sections 13.3 and 13.4), Hubbard proposes that at the phonology/phonetics interface, the overall duration of words in nonstress languages like Luganda and Runyambo is first computed on the basis of mora count, with the durations of individual segments subsequently adjusted, accordion-like, so as to satisfy language-specific and universal segmental and intersegmental durational effects. This mora-based model of phonetic timing contrasts with the standard assumption that the segment constitutes the most relevant unit of programming for duration. Hubbard's Figure 13.2 illustrates her point: these Runyambo examples show almost perfect duration constancy under mora count for three-mora and four-mora words, with accordion-like internal durational adjustments based on segmental content. The relative "stretching" of /s/ at the expense of neighboring segments is particularly noteworthy in the minimal pair *kubona/kusona*, where the inherent length of the /s/ apparently causes the preceding /k/ and the following /o/ to shorten. In the pair *kugooba/kusiiba*, the inherent length of the /s/ is essentially accommodated by the following comparatively short /ii/, though this effect may not result from a compensatory adjustment, since high vowels are inherently shorter than other vowels to begin with.

If valid, Hubbard's model provides evidence of a phonetic nature for a theory of phonology that incorporates the mora, rather than segmental slots, as timing units.

14.3 Discussion

14.3.1 Word and word size

Hubbard's measuring unit is the mora. As she emphasizes, however, "it is not the case that every phonologically moraic sequence has the same duration"; rather her contention is that over the domain of the word, there is a constancy of duration measurable in terms of mora count. The word is thus the relevant domain of measurement. If correct, this result could provide phonetic validation for the notion of "word" used in phonology (how the word is defined in the languages considered needs to be spelled out precisely, at both the phonological and phonetic levels).

In the data given, word size ranges from three to eight moras. Interestingly, the average duration of a mora seems to shrink as the number of moras increases in the word. Although the statistical significance of this observation ought to be verified, Table 14.2, derived from Hubbard's Table 13.3, does appear to reflect such an overall trend (the diverging Luganda data for six- and seven-mora words are due to the special durational effect of long vowels in this language, which is discussed further below).

If this trend is indeed operational, it requires an explanation and would constitute another factor to be incorporated into the proposed timing algorithm at the phonology/phonetics interface. The inclusion in the data of words shorter than three moras would be useful to test the robustness of this preliminary observation, but there are no monosyllabic words in these languages, and bisyllabic words are quite rare (Kathleen Hubbard, personal communication).

Table 14.2. Word size and average mora duration (in ms) for Runyambo (left) and Luganda (right).

Mora count	Duration	Average mora duration	Mora count	Duration	Average mora duration
3	476	159	3	426	142
4	550	138	4	545	136
5	658	132	5	604	121
6	786	131	6	810	135
7	859	122	7	867	124
8	957	120	8	901	113

14.3.2 Mora count

In establishing the role of mora count in the determination of word duration, Hubbard shows that this correlation is statistically superior to that between word duration and syllable count. It might be appropriate as well to test the correlation between word duration and segment count, in order to see whether statistics-buttressed evidence from phonetic timing could be brought to bear on X-Theory, which, in contrast to Moraic Theory, views each phonetically realized segment as dominated by its own timing unit, long segments occupying two slots (cf. Levin, 1985, and Lowenstamm & Kaye, 1986, among others). My own rapid examination of the data, performed without the benefit of sophisticated statistical analysis, indicates that as a correlate of word duration, segment count is inferior to mora count. The relevant data presented in Tables 14.3 and 14.4 are derived from Hubbard's Tables 13.1 and 13.2 respectively.

Table 14.3. Correlation between word duration (in ms) and mora count vs. segment count for Runyambo.

	Segment count	Mora count	Duration range	Mean duration
	6	3	448–488	471
*	7	4	528–575	549
*	8	4	513–581	555
**	9	5	675	675
**	10	5	621–677	649
	11	6	772–779	776
	12	6	807	807
	13	7	849	849
	14	7	874	874
	15	8	957	957

Table 14.4. Correlation between word duration (in ms) and mora count vs. segment count for Luganda.

	Segment count	Mora count	Duration range	Mean duration
	6	3	426	426
	7			
	8	4	538–553	546
	9			
	10	5	599–610	605
	11	6	769–852	810
	12			
***	13	7	869–914	892
***	14	7	817	817
	15			
	16	8	901	901

On phonetic evidence for the phonological mora

In these two tables, asterisks point to the problems faced by segment count as a correlate of word duration: the rows marked by the same number of asterisks exhibit, contrary to expectations, either an overlap in duration range and/or a reversal in mean duration. In each of the three cases thus identified, mora count groups together the offending lines, thereby eliminating the problems.

While mora count appears superior to segment count as a correlate for word duration, it is not without its own difficulties, in particular with respect to Luganda. These difficulties are not immediately visible in Hubbard's Table 13.3 (because it contains only average word durations), but they appear clearly in Table 14.4, which shows how duration ranges actually overlap for Luganda words with six, seven, and eight moras. The same difficulties are also reflected in the high variability in duration increments contributed by each mora in Luganda, as compared to Runyambo (see Table 14.5, derived from Hubbard's Table 13.3).

Although the average duration increment is basically the same in both languages (just under 100 ms), the actual range in Luganda reaches 172 ms (206–34), compared to just 55 ms (128–73) for Runyambo. Clearly, contrary to Hubbard's hypothesis, extending Luganda words "one mora at a time" cannot be said to result in "roughly constant increments" in duration.

The source of the problem can be tracked down to Luganda's long-vowelled syllables, as the words listed in Table 14.6 illustrate (data taken from Hubbard's Table 13.2).

Table 14.5. Duration increments (in ms) per mora; Runyambo on the left and Luganda on the right.

Mora count	Duration	Duration increment	Mora count	Duration	Duration increment
3	476		3	426	
4	550	74	4	545	119
5	658	108	5	604	59
6	786	128	6	810	206
7	859	73	7	867	57
8	957	98	8	901	34

Bernard Tranel

In Table 14.6, the words in (a) contain only short vowels, whereas those in (b) contain one long vowel in addition to short vowels. The six-mora word with a long vowel is longer than the seven-mora word with only short vowels; in turn, the seven-mora word with a long vowel is longer than its seven-mora counterpart with only short vowels, and comparable in length to the eight-mora word with only short vowels. These examples show that long vowels in Luganda contribute inordinately to total word duration, as Hubbard's figures in her Table 13.4 confirm: whereas Runyambo long vowels are about twice as long as short vowels, Luganda long vowels are two and a half times longer than short vowels. [1] Under the standard assumption that short vowels are monomoraic and long vowels bimoraic, the Luganda high duration ratio of long to short vowels will necessarily weaken the correlation between word duration and mora count, and such weakening would only worsen with the possibility of more than one long vowel per word. Using for purposes of illustration a long-to-short duration ratio of three to one, consider the relative durations of the three hypothetical five-mora words in Table 14.7.

Table 14.6. Vowel length, mora count, and word duration (in ms) in Luganda.

	Luganda word	Mora count	Duration
(a)	balimiralimira	7	817
	bamulimiralimira	8	901
(b)	baagulirira	6	852
	baamugulirira	7	914

Table 14.7. The role of long vs. short vowels in word duration.

Word type	Mora count	Relative word duration
a. CVCVCVCVCV	5	5 (1+1+1+1+1)
b. CVVCVCVCV	5	6 (3+1+1+1)
c. CVVCVVCV	5	7 (3+3+1)

194

Even though the three word types in Table 14.7 have the same number of moras (namely five), and should thus all be of comparable duration, word (b) would in fact have the same duration as a six-mora word with only short vowels, and word (c) the same duration as a seven-mora word with only short vowels. Out of the 25 Luganda words used by Hubbard in her computations, only four contained a long vowel (Kathleen Hubbard, personal communication). In sum, at least for Luganda, it seems that if more words with (more) long vowels were included in the data, the robustness of mora count as a correlate of word duration could deteriorate beyond recognition.

Merely counting moras thus seems insufficient to establish phonetic timing accurately. As we have just seen, languages may differ in the duration ratio assigned to long (bimoraic) vs. short (monomoraic) vowels. There is another aspect in which sheer mora count yields incorrect information regarding duration. Within a syllable, mora count typically provides a binary distinction: one mora vs. two. But with respect to vowel duration, there is, as shown in Table 14.8, a three-way distinction in both Runyambo and Luganda: short~pre- NC~long (the data in this table come from Hubbard's Table 13.4).

Table 14.8. Vowel durations (in ms), and ratios to short vowel in parentheses.

Language	Short vowel	Pre-NC vowel	Long vowel
Runyambo	110	168 (1.5)	215 (1.9)
Luganda	98	192 (2)	240 (2.5)

Consider now the diagrams in (2). As shown in (2a), this three-way distinction is very nicely accommodated moraically in Runyambo, owing to the "shared mora" structure that obtains in the intermediate pre-NC case. Thus, in this language, the three vowel duration types actually correlate with moraic structure: a short vowel is phonologically monomoraic and a long vowel (phonetically approximately twice as long as a short vowel) is phonologically bimoraic; the intermediate pre-NC vowel (one and a half time as long as a short vowel) is also attached to two moras, but the time allocated to the second mora is shared with the following nasal consonant. For Luganda, however, moraic structure does not allow a three-way distinction; as shown in (2b), although of distinct durations, a pre-NC vowel and a long vowel have the same bimoraic structure.

Bernard Tranel

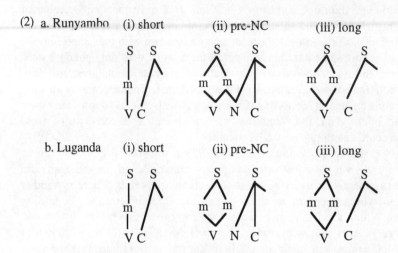

(2) a. Runyambo (i) short (ii) pre-NC (iii) long

b. Luganda (i) short (ii) pre-NC (iii) long

As far as vowel duration is concerned, the moraic structures in (2b) would in fact be appropriate for a third Bantu language, CiYao, which observes a two-way distinction (see Hubbard's Table 13.5): short vowels on the one hand (about 61 ms), and pre-NC and long vowels on the other (both about 131 ms). Another Bantu language, CiTonga, also has a two-way durational distinction, but with short and pre-NC vowels falling together (both about 100 ms) against long vowels (about 240 ms) (see Hubbard's Table 13.5); these facts could be moraically accommodated by assuming that in CiTonga the vowel and the nasal consonant in VNC sequences each occupy a single mora. It would be interesting to determine whether the phonologies of CiYao and CiTonga justify such moraic structures (i.e., whether, phonologically, the moraic status of nasal consonants in VNC sequences is different in these languages?)

Altogether, Luganda appears to be the problematic case regarding the correlation between duration and mora count, (i) by having long (bimoraic) vowels of unexpected duration, and (ii) by having a phonology yielding a two-way moraic contrast, when there is in fact a three-way durational contrast. It is interesting to note, however, that the duration of pre-NC vowels in Luganda is approximately twice that of short vowels, as predicted by the corresponding phonological moraic contrast (compare (2bi) vs. (2bii)). The puzzle may thus be reduced to the extra duration allotted to the long vowels in this language. This extra duration could be explained away functionally by assuming that the long vowels must be kept distinct from the pre-NC vowels. This account, however, would further require an elucidation of the contrary situation found in CiYao, where the duration of pre-NC vowels merges with that of long vowels.

At any rate, mora count, as ultimately delivered at the output of the phonological component, seems too rough a yardstick to determine overall word

196

duration accurately. Timing algorithms must apparently include a component that will, on a language-specific basis, provide the appropriate duration ratios between long and short vowels. In this respect, it would be interesting to find out the range of ratios allowed across languages, as well as the range of ratio variations tolerated across speakers of the same language (see note 1).

A related issue concerns geminate consonants, which according to Hubbard, occur in Luganda (but not in Runyambo). A fourth phonological structure, one involving vowels before geminate consonants, must therefore be added to the three already given in (2b) for Luganda. (Here, (3i–iii) repeat the structures in (2b).) As (3iv) shows, phonologically, a vowel and the first part of a following geminate consonant form a bimoraic sequence (each occupying a mora in the syllable), just as a long vowel gives rise to a bimoraic syllable (see 3iii).

(3) Luganda   (i) short   (ii) pre-NC   (iii) long   (iv) pre-GC

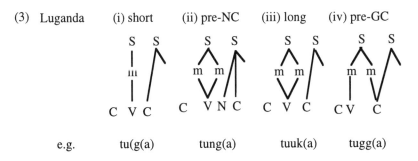

e.g.   tu(g(a)   tung(a)   tuuk(a)   tugg(a)

As Hubbard's Figure 13.3 indicates, a bimoraic structure of the kind presented in (3iv) yields a duration type for the sequences shown which is unsurprisingly longer than the monomoraic case in (3i), but unexpectedly shorter than the other two bimoraic cases in (3ii) and (3iii).

For the sake of completeness, I note here that Hyman (1992: 262–263) in effect suggests the existence of a fifth type of moraic structure in Luganda, one involving stems beginning with VNC sequences. According to Hyman, because of a general constraint in the language against stem-initial long vowels, such vowel-initial stems do not undergo the standard processes of Vowel Spread and Nasal Delinking whose results are illustrated in (3ii); rather, as shown in (4a), the vowel and the nasal consonant each remain dominated by a single mora (the general situation I suggested earlier for CiTonga).

Phonetic measurements involving words containing this additional type of bimoraic stems would be of interest. All the more so, since in all the examples given by Hyman, such as (4b), the initial vowels in these stems actually end up phonetically lengthened because of another process, i.e., prevocalic glide formation in prefixes like /ku-/ or /tu-/. In these cases, the stem vowel spreads to the prefixal mora, presumably yielding yet another moraic structure, namely a trimoraic syllable.

(4) a.

```
        S   S            (b) /... tu-end-a/      → [...tweːndâ]
       /\  /\  ⌐
       m m
       | |
       V N  C
```

e.g. end-

Hubbard's proposed timing algorithms for Luganda and Runyambo are based on mora count and subsequent segmental adjustments within words. My own interpretation of her data suggests the need for a more refined consideration of moraic structures and their segmental contexts on a language-specific basis. The case of Luganda, in particular, seems to show that the types of segments that head moras (bimoraic V vs. bimoraic VC), and the nature of the following segments (NC vs. C after bimoraic V), are of crucial importance in determining phonetic timing, beyond simple mora counting.

With respect to geminate consonants, I note finally that the moraic structures of Bantu VNC sequences make interesting testable duration predictions. Although Hubbard states that geminate consonants do not occur in Runyambo (in the sense that Runyambo does not have structures of the type (3iv) found in Luganda), Runyambo nasal consonants in VNC sequences actually exhibit the structure typical of geminate consonants: as (2aii) shows, the nasal melody branches into a (shared) mora and an onset. This nasal melody should therefore be of comparatively longer duration than a non-branching, purely onset case, such as the same nasal melody in Luganda (see 2bii). On the other hand, it should not (everything else being equal) be as long as a Luganda geminate consonant, such as that in (3iv), because of mora sharing.

14.4 Conclusion

In my view, Hubbard presents a good case for the phonological mora as an essential ingredient in the determination of phonetic timing. Overall, my remarks simply suggest that at least for Luganda, the proposed timing algorithm needs to be supplemented with computations involving consideration of the identity and context of mora heads.

I note that such information has been deemed necessary for phonological operations as well: for example, in line with proposals by Steriade (1990) and Hyman (1992) that "only a subset of moras [may be] tone-bearing in a given language" (Hyman, 1992: 264), Hubbard concludes for Bantu that "a weak mora dominating a non-vocalic segment may not bear tone".

With respect to the phonetic interpretation of phonological moras, language-specific information seems to be required as well in other, unrelated languages. For example, Hayes' treatment of Cahuilla's morphological process of "intensification", whereby a consonant receives greater length, relies on a language-internal contrast between light (monomoraic) and heavy (bimoraic) CVC syllables, as in (5a) and (5b), respectively (Hayes, 1991: 117).

(5)   a. [wélnet] "mean one"   b. [wéllnèt] "very mean one"

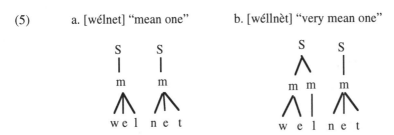

The gemination of the / l / in the intensified form (5b) is captured by making this segment moraic. But moraic coda consonants are not generally interpreted as having extra length (unless they also branch into an onset, as in the case of ambisyllabic geminates). Thus, if Hayes' analysis is correct, Cahuilla requires a special phonetic reading of moraic coda consonants.

The diagrams in (5) prompt a few final remarks. Observe that onset consonants are linked to moras in (5), rather than directly to syllable nodes, as they were in all the other similar diagrams in Hubbard's, and in this paper. At issue here is the mode of prosodic attachment for non-moraic consonants (strict vs. weak layering).[2] Under strict layering, all segments are connected to syllable nodes through moras. Hubbard's hypothesis on the central role of the mora in phonetic timing might be usefully recast within this type of phonological representation where moras exhaustively dominate all melodies. On the other hand, with strict layering, the phonetic interpretation of moraic information becomes less transparent, because non-moraic consonants are represented as if they shared a mora with syllable heads. If the notion of "shared mora" has timing significance, as claimed in the case of Runyambo's VNC sequences (see (2aii) above), an awkward ambiguity arises for phonetic interpretation: which consonants truly share a mora with a vowel and which do not? This ambiguity can be resolved universally for onset consonants, given the standard assumption that onset consonants never contribute weight (i.e., are always non-moraic, that is, never strictly speaking share a mora with a vowel); but for coda consonants, which may moraically contrast, it would seem that the ambiguity can only be lifted on a language-specific basis. Given strict layering,

Bernard Tranel

then, the resolution of this ambiguity would constitute another example where phonetic timing must draw on moraic information that goes beyond simple mora count.

Notes

* Many thanks to Bob Ladd for presenting my comments at the conference in my absence. Additional thanks to him and also to Amalia Arvaniti, Bruce Connell, Kathleen Hubbard, Ian Maddieson, and two anonymous reviewers for providing useful feedback.

1 Data from another Luganda speaker reveal long vowels that are more than three times as long as short vowels (Maddieson, 1993: 12). As pointed out by Kathleen Hubbard (personal communication), the ratio for this other speaker may be particularly skewed because of the short vowels, which he pronounced inordinately short (73 ms vs. 98 ms for her speaker). The two Luganda speakers otherwise exhibit remarkably close average durations for both pre-NC vowels (191 ms vs. 192 ms) and long vowels (237 ms vs. 240 ms).

2 For various practices in this regard, see, among others, Hyman (1985), McCarthy & Prince (1986), Zec (1988), Hayes (1989), Itô (1989), Steriade (1990), Hayes (1991), Tranel (1991), McCarthy & Prince (1993). Broselow (in press) provides some recent discussion on the topic. See also Katada (1990) and Kubozono (this volume) for interesting Japanese evidence regarding the status of onset consonants. See also Beckman (this volume) for remarks on strict layering above vs. below the level of the syllable.

References

Broselow, E. In press. Skeletal positions and moras. In J. Goldsmith (ed.), *A Handbook of Phonological Theory*. Oxford: Blackwell

Hayes, B. 1989. Compensatory lengthening in Moraic Phonology. *Linguistic Inquiry* 20: 253–306.

Hayes, B. 1991. Metrical stress theory: principles and case studies. Ms, University of California, Los Angeles.

Hyman, L. M. 1985. *A Theory of Phonological Weight*. Dordrecht: Foris.

Hyman, L. M. 1992. Moraic mismatches in Bantu. *Phonology* 9: 255–265.

Itô, J. 1989. A prosodic theory of epenthesis. *Natural Language and Linguistic Theory* 7: 217–259.

Katada, F. 1990. On the representation of moras: evidence from a language game. *Linguistic Inquiry* 21: 641–646.

Levin, J. 1985. A metrical theory of syllabicity. Ph.D. dissertation, MIT.

Lowenstamm, J. & J. Kaye. 1986. Compensatory lengthening in Tiberian Hebrew. In L. Wetzels & E. Sezer (eds.), *Studies in Compensatory Lengthening*. Dordrecht: Foris, 97–132.

On phonetic evidence for the phonological mora

Maddieson, I. 1993. Splitting the mora. *UCLA Working Papers in Phonetics* 83: 9–18.
McCarthy, J. & A. Prince. 1986. Prosodic morphology. Ms, University of Massachusetts, Amherst and Brandeis University.
McCarthy, J. & A. Prince. 1993. Prosodic morphology I: constraint interaction and satisfaction. Ms, University of Massachusetts, Amherst and Rutgers University.
Steriade, D. 1990. Moras and other slots. Ms, University of California, Los Angeles.
Tranel, B. 1991. CVC light syllables, geminates and Moraic Theory. *Phonology* 8: 291–302.
Zec, D. 1988. Sonority constraints on prosodic sructure. Ph.D. dissertation, Stanford University.

Part III
Articulatory Organization

15
Prosodic patterns in the coordination of vowel and consonant gestures

CAROLINE L. SMITH*

Both autosegmental representations (e.g. McCarthy, 1981, 1982, 1989; Prince, 1987; Archangeli, 1985; Steriade, 1986) and analyses of articulatory and acoustic data (e.g. Joos, 1948; Öhman, 1966, 1967; Fowler, 1980, 1981, 1983) suggest that vowels and consonants can appear independent of one another. In phenomena such as vowel harmony, phonological processes involving vowels sometimes operate as if an intervocalic consonant were absent; likewise, consonantal harmony processes or co-occurrence restrictions may ignore intervening vowels. In speech production, it has been suggested that there are distinct, identifiable vowels and consonants, but that the two classes of sounds may be produced at least partially simultaneously. It is hypothesized that these periods of simultaneous production ("coproduction", as discussed in Fowler, 1980) are responsible for the context-dependent influences of vowels on consonants, and vice versa.

This study focuses on the organization of the temporal relations between vowels and consonants. It is proposed that languages may choose among alternative ways of coordinating vowels and consonants, and that these alternatives underlie differing prosodic properties that languages exhibit, such as the timing patterns traditionally described as stress-, syllable- or mora-timing. The approach taken here involves defining consonants and vowels in terms of articulatory gestures, following Browman and Goldstein's Articulatory Phonology (e.g. Browman & Goldstein, 1986, 1992). This framework provides a phonological description that explicitly specifies how consonants and vowels are produced, making it possible to predict how differences in articulatory coordination could result in different prosodic characteristics.

In Articulatory Phonology, a gesture is both a primitive of phonological representation and an abstract, dynamic unit of action that controls the coordinated movement of one or more articulators. The spatial and temporal properties of each gesture are specified in terms of tract variables (Saltzman, 1986; Saltzman & Kelso, 1987; Saltzman & Munhall, 1989). These are variables such as Lip Aperture or Tongue Body Constriction Degree, which are characterized by categorically valued descriptors. These descriptors specify the parameters of the task(s) involved in producing the gesture, a task typically being the formation of a constriction in some part of the vocal tract. For instance, in a bilabial gesture such as for /p/, the goal, specified using the Lip Aperture tract variable, is to close the lips together. Temporally, the gesture is specified by the parameters of the tract variable(s) that determine the time course of the movements associated with that gesture (Browman & Goldstein, 1986, 1990a, b, 1992; Saltzman, 1986; Saltzman & Kelso, 1987; Saltzman & Munhall, 1989).

In Articulatory Phonology, gestures are abstract phonological units; by positing a relation between tract variables and actual articulators, the gestures can be associated with the measurable movements of the articulators for the different vowels and consonants. In this way the temporal characteristics of a gesture can be estimated from movement in the part of the vocal tract that would be controlled by that gesture. Of course, measuring the movements of just one articulator is at best an approximation, because a gesture typically involves multiple articulators. For instance, a bilabial closing gesture involves one tract variable (Lip Aperture), but several articulators – the jaw, lower and upper lips.

Because duration is an intrinsic property of gestures, they are well suited to serve as the units of representation in processes that crucially involve the temporal extent of phonological properties. (Steriade's, 1990 gestural analysis of Dorsey's Law provides an example of such a process.) In order to use gestures to represent such processes, it is desirable to specify a structure for the temporal relations among the gestures. It would be expected that only a limited set of the possible temporal relations among gestures would be stable in a given language (Goldstein, 1989). Because gestures are defined in terms of possible vocal tract goals, they are inherently constrained by the physical possibilities of the vocal tract. Their representation is additionally constrained in Articulatory Phonology by limits on the permissible values for dynamic parameters, and can be further constrained by a specific model of the temporal coordination between vowels and consonants.

15.1 Models

Two models of this coordination will be compared here. Both models have been proposed as representations of consonant–vowel relations in English, although they also apply to other languages as well (or better).

In one of these models, each oral gesture is coordinated with the oral gesture preceding it and the one following it (Browman & Goldstein, 1990a); thus, consonants and vowels are mutually coordinated. Vowels can be coordinated with respect to consonants, and vice versa, rather than being exclusively coordinated with other vowels. This arrangement means that the temporal properties of consonants can affect vowels, either as a result of the properties of individual consonants or as a function of the number of consonants. How such an effect comes about depends on exactly how the consonants and vowels are coordinated. For example, in a VCV sequence, suppose one phase of the consonant's production (e.g. the achievement of closure) is coordinated with the preceding vowel and that the following vowel is coordinated with respect to a later phase in the consonant (e.g. its release). If the duration of the consonant were to increase, the time between the two phases of the consonant, and hence between the vowels, might be expected to increase. This model, illustrated on the left-hand side of Figure 15.1, will be referred to as "combined vowel-and-consonant timing".

The other model gives special status to vowels. Öhman (1967) proposed a model of vowel-to-vowel coarticulation in which the production of individual consonants is superimposed on the continuous production of vowels. Similarly, Fowler (1983) summarized a variety of experimental and phonological evidence suggesting that, at least for a sequence of stressed monosyllables, vowels are produced continuously and consonants are coordinated with them. That is, consonants are produced separately from vowels but organized temporally with respect to them; since the production of vowels is continuous, consonants will overlap them (Fowler, 1983).

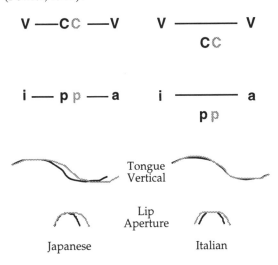

Figure 15.1. Two possible models of coordination between consonant and vowel gestures: the combined vowel-and-consonant model on the left, and the vowel-to-vowel model on the right.

One problem in comparing the model suggested by Fowler with the combined vowel-and-consonant model is that the two models are based on somewhat different concepts of vowel production. If the vowels and consonants are both defined in terms of discrete articulatory gestures, as in Articulatory Phonology, then the production of vowels is not a strictly continuous cycle as it is in Fowler's model. The kind of vowel-based model assumed here is similar to Fowler's, in that it retains the independence of vowels from consonants that characterizes Fowler's model, but it treats each vowel as a discrete gesture that must be coordinated with other vowel gestures. In this model, the oral gesture for each vowel is coordinated with the oral gesture for the preceding vowel, and each consonantal oral gesture is also coordinated with the oral gesture for the preceding vowel.

In this kind of model, consonants are essentially irrelevant to the temporal organization of the vowels, which is dependent on the foot structure (patterning of the stressed and unstressed units). The production of vowels should not be affected by the number of consonants or by any other property of them, such as inherent differences in duration among types of consonants. This prediction contrasts with the prediction of the combined vowel-and-consonant model that the differences in the consonant(s) would affect the vowels. The right-hand side of Figure 15.1 represents this model similar to Fowler's , and will be referred to as "vowel-to-vowel timing".

The distinction between these two possible ways of coordinating vowels and consonants can be seen when the duration of the intervocalic consonant changes. The lower half of Figure 15.1 compares the predictions of the two models for utterances with single and geminate consonants. Stylized traces of tongue and lip movements for the sequence /ipa/ are shown by black lines. When the intervocalic consonant is a geminate /p/ (as shown by the light gray lines in the figure) rather than a singleton, the combined vowel-and-consonant model predicts a reorganization in the timing of the movements associated with the vowels. As the left-hand side of Figure 15.1 suggests, this might be a delay in the second vowel until after the longer consonant has been produced, illustrated by the Lip Aperture trace showing a longer period of closure. But, as shown on the right, in vowel-to-vowel timing, where the coordination of the vowels is independent of the consonant, the prediction would be that no change would occur in the movements associated with the vowels.

These two models reflect, at the very least, different logical possibilities for coordinating consonant and vowel events. It is hypothesized here that both do occur, but that they are found in languages with different prosodic structures, with the vowel-to-vowel model of organization underlying languages whose rhythm has been described as being based on vowels ("stress-" or "syllable-timed"), and the combined vowel-and-consonant model underlying languages that have been described as "mora-timed". The best-known example of a mora-timed language is Japanese (Vance, 1987), in which both vowels and coda consonants "count" in determining the number of moras. Examples of mora-counting in Japanese are given in Table 15.1.

Conversely, for languages in which the rhythm is determined primarily on the basis of the vowels, vowel-to-vowel timing seems more appropriate. Italian will be used here as an example of this kind of language. There is considerable debate over whether Italian is best classified as stress-timed or as yllable-timed (see e.g. Dauer, 1983; Bertinetto, 1983); what is relevant (and widely accepted) is that its rhythm is centered around the vowels; thus, it is in a different category from Japanese. In this study it is the two models of emporal organization of gestures that are being compared, but it is also suggested that these models provide a way of understanding differences between languages that fall into the different rhythm categories known as syllable- and mora-timing.

Table 15.1. Number of moras in Japanese words.

a	"oh!"	1 mora	*kan*	"building"	2 moras
ka	"mosquito"	1 mora	*kana*	(orthography)	2 moras
an	"bean jam"	2 moras	*kanna*	"plane"	3 moras

These two models of temporal organization have been formulated here in terms of an abstract level of gestural control, but to test whether they accurately model consonant–vowel relations in Japanese and Italian requires data showing the actual movements of the articulators that are associated with these gestures. In this study, articulatory data were collected that make it possible to measure the continuous movements associated with the vowel and consonant gestures and examine their temporal behavior. By using articulatory data, it is possible to separate movements associated with consonants, for example lip movement for bilabials, from movements of the tongue associated with vowels. These gestures cannot be measured separately in acoustic data where there is only one channel of data that incorporates both vowels and consonants.

15.2 Experimental method

In this experiment, such movements were measured using the NIH X-ray microbeam facility at the University of Wisconsin, Madison (Nadler, Abbs & Fujimura, 1987; Westbury, 1991). This system recorded the movements of the articulators by means of a microscopic X-ray beam that tracks tiny gold pellets attached to the midline of the tongue, the upper and lower lips, and the lower incisor (to measure jaw movement).

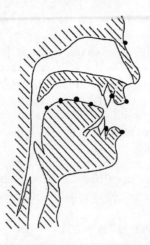

Figure 15.2. Mid-sagittal cross-section of the vocal tract, showing approximate positions of the microbeam pellets on the speaker's articulators (after Abbs & Nadler, 1987).

Figure 15.2 shows a midsagittal cross-section of the vocal tract indicating the approximate positions of the pellets on the articulators for the speakers in this experiment.

Microbeam data consist of trajectories of the pellets in a two-dimensional coordinate system over time, thus showing the movements of the articulators.

Three speakers each of Japanese and Italian produced disyllabic nonsense words consisting of the vowels /a/ and /i/ with single and geminate intervocalic consonants. The target utterances are shown in Table 15.2. These utterances were produced within carrier phrases designed to provide phonetically similar contexts in the two languages: *Boku wa _____ mo aru* ("I have a _____, too.") for Japanese, and *Dica _____ molto* ("Say _____ again and again") in Italian.

Table 15.2. Target utterances.

map(p)i	mip(p)a
mat(t)i	mit(t)a
mam(m)i	mim(m)a
man(n)i	min(n)a

210

Note that utterances of the form /matti/ were not collected for Japanese because a rule of palatalization changes the [t] to [tʃ] before [i]. Experimental constraints resulted in considerable variation in the number of tokens per utterance produced by the speakers: for the Japanese speakers (J1–J3), there were typically 15–20, for Italian speaker 1, about 10, and for the other two Italian speakers (designated I2 and I3), about five.

The positions of the microbeam pellets over time were recorded, and traces of their horizontal and vertical movements were used to measure the intervals between various significant events. The pellet traces chosen for measurement were those that could be most directly associated with tract variables involved in the production of the vowel and consonant gestures. In this way a connection could be made between significant events in the articulatory movements and in the gestures. For most speakers, four pellets were attached to the tongue, as in Figure 15.2, and the horizontal movement of the rearmost pellet and vertical movement of next-rearmost were associated with the vowel gestures.[1] Consonantal gestures for bilabials were associated with the Lip Aperture trace, calculated as the vertical distance between the upper and lower lip pellets.

The locations of the measured events were determined algorithmically. For example, movement onset was identified as the time when the velocity of the movement exceeded zero by a predetermined threshold, and the achievement of the target of a gesture was associated with the time at which the velocity of the movement slowed down to no greater than the threshold value, and approached a displacement plateau. For the tongue movement traces, this threshold was ±10% of the most extreme velocity recorded for a particular trace for a given speaker.

15.3 Results

The different timing patterns that were observed in these utterances will be illustrated by individual tokens, representative of statistically significant effects.[2] For details of the statistical analyses, see Smith (1992).

In Figure 15.3, Japanese speaker J1's production of the utterance /mipa/ is illustrated by the lower of the two acoustic waveforms and the solid black lines in the articulatory movement traces. The vertical lines in the movement traces indicate the times at which the tongue approached the target locations for the vowel gestures. To test the hypothesis that Japanese shows re-organization of the timing between the vowel gestures when the duration of the consonant increases, this utterance was compared to the corresponding utterance with a geminate /p/, shown in Figure 15.3 in the top acoustic waveform and the light gray lines in the movement traces.

The two utterances are lined up in this figure at the offset of the initial /m/ in the Lip Aperture movement trace. Notice that in the utterance with a geminate intervocalic consonant, the second vowel reaches its target position later relative to the first vowel, and the plateau region for the first vowel is longer preceding the geminate. These differences between the utterances with single and geminate consonants were statistically significant for all Japanese speakers. The change in the relation between the vowels that is observed when the consonant is a geminate suggests that the combined vowel-and-consonant timing model is appropriate for Japanese.

Japanese speaker 1

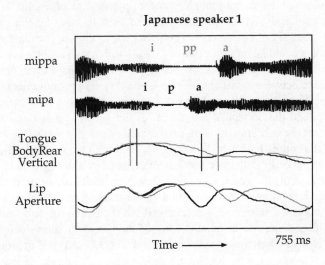

Figure 15.3. Productions of /mipa/ (dark lines) and /mippa/ (light lines) by Japanese speaker J1. The vertical lines mark the times of achievement of target in the tongue movement associated with the vowel gestures.

The contrast between single and geminate consonants shows up in quite a different way in Italian. Productions of /mipa/ and /mippa/ by Italian speaker I1 are shown in Figure 15.4. For this speaker, when the intervocalic consonant is a geminate, the movements of the tongue associated with the vowels remain essentially unchanged from the utterance with a single intervocalic consonant. In particular, the times at which the two vowels reach their target positions (shown by the vertical lines) are virtually the same in the utterances with single and geminate consonants. This result suggests that the consonant has not affected the relative timing of the vowels. For this speaker, there was no significant difference in the interval between vowel targets between utterances with single and geminate consonants. As predicted by the vowel-to-vowel timing model, the vowels seem to be coordinated independently of the consonant.

For speakers I2 and I3 (results for speaker I3 are shown in Figure 15.5), there was a small, statistically significant shortening[3] of the duration of the interval between vowel targets with an intervening geminate consonant. Whereas in Japanese the interval between vowel targets was longer with a geminate

212

intervocalic consonant, for Italian speakers I2 and I3 this interval was slightly shorter. Although these two Italian speakers showed some changes in vocalic durations when the intervocalic consonant was longer, they resembled speaker I1 in that the total duration of the articulatory movements from start to finish of the utterances were extremely similar regardless of the length of the intervocalic consonant. For speakers I2 and I3 there seems to be a trade-off in the durations of the interval from the target to the offset of the first vowel and the interval from the offset of the first vowel to the target of the second vowel. Note that in the utterance with the geminate consonant, the plateau region for the first vowel is shorter but the interval from the offset of the first vowel to the target of the second vowel is much longer, with the result that the time from vowel target to vowel target is not very different from that observed with the single consonant.

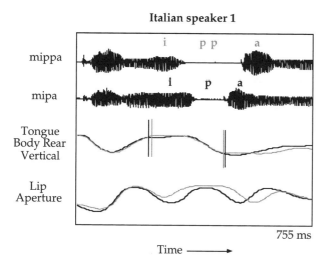

Figure 15.4. Productions of /mipa/ (dark lines) and /mippa/ (light lines) by Italian speaker I1. The vertical lines mark the times of achievement of target in the tongue movement associated with the vowel gestures.

This pattern suggests that since the tendency for speakers I2 and I3 is that the target-to-target interval does not vary much, all the Italian speakers are more alike than may initially appear to be the case. Nonetheless, the fact that speakers I2 and I3 do show a difference between the single and geminate utterances for the interval between vowel targets, implies that the length of the consonant may affect the vowels to some extent. Therefore, speakers I2 and I3, who behaved similarly, contradict the strongest form of the vowel-based hypothesis, which predicted that the vowels would be unaffected by a change in the consonants. The strong form of the vowel-to-vowel timing hypothesis is completely borne

213

out only for Italian speaker I1. However, all the Italian speakers clearly differ from the Japanese speakers. It remains unclear, however, to what extent the patterns shown by the Italian speakers can be described by the vowel-based hypothesis alone.

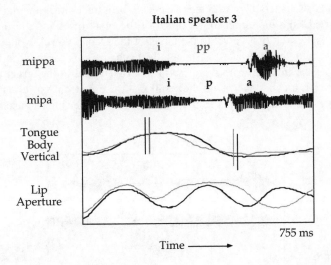

Figure 15.5. Productions of /mipa/ (dark lines) and /mippa/ (light lines) by Italian speaker I3. The vertical lines mark the times of achievement of target in the tongue movement associated with the vowel gestures.

15.4 Modeling

To illustrate how the measured durational changes between utterances with single and geminate consonants could arise from limited changes to the relations among gestures, models of timing were constructed for Japanese and Italian, with the timing relations among the gestures specified in terms of phasing. The modeling was done by manipulating parameters that specify the temporal characteristics of the individual vowel and consonant gestures and their relative phasing. For each speaker, these parameters were manipulated to create the best possible model structured in accordance with the hypothesized timing organization; that is, the models for Japanese speakers used the vowel-and-consonant organization and the models for Italian speakers the vowel-to-vowel organization. The basic structures for the models are shown in Figure 15.6, where the rounded boxes represent consonant and vowel gestures and the lines between them show the phasing relations that were specified in the models.

The coordination of vowel and consonant gestures

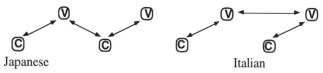

Japanese   Italian

Figure 15.6. Intergestural phasing relations used in the models.

Figure 15.7 illustrates how the differences between utterances with single and geminate consonants were modeled; the boxes represent abstract gestures and the lines between them connect phases in the gestures that were specified to occur at the same times. The black lines correspond to the model for the utterance with a single consonant, and the light gray lines show the model for the utterances with a geminate consonant. These diagrams are drawn to scale, and the width of the boxes reflects the measured durations, for one speaker of each language (J1 and I3), of the movements associated with the different gestures.

These models were used to predict durations of intervals between pairs of events that had been identified in the articulatory movements, such as the events marked by vertical lines in Figures 15.3, 15.4, and 15.5. The differences in these durations between the utterances with single and geminate consonants were then

Japanese speaker 1

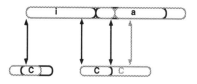

Italian speaker 3

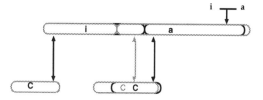

Figure 15.7. Structures of the models for Japanese and Italian. Each box corresponds to a gesture: the width is scaled to the mean duration of the articulatory movements associated with that gesture, from onset to end of the period of activation, for the individual speaker.

215

calculated, and the predicted and measured differences were compared. The modeling procedure minimized the number of parameters whose values varied between the utterances with single and geminate consonants, while optimizing the r^2 correlation between the measured and predicted differences in durations. For each speaker, one model was optimized using the structure hypothesized for that speaker's language. The same model was used for Italian speakers I2 and I3. In addition, all of these models were tested on the data for every speaker, so that both structures were tested on speakers of both languages. Speakers of each language were best modeled (that is, the fit had the highest r^2) by the models using the structure that had been hypothesized to reflect the patterns of their language. Even when using models optimized for other speakers, better fits were found with models for speakers of the same language, which lends support to the initial assumption that the two languages require models with different structures. A sample of the modeled r^2 values is given in Table 15.3, which shows results for utterances of the form $miC(C)a$.[4] The entries in the table are the r^2 values between the differences between the measured interval durations in single and geminate utterances and the differences predicted by the models developed for each of the speakers. Results for utterances of the form $miC(C)a$ are shown here. The models are named for the speaker(s) they were developed for; r^2 values for speakers' own models are in boldface in the table. Variables were the phasing relations between pairs of gestures; the stiffness of the vowel gestures was also varied between utterances with single and geminate consonants for models J3, I1, and I2 & 3.

This kind of modeling has the advantage of capturing the numerous measured differences between utterances with singleand geminate consonants with relatively few parameterized differences, reducing much variability to a few

Table 15.3. Fits of the durational differences between utterances with single and geminate consonants for the intervals between articulatory events.

	Japanese-style models (V-and-C)			Italian-style models (V–V)	
Speaker	J1	J2	J3	I1	I2&I3
J1	**.91**	.57	.89	.31	.26
J2	.69	**.92**	.68	.74	.73
J3	.90	.53	**.99**	.02	.01
I1	.02	.00	.03	**.93**	.80
I2	.15	.00	.23	.66	**.88**
I3	.20	.24	.16	.83	**.96**

interpretable differences. The similarity of the models obtained for the three Italian speakers suggests that they were all showing similar temporal organization, despite the superficial differences among them.

15.4.1 Gestural representation of geminates

Since the two structures for temporal organization are being contrasted with respect to differences due to consonantal length contrast, the criterion of goodness-of-fit for the models was how accurately they predicted the pattern of differences, between single and geminate utterances. Thus a crucial aspect of the models is how the single/geminate contrast is represented, in two ways – the specific consonantal gesture(s) and the differences in the utterance as a whole that result from this contrast. The modeling procedure outlined above assesses the overall validity of the representation; it remains to consider how the length contrast should be modeled in the consonantal gesture.

In both the models shown in Figure 15.7, a geminate consonant was modeled as one gesture with different parameter values from those for the gesture for a single consonant. In both languages the interval during which the lips or tongue tip remained in a closed position was significantly longer for the geminate than for the single consonant. This pattern was modeled by having the gesture for a geminate consonant remain active for a longer time after reaching its target position than the gesture for a single consonant.

For the Japanese speakers, and Italian speakers I1 and I3, in addition, the lips moved more slowly when forming the constriction for a geminate than a singleton, so the duration of the movement towards the target was significantly longer. This difference was modeled by reducing the stiffness of the gesture for the geminate versus the single consonant. Both the longer period of activation and the decreased stiffness have the effect of increasing the duration of the gesture for a geminate. These parameter changes are schematized in Figure 15.8. These models require specification of the characteristics of the movement forming a constriction and, for consonants, the duration of the period of activation. For vowels, the end of the period of activation was not specified; how long the gesture remains active depends on the timing of the following gestures.

The models presented here, which represent geminate consonants by a single gesture, offer an economical way of getting a good correspondence with the articulatory data. While the goal of the modeling was to achieve a good fit of the data, ideally the model should reflect the phonological structure of the utterances being modeled. Conceptually, a model using two gestures to represent a geminate may be more appealing. In Articulatory Phonology, phonological contrasts (such as presence or absence of voicing) are represented by the presence or absence of a gesture. Thus, adding a gesture to geminate a consonant

Single consonant    **One-gesture geminate**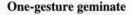

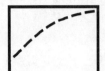   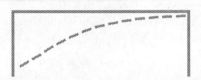

Figure 15.8. Hypothetical gestural representation (box) and resulting trajectory of a tract variable towards its target (dashed line) for gestures associated with single and geminate consonants, with the geminate consonant modeled as a single gesture having lower stiffness and a longer period of activation than the single consonant.

would better match the representation of other kinds of phonological contrasts. This seems appropriate for languages such as Japanese and Italian, in which consonant length is phonologically contrastive. A two-gesture representation also reflects the fact that phonologically, geminates often seem to behave like two units (see e.g. Schein & Steriade, 1986).

In a two-gesture representation of geminates, the parameters (stiffness and phasing) for each of the two gestures in a geminate would have to be specified, as for any other gesture. If each of these gestures had the same parameter values as the gesture for a single consonant, then the total duration of the geminate would be greater than that of a single consonant. But exactly how much greater would depend on the phasing between the two gestures. This phasing relation might well vary between languages. Figure 15.9 illustrates two possible phasing relations between the two gestures of a geminate. The total duration of the geminate would, of course, be greater in the right diagram in Figure 15.9. However, in order for two gestures to form a geminate, rather than two separate consonants, they must be timed in such a way that the articulators maintain the target configuration of the vocal tract. In the right diagram of Figure 15.9, the delay between the two gestures may be too great to maintain the target configuration. The extent of overlap between the two hypothetical gestures cannot be determined from the data: in the movement traces the geminates, like the singletons, had a single articulatory maximum, i.e., they showed up as a single hump. Thus relating this two-gesture model to the articulatory data is problematic.

The most constrained form of the two-gesture model would be to assume that each of the two gestures has the same parameters as the gesture for a single consonant. However, recall that for most of the speakers the movement to form a geminate closure was significantly slower than for a single closure. This implies that if a geminate consists of a pair of gestures, at least the first one would have to have a lower stiffness than if it were alone. Thus, even for a two-gesture model, the dynamic parameters for a geminate consonant have to be different from the parameters for a single consonant. This means that a two-gesture model effectively requires two changes to represent a single phonological contrast, rather than the one change (the parameter values) that is required by the one-

Two-gesture geminates

Figure 15.9. Model of a geminate consonant as two gestures. The figure illustrates a hypothetical gestural representation (box) and resulting trajectory of a tract variable towards its target (dashed line) for two alternate phasing relations between the two gestures of the geminate.

gesture representation. For this reason, the two-gesture model appears to be a more costly approach.

15.4.2 Generalization of results for geminates to utterances with intervocalic clusters

Because the single and geminate consonants contrast only in the time domain, they were used in this study for the comparison of the timing structures of Japanese and Italian. However, to ensure that the observed differences between the utterances with single and geminate consonants were general effects of durational differences, and not particular to geminates, utterances with the homorganic cluster /mp/ were also measured and compared to the utterances with geminates.[5] There were very few statistically significant differences in the durations of the various measured intervals, and where there were differences, they were similar in magnitude to the small differences that had been observed between oral and nasal geminates – that is between /pp/ and /mm/, /tt/ and /nn/. In general, durations of the measured intervals in utterances with the intervocalic cluster seemed to be mostly dependent on the nasality of the adjacent part of the cluster: that is, measures relating to the first part of the utterance tended not to differ between /mp/ and /mm/, and measures of the second part tended to pattern similarly in /mp/ and /pp/. This suggests that the cluster does not differ from the geminates in any way relating to length, but that it does constitute a sequence with respect to nasality.

The /mp/ cluster tested in this experiment could be represented as a single labial gesture with coordinated velic opening and closing gestures. However, heterorganic clusters would have to be specified using two or more oral gestures; thus in general, clusters cannot be distinguished from single consonants merely by altering the parameters of a single gesture. Therefore, if a single-gesture representation is adopted for geminates, it could not be extended to clusters. This restriction seems undesirable, since it appears that the cluster and the geminates pattern in the same way with respect to durational effects. The similar patterning

Caroline L. Smith

of clusters and geminates supports the proposal for representing geminates as two gestures, rather than one.

15.5 Conclusion

The results presented here show how minimal manipulation of structural relations organizing dynamic primitives (gestures) can give rise to complex, inter-related surface iming patterns. One of the principal advantages of Articulatory Phonology is that the intrinsic duration of gestures facilitates the representation of emporal relations. The patterns of temporal organization observed among articulatory gestures can vary among languages, but seem to vary in a way that corresponds to the traditional descriptions of languages' rhythms, and can be described in terms of how different gestures are coordinated in time. Steriade's (1990) work has also suggested that some phonological processes may be interpretable as changes in the phasing of consonants and vowels relative to each other. In the framework of Articulatory Phonology, the account of the patterning of such phonological processes is related to cross-linguistic differences in rhythmic units and durational patterns. Different structural relations among gestures are one of the ways that languages create different rhythms.

Notes

* This work was supported by NSF grant BNS 8820099 and NIH grant DC 00121 to Haskins Laboratories. Support during the preparation of this manuscript was provided by a fellowship from the Fondation Fyssen. I thank Cathe Browman, Louis Goldstein, Ian Maddieson, and Ignatius Mattingly for advice and comments on various versions of this material, but do not wish to imply that any of them is responsible for remaining flaws.

1 Only two tongue pellets could be used with speaker I3, so the horizontal and vertical movements of the rearmost pellet were measured.
2 Each movement trace was analyzed individually, and separate analyses of variance were performed for each vowel pattern (*a-i* and *i-a*) for each speaker. The factors in these analyses were length and nasality of the intervocalic consonant. The significance level for results reported here was $p < 0.05$.
3 Statistically non-significant in the vertical movement of the Tongue Body for speaker I3.
4 Exceptionally, Table 15.3 shows that the Italian models fit this set of utterances from Japanese speaker J2 quite well: this goodness-of-fit was not found in the *maC(C)i* utterances.

5 It was not possible to make a direct statistical comparison between the utterances with single consonants and those with clusters.

References

Abbs, J. H. & R. D. Nadler. 1987. *User's Manual for the University of Wisconsin X-Ray Microbeam.* Madison, WI: Waisman Center.

Archangeli, D. 1985. Yokuts harmony: coplanar representation in nonlinear phonology. *Linguistic Inquiry* 16: 335–372.

Bertinetto, P. M. 1983. Ancora sull'italiano come lingua ad isocronia sillabica. In *Scritti Linguistici in onore di Giovan Battista Pellegrini* II. Pisa: Pacini, 1073–1082.

Browman, C. P. & L. Goldstein. 1986. Towards an articulatory phonology. *Phonology Yearbook* 3: 219–252.

Browman, C. P. & L. Goldstein. 1990a. Tiers in articulatory phonology, with some implications for casual speech. In J. Kingston & M. E. Beckman (eds.), *Papers in Laboratory Phonology I: Between the Grammar and the Physics of Speech.* Cambridge: Cambridge University Press, 341–376.

Browman, C. P. & L. Goldstein. 1990b. Gestural specification using dynamically–defined articulatory structures. *Journal of Phonetics* 18: 299–320.

Browman, C. P. & L. Goldstein. 1992. Articulatory phonology: an overview. *Phonetica* 49: 155–180.

Dauer, R. M. 1983. Stress-timing and syllable-timing reanalyzed. *Journal of Phonetics* 11: 51–62.

Fowler, C. A. 1980. Coarticulation and theories of extrinsic timing control. *Journal of Phonetics* 8: 113–133.

Fowler, C. A. 1981. A relationship between coarticulation and compensatory shortening. *Phonetica* 38: 35–50.

Fowler, C. A. 1983. Converging sources of evidence on spoken and perceived rhythms of speech: cyclic production of vowels in monosyllabic stress feet. *Journal of Experimental Psychology: General* 112: 386–412.

Goldstein, L. 1989. On the domain of the Quantal Theory. *Journal of Phonetics* 17: 91–97.

Joos, M. 1948. *Acoustic Phonetics* (Language Monographs No. 23). Baltimore: Linguistic Society of America at the Waverly Press.

McCarthy, J. J. 1981. A prosodic theory of nonconcatenative morphology. *Linguistic Inquiry* 12: 373–418.

McCarthy, J. J. 1982. Prosodic templates, morphemic templates, and morphemic tiers. In H. van der Hulst & N. Smith (eds.), *The Structure of Phonological Representations, Part I.* Dordrecht: Foris, 191–224.

McCarthy, J. J. 1989. Linear ordering in phonological representation. *Linguistic Inquiry* 20: 71–99.

Nadler, R. D., J. H. Abbs & O. Fujimura. 1987. Speech movement research using the new x-ray microbeam system. *Proceedings of the XIth International Congress of Phonetic Sciences.* Tallinn, 1: 221–224.

Caroline L. Smith

Öhman, S. E. G. 1966. Coarticulation in VCV utterances: spectrographic measurements. *Journal of the Acoustical Society of America* 39: 51–168.

Öhman, S. E. G. 1967. Numerical model of coarticulation. *Journal of the Acoustical Society of America* 41: 310–320.

Prince, A. 1987. Planes and copying. *Linguistic Inquiry* 18: 491–509.

Saltzman, E. 1986. Task dynamic coordination of the speech articulators: a preliminary model. In H. Heuer & C. Fromm (eds.), *Generation and Modulation of Action Patterns*. Experimental Brain Research Series 15. New York: Springer-Verlag, 129–144.

Saltzman, E. & J. A. S. Kelso. 1987. Skilled actions: a task–dynamical approach. *Psychological Review* 94: 84–106.

Saltzman, E. & K. G. Munhall. 1989. A dynamical approach to gestural patterning in speech production. *Ecological Psychology* 1: 333–382.

Schein, B. & D. Steriade. 1986. On geminates. *Linguistic Inquiry* 17: 691–744.

Smith, C. 1992. The temporal organization of vowels and consonants. Ph.D. dissertation, Yale University.

Steriade, D. 1986. Yokuts and the vowel plane. *Linguistic Inquiry* 17: 29–146.

Steriade, D. 1990. Gestures and autosegments: comments on Browman and Goldstein's "Gestures in Articulatory Phonology". In J. Kingston & M. E. Beckman (eds.), *Papers in Laboratory Phonology I: Between the Grammar and Physics of Speech*. Cambridge: Cambridge University Press, 382–397.

Vance, T. J. 1987. *An Introduction to Japanese Phonology*. Albany, NY: State University of New York Press.

Westbury, J. R. 1991. The significance and measurement of head position during speech production experiments using the X-ray microbeam system. *Journal of the Acoustical Society of America* 89: 1782–1791.

16
"Where" is timing? Comments on Smith

RICHARD OGDEN*

16.1 Caroline Smith's main points

At the heart of Smith's (henceforth CS) study is an attempt to describe rhythm adequately in an Articulatory Phonology framework. Two models of vowel and consonant organization are investigated, and CS suggests that these models of gestural coordination may give rise to timing patterns traditionally described as syllable- and mora-timing. If the primitives of phonological statement are gestures, then a gestural understanding of syllable- vs. mora-timing is important, since it helps to make it clearer how a purely gestural definition of "syllable" or "mora" (i.e. one in terms of the primitives of the statement) could be given. Some durational characteristics of rhythmical pieces apparently fall out from the articulatory model. CS's work makes a useful contribution to Articulatory Phonology in exploring the different possible timing relations that can hold between gestures of different types and in relating these to rhythm more generally.

The relationship between consonants and vowels may be more complex than just linear sequencing. Different organization of consonant and vowel gestures in relation to one another gives rise to syllable- vs. mora-timing.

Syllable-timing, as exemplified by Italian, has vowels coordinated with one another and consonants overlaid on to the vowels. CS calls this "vowel-to-vowel timing", and it seems to be an instantiation of Fowler's (1980) coproduction model. In mora-timing on the other hand, as exemplified by Japanese, consonants are coordinated with vowels and vice versa. CS calls this "combined consonant-and-vowel timing." Observable differences in vowel durations (i.e. observations on the "output," Browman & Goldstein 1992) are a product of differences in the way consonant and vowel gestures are overlaid (all other

223

things being equal), which in turn depends upon what form of timing a language employs.

16.2 Some general observations

The terms "consonant" and "vowel" in Articulatory Phonology need formal definition. Gestures are not of themselves consonantal; it is the degree of stiffness specified in the task dynamic model which determines consonantality (Browman & Goldstein, 1990: 306). In this way, in Articulatory Phonology, the distinction between consonants and vowels is less rigid than in other phonologies, and this seems to be an attractive property of it. Consonants and vowels are products of the gestural score, the output. I wonder therefore what sense it makes to talk about the relative timing of 'consonant and vowel gestures' as CS does; "consonant" and "vowel" are no more than shorthand terms in Articulatory Phonology, but it is a mistake to allow shorthand terms to become longhand ones. As it stands, CS's model of timing relies on consonant and vowel as special categories in the phonology; this should be formalized more rigorously.

Duration is an intrinsic property of gestures. However it seems to me that the stiffness of the gestures with respect to one another (stiffness being what determines duration), is not predictable on this purely physical basis, but needs stating explicitly. What degree of stiffness can be associated with any particular gesture? The answer, as I hope to show, is language-specific, and cannot be said to fall out from general physical descriptions. Furthermore, I shall show that rhythm and gemination are not *merely* about timing.

Structure, syntagmatic relations, could be more appropriately seen as the driving factor behind rhythm, regardless of whether rhythm is syllable-based or mora-based. Exploring syntagmatic relations is an important part of studying the rhythms of languages, where rhythm can be stated with reference to at least: duration, amplitude, and fundamental frequency; perhaps also vowel qualities and terms in C-systems.[1] I shall go on to look at this matter in more detail in relation to Finnish.

16.3 Timing and rhythm in Baltic-Finnic

Finnish is said to have both long and short consonants and vowels, and there are almost no restrictions on the combinations of long and short which appear in Finnish. It is worthwhile, however, to look closely at phonetic data because the situation is not as simple as one might expect from a cursory reading of the literature, nor from the phonemic transcriptions so often used to represent Finnish phonetics. The broad phonetic transcriptions in (1) are from the speech of a native of Kuopio, in Savo.

It is, I think, a mistake to look only at the durations of the consonantal or vocalic portions in isolation. Equally important are the relations that obtain over the disyllabic piece.[2] So in the word for "flower" (nominative form) we find a long consonantal portion followed by a very short vocalic portion and in the genitive form a short consonantal portion followed by a "half-long" vocalic and another consonantal portion. There are durational differences throughout the word. An analysis which looks only at whether the consonant is "geminate" or not misses this important observation, which is of course crucial to the description of rhythms in Finnish. Such an analysis is the "standard" one found in generative phonology (e.g. Keyser & Kiparsky, 1984), which without exception uses phonemic material. Phonemic material is highly impoverished from a phonetic point of view.

[kukɑ·n]	"flower" (gen. sg.)	[kukːǎ]	"flower" (nom sg)
[kukɑːn]	"anyone"		
[sɑli·]	"hall"	[sɑlˑmǐ]	"straits, sound"
[tuli·]	"fire"	[tulːĭ]	"customs"

Note that there are four degrees of length marked in these broad transcriptions (cf. also Wiik, 81:105): [v̌], [v], [vˑ], [vː], where [v] stands for any symbol. Three of these degrees of duration (very short, short and half-long) are relevant to the description of Finnish **short**[3] consonants and vowels. That this is not just an impression is confirmed by Lehtonen (1970), an extensive study of the durations of consonantal and vocalic segments in the acoustic domain. Lehtonen recorded 10 native speakers producing words of particular CV structures in a test frame and measured and compared the durations of consonantal and vocalic portions to see what relations held between adjacent segments. A summary of these measurements appears in Figure 16.1.

I shall focus on the vocalic portions of the second syllable. These durations fall into three groups (all four transcribed durations can be illustrated only with reference to *both* syllables), which I shall call very short (about 50 ms), half-long (about 100 ms) and long (from 120 ms upwards). These are transcribed as [v̌], [vˑ], [vː] respectively. It can be seen that all but two vocalic portions in Lehtonen's data can be classified as long or very short. The portions of half-long duration occur after initial syllables with the general phonetic shape CV– (the first two examples at I in the diagram). Long vocalic portions are found in this position (the last two examples of I–IV), while very short ones are not. Very short vocalic portions are exemplified in the first two examples of II–IV in the diagram. These occur when the general phonetic shape of the first syllable is

Richard Ogden

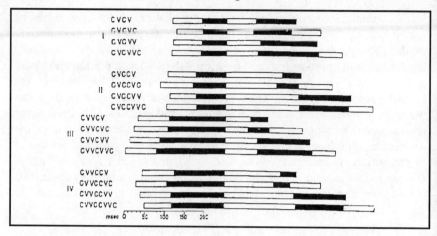

Figure 16.1. Durational distribution of consonantal and vocalic portions in different disyllabic word structures. Consonants are symbolized with blank and vowels with black bars. (From Lehtonen, 1970).

CVC, CVV or CVVC. We may therefore conclude that vocalic portions of half-long duration are exponents of phonologically **short** Vs. In other words, **short** Vs have as their exponents vowels of half-long duration after a preceding **light** syllable (one mora, μ), but vowels of very short duration after a preceding **heavy** syllable (two moras, μμ). In the first case, the second syllable vowel is associated with the word's second mora, in the second case it is associated with the word's third mora.

Wiik (1991) proposes that the Baltic-Finnic languages, which include Finnish, are neither mora-timed nor syllable-timed (nor for that matter stress-timed), but are *foot-timed* Wiik's analysis is that Finnish counts moras. Heavy syllables have two moras, and light ones have one mora. A syllable has only one or two moras in Finnish; it cannot be overlong, i.e., have three moras, even though long vowels can be followed by long consonants.

Lehtonen's results can in general be seen to support Wiik's claim. But why should there be portions we can describe as half long at all? After all if there are only two contrastive categories at the phonological level (**short** and **long**), why should there be *three* clusters of durations at the phonetic level (very short, half-long, long)? The answer, I think, lies in Wiik's suggestion, that the second mora of Baltic-Finnic words is associated with extra duration at the phonetic level. In other words, the exponents of a unit in μ2 will include longer duration than the "same" unit in μ1. In Estonian (a close relative of Finnish, whose quantity system is the subject of much debate), we see long vocalic portions as well as F_0 contours focused on the material which expones μ2 (cf. Lehiste, 1975), as in the spectrograms and F_0 traces in Figure 16.2, of the words [sʏnɑ·], "word", and

226

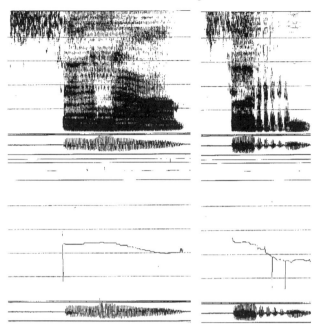

Figure 16.2. Wide-band spectrograms and F_0 plots of Estonian [sɤnɑˑ], "word", and [sɤrˑm], "finger".

[sɤrˑm], "finger". As Lehtonen writes, in Finnish the first two moras constitute a timing unit. Wiik calls this and also three-mora structures a foot, and for him the foot is an essential unit of Baltic-Finnic timing.

Let us return to the questions CS raises. The duration of the second syllable's vocalic portion depends on whether the preceding syllable is **heavy** or **light**, so **CV** structure in just the *second* syllable is not enough to explain duration. The vocalic portions of half long duration cannot be the exponent of one and a half **V**s (with **short** as **V** and **long** as **VV**) according to current ideas, because timing in most modern phonology is seen as categorial rather than gradient. In the Finnish words for "flower" we could describe the differences in timing as differences in the association of **C**s and **V**s to moras, in turn determined by grammatical structure; moras, instead of being determined by **CV** structure, could drive **CV** structure, if we understand **CV** to mean a broad phonetic rather than a strictly abstract and phonological level of description.[4] This seems broadly compatible with the conclusion reached by CS that modeling geminates with one gesture is more economical than using a two-gesture approach; it overcomes difficulties of answering the question "where does the second C come from?"

227

CS's model suggests that vowel-to-vowel duration in syllable-timed languages (modeled by vowel-to-vowel coordination) is a product of the number of consonant gestures overlaid onto a vowel gesture. Could it be that in structures with a **heavy** first syllable the second vowel is short and in structures with a **light** first syllable it is longer because there are more consonants in the first case than in the second? Perhaps. But this does not explain why in generalized phonetic structures of the form $CVC_1CV\ C_1$ is so long and longer than in CVC_1V structures. The mora-timing model (combined consonant and vowel timing), however, predicts that the vowels will have more or less equal duration whichever syllable they occur in. It could only account for different vowel durations if the gestures had different context-sensitive degrees of stiffness: and if that were the case, there would have to be three contrasting lengths in the phonology. There is no clear statement of the definition of phonological "sameness" in Articulatory Phonology, so it remains unclear to me what it would mean to say "three contrasting lengths" in terms of Articulatory Phonology.

Vowel-to-vowel timing will not necessarily predict syllable weight because weight can depend on the number of medial Cs. Some way to relate the fact that material in the second mora (whether consonantal or vocalic) is longer than in the first mora is also needed – there is no way to relate these two facts without some notion of higher structure. Some higher unit of organization, or some way of counting Vs and Cs is required. According to Wiik and Lehtonen, feet – or groups of moras – rather than individual moras are the domain of timing. Can "foot," "mora," "syllable," "heavy" or "light" be given definitions in terms of the primes of Articulatory Phonology, i.e., gestures? CS offers a partial answer to this question, expressed in terms of the way gestures are timed in relation to each other. But unless and until "consonant gesture" and "vowel gesture" can be replaced with some more formal and rigorous definition in terms of Articulatory Phonology's primes, it cannot be fully answered.

Rhythm, which is in part what moras and syllables are meant to explain, is not just a matter of timing slots, nor of syllables or moras alone. Rhythm is a product of temporal relationships. English *patter* does not have the same rhythm as Finnish *pata*, although both words could be characterized as CVCV, since they both have two light syllables and according to a moraic description two moras. They both make up one foot. No one has yet offered an explanation for how observable rhythmical differences can be explained by general principles of phonetic implementation or through the intrinsic durations of gestures. I believe, like the Firthians, that timing relations must be an integral part of the statement of *phonetic exponency* rather than part of the phonological statement *per se*. I see Articulatory Phonology primarily as part of a theory of phonetic exponency, not of phonology.

Phonology need only express a relationship between its terms; its main function is to state that there are contrasts. Saying *how those contrasts are realized* is part of the statement of phonetic exponency, whether in the parametric, or more controversially, in the temporal domain. Coleman (1994) and Ogden (1992) have shown how timing is handled in a neo-Firthian framework for speech synthesis. The most explicit Firthian statement on timing comes from Jack Carnochan: "order and place in structure do not correlate with sequence in time . . . there is no time in structure, there is no sequence in structure; time and sequence are with reference to the utterance, order and place are with reference to the structure" (Carnochan, 1962: 158). At least part of this is echoed by McCarthy (1989: 90ff.) but he does not take the abstraction as far as the Firthians. Articulatory Phonology is developing comparatively simple explanations of some complex speech processes, but it seems to offer little in the way of formal definition of what could be contrastive, or how contrast is formally defined in gestural terms. There is so far no adequate characterization of what counts as same or different, particularly in the temporal domain.

16.4 The representation of geminates

Let us now go on to consider how to represent geminates. Phonetically long portions are treated as geminates and phonetically short portions as singletons (cf. Clements, 1986: 39). CS has two suggestions on how to represent them using Articulatory Phonology. One is to combine two gestures, the other is to make one gesture particularly long by reducing its stiffness. This latter option corresponds well with the slower movement into a geminate closure which CS observes. Both possibilities she considers involve timing as the crucial distinguishing factor. The Firthian view is that gemination is not necessarily *just* a temporal phenomenon.

In Finnish, a good case can be made for an abstract description of geminates. Pairs like the following can be observed:

(2)   [matːŏ]   [matoˑn]   "rug" (nominative & genitive singular)

[matoˑ]   [madoˑn]   "worm" (nominative & genitive singular)

while forms like [madoˑ] and [matːŏn] are not just unattested but unattestable: they are not well-formed words. When the second syllable is *closed* and *short* only two possible syllable-initial apical plosives are found, [t] and [d]. When it is *open*, only [tː] and [t] are found. Thus there is only one two-way contrast which we can label as **g** and **ng** respectively, where **g** is a mnemonic for "gemination". The exponents of gemination must be stated with reference to

Richard Ogden

syllable-level phonological categories. **g** and **ng** also have implications for the durations of vocalic portions in the second syllable. The figures below (**p** in Figure 16.3 represents a three-term plosivity system) are a first (and imperfect) attempt at describing the phonological structures for the broad phonetic transcriptions in (1) and (2). Note that there is no "deletion", and need not be any (i.e., the rewriting of CC as C) (cf. Ogden 1993).

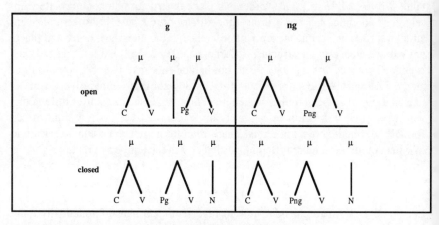

Figure 16.3. Possible structures for some Finnish nominals.

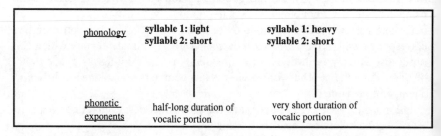

Figure 16.4. The relationship of phonological category to phonetic exponents: Note the importance of structural information.

Exponents can be stated in terms of articulation or acoustics, or both. If CS's theory is right, some of the durational facts about Finnish (such as the very short vowels in the second syllable after a heavy initial syllable) might fall out from the articulatory model and the way gestures are coordinated with each other; but note that according to the Firthian view this is part of the phonetic exponency rather than part of the phonological statement, because in the Firthian view phonological statements are entirely abstract. The phonological statement is devoid of phonetic content, and is set up only on the bases of contrast and identity. This is in stark contrast with Articulatory Phonology, whose terms are

230

simultaneously primitives of phonological representation and a unit of action that controls movements of articulators.

When discussing the half-long vowel of the second syllable in Finnish, I analyzed it as a *short* vowel phonologically. I could have said that there are three degrees of *length* in the second syllable; the arguments in favor of this would be purely phonetic and not phonological. In treating a vocalic portion of half-long duration as phonologically **short**, time is part of the statement of phonetic exponency, *with reference to structure* – this reference to structure is essential. In this case the relevant part of structure would be the weight of the preceding syllable. The classic generative view of Finnish, as epitomized by Keyser & Kiparsky (1984), uses two contrastive lengths at the phonological level, thereby abstracting duration away. So by saying that time is part of the statement of phonetic exponency, I am not suggesting that we do anything new; just that the principle should be applied thoroughly, and crucially, that statements of exponency should be made, otherwise the phonological terms have no meaning because it would not be possible to connect the phonological statement back to the phonic material on which it is based; thus it is not amenable to verification. The other option is to end up with all sorts of inelegancies in the statement which have no phonological, only a phonetic, basis.

CS's interpretations of "geminate" are based on the idea that gemination is a purely temporal phenomenon; i.e., geminates involve longer hold phases, or two gestures vs. one gesture, and nothing more. However in Malayalam (Local & Simpson, 1988) gemination as a term involves at least: phonatory quality, resonance of consonantal and vocalic portions (with "geminates" being typically darker in quality), different rhythmic relations between adjacent syllables, tense vs. lax articulations, and different patterns of variability associated with geminate vs. non-geminate pieces (see Figure 16.5). Gemination is also a term in the wider grammatical statement, part of the statement of the structures of transitive and intransitive verbs.

How can a form of statement whose categories are essentially phonetic, like Articulatory Phonology, capture all this information without redundancy, and without also the arbitrary choice of the primacy of one phonetic feature over others (cf. Sprigg, 1961)? As long as gestures are the primes of the analysis, it is hard to see how structural constraints or language-specific conventional phonetic associations, such as those in Malayalam, can be stated formally.

Finnish presents a different case from Malayalam: words that alternate CVCCV and CVCVC at the broad phonetic level display rhythmic alternations which we can characterize as a difference in the way moras associate with other material. The observable durational and rhythmical patterns in the language can be fairly satisfactorily explained by an analysis which makes use of moras and the phonological structure $CVC^{\pi}V$, where π stands for the prosodic system of **g**

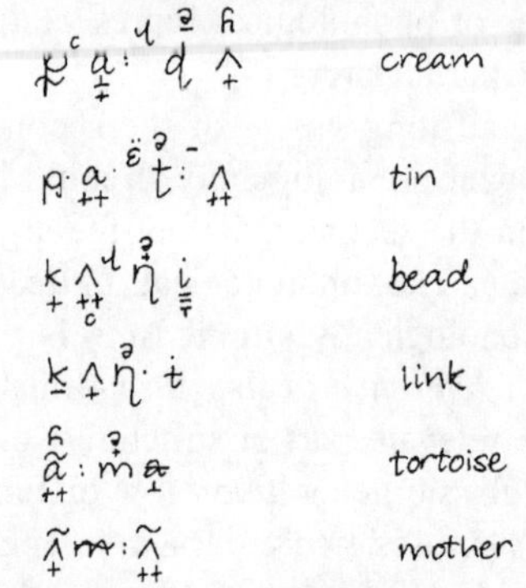

Richard Ogden

cream

tin

bead

link

tortoise

mother

Figure 16.5. Some Malayalam geminate/non-geminate minimal pairs, from Local & Simpson (1988).

and **ng**. Interestingly, CS's preferred analysis of geminates as one gesture rather than two ties in somewhat with the analysis I have proposed here for Finnish.

16.5 Conclusions

Timing between gestures with different degrees of constriction may be an important characterization of the relationships which can hold between gestures in languages. Such a characterization and its concomitant assumptions cannot however explain rhythm adequately because it assumes that:

(i) No criteria are given for deciding whether two gestures are temporally "the same" or "different" (the basis of phonological as opposed to phonetic statement). This potentially produces as many durational categories as there are degrees of stiffness, which is phonologically uneconomical. Given a gradient set of degrees of stiffness, it is hard to see how categorial distinctions are made. If degrees of stiffness are driven by some more abstract structure, we need to ask what the nature of that structure is.

(ii) CS treats gemination as a purely temporal phenomenon. Its domain may be much wider than just the consonant, as CS shows. The way in which gestures are coordinated with respect to one another may explain some of the other differences between geminate vs. non-geminate pieces (such as vocalic resonance), but it remains an open question how and whether regular groupings of phonetic features which are language-specific can be stated more generally.

Timing can be seen as an essential part of the statement of the phonetic exponency of phonological units. Terms like "mora" and "geminate" cannot be universally defined on the basis of gross phonetic characterization; abstract phonological study of individual languages and their metrical systems is needed along with the statement of their phonetic exponents to determine whether such

232

"Where" is timing?

terms mean anything in a more general sense. In this way the categories "mora", "geminate" etc. are of the same type as "voice" or "obstruent": abstract phonological categories whose phonetic exponents are arbitrary but systematic within a given language.

Notes

* My thanks to John Local, Caroline Smith and two anonymous reviewers for their help in writing this.

1 For example, in Sámi, the C-system between the second and third syllables in the foot is different from that between the first and second syllables in the foot (Sammallahti, 1977: 133, 180). "C-system" is used as a phonological term; consonant-system as a phonetic one.

2 The Firthian term "piece" is intentionally used as a non-committal term in working out the categories of the phonology on the basis of the phonetic substance.

3 I use the convention that phonological material appears in bold.

4 I do not wish to imply that a broad phonetic level of description is the output of the phonology. Firthian phonology is monostratal; cf. Local (1992), Coleman (1992), Ogden (1992, 1993).

References

Browman, C. & L. Goldstein. 1990. Gestural specification using dynamically-defined articulatory structures. *Journal of Phonetics* 18: 299–320.

Browman, C. & L. Goldstein. 1992. Articulatory Phonology: an overview. *Phonetica* 49: 155–180.

Carnochan, J. 1962. Gemination in Hausa. *Studies in Linguistic Analysis*, special volume of the Philological Society, 149–181.

Clements, G. N. 1986. Compensatory lengthening and consonant gemination in LuGanda. In Leo Wetzels & Engin Sezer (eds.), *Studies in Compensatory Lengthening*. Dordrecht: Foris, 37–77.

Coleman, J. C. 1992. 'Synthesis by rule' without segments or rewrite rules. In G. Bailly & C. Benoit (eds.), *Talking Machines*. Amsterdam: North-Holland Elsevier, 43–60.

Coleman, J. C. 1994. Polysyllabic words in the YorkTalk synthesis system. In P. Keating (ed.), *Phonological Structure and Phonetic Form: Papers in Laboratory Phonology III*. Cambridge: Cambridge University Press, 293–324.

Fowler, C. A. 1980. Coarticulation and theories of extrinsic timing. *Journal of Phonetics* 8: 113–133.

Keyser S. J. & P. Kiparsky 1984. Syllable structure in Finnish phonology. In M. Aronoff, & R.T. Oehrle (eds.), *Language Sound Structure*. Cambridge, MA: MIT Press, 7–31.

Richard Ogden

Lehiste, I. 1975. Experiments with synthetic speech concerning quantity in Estonian. *Congressus Tertius Internationalis Fenno-Ugristrarum. Pars I Acta Linguistica.* Helsinki: Suomalais-Ugrilainen Seura, 254–269.

Lehtonen, J. 1970. *Aspects of Quantity in Standard Finnish.* Jyväskylä: Gummerus.

Local, J. K. 1992. Modeling assimilation in a non-segmental rule-free phonology. In G. J. Docherty & D. R. Ladd (eds.), *Papers in Laboratory Phonology II: Gesture, Segment, Prosody.* Cambridge: Cambridge University Press, 190–223.

Local, J. & A. Simpson. 1988. The domain of gemination in Malayalam. In D. Bradley, E. J. A. Henderson, & M. Mazaudon, (eds.), *Prosodic Analysis and Asian Linguistics: to Honour R. K. Sprigg. Pacific Linguistics*, Series C no. 104: 33–42.

McCarthy, J. J. 1989. Linear order in phonological representation. *Linguistic Inquiry* 20: 71–99.

Ogden, R. A. 1992. Parametric interpretation in YorkTalk. *York Papers in Linguistics* 16: 81–99.

Ogden, R. A. 1993. What Firthian Prosodic Analysis has to say to us. *Edinburgh Working Papers in Cognitive Science* 8 *(Computational Phonology)*: 107–127.

Palmer, F. R. (ed). 1970. *Prosodic Analysis.* London: Oxford University Press.

Sammallahti, P. 1977. *Norjansaamen Itä-Enontekiön murteen äänneoppi* [The synchronic phonology of Eastern Enontekiö dialect of Norwegian Lappish]. Helsinki: Suomalais-Ugrilaisen Seuran Toimituksia 160.

Sprigg, R. K. 1961. Vowel harmony in Lhasa Tibetan: prosodic analysis applied to interrelated vocalic features of successive syllables. *Bulletin of the School of Oriental and African Studies* 24: 116–38. Also in F. R. Palmer (ed.), 1970, 230–252.

Wiik, K. 1981. *Fonetiikan Perusteet.* Juva WSOY.

Wiik, K. 1991. On a third type of speech rhythm: foot timing. *Proceedings of the XIIth International Congress of Phonetic Sciences*, Aix-en-Provence, 3: 298–301.

17

Asymmetrical prosodic effects on the laryngeal gesture in Korean

SUN-AH JUN*

17.1 Introduction

It is well established that prosody conditions segmental and suprasegmental features. In English, for example, segments are lengthened at the end of a phrase (e.g. Oller, 1973; Beckman & Edwards, 1990), and the "gestural magnitude" of /h/ is weakened word medially or in deaccented words (Pierrehumbert & Talkin, 1992). Additionally, Keating, Linker & Huffman (1983) show that many languages have different allophones for voiced or voiceless stops depending on position within the word or the phrase. However, such effects are often not symmetrical with respect to the edges of a prosodic unit. For example, in German, voiced stops often become voiceless word initially as well as word finally, but this causes neutralization only word finally, where the contrasting voiceless stop is not aspirated.

Korean also has such prosodically conditioned strengthenings and weakenings of laryngeal features, and asymmetries between word initial and word final position. In syllable initial position, there is a three-way contrast among aspirated, tense, and lenis voiceless obstruents, but this contrast is preserved only in the initial position of a word in isolation. In word medial onset position, the lenis stops are voiced between sonorants. In syllable final position, the distinction is neutralized completely to an unreleased lenis stop. The weakening processes in word medial and syllable final position have been described by phonologists (e.g. Cho, 1987; Kim-Renaud, 1974; Kang, 1992) as Lenis Stop Voicing and Coda Neutralization, respectively.

In Jun (1990a, 1990b, 1993), I show that Lenis Stop Voicing applies to a word initial lenis stop if the word and the preceding word are uttered in the same prosodic domain, higher than the Prosodic Word level, and equal to the

235

Phonological Phrase proposed in the theory of Prosodic Phonology (Selkirk, 1986; Nespor & Vogel, 1986; Hayes, 1989). I call this higher level an *Accentual Phrase* because this level is defined on the basis of the intonational pattern of an utterance (see section 17.2). I propose that the domain of Lenis Stop Voicing is the Accentual Phrase.[1] Since Lenis Stop Voicing is a domain span rule in Selkirk's (1986) sense (applying anywhere within a certain domain), all intersonorant lenis stops both in onset and coda position are claimed to be voiced if the lenis stop is within the Accentual Phrase, α, as shown in (1) (Jun, 1993).

(1)

$$\left[\begin{array}{l} \text{-cont, -constricted glottis} \\ \quad\quad \text{-spread glottis} \end{array} \right] \rightarrow \text{[+voice] / } \alpha(\text{ ...[+voice]\_\_\_[+voice]... })\alpha$$

However, to my knowledge, the voicing of word final lenis stop at the end of an Accentual Phrase or a Phonological Phrase has not been studied.

In this paper, I focus on the voicing of the coda lenis stop at the end of the Accentual Phrase as in {kimba p}{ərənni } "Was the sushi frozen?" (/kimpap/ "sushi", /əl-əss-ni/ "to freeze-past-Q"). (Throughout this paper, Accentual Phrases are given in phonetic transcription and enclosed in curly brackets.) Acoustic data show that word final lenis stops very often become voiced across an Accentual Phrase boundary. Furthermore, the domain of /l/-Flapping confirms that the Accentual Phrase final lenis stop is voiced when it is resyllabified as the onset of the initial syllable of the following Accentual Phrase. Moreover, the durational relationship between the lenis stop and the adjacent segments in different prosodic positions suggests that voicing of a lenis stop is not a categorical change, but a by-product of prosodic structure. In the last section, the phonetic nature of the rule is interpreted in terms of gestural overlap and reduction based on Browman and Goldstein's (1990) model. This experiment shows the importance of the underlying prosodic structure in the realization of phonetic features. That is, a resyllabified onset lenis stop is different from an underlying onset lenis stop in terms of the magnitude of glottal gesture.

Before introducing the experimental methods, I briefly introduce the definition of the Accentual Phrase and its relation to Lenis Stop Voicing based on Jun (1989, 1990a, 1990b, 1993).

17.2 The Accentual Phrase

The Accentual Phrase is a grouping of Prosodic Words defined on the basis of the tonal pattern of an utterance. In the Seoul dialect, the tonal pattern of an Accentual Phrase is a final rise, L(H)LH, with the first High optionally appearing when the phrase is longer than four or five syllables. In the Chonnam dialect, the characteristic pattern is an initial rise-fall or fall, either LHL or HHL. The choice of pattern is determined by the laryngeal features of the first segment of the Accentual Phrase: when the segment has either [+spread glottis] (aspirated consonants and /s/) or [+constricted glottis] (tense consonants), the Accentual Phrase has the HHL pattern; otherwise it has the LHL pattern.

I show in Jun (1993) that the Accentual Phrase is the domain of several postlexical phonological rules, and that Lenis Stop Voicing is one of them. Figure 17.1 illustrates the voicing of a lenis stop in different positions in the Accentual Phrase produced by a Seoul speaker for the sentence given in (2). The X-axis shows time and the Y-axis fundamental frequency in Hz. (This format is used for all pitch track figures in this paper.)

(2)   jəlme-ka   tal-ass-ni

"the fruit - NOM"   "sweet-past-Q marker" => "Was the fruit sweet?"

The Accentual Phrases in Figure 17.1(a) have a final rise with an initial High being undershot, but the Accentual Phrase in Figure 17.1(b) has both an initial

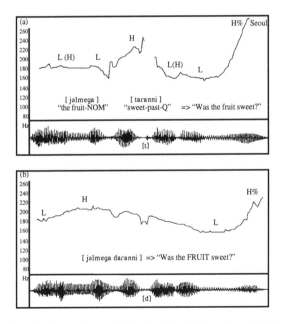

Figure 17.1. Pitch tracks and waveforms of *jəlmeka talassni* in two Accentual Phrasings by S2, forming (a) two Accentual Phrases as in {jəlmega}{ taranni } and (b) one Accentual Phrase as in {jəlmega daranni }.

237

rise and a final rise.[2] As shown by the absence of sinusoidal waveform and the broken line on the pitch track in Figure 17.1(a), the Accentual Phrase initial lenis stop is voiceless, [t]. However, the same lenis stop is voiced, [d], in the middle of the Accentual Phrase as shown in Figure 17.1(b). Figure 17.2 shows the same effect, but differs from Figure 17.1 in that this utterance is produced by a Chonnam speaker, thus having a different verbal ending and an initial rise contour, LHL.

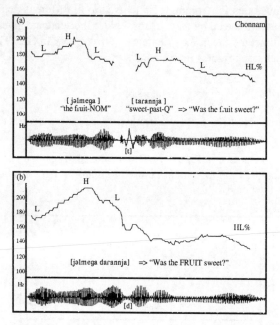

Figure 17.2. Same as Figure 17.1 produced by a Chonnam speaker, C1.

17.3 Experimental methods

17.3.1 Subjects

Three Seoul speakers (S1: female, S2: male, and S3: male) and three Chonnam speakers (C1: female, C2: male, and C3: male) participated in the experiment. All subjects were in their late twenties or early thirties.

17.3.2 Material

Five pairs of two word sentences (listed in Table 17.1) were constructed so that one sentence of the pair has a lenis stop at the beginning of the second word,

Table 17.1. Corpus sentences for voicing, in phonemic transcription. Sentences in brackets show a morpheme breakdown indicated by "-".

1. a. jəlme<u>ka ta</u>las sni (namu) "Was the fruit sweet? (the tree)"
   /jəlme-ka tal-ass-ni/ "the fruit-NOM" "sweet-past-Q"
   b. jəlme<u>kas a</u>lassni (namukas)[3] "Did you know the fruit-hat? (the tree-hat)"
   /jəlme-kas al-ass-ni/ "the fruit-hat" "to know-past-Q"

2. a. ant<u>ʃu ka</u> lassni (salku) "Did you grind the snacks to eat with drink? (the apricot)"
   /antʃu kal-ass-ni/ "the snacks to eat with drink" "to grind-past-Q"
   b. p ant<u>ʃuk a</u>lassni (sokɨm) "Did you know the paste? (the salt)"
   /pantʃuk al-ass-ni/ "the paste" "to know-past-Q"

3. a. tʃam<u>pa pə</u>ljəssni (opa) "Did you throw away the jacket? (the overcoat)"
   /tʃampa pəli-əss-ni/ "the jacket" "to throw away-past-Q"
   b kimp<u>ap ə</u>ləssni (pokkɨmpap) "Was the sushi frozen? (the fried rice)"
   /kimpap əl-əss-ni/ "the sushi" "to frozen-past-Q"

4. a. sal<u>ku ka</u>lassni (antʃu) "Did you grind the apricot? (the side food for liquor)"
   /salku kal-ass-ni/ "the apricot" "to grind-past-Q"
   b. su<u>kuk a</u>lassni (nantʃʰo) "Did you know the water mum? (the lily)"
   /sukuk al-ass-ni/ "the water mum" "to know-past-Q"

5. a. tʃaŋsin <u>ku ta</u>lassni (tʃaŋnankam) "Did you wear the ornament? (the toy)"
   /tʃaŋsinku tal-ass-ni/ "the ornament" "to wear-past-Q"
   b. tʃaŋsin<u>kus a</u>lassni (nelimkus) "Did you know 'tʃaŋsin-shamanism ceremony'?"
   ("descending shamanism ceremony")
   /tʃaŋsin-kus al-ass-ni/ "tʃaŋsin-shamanism ceremony" "to know-past-Q"

while the other sentence of the pair has the same lenis stop at the end of the first word. Except for this prosodic difference, the contexts surrounding the lenis stops were the same. The target segments and the relevant context segments are underlined.[4] The word in parentheses after each sentence was used to trigger contrastive focus.

17.3.3 Methods

These sentences were placed in semi-random order, so that no sentence immediately followed the other sentence from the pair. This strategy was employed to avoid putting emphasis on the difference. Subjects were asked to read the list in two different Accentual Phrasings 10 times each at normal speech rate. First, they read the list of sentences without contrastive focus, and without considering the word in parentheses. In this reading, they nearly always produced the sentence as two Accentual Phrases, one for each word within the sentence. For the second reading, subjects were asked to read each sentence by contrasting the first word with the word in parentheses, thus facilitating the production of the whole sentence in one Accentual Phrase. An example is shown in (3). (The verbal endings given in this paper are for the Seoul speakers. For Chonnam speakers, [-nja] was substituted for [-ni].)

(3) Given: jəlme-ka talassni? (namu) "Was the fruit sweet? (the tree)"
    Read: { jəlmega daranni }{ namuga daranni }?
    "Was the fruit sweet or was the tree sweet?"

For each utterance, the target lenis stop and context segments were analyzed for voicing using a Kay Sonagraph Model 5500 and the pitch track was checked for Accentual Phrasing. The audio waveform and amplitude were displayed simultaneously in the upper window, thus providing further cues to segmentation. The durations of the target lenis stop, underlyingly Accentual Phrase final or initial, as well as the duration of the following and preceding vowels, were measured using the spectrogram display. The durations of adjacent vowels were measured to see whether a segment shows any difference in duration depending on its position relative to the Accentual Phrase. In addition, I measured the word medial lenis stop (except for 3(b) in Table 17. 1, where /p/ is produced as [p̚]) to compare its duration with that of the word initial/final lenis stop. For the lenis stop, the duration was measured to include closure duration and any portion after the release (i.e., VOT). The duration of the vowel preceding the target lenis stop was measured from the point where the first formant of the vowel had a clear amplitude (usually immediately after the stop release) to the point where the formant ceases (usually at the beginning of closure of the target lenis stop). The duration of the vowel following the target lenis stop was measured from the first formant onset to the onset of a flap.

17.4   Results and Discussion

17.4.1 Voicing of the Accentual Phrase final lenis stop and resyllabification

As in my earlier work, onset stops are mostly voiceless in Accentual Phrase initial position, and voiced in Accentual Phrase medial position. But, for all subjects, word final coda stops are voiced most of the time. Out of 300 tokens (5 sentences × 6 subjects × 10 repetitions) for each prosodic condition, 5 to 10% of

240

tokens show an exception to this voicing pattern; 10.67% were voiced at Onset/A-initial position, 4.78% were voiceless at Onset/A-medial position, 8.36% were voiceless at Coda/A-final position, and 4.76% were voiceless at Coda/A-medial position. Depending on the position of the target lenis stop relative to a Prosodic Word or an Accentual Phrase, I defined four prosodic positions as in Table 17.2. Figure 17.3 shows the percentage of voiced versus voiceless lenis stops in the four prosodic positions.

Contrary to my prediction, the lenis stop seems to differ in its voicing depending on which edge of an Accentual Phrase it occurs in. Only the lenis stop in the Accentual Phrase initial position remains voiceless, while that in the Accentual Phrase final position is not. Accordingly, the data do not support the claim that

Table 17.2. Four prosodic positions of the target lenis stop.

	Prosodic Position	Word	Accentual Phrase
1	Onset/A-initial	beginning	beginning
2	Onset/A-medial	beginning	middle
3	Coda/A-final	end	end
4	Coda/A-medial	end	middle

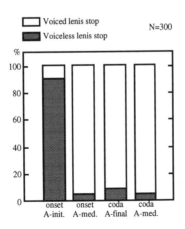

Figure 17.3. Percentage of voiced versus voiceless lenis stop in four prosodic positions combining data from six subjects (N=300).

241

Lenis Stop Voicing is a domain span rule. The Lenis Stop Voicing rule may apply anywhere except at the beginning of an Accentual Phrase.

However, there is a problem with this analysis. In Korean, a coda is resyllabified as an onset within a word and across word boundaries. Cho (1987) and Kang (1992) claim that the domain of resyllabification is the Intonational Phrase, a prosodic level higher than the Phonological Phrase. However, to my knowledge, there is no available phonetic data concerning the domain of resyllabification. To determine whether the coda lenis stop is resyllabified within the Intonational Phrase, i.e., across the Accentual Phrase boundary, the domain of another phonological rule, /l/-Flapping, was examined in a pilot study.

In Korean, /l/ only surfaces in a coda position, unless it is part of a geminate. By /l/-Flapping, /l/ becomes a flap, [ɾ] intervocalically and is realized as an onset to the following syllable. That is, the allophones of /l/ are assumed to be syllabically determined. In the pilot study, I examined the domain of /l/-Flapping, using five sentences. Each sentence had an object NP ending in /l/ and a verb beginning with a vowel. The same six subjects read each sentence in two different Accentual Phrasings 10 times each; one in one Accentual Phrase and the other in two Accentual Phrases with each word forming one Accentual Phrase.

The results show that resyllabification *can* occur across any word boundaries within an Intonational Phrase. The frequency of flapping varied across speakers but all speakers produced a flap across an Accentual Phrase boundary ranging from 65% to 98% of the time.[5] Thus, I assume that any coda can be resyllabified to be the onset of the initial syllable of the following Accentual Phrase, provided the Accentual Phrase is vowel-initial. Since an obstruent coda is neutralized to an unreleased lenis stop, and since the unreleased stop is shown to have a small but still open glottal configuration, i.e., is voiceless, (Sawashima *et al.,* 1980), I assume that a coda stop that is not resyllabified to an onset is unreleased and thus voiceless, while a resyllabified coda stop is released and becomes voiced. This means that the Accentual Phrase final lenis stop is resyllabified most of the time.[6] To reflect the resyllabification, I hereafter use the term *Coda/A-initial* instead of Coda/A-final, when referring to this prosodic position.

The pitch contours and the corresponding segmental realization in Onset/A-initial position are shown in Figure 17.1(a) and those in Onset/A-medial position are shown in Figure 17.1(b). Accentual phrasings and the corresponding segmental realizations in Coda/A-initial and Coda/A-medial position are shown in Figure 17.4. The voicing of lenis stops in each prosodic position is outlined in (4). The arrows in (4c) and (4d) indicate resyllabification. Here, a dot indicates a syllable boundary.

As expected, the underlying onset or coda /t/ is voiced in Accentual Phrase medial position, (4b) and (4d), whereas the underlying onset /t/ is voiceless at the beginning of the Accentual Phrase, (4a). However, the resyllabified word initial /t/, as in (4c), is still *voiced*, as shown in Figure 17.4 (a). Thus, even though the tonal pattern of Figure 17.4 (a) is different from those of Figure 17.1 (b) and Figure 17.4 (b), all three are alike in terms of segmental realization. It was often difficult to distinguish between types (4b) and (4d) solely by listening, but type (4c) was easily distinguished due to the different tonal pattern.

(4) jəlmeka talassni?   "Was the fruit sweet?"

  a. {jəlmega} {taranni} ⇒ [jəl.me.ga.ta.ran.ni] : Onset/A-initial

  b. {jəlmega daranni } ⇒ [jəl.me.ga.da.ran.ni] : Onset/A-medial

  jəlmekat alassni?   "Did you know the 'fruit hat'?"

  c. {jəlmegad} {aranni } ⇒ [jəl.me.ga.da.ran.ni] : coda/A-initial

  d. {jəlmegad aranni } ⇒ [jəl.me.ga.da.ran.ni] : coda/A-medial

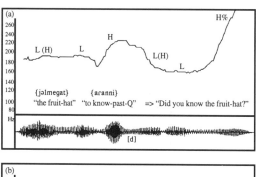

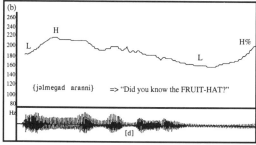

Figure 17.4. Pitch tracks and waveforms of lenis stop in two prosodic positions: (a) Coda/A-initial, (b) Coda/A-medial. The sentence is from Table 17.1(1b) (speaker: S2).

243

In summary, we can predict most of the voicing data in terms of the underlying prosodic context of the lenis stop; a lenis stop is voiceless only when it is an underlying onset at the beginning of an Accentual Phrase, but voiced otherwise.

17.4.2 Duration of lenis stop and adjacent segments in different prosodic positions

Figure 17.5 shows the mean durations of the vowel preceding the target lenis stop (lightly shaded bar), the target lenis stop (white bar), and the following vowel (dark shaded bar) plotted in the four different prosodic positions: Onset/A-initial, Onset/A-medial, Coda/A-initial, and Coda/A-medial position. The mean value of the word medial lenis stop is shown on the first row for each subject. (Here, this value is only based on the word medial lenis stop between vowels.)

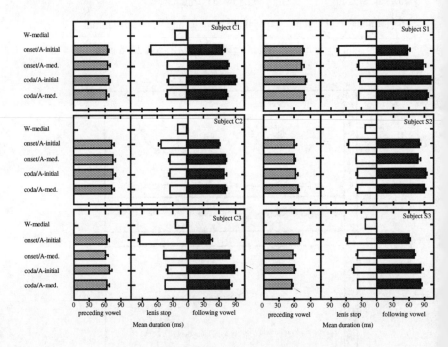

Figure 17.5. The mean duration of the word medial lenis stop, the vowel preceding the target lenis stop, the target lenis stop, and the following vowel in four different prosodic conditions (Onset/A-initial, Onset/A-medial, Coda/A-initial, and Coda/A-medial) for each subject. A standard deviation is shown on top of each bar.

244

For all subjects, there is a significant main effect of prosodic position on the target lenis stop duration (ANOVA for all: $p < 0.0001$, $df = 4$; $F_{C1} = 119.7$, $F_{C2} = 34.3$, $F_{C3} = 279.9$, $F_{S1} = 94.7$, $F_{S2} = 53.9$, $F_{S3} = 56.3$). The result of a *post hoc* test (Tukey, $\alpha = 0.01$) shows effects of Prosodic Word boundary and Accentual Phrase boundary: the word initial and final lenis stops are significantly longer than the word medial lenis stop, and the target onset lenis stop is significantly longer Accentual Phrase initially than Accentual Phrase medially. This agrees with the results of Jun (1990a) regarding the duration of VOT of aspirated stops.

In addition, for all subjects, the target lenis stop is significantly longer in Onset/A-initial position than in Coda/A-initial position (Tukey, $\alpha = 0.01$). However, the target lenis stop is not significantly different among onset/A-med, Coda/A-initial, and coda/A-med. The vowel following a lenis stop also shows a significant main effect of prosodic position (ANOVA for all: $p < 0.0001$, $df = 3$; $F_{C1} = 27.3$, $F_{C2} = 18.0$, $F_{C3} = 123.8$, $F_{S1} = 103.2$, $F_{S2} = 11.2$, $F_{S3} = 33.5$). Except S2, vowels following Onset/A-initial lenis stops are significantly shorter than vowels following lenis stops in all other positions (Tukey, $\alpha = 0.01$). At the same time, vowels following Coda/A-initial lenis stops are in general longer than vowels following lenis stops in all other positions (significant at $\alpha = 0.01$ for C1, C3, S1). In fact, the vowel following Coda/A-initial lenis stop is the underlying initial segment of the Accentual Phrase. Thus, it seems that the left edge of the Accentual Phrase is strong in Korean; it shows a lengthening effect. To see if the right edge of the Accentual Phrase shows the same effect, the duration of the vowel preceding the target lenis stop was examined. For all subjects, there is no significant difference among the four prosodic positions; there is no lengthening effect at the end of the Accentual Phrase. Thus, the boundary effect is not necessarily symmetrical at this level. But, at the same time, the prosodic boundary effect on the segment is not uniform: in Korean, Accentual Phrases show a left edge lengthening while the Intonational Phrase shows a right edge lengthening (Jun, 1992). Also the domains and patterns of these lengthening effects are not universally the same: for example, unlike Korean, English has a right boundary effect at both the Word level and the phrase level (Beckman & Edwards, 1990; Crystal & House, 1990).

17.4.3 The representation of lenis stop voicing

Since the word final lenis stop is shown to be mostly voiced at the boundary of the Accentual Phrase, we can no longer claim that the domain of the Lenis Stop Voicing in Korean is the Accentual Phrase. Rather, we can say that a lenis stop becomes voiced everywhere except in underlying Accentual Phrase initial position. But the question is whether Lenis Stop Voicing is indeed a categorial rule. To determine the categoriality of this phenomenon, the durations of individual tokens of the target lenis stop are plotted against the following vowel in three prosodic positions: Onset/A-initial, Onset/A-medial and Coda/A-initial. This is shown in Figure 17.6. If the rule is categorial, we would expect two separate groups of consonant durations: longer duration for the voiceless lenis stop and shorter duration for the voiced lenis stop. Here, a token was counted "voiced" if voicing continues through for the duration of the consonant, while all partially or fully voiceless ones were considered "voiceless". The lenis stops in Coda/A-medial position showed a similar pattern to that of Onset/A-medial position. For graphing convenience, only the lenis stops in Onset/A-medial position are plotted.

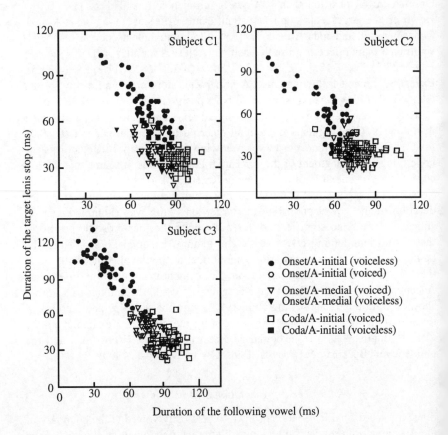

Figure 17.6. The duration of the target lenis stop against the following vowel, for each subject, in three different prosodic positions: Onset/A-initial, Onset/A-medial and Coda/A-initial position. Tokens of voiced lenis stop are indicated by a filled circle/triangle/square, and tokens of voiceless lenis stop are indicated by an empty circle/triangle/square.

For all subjects, there is no separation of data clouds between voiced and voiceless lenis stop duration. Rather, the duration of the lenis stop is negatively correlated to that of the following vowel; that is, it seems that the duration of the lenis stop is trading off with that of the following vowel. Furthermore, no subject shows a clear separation between the groups of the data for the different prosodic positions. Subject C3 seems to have a better separation between the tokens in Onset/A-initial position and the tokens of the other two groups. However, if we compare voiced tokens with voiceless tokens in the same prosodic position, we can clearly see that the voicing of the lenis stop is predicted by the relative duration of the lenis stop and the following vowel: i.e., longer stops followed by shorter vowels tend to be voiceless and shorter stops followed by longer vowels tend to be voiced.

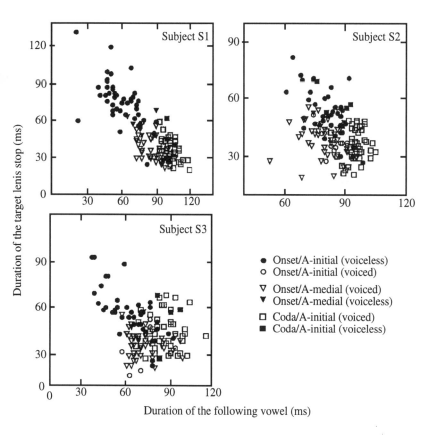

Figure 17.6. (continued)

This result suggests that voicing is a function of duration. This duration-sensitive voicing is further supported by the fact that the lenis stop is more likely to be voiced in faster speech (Jun, 1990a, 1993). Thus, the voice/voiceless distinction is not a categorial change. This non-categoriality is also supported by Jun & Beckman (1993), who found that the voicing of a lenis stop in Accentual Phrase medial position is influenced by segmental context: a lenis stop is more often voiceless when it is preceded by an aspirated stop and a high vowel, or followed by a high vowel and an aspirated stop, than when it is flanked by a high vowel and a lenis stop. That is, a lenis stop is more likely to be voiced in faster rate, in shorter duration, and next to a segment with a stronger voicing gesture. This characteristic of gradient voicing supports the interpretation that Lenis Stop Voicing in Korean is not a phonological rule.[7] Rather, lenis stop voicing itself is a gradient process, whose output is determined by the effects of prosodic position on the strength of glottal gestures and coproduction. This interpretation is also supported by Silva (1992) who claims that lenis stop voicing is due to the word internal weakening and that phrase edge strengthening is based on closure duration and percent of closure voicing data.[8]

To explain the different patterns of lenis stop voicing relative to the Accentual Phrase as well as the gradient nature of voicing, I posit a gradation of strengths for the realization of the glottal gesture of the lenis stop. At one end of the continuum is the lenis stop associated with a syllable at the left edge of the Accentual Phrase, i.e., Onset/A-initial lenis stop. Here, all the gestures for the segment, including the glottal opening gesture and oral gesture, are "strong", having a larger amplitude and longer duration. At the other end of the continuum is the lenis stop associated with a syllable anywhere inside the word. Here, the gestures for the segment are "weak", having a smaller amplitude and shorter duration. When a lenis stop is associated with the left edge of the word but within the Accentual Phrase, and when a lenis stop is an underlying coda but is associated with the left edge of the following Accentual Phrase (due to resyllabification), the gestures for both segments possess values intermediate between these two extremes. Thus, even though the coda lenis stop is associated with the left edge of the Accentual Phrase, the glottal opening gesture is not as strong as that of an onset associated with the left edge of the Accentual Phrase.

To distinguish these two cases, we need to know whether the Accentual Phrase initial lenis stop is underlyingly a coda (word final) or an onset (word initial). Schematic representations of the prosodic structures conditioning the two extremes of the continuum and the Coda/A-initial type lenis stop are shown in (5).

Here, α is an Accentual Phrase, ω a Prosodic Word, and [F] is the bundle of features specifying the lenis stop. The horizontal line separates the prosodic specification plane from the associated segmental features. (5a) is the representation for the Accentual Phrase initial onset lenis stop, and (5b) is the representation for the coda stop resyllabified across the Accentual Phrase boundary. (5c) is the representation for the word medial lenis stop. To represent the different voicing patterns of the underlying onset vs. coda Accentual Phrase initial lenis stops, [F] is associated with one Accentual Phrase in (5a) but two Accentual Phrases in (5b).[9] Browman & Goldstein (1990) explain intervocalic voicing assimilation as a reduction in the magnitude of the glottal opening gesture responsible for voicelessness. That is, if the magnitude of the opening is reduced sufficiently, devoicing might not take place at all. Based on data from Japanese, Hirose, Niimi, Honda & Sawashima (1985) suggest that if the magnitude of the abduction gestures is slightly reduced, the critical value of vocal fold separation for devoicing might not be reached.

(5) Schematic representation of the prosodic structure conditioning the two extremes of the continuum and the Coda/A-initial type lenis stop.

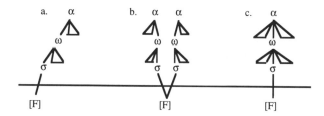

However, in addition to the different amplitude of the glottal gesture, the negative gradient relationship between lenis stop and the following vowel, shown in Figure 17.6, suggests that there is gestural overlap between the lenis stop's glottal opening gesture and the following vowel's glottal closing gesture. That is, the different degrees of overlapping between the glottal opening and closing gestures and the different degrees of amplitude of the glottal gesture would produce the gradient voicing output. The hypothetical gestural score for a lenis stop, here [t], in different prosodic positions is given in (6). Only the glottal tier is shown. The height of the box indicates degree of opening (aperture) or closing (closure) of the glottal gesture and the width of the box indicates this gesture's duration. The white boxes represent the glottal opening gesture and the shaded boxes represent the glottal closing gesture.

For the Accentual Phrase initial lenis stop, (6a), the opening gesture would be larger and longer, overlapping and hiding the vowel's glottal closing gesture, while for the resyllabified phrase initial lenis stop, (6b), the opening gesture would be smaller and shorter and overlapping less with the following vowel. This weaker opening glottal gesture would probably result in voicing and the following vowel will be longer than that in (6a) due to less overlap with the glottal opening gesture. For the word medial lenis stop, (6c), the opening glottal gesture would be the smallest and shortest, thus voicing could easily occur as suggested by Browman & Goldstein (1990).[10]

(6) Hypothetical score of overlapping glottal gestures

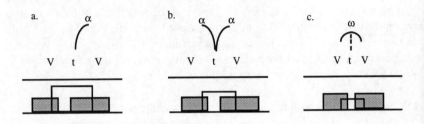

17.5 Conclusion

In contrast to word initial lenis stops in Korean, which are almost always voiceless at the beginning of the Accentual Phrase, word final lenis stops are voiced in resyllabified Accentual Phrase initial position. The data show that the voicing of lenis stops depends on their duration relative to the following vowel and that their duration is determined by their prosodic position. Therefore, I propose that the Lenis Stop Voicing rule in Korean is not a phonological rule, but a by-product of some other effect of prosodic position on the gestural amplitude and overlapping, thus producing a continuum of voicing. To distinguish the different duration patterns of lenis stops, and the resulting difference in the voicing patterns of these stops, I suggest different prosodic representations utilizing the coda/onset information. The lenis stop voicing pattern in Korean illustrates that the information of prosodic structure is reflected in the phonetic realization of the segment.

Notes

* I would like to thank Mary Beckman, Gerry Docherty, Catherine Browman, Louis Goldstein, Michel Jackson, Janet Pierrehumbert, and two anonymous reviewers for their comments and suggestions. I would also like to acknowledge the financial support of the OSU and UCLA Linguistics departments. The work reported in this paper was also supported by the NSF under Grant No. IRI-8858109 to Mary E. Beckman.

1 Cho (1987, 1990), Kang (1992) and Silva (1989, 1992) propose the Phonological Phrase as the domain of Lenis Stop Voicing based on either Selkirk's (1986, 1990) end-based theory, or Nespor and Vogel's (1986) relation-based theory.

2 The final rise in Figure 17.1(b) and that of the second Accentual Phrase in Figure 17.1(a) are due to the intonational phrase boundary tone (H%) for an interrogative sentence.

3 The word final coda /s/ is realized as [t] due to Coda Neutralization, thus becoming a minimal pair with the sentence in (1a). The same is true for the word final /s/ in (5b).

4 The words *jəlmekat* in (1b) and *tʃaŋsinkut* in (5b) in Table 17.1 are not real but possible words. Subjects had no trouble understanding the possible meanings.

5 The percentage was a little higher (70–100%) within an Accentual Phrase for every speaker. It seems that /l/-Flapping depends on the force of articulation: more emphasis given to a coda results in less /l/-Flapping. Thus, flapping happens more often in fast and casual speech.

6 Comparing the voicing data with the /l/-Flapping data, it seems that a lenis stop is more likely to be resyllabified than /l/. I think this is because there are two strategies for /l/ resyllabification: by flapping /l/ or by geminating /l/. I found from acoustic data that some speakers lengthen the coda /l/, thereby making it also function as an onset. This /l/-gemination seems to be the result of emphasizing the coda /l/. To clarify this phenomenon, articulatory data, as well as more acoustic data, are needed.

7 There were also different degrees of voicing within a stop closure, as claimed by Silva (1992); the shorter the stop, the higher the percentage of voicing. But this kind of gradience is not incorporated in my analysis here.

8 His phrase edge was mainly phrase initial. Moreover, since his PE (phrase initial) category is based on the syntactic structure of a sentence, his results are not comparable with mine in terms of voicing with respect to duration.

9 The weak gesture of the underlying coda can also be shown in English Flapping data. In English, /t/ can be a flap across a word boundary if the /t/ is a coda and also becomes an onset (ambisyllabic). On the other hand, a word initial onset /t/ can never be a flap (Kahn, 1976); e.g. *eat*[ɾ] *again* vs. my *t*[tʰ]*omato*.

10 This kind of overlapping of consonant and vowel gestures was also used to explain vowel-to-vowel coarticulation across consonants in Öhman (1966) and later literature, and Fowler (1980).

References

Beckman, M. E. & J. Edwards. 1990. Lengthenings and shortenings and the nature of prosodic constituency. In J. Kingston & M. E. Beckman (eds.), *Papers in Laboratory Phonology I: Between the Grammar and Physics of Speech.* Cambridge: Cambridge University Press, 152–178.

Browman, C. P. & L. Goldstein. 1990. Tiers in articulatory phonology, with some implications for casual speech. In J. Kingston & M. E. Beckman (eds.), *Papers in Laboratory Phonology I: Between the Grammar and Physics of Speech.* Cambridge: Cambridge University Press, 341–376.

Cho, Y. Y. 1987. *The Domain of Korean Sandhi Rules.* Paper presented at the 62nd LSA meeting.

Cho, Y. Y. 1990. Syntax and phrasing in Korean. In S. Inkelas & D. Zec (eds.), *The Phonology–Syntax Connection.* Chicago: University of Chicago Press, 47–62.

Crystal, T. & A. House. 1990. Articulation rate and the duration of syllables and stress groups in connected speech. *Journal of the Acoustical Society of America* 88: 101–112.

Fowler, C. 1980. Coarticulation and theories of extrinsic timing. *Journal of Phonetics* 8: 113–133.

Hayes, B. 1989. The prosodic hierarchy in meter. In P. Kiparsky & G. Youmans (eds.), *Perspectives on Meter.* New York: Academic Press, 203–260.

Hirose, H. , S. Niimi, K. Honda & M. Sawashima. 1985. The relationship between glottal opening and tranglottal pressure difference during consonant production. *Annual Bulletin of the Research Institute of Logopedics and Phoniatrics* 19: 55–64.

Jun, S-A. 1990a. *The domains of laryngeal feature lenition effects in Chonnam Korean.* Paper presented at the 119th ASA meeting.

Jun, S-A. 1990b. The prosodic structure of Korean – in terms of voicing. In E-J. Baek (ed.), *Proceedings of the 7th International Conference on Korean Linguistics.* Toronto: University of Toronto Press, 87–104.

Jun, S-A. 1992. The Domain of Nasalization and the Prosodic Structure in Korean. In H. Sohn (ed.), *Korean Linguistics* 7: 11–29.

Jun, S-A. 1993. *The Phonetics and Phonology of Korean Prosody.* Ph.D. dissertation, The Ohio State University.

Jun, S-A. & M. E. Beckman. 1993. A gestural-overlap analysis of vowel devoicing in Japanese and Korean. Paper presented at the 67th LSA meeting.

Kahn, D. 1976. Syllable-based generalizations in English phonology, Ph.D. dissertation, MIT.

Kang, O. 1992. Korean prosodic phonology. Ph.D. dissertation. University of Washington.

Keating, P., W. Linker & M. Huffman. 1983. Patterns in allophone distribution for voiced and voiceless stops. *Journal of Phonetics* 11: 277–290.

Kim-Renaud, Y-K. 1974. Korean consonantal phonology. Ph.D. dissertation, University of Hawaii.

Nespor, M. & I. Vogel. 1986. *Prosodic Phonology.* Dordrecht: Foris.

Öhman, S. 1966. Coarticulation in VCV utterances: spectrographic measurements. *Journal of the Acoustical Society of America* 41: 310–320.

Oller, D. K. 1973. The effect of position in utterance on speech segment duration in English. *Journal of the Acoustical Society of America* 54: 1235–1247.

Pierrehumbert, J. & D. Talkin. 1992. Lenition of /h/ and glottal stop. In G. J. Docherty & D. R. Ladd (eds.), *Papers in Laboratory Phonology II: Gestures Segment, Prosody.* Cambridge: Cambridge University Press, 90–116.

Sawashima, M., H-S. Park, K. Honda & H. Hirose. 1980. Fiberscopic study on laryngeal adjustments for syllable-final applosives in Korean. *Annual Bulletin of the Research Institute of Logopedics and Phoniatrics* 14: 125–138.

Selkirk, E. O. 1984. *Phonology and Syntax: the Relation between Sound and Structure.* Cambridge, MA: MIT Press.

Asymmetrical effects on the laryngeal gesture

Selkirk, E. O. 1986. On derived domains in sentence phonology. *Phonology Yearbook* 3: 371–405.
Silva, D. J. 1989. Determining the Domain for Intervocalic Stop Voicing in Korean. In S. Kuno *et al.* (eds.), *Harvard Studies in Korean Linguistics III*, Cambridge, MA: Harvard University Press, 177–188.
Silva, D. J. 1992. The phonetics and phonology of stop lenition in Korean. Ph.D. dissertation, Cornell University.

18

On a gestural account of lenis stop voicing in Korean: comments on Jun

GERARD J. DOCHERTY

18.1 Introduction

As well as providing interesting data on the phonetic characteristics of Korean, and building on her previous work investigating prosodically based variation in the production of Korean stops (e.g. Jun, 1990), Jun's paper addresses issues which are at the heart of laboratory phonology. The point of departure for this study is previous work (by Jun herself and others) showing that the realization of lenis stops in Korean is subject to word- and higher-level prosodic conditioning. Word-initially, lenis stops are produced with a glottal opening and closing gesture, word-medially (and intervocalically) they are produced as voiced, and word-finally with only a small glottal opening. However, in casual connected speech, these word-level constraints appear to be overridden by a higher level of conditioning based on the Accentual Phrase (henceforth "AP", defined as a prosodic unit intermediate in size between the prosodic word and the intonational phrase). Word-initial lenis stops are voiced intervocalically within the AP, but voiceless in AP-initial position. This alternation is captured in the AP-conditioned lenis stop voicing rule. In the study described in this paper, Jun focuses on lenis stops which are in word-final position, but which in connected speech are assumed to be resyllabified across an AP boundary, with the result that they are postlexically in AP-initial position. However, despite the fact that they are now in AP-initial position, they are most often realized as voiced, contrary to the lenis stop voicing rule. This, and accompanying data showing a trade-off between the durations of lenis stops and following vowels, prompts Jun to raise the following question: is the voicing of lenis stops best accounted for by invoking a categorial phonological rule (such as the lenis stop voicing rule) or by appealing to a prosodically modulated phonetic process of gestural overlap

254

along the lines suggested by Browman and Goldstein's framework of Articulatory Phonology? Evidence is presented which is claimed to suggest that the former type of explanation may not be appropriate, and subsequently Jun outlines a possible phonetic account. Before looking more closely at this account, I will comment briefly on Jun's reasons for leaning in this direction.

18.2 On interpretation of data

Jun's case for adopting a phonetic as opposed to a phonological account of lenis stop voicing is based on the findings of the experiment reported in the present paper, backed up by the results of previous studies (Jun, 1990, 1993; Jun & Beckman, 1993; Silva, 1992) which seem to point in the same direction. Taken together, these findings do constitute good grounds for hypothesizing that Korean lenis stop voicing may be phonetically motivated along the lines suggested by Jun, and that the conventional account, couched in categorial phonological terms, should be drawn into question. What Jun's results do not do however is provide the means for deciding whether the "phonological rule" account can safely be rejected.

Jun's argument for a phonetic, non-categorial account of lenis stop voicing is hinged on her interpretation of the relative durations of the lenis stop closure and following vowel in three prosodic positions: Onset/AP-initial, Onset/AP-medial, Coda/AP-initial. This data is used to determine whether the voicing of the lenis stop is a categorial change. The findings are as follows. Whilst there is considerable overlap in both C and V durations across the three prosodic positions, there seems to be something of a trade-off between the acoustic durations of consonants and following vowels, with onset/AP-initial stops (which are voiceless) tending to have relatively long duration and being followed by relatively shorter vowels, and stops in other positions (which are voiced) tending to have relatively shorter durations and being followed by vowels with relatively longer durations (although note that this trade-off is not apparent across all speakers – see S2, Figure 17.6, where the vowel duration following onset/AP-initial stops is not noticeably different from that following onset/AP-medial stops).

It is not immediately obvious why these results support the interpretation that lenis stop voicing in Korean does not arise as the consequence of a categorial phonological rule. Jun focuses on the fact that there is a tendency for voiced lenis stops to have shorter duration in conjunction with longer following vowels, whereas the voiceless lenis stops have a tendency to be produced with longer duration and shorter following vowel durations. Note however that there is a good deal of overlap between the voiced and voiceless alternants in the CV duration space. In the data for all the speakers there is a large area where it would be impossible to predict whether a stop is voiced or voiceless. Any predictive (and, indeed, explanatory) power of stop duration requires further data and testing before it can be safely asserted. However, given a degree of negative correlation between stop duration and the presence of voicing (no indication is given whether this is statistically significant or not), Jun raises the hypothesis that voicing may arise as a result of the shorter duration (and of course this is built in to the gestural account which is then proposed). Whilst of course, it is possible to raise this hypothesis, and it is a very challenging one, what these results do not do is allow a rejection of the possibility that voicing is in fact specified by a categorial phonological rule.

Jun's argument is that if lenis voicing is a categorial rule, this would give rise to a separation in CV duration space of the voiced and voiceless tokens, as opposed to an overlapping distribution. No reasons are presented for this assertion, and there seems no reason to expect that the phonological categories voiced and voiceless need *necessarily* be phonetically distinct with respect to every parameter involved in their production. For example, whilst voice onset time measures in English are a prime example of a phonetic parameter which does seem to reflect a phonological contrast by way of more-or-less non-overlapping distributions for voiced and voiceless stops, other parameters, such as the extent of closure voicing in stops, or the extent of voicing during fricatives, show considerable overlap across the two phonological categories of voiced and voiceless (Docherty, 1992). At the same time, it is also possible to find instances of separate distributions underlying a *single* phonological category. For example, many English speakers demonstrate a bimodal distribution in their voice onset time scores for phonologically voiced stops in post-pausal position (Lisker and Abramson, 1964). Jun's observations (a) that voiced and voiceless lenis stops overlap considerably in CV duration space, and (b) that there is a degree of trade-off between the acoustic durations of con-sonants and following vowels, are not, in themselves, strong indicators that lenis stop voicing cannot be a categorial alternation. An alternative description of the duration results presented by Jun might be that the Onset/AP-initial stops vary in duration to a relatively large extent, whereas the lenis stops in other positions vary a lot less. And of course, the tendency for the onset/AP-initial stops to be longer may just reflect the finding, which Jun points out elsewhere in her paper, that the left-edge of the AP in Korean shows a lengthening effect;[1] or alternatively we might hypothesize that it is a reflection of the time requirements for achieving a glottal opening and closing such that the glottis is adducted again prior to the release of the stop.

Of course, I am speculating here, but the point I wish to make is that whilst Jun's data provide a good basis for proposing a rival explanatory hypothesis (indeed, as pointed out by Jun & Beckman, 1993, the durational trade-off is what we might expect to see if lenis stop voicing arises as a result of overlap of vowel and stop gestures), they do not supply the crucial evidence required to test the two rival accounts. Indeed, as Jun herself points out the findings could be captured by a single phonological rule stating that "a lenis-stop becomes voiced in all positions but the underlying accentual-phrase initial position". However, Jun does not explore the motivation for discarding this hypothesized categorial rule.

18.3 Lenis stop voicing as a "by-product"

The interpretation of the duration measures just discussed leads Jun to the view that voicing of lenis stops in Korean is a phonetic rather than a phonological phenomenon. In commenting on this phonetic account, firstly, it is important to note what Jun means by "phonetic". This term is applied to an aspect of performance which is a "by-product" of some other aspect of the production of an utterance, as opposed to being specifically governed by that part of the grammar which specifies the detailed language-specific aspects of speakers' performance – I will comment more on this below. The proposed explanation is embedded in the framework offered by Browman and Goldstein's (1986, 1990, 1992a, 1992b) Articulatory Phonology. Jun assumes that lenis stops are characterized by a glottal opening/closing gesture (referred to henceforth as a glottal abduction gesture). This is always present whenever a lenis stop is produced but with different activation intervals and magnitudes in different prosodic contexts. In some (prosodically weak) cases, the abduction falls below the threshold required to achieve a cessation of voicing, and, as a result, voicing continues throughout the stop into the next vowel. Furthermore, in the weak environments, there is greater overlap of the vowel and consonant gestures on the glottal tier. This combination of prosodically modulated truncation of the glottal gesture and overlap of stop and adjacent owel gestures leads to the production of what Jun refers to as "the gradual voicing output". There are a number of aspects of this account which merit comment. We are given no explanation of why, in the gestural score, the lenis stop is assigned a glottal abduction gesture when its feature representation is specified by Jun as [–spread glottis, –constricted glottis]. The aspirated stop in Korean, specified phonologically in the paper as [+spread glottis], is presumably also assigned a glottal abduction gesture in the gestural score (although, one would surmise, with a different phasing relationship with respect to the supralaryngeal occlusion gesture). As is shown elsewhere in this volume (especially in the contribution by Zsiga), there is a need to explore the nature of the links between a phonological feature representation and the gestural score. The association of a [-spread glottis] feature representation with a glottal abduction gesture in the gestural score certainly requires an explanation. It is interesting to note that the alternation being studied in this paper is quite different from the palatal

257

Gerard J. Docherty

assimilation alternations looked at by Holst & Nolan (this volume) and Zsiga (this volume) where there is demonstrable "output" gradience. Jun refers to "gradual voicing output", the "graduality of voicing" and to a "continuum of voicing". However, it is not clear in what sense the voicing is gradient. It is certainly possible to conceive of there being different degrees of overlap and co-production of the C and V gestures, but Jun's results show that lenis stops are produced as either voiced or voiceless depending on their prosodic and word context. It is possible that this lack of understanding on my part is because I am adopting what Browman & Goldstein (1992a) refer to as an "output" analysis focusing on the surface articulation/acoustics, as opposed to an "input" analysis focusing on the articulatory gestural organization. However, Jun does talk about a "gradual voicing *output*" [my emphasis – GJD], and I am not sure what this is referring to. For example, Jun's study shows that Korean lenis stops in word-medial position are just as voiced as the coda stops – i.e., there is no sense of a continuum of voicing here, and Jun does not specify what we would have to look for to demonstrate that the medial stops are at the end of the voicing continuum whilst the word-final stops are somewhere in the middle of that continuum.

Jun's account predicts a "gradation of strengths for the realization of the glottal gesture of the lenis stop". Jun asserts that all the tiers in the gestural score are affected by the relative strength of the prosodic environment. If this is the case, in prosodically weak environments we might expect to see some signs of weakening of the supralaryngeal gestures (as well as of the glottal gestures), or possibly some measurable increase in the velocity of the lingual gesture as a consequence of the shorter time-span available for achieving the target occlusion. It is certainly true that in the weakest environment (word-medially), the measured duration of the stop is shorter than in other environments (although because of gestural overlap the measurable stop duration may not be an accurate reflection of the activation interval of the underlying lingual gesture corresponding to that stop, and recall that it is this latter feature which Jun's prediction refers to). However, further investigation will be required for this particular part of Jun's proposal to be pursued in greater detail. If, on the other hand, it is just the glottal tier that is being weakened, then we might expect the gradual incursion of voicing into the interval associated with the consonant to lead to some partially devoiced lenis stop tokens. Jun's account would predict that lenis stops in the strongest prosodic environment (onset/AP-initial) will be voiceless, and that those in the weakest prosodic environment (word-medial) will be voiced. In environments of intermediate prosodic strength, we might expect to see partially voiced tokens reflecting the partial overlap of the vowel voicing gesture into the interval during which there is a stop closure. The weaker the prosodic strength associated with a lenis stop, the greater the amount of voicing there should be, until the weakest environments, in which voicing

258

continues throughout the occlusion. Jun does not report any cases of partially devoiced lenis stops (this of course is one reason why the notion of "continuum of voicing" is difficult to come to terms with). However, another recent study of Korean lenis stops (Silva, 1992) *has* reported a significant incidence of partially devoiced tokens in what is referred to as word-edge position. This apparent conflict between Silva's and Jun's results regarding the occurrence of partially devoiced tokens suggests that this may indeed be a productive area for testing Jun's gestural overlap hypothesis. What does it mean to say that glottal abduction and voicing gestures can overlap? In discussing precisely this notion (gestural blending on the same glottal tier), Beckman, de Jong, Jun & Lee (1992) rightly draw attention to work by Munhall & Lofqvist (1992) showing gradual rate-dependent blending of glottal abduction gestures in sequences of voiceless consonants (such as the medial sequence in *kiss Ted*). However the blending of two identical gestures is quite a different process to the proposed blending of two antagonistic gestures. Browman & Goldstein (1990: 362) point out that, "Gestures on the same articulatory tier cannot overlap without perturbing each other, since the same vocal tract variables are employed but with different targets. [In Munhall & Lofqvist's data the same variables are involved but with the same targets – GJD.] Thus even a partial overlap of gestures on the same tier leads to a blending of the observed output characteristics of the two gestures." And of course Browman and Goldstein have used this to propose extremely interesting accounts of different types of contextual variation. Jun argues that this blending (of glottal abduction and voicing gestures) results in a continuum of voicing in the production of the stop, but the blending would presumably also have an effect on voicing during the portion of the vowel which is overlapped with the later stages of the consonant abduction gesture.

   One way in which this might be examined further would be to carry out a laryngographic study along the lines described by Lindsey, Davies & Fourcin (1986). In this study, the open phase of the laryngograph waveform $(Lx)^2$ was tracked during the voiced intervals of V-voiceless C-V sequences. It was found that the open phase was greater during the portion of the vowel immediately before the abduction of the vocal folds for the voiceless consonant. Lindsey *et al.* interpreted these findings as illustrating coarticulatory influence of the consonant glottal gesture on the glottal gestures for the adjacent vowels. In the light of Jun's results, it would be interesting to investigate whether the gradient gesture overlap predicted by the different strengths of prosodic modulation is reflected in the extent to which the open phase in the vowel Lx waveform demonstrates coarticulatory influence from an adjacent lenis stop. Jun's account would be supported by a finding that the greatest effect on the open phase during the vowel would be found in the prosodically weakest environment (word-medially) where maximum gesture overlap is claimed to take place, with progressively less influence being found in the prosodically stronger environments.[3]

Jun's motivation for proposing this gestural account of lenis stop voicing, and the account itself are hinged on modulation of gestural overlap of a stop and a following vowel. However, all of the stops considered are in a V_V frame (with a range of different boundary conditions applying between the different components of the frame). The question arises whether there is any prosodically induced alteration in the gestural overlap between the lenis stops and the *preceding* vowel. The only evidence relevant to this presented in the paper is the finding that there is no trade-off in the durations of preceding vowels and following lenis stops. This is reflected in Jun's gestural overlap hypothesis by the fact that the phasing relationship between the glottal gesture for the preceding vowel and the glottal gesture for the lenis stop remains constant under different prosodic conditions. For this aspect of Jun's account to be supported what we need is an account of the independent principles which determine that the gestural interaction is between the stop and the following vowel only.

In Jun's account, intervocalic lenis stop voicing is interpreted as a gesture lenition process, as opposed to an assimilation process. It is based on the proposal that a glottal abduction gesture is always present and produced for a lenis stop, but that it is truncated or lenited in prosodically weak environments. Future work must test this hypothesis, with an obvious place to start looking being the laryngeal contribution to voiced lenis stops in prosodically weak environments. Firstly, is there any evidence of a glottal abduction gesture? If not, can any difference be discerned between voiced lenis stops in Korean and intervocalic phonetically and underlyingly voiced stops in other languages? If there is evidence of a glottal gesture, this would of course speak quite strongly for Jun's account. If there is no sign of the hypothesized glottal gesture, then it would seem that Jun's account would be weakened. There is very little in the literature which addresses this issue. However, in Kagaya's (1974) fiberscopic study of Korean stops there is at least some evidence suggesting that glottal opening need not be found in Korean lenis stops, specifically in word-medial lenis stops. Of course, it is possible that fiberoptic endoscopy would not be the best way of looking for the presence of a glottal gesture in the prosodically weakest position – the gesture may be so truncated that it may only be detected by electromyographic monitoring of the abductor muscles. This is a matter for future study. In summary, Jun's account of lenis stop voicing as a by-product of other aspects of coproduction is extremely interesting and raises a number of issues which could be tested empirically, but I am forced to conclude that it contains sufficient unanswered questions that it cannot, at this stage, allow us to reject the other possible explanation.

18.4 Gestural and phonological explanations

Jun's proposals form part of a larger picture together with other papers in this volume by Zsiga, Holst & Nolan, and Browman, and recent articles such as those by Kingston & Cohen (1992) and Browman & Goldstein (1992a). This strand of work has focused on Browman & Goldstein's (1992a) claim that allophonic variation can only arise from differences in phasing and magnitude of the gestures specified in the gestural score for an utterance. Jun's study reveals yet another area where a gestural account of variability is a possibility meriting further investigation.

I would like to conclude by making a general point regarding the focus of this on-going debate. According to Browman & Goldstein (1992b: 28) "all of the language-particular phonetic/phonological structure must reside in the gestural score." The scenario which emerges from several papers in this volume (including Jun's) is that what cannot be accounted for by gesture phasing and magnitude must be accounted for by categorial phonological feature rules, and vice versa. In this paper, Jun opts for the former type of explanation, whereas Holst and Nolan appeal to both types, as does Zsiga. However, I would like to draw attention to the fact that there are numerous phonetic phenomena which fall into what appears to be a gap between these two types of explanation. Zsiga (this volume) refers to these briefly when she mentions the temporal relations which need to be specified in a hypothesized mapping from a feature geometry to a gestural score. What I am referring to are those systematic language-particular aspects of a speaker's performance which apparently do not "fall-out" from anything else, which are too fine-grained to be accounted for in a feature geometry based on abstract and discrete feature categories, but which are conceivably part of "the grammar" in the broadest sense of the word (i.e., part of what it is that speakers do in order to be native speakers). It is interesting, in the context of this paper, to note that the timing of voicing in stops is one area where some thought has been given to this aspect of performance. This whole area has been addressed in some detail in two papers by Keating (1984, 1990). Referring specifically to contrasts arising from laryngeal features, Keating (1984: 288) points out that a fundamental problem in accounting for the relationship between phonological categories and their realization in different languages and different contexts in the same language is the attempt to use "physical features describing specific articulatory states, both to represent phonetic categories and to serve as the basis for phonological representation". Keating suggests that there is a need for what she labels an intermediate phonetic category representation. This is described in Keating (1990: 323) as "the output of the phonology . . . the same thing as a 'derived phonological representation' . . . a somewhat more elaborated output than normally assumed by phonologists". It is conceived of as a means of stating the language-specific phonetic interpretation of phonological categories. So, whilst many papers in

Gerard J. Docherty

this volume have effectively been proposing a dichotomy of explanations, it is important to highlight that there exists a diversity of systematic phonetic characteristics of languages/accents, which seem to fall outside the scope of these explanations. As pointed out by Docherty (1992), we are a long way short of a satisfactory account of these aspects of phonetic realization, yet they are presumably absolutely central to laboratory phonology's goal of elucidating how (in Beckman and Kingston's words) "the discrete symbolic or cognitive units of the phonological representation of an utterance map onto the continuous psychoacoustic and motoric functions of its phonetic representation" (Beckman & Kingston, 1990: 1).

18.5 Concluding comments

The importance of Jun's paper lies in its challenging hypothesis that consonant voicing (like many other aspects of speech performance) may be accountable for in terms of gestural overlap and magnitude. Furthermore, the hypothesis has the attraction of having a number of testable components. This research will force those who have worked on voicing in obstruents in other languages to look again at their data and at commonly held suppositions about what factors might account for it, and to weigh up the evidence for a gestural account. In the process, this work will have provoked a deeper understanding of this aspect of the junction between phonetics and phonology.

Notes

1 The fact that this left-edge lengthening is not found in coda/AP-initial stops may be a relevant observation to the question of whether these stops are resyllabified or not. Based on a pilot study of /l/-flapping in Korean, Jun assumes that all coda lenis stops in underlying AP-final position are resyllabified to become postlexically AP-initial. If this is the case, it is pertinent to ask why the "resyllabified" stops do not demonstrate the left-edge lengthening as demonstrated by onset/AP-initial stops. It may be that prosodic strengthening is somehow blind to re-syllabification, or that re-syllabification is an extremely late stage of the derivation of an utterance; or it may even be questionable whether re-syllabification actually occurs at all in every case of a coda/AP-final lenis stop (recall that this is an assumption built in to Jun's analysis). There is clearly an issue here to be pursued further in future work.

2 The open phase was defined by Lindsey *et al.* (1986: 168) as follows. "The open and closed phase plots ... are derived from the Lx waveform by taking the upper 70% of the peak-to-peak amplitude of each cycle to represent the closure of the glottis, and the lower 30% to represent an open glottis, and by measuring the respective durations of each portion."

3 One confounding factor for this prediction might be the facet of Jun's proposal which claims that lenis stop glottal abduction gestures will be extremely truncated in prosodically weak environments. So whilst gesture overlap will be at its maximum in these environments, the glottal gesture will be at its weakest. This means that we might expect to see relatively little effect of the consonant gesture on the vowel Lx signal in both prosodically strong and (for the reason just given) in the prosodically weakest positions, with maximum coarticulatory influence showing up in environments of intermediate prosodic strength.

References

Beckman, M. E. & J. Kingston 1990. Introduction. In J. Kingston & M. E. Beckman (eds.), *Papers in Laboratory Phonology I: Between the Grammar and Physics of Speech*. Cambridge: Cambridge University Press, 1–16.

Beckman, M. E., K. de Jong, S-A. Jun & S-h. Lee. 1992. The interaction of coarticulation and prosody in sound change. *Language and Speech* 35: 45–58.

Browman, C. & L. Goldstein. 1986. Towards an articulatory phonology. *Phonology Yearbook* 3: 219–252.

Browman, C. & L. Goldstein. 1990. Tiers in articulatory phonology with some implications for casual speech. In J. Kingston & M. E. Beckman (eds.), *Papers in Laboratory Phonology I: Between the Grammar and Physics of Speech*. Cambridge: Cambridge University Press, 341–376.

Browman, C. & L. Goldstein. 1992a. Articulatory phonology: an overview. *Phonetica* 49: 155–180.

Browman, C. & L. Goldstein. 1992b. "Targetless" schwa. In G.J. Docherty & D.R. Ladd (eds.), *Papers in Laboratory Phonology II: Gesture, Segment, Prosody*. Cambridge: Cambridge University Press, 26–56.

Docherty, G. J. 1992. *The Timing of Voicing in British English Obstruents*. Berlin: Foris.

Jun, S-A. 1990. The prosodic structure of Korean – in terms of voicing. In E-J. Baek (ed.), *Proceedings of the Seventh International Conference on Korean Linguistics*. Toronto: University of Toronto Press, 87–104.

Jun, S-A. 1993. The phonetics and phonology of Korean prosody. Ph.D. dissertation. The Ohio State University.

Jun, S-A. & M. E. Beckman. 1993. A gestural-overlap analysis of vowel devoicing in Japanese and Korean. Paper presented at the annual meeting of the Linguistic Society of America, Los Angeles, January 1993.

Kagaya, R. 1974. A fiberscopic and acoustic study of the Korean stops, affricatives, and fricatives. *Journal of Phonetics* 2: 161–180.

Keating, P. 1984. Phonetic and phonological representation of stop consonant voicing. *Language* 60: 286–319.

Keating, P. 1990. Phonetic representations in a generative grammar. *Journal of Phonetics* 18: 321–334.

Kingston, J. & A. Cohen 1992. Extending articulatory phonology. *Phonetica* 49: 194–204.

Lindsey, G., P. Davies & A. Fourcin. 1986. Laryngeal coarticulation effects in English VCV sequences. *Speech, Hearing and Language* 2: 167–176. Department of Phonetics and Linguistics, University College London.

Lisker, L. & A. Abramson. 1964. A cross-language study of voicing in initial stops: acoustic measurements. *Word* 20: 384–422.

Munhall, K. & A. Lofqvist. 1992. Gestural aggregation in speech: laryngeal gestures. *Journal of Phonetics* 20: 111–126.

Silva, D. 1992. The phonetics and phonology of stop lenition in Korean. Ph.D. dissertation. Cornell University.

19

A production and perceptual account of palatalization

DANIEL RECASENS, JORDI FONTDEVILA, and
MARIA DOLORS PALLARÈS*

19.1 Introduction

Some phonologists have treated alveolopalatals (/ɲ/ as in French [beˈɲe] *baigner* "to bathe"; /ʎ/ as in Spanish [ˈʎaβe] *llave* "key") as complex segments (Keating, 1988, 1991; Avery & Rice, 1989; Lahiri & Evers, 1991). In their opinion these consonants are specified for a Coronal Node and a Dorsal Node, as in (1), thus requiring two independent and simultaneous commands for the activation of the tongue front and the tongue dorsum. According to this view alveolopalatals would not differ essentially from palatalized alveolars (such as /nʲ/ in Russian [konʲ] "horse").

(1)

This hypothesis accounts presumably for several aspects of the behavior of alveolopalatals. The fact that the two lingual articulators under presumed active control are located close to each other may explain why these consonants show a great deal of linguopalatal contact extending along both the alveolar zone and the palatal zone (Keating, 1988).

In addition, the complex nature of alveolopalatal consonants may account for changes like /nj/ becoming /ɲ/. According to Lahiri & Evers (1991), if /j/ is also treated as a complex alveolopalatal consonant, the segmental elements of the sequence /nj/ can easily merge into /ɲ/ through spreading of the feature [-ant] from /j/ to /n/ within the Coronal Node, as in (2). In this way the two gestural components of the input segment /j/ are preserved throughout the derivation.

(2)

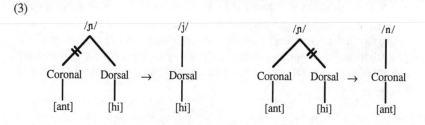

The decomposition of /ɲ/ into /jn/ (see section 19.3) could be treated in a related fashion.

Within the framework of Autosegmental Phonology, the simplification of alveolopalatals into palatal or alveolar consonants is obtained through delinking of the coronal or dorsal node, respectively, shown in (3) (Lipski 1989).

(3)

In this paper we will use descriptive and experimental data for the consonant /ɲ/ in order to show that these and other processes (sound changes, cases of phonetic variability and phonological alternations) can be explained assuming that alveolopalatals are simple, noncomplex segments. Moreover, it will be argued that alveolopalatals and palatalized dentalveolars cannot be assigned the same phonological representation.

19.2 Segmental coalescence

The consonant /ɲ/ can be generated from a sequence of alveolar /n/ followed by a palatal segment (usually /j/). Less often /ɲ/ originates from the reverse cluster, /jn/, (Southeastern Catalan ['kuɲə] for ['kuᵢnə] *cuina* "kitchen"), which accords with progressive assimilatory and coarticulatory phenomena being less frequent

266

than regressive ones. We hypothesize that /nj/ > [ɲ] should be characterized as a coalescence process between two simple segments into a simple alveolopalatal segment. Moreover, this is not a categorical but a gradual change, involving different degrees of overlap between the tongue front and the tongue dorsum gestures. It can be split into two consecutive subprocesses, i.e., gestural blending and segmental merging proper.

19.2.1 Gestural blending

Tongue dorsum raising during /n/ in anticipation of the following palatal segment may not affect the place of alveolar articulation. EPG data for Catalan (Recasens, 1984) reveal the existence of a shorter time interval between the periods of maximum alveolar contact and maximum palatal contact for [nj] in the sequences /anja/ and /unju/ (15–30 ms) than for [ni] in the sequences /ani/ and /uni/ (60 ms). In spite of the maximum alveolar and palatal contact coming closer to each other in the former vs. the latter sequence, the place of alveolar articulation for /n/ remains at the same location; alveolar closure is quite front, thus leaving room for the tongue dorsum to approach the palatal zone in anticipation of the following /j/ or /i/.

At a more advanced stage in the palatalization process tongue dorsum raising may involve closure retraction and active laminal involvement; closure extends all along the alveolar zone and may even reach the prepalate. This realization, [ŋ], is often heard as a palatalized sound, as for /n/ before /i/ and /e/ in Roumanian dialects (Nandris, 1963, and *ALR*; see Dukelski, 1960 for palatographic evidence), and occasionally before /i/ in French dialects (Pignon, 1960; see Straka, 1979, for palatographic evidence).

It is hypothesized that more considerable shortening of the time interval between the two lingual gestures in the sequence /nj/ may cause gestural blending (see Browman & Goldstein, 1989, for this notion). The outcome is an articulation which is intermediate between the two original gestures, i.e., lamino-predorso-alveolo-prepalatal. This modification of place of articulation may or may not be accompanied by a withdrawal of the front alveolar closure, as indicated by the fact that /ɲ/ itself is articulated with different degrees of closure fronting depending on speaker and other factors (compare the realizations of Catalan /ɲ/ for speakers JP and DR or JC at frame 3 in Figure 19.1). This case of blending is most probably found in languages in which /ɲ/ does not have phonemic status, such as English (in the word *onion*, much in the same way as /sj/ > [ʃj] in the phrase *bless you*), and Japanese.[1] Indeed, EPG data reported by Miyawaki, Kiritani, Tatsumi & Fujimura (1974) show that, in comparison to non-palatalized /n/ before /u/, palatalized /n/ before /i/ and /j/ in Japanese entails considerable closure retraction and no trace of central closure at the front alveolar zone; according to linguopalatal configurations in Miyawaki *et*

a ɲə

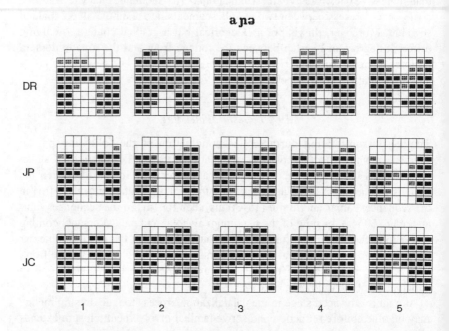

Figure 19.1. Linguopalatal configurations at five equidistant frames along the closure period for /ɲ/ in the sequence [aɲə] (three Catalan speakers DR, JP and JC), where 1 = closure onset, 3 = closure midpoint and 5 = closure offset. Data were collected with the Reading EPG system (Hardcastle, Jones, Knight, Trudgeon & Calder, 1989). The alveolar zone is located along the four front rows of electrodes; the palatal zone is found along the four back rows. Percentages of electrode activation are represented as follows: (black) 80–100%; (gray) 40–80%; (white) 0–40%.

al., this closure backing mechanism causes an increase in tongue dorsum constraint, thus preventing this tongue region from being affected by coarticulatory effects associated with following /j/ vs. /i/.

Data are needed to investigate the extent to which temporal overlap between the two supposedly blended gestures is partial or complete. Absorption of the second segment of the sequence has been acknowledged as an extreme case of palatalization (Bhat, 1974), and it is certainly the case that [ɲ] may be heard instead of [ɲj] as a realization of underlying /nj/.

19.2.2 Segmental merging

Complete gestural blending results in simultaneous activity of the tongue front and the tongue dorsum; EPG data show temporal overlap between the maximum alveolar and maximum palatal contact periods (Recasens, 1984). At this stage the alveolopalatal articulation ([ɲ]) may acquire phonological status and is no longer found in free alternation with the biphonemic cluster, as shown by the Spanish minimal pair ['kuna] (*cuna* "crib") / ['kuɲa] (*cuña* "wedge", from Latin CUNEA). Minimal pairs with the cluster /nj/ and the phoneme /ɲ/ can be found in Romance languages (e.g. Italian *Campania* "region in Southern Italy"/ *campagna* "countryside"; Spanish *uranio* "uranium"/ *huraño* "grump").

There are two classes of simple consonants involving active contact at the palatal zone, alveolopalatals (Catalan /ɲ/) and palatals proper (Catalan /j/) (Recasens, 1990). What is transcribed as the same sound may belong to the former or latter category depending on the language; thus, e.g. /ɲ/ and /c/ are usually alveolopalatal in the Romance languages but palatal in some African languages (Ibibio: Connell, 1992; Ngwo: Ladefoged, 1968).

The following arguments (a, b, and c) can be adduced in support of the non-complex status of alveolopalatals.

(a) Alveolopalatals are often produced with the back of the blade and the front predorsum. Since these two lingual regions can act as primary articulators in the production of other sounds, one could be lead to believe that they also act as independent articulators in the production of alveolopalatals. However, two immediately adjacent tongue regions contributing simultaneously to the formation of one and the same place of articulation are not likely to be separately controlled (see also Keating, 1993, for a similar remark).

(b) Full lingual contact at the postalveolo–prepalatal zone is found during the entire closure period of /ɲ/ (see Figure 19.1; Recasens, Fontdevila & Pallarès, in press b), which may be taken in support of alveolopalatals being produced with one articulator at a single, localized place of articulation. A contact increase towards the front and back palate before closure midpoint (i.e., from frame 1 through frame 3 in the figure) is not caused by simultaneous activation of a tongue front gesture and a tongue dorsum gesture but results presumably from an increase in lingual contact pressure level at the place of articulation. In fact, a large dorsopalatal contact surface is not a necessary attribute of alveolopalatals; indeed, speakers showing less laminopredorsal contact at the place of articulation (e.g. speaker JP as compared to speaker DR in Figure 19.1) allow less tongue dorsum raising and less dorsopalatal contact to occur.

(c) If the tongue dorsum were activated for /ɲ/, this consonant should exhibit at least the same amount of dorsopalatal contact as /j/ (English [jɛs] *yes*); coupling effects between the tongue front and the tongue dorsum could even convey additional contact for the alveolopalatal consonant. Data from five Catalan speakers (Recasens *et al.*, in press b) show instead less dorsopalatal contact for /ɲ/ than for /j/, thus suggesting that the former consonant undergoes no active dorsal control; moreover, /ɲ/ turns out to be more variable than /j/, both across repetitions of the same sequence and across vowel environments. These results indicate that the two areas of lingual articulation in alveolopalatals are too close to one another to be considered as contributing to the formation of a complex segment.

If no palatal gesture is involved in the production of alveolopalatals, what is it that speakers interpret as a [j]-like segment when listening to prevocalic /ɲ/? This auditory-perceptual effect is associated with the presence of an uncontrolled, [j]-like lingual configuration at closure offset caused by the alveolopalatal release not being abrupt but proceeding gradually from front to back in languages such as Catalan, Italian, and French (see frames 4 and 5 in Figure 19.1; also Bothorel, Simon, Wioland & Zerling, 1986). This [j]-like segment is usually audible to speakers of languages lacking the phoneme /ɲ/ (English), since they always tend to identify alveolopalatals as a blended version of /nj/. Its perceptibility may also be related to articulatory differences in the production of /ɲ/ (perhaps in cases where the consonant exhibits a very front closure location), as implied by the transcriptions [ɲj] and [nj] for the alveolopalatal phoneme in French dialects (*baigner, agneau, oignon, saigner*; *ALF: ALEC, ALEP, ALEB*), and as shown by some palatographic data in the literature (Straka, 1979).

19.3 Segmental decomposition

The decomposition of /ɲ/ into [in] can also be accounted for without assuming that a dorsal gesture is present in the alveolopalatal consonant. Segmental decomposition often occurs in syllable coda (see Ohala & Kawasaki, 1984, for other processes taking place in the same contextual position). The word final consonant may be realized as [in], [iŋ] or [iɲ].[2] In contemporary Majorcan Catalan, word final /ɲ/ is realized as [i] + a nasal stop in preconsonantal position; the nasal agrees in place with the following consonant ([aɲ] *any* "year," [aim 'bɔ] *any bo* "good year") (also Straka, 1979, for Czech /ɲ/).

In our opinion segmental decomposition may result from listeners assigning segmental status to the [j]-like acoustic formant transitions associated with the consonantal gesture in prepausal position. Those transitions often start at vowel offset (F_2, F_3, . . .) and continue during murmur onset with a higher number (F_2-N_3, F_3-N_4, and so on) because of the presence of a fixed N_2 formant during the murmur which is exclusively dependent on the nasal cavity. The perceptual relevance of these formant transitions has been validated in a natural speech synthesis experiment with final VC syllables made up of the vowels /i/, /a/ and /u/, and the nasal stops /m/, /n/ and /ɲ/ (Catalan: Recasens & Martí, 1990). Pitch pulses were removed in several steps according to two conditions: (murmurs condition) from the third pitch pulse before vowel offset (−3) until the ninth pitch pulse after murmur onset (+9); (vowels condition) starting at pitch pulse +9 back to pitch pulse −3. Percent correct responses for /ɲ/ show that signal truncation affects mostly the identification of the syllable /aɲ/ in the murmurs condition; progressive removal of pitch pulses from vowel offset to murmur onset reduces the percent correct responses from almost 100% to 20%. In the other cases, correct identification scores undergo fewer modifications: they remain either low (for /iɲ/ in both conditions and for /uɲ/ in the vowels condition) or high (for /aɲ/ in the vowels condition and for /uɲ/ in the murmurs condition). Spectrographic displays suggest that the dynamic information contained in the long and rising formant transitions proceeding from the vowel into the murmur are highly relevant cues for the identification of /ɲ/ when preceded by the vowel /a/ in prepausal position. Formant transitions contribute little to consonantal identification in the other word final syllables because of their low amplitude (/uɲ/) or small frequency range (/iɲ/).

In order to study more precisely the role of the formant transitions in the identification of /aɲ/ we compared their acoustic and articulatory salience in the final syllable /aɲ/ to that in the VC portion of the intervocalic sequence /aɲa/. Special attention was given to the F_2-N_3 transitions and to the rising trajectories

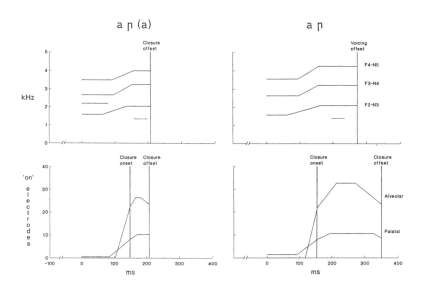

Figure 19.2. Formant trajectories (top) and linguopalatal contact trajectories (bottom) for /aɲ/ in the intervocalic sequence /aɲa/ (left) and in the final sequence /aɲ/ (right). Both signals are displayed simultaneously; data correspond to the Catalan speaker DP. Acoustic formant transitions occur between the vowel steady-state period and the murmur steady-state period; formant trajectories are represented until closure offset (intervocalic sequence) and until voicing offset (final sequence). Rising lingual contact trajectories from the vowel until maximum contact during the closure period are displayed independently for the alveolar zone and for the palatal zone; they are followed by a platform of maximum contact and a final period of contact decrease before closure offset.

in dorsopalatal contact (see Figure 19.2), since they are positively correlated (Recasens, Fontdevila & Pallarès, in press a).

Table 19.1 shows that the F_2-N_3 transitions exhibit a larger frequency range and a longer duration in final vs. intervocalic position; moreover these position-dependent differences are matched by the ranges and durations of the dorsopalatal contact trajectories. Ratio values indicate that an increase in the duration of the final transitions is to a large extent independent of the duration of the vowel (which is also longer in final vs. intervocalic position).[3] Overall, spatiotemporal data confirm that the acoustic VC transitions and their corresponding articulatory trajectories are particularly salient in final position which may very well favor segmental decomposition.

Table 19.1. Top: ranges of the F_2–N_3 transitions (in Hz) and rising dorsopalatal contact trajectories (in number of "on" electrodes) for /aɲ/ in the sequences /aɲ/ and /a ɲa/. Bottom: durations (in ms) of the same transitions and contact trajectories. Significant differences are marked with a bracket; standard deviations are included within parentheses. Data correspond to Catalan speakers DR, JP and DP.

		F_2–N_3 (Hz)	EPG ("on" electrodes)
DR	aɲ	769.80 (111.30)	⌈ 18.60 (2.07)
	aɲ(a)	640.00 (71.63)	⌊ 15.20 (2.17)
JP	aɲ	952.33 (137.99)	⌈ 18.00 (0.00)
	aɲ(a)	891.60 (192.41)	⌊ 11.60 (2.70)
DP	aɲ	525.80 (115.76)	9.20 (1.30)
	aɲ(a)	452.40 (82.13)	9.80 (0.84)
		F_2–N_3 (ms)	EPG (ms)
DR	aɲ	⌈ 140.20 (21.88)	⌈ 121.00 (8.94)
	aɲ(a)	⌊ 83.60 (7.30)	⌊ 97.00 (12.55)
JP	aɲ	162.33 (57.50)	120.00 (13.23)
	aɲ(a)	115.80 (24.48)	101.00 (44.78)
DP	aɲ	99.40 (34.56)	102.00 (20.19)
	aɲ(a)	73.40 (11.50)	85.00 (12.25)

A production and perceptual account of palatalization

Table 19.2. Top: time intervals between alveolar contact maximum and closure onset (left column), and between palatal contact maximum and closure onset (central column); ratios between both intervals are given in the right column. Bottom: time intervals between closure onset and onset of the rising alveolar contact trajectories (left column), and between closure onset and onset of the rising palatal contact trajectories (central column); ratios between both intervals are given in the right column. Data correspond to /aɲ/ in the sequences /aɲ/ and /aɲa/ (Catalan speakers DR, JP and DP). Significant differences are marked with a bracket; standard deviations are included within parentheses.

		Alv$_{max}$ - Cl$_{ons}$	Pal$_{max}$ - Cl$_{ons}$	Ratio
DR	aɲ	45.00 (25.74)	50.00 (8.66)	0.92 (0.57)
	aɲ(a)	27.00 (9.08)	46.00 (14.32)	0.62 (0.25)
JP	aɲ	⌈ 43.33 (7.66)	53.33 (20.21)	0.87 (0.25)
	aɲ(a)	⌊ 21.00 (8.22)	33.00 (30.54)	0.26 (0.61)
DP	aɲ	⌈ 57.00 (5.70)	38.00 (22.53)	3.63 (5.25)
	aɲ(a)	⌊ 16.00 (8.94)	17.00 (23.61)	0.29 (1.67)
		Cl$_{ons}$ - Alv$_{ons}$	Cl$_{ons}$ - Pal$_{ons}$	Ratio
DR	aɲ	⌈ 35.00 (3.54)	⌈ 71.00 (4.18)	0.49 (0.03)
	aɲ(a)	⌊ 29.00 (2.24)	⌊ 51.00 (4.18)	0.57 (0.08)
JP	aɲ	⌈ 26.67 (2.89)	66.67 (7.64)	⌈ 0.40 (0.07)
	aɲ(a)	⌊ 43.00 (10.37)	72.00 (21.97)	⌊ 0.61 (0.09)
DP	aɲ	39.00 (4.18)	64.00 (11.94)	0.62 (0.11)
	aɲ(a)	49.00 (10.84)	69.00 (12.94)	0.71 (0.10)

The salience of the [j]-like formant transitions for final vs. intervocalic /aɲ/ can also be related to a longer delay of the alveolar contact maximum with respect to the dorsopalatal contact maximum during closure; as shown in Table 19.2 (top), in comparison to its intervocalic counterpart, final /aɲ/ shows higher ratio values between the time intervals Alv$_{max}$ – Cl$_{ons}$ (i.e., from closure onset until alveolar contact maximum), and Pal$_{max}$ – Cl$_{ons}$ (i.e., from closure onset until palatal contact maximum). Another measure of relative timing contributing to the salience of the final vowel transitions is an earlier onset of the rising dorsopalatal contact trajectory with respect to the rising alveolar contact trajectory during the preceding vowel /a/; indeed, in comparison to its intervocalic counterpart, final /aɲ/ shows lower ratios between the time intervals Cl_{ons} – Alv_{ons} (i.e., from the onset of the alveolar contact trajectory during V1 until closure onset) and Cl_{ons} – Pal_{ons} (i.e., from the onset of the palatal contact trajectory until closure onset) (Table 19.2, bottom).

In summary, there are several events causing the appearance of longer dorsopalatal trajectories and longer F_2–N_3 transitions in final vs. intervocalic position.

19.4 Gestural reduction

Alveolopalatal /ɲ/ can also be realized as [n] or as [j]. In our view, these outcomes do not result from the loss of an apicoalveolar or a dorsopalatal gesture (i.e., from delinking the featural contents of either the Coronal Node or the Dorsal Node within the Autosegmental Phonology framework) but from articulatory changes affecting a simple alveolopalatal gesture.

Similar to segmental decomposition, the process /ɲ/ > [n] or [ŋ] occurs mostly in syllable coda position.[4] In present-day Alguerese Catalan, word final /ɲ/ is realized as a nasal stop agreeing in place with the following consonant ([aɲ] *any* "year", [am 'bɔ] *any bo* "good year"), and Spanish shows alternations between intervocalic [ɲ] and word final [n] (*desdeñar* "to disdain" ~ *desdén* "scorn"). We would like to think that this outcome is arrived at if listeners fail to hear the [j]-like formant transitions (e.g. when /ɲ/ is produced with little tongue dorsum raising); a fronted realization of the alveolopalatal consonant could be interpreted as /n/ in these circumstances. The EPG data analyzed in this paper reveal indeed more alveolar contact fronting for prepausal vs. intervocalic /ɲ/ at the closure midpoint in the case of those Catalan speakers (JP and DP) allowing longer delays in the achievement of the alveolar contact maximum (Alv_{max}) during the closure period. No differences in dorsopalatal contact size or in nasal formant frequency values are found between the two consonantal realizations but could presumably occur in faster speech or in preconsonantal position.

The change /ɲ/ > [j] is also documented.[5] It may be attributed to the absence of a complete central closure in reduced realizations of the alveolopalatal consonant (Farnetani, 1990; Straka, 1979). Nasalized [j̃] is then reinterpreted as [j]. This change could also be due to the failure to perceive the nasal formants if the closure period is particularly short (e.g. in preconsonantal position) or is produced with low amplitude level and partial devoicing (e.g. in prepausal position; see voicing offset bar in Figure 19.2).

19.5 Gestural strengthening

Alveolopalatals do not always originate from clusters composed of an alveolar consonant and a following dorsopalatal segment, but from initial / n / or geminate /nn/ as well. Both cases are problematic for defenders of the complex nature of alveolopalatals since neither /n/ nor /nn/ involve the presence of a dorsal gesture.

The evolution of initial /n/ into [ɲ] appears to be related to articulatory gestures being especially prominent in this contextual position (Ohala & Kawasaki, 1983; Farnetani & Recasens, in preparation; Browman, personal communication). Gestural reinforcement is favored presumably by gestural blending before high vowels.[6] There is some palatographic evidence for contact spreading along the alveolar zone for initial /ɲ/ before any vowel and in emphatic pronunciation (Straka, 1979).

The reinforcement of geminate /nn/ is well documented in some Romance languages (Spanish ['aɲo] *año* and Catalan [aɲ] *any*, from Latin ANNUM "year"). The suggestion that lingual geminates may be produced with more tongue dorsum raising than their singleton equivalents renders this change highly plausible (Javkin, 1979; Farnetani, 1986).

19.6 Palatalized dentalveolars

The relationship between alveolopalatal consonants (/ɲ/) and palatalized dentalveolar consonants (/nʲ/ in the Russian word [konʲ] "steed" or in the Estonian word [onnʲ] "hut") is of interest here since they are both treated as complex segments within the framework of Autosegmental Phonology. We will show however that the articulation of the two consonantal categories differs in crucial respects.

Palatalized consonants can be characterized as complex segments involving two relatively independent articulators. Palatalization is manifested by a secondary tongue dorsum gesture superimposed onto most primary places of articulation. The independent status of the dorsal gesture can be easily observed in palatalized consonants using a non lingual primary articulator such as palatalized bilabials. Palatalized dentalveolars are thus realized by means of two simultaneous lingual gestures leading towards a primary front lingual closure or constriction and a secondary dorsal [j]-like constriction (Öhman, 1966).

Some consistent articulatory differences between alveolopalatals and palatalized dentalveolars are in agreement with the non-complex nature of the former class of sounds and the complex status of the latter.

(a) The place of closure or constriction with the tongue front is more advanced for palatalized dentalveolars than for alveolopalatals. X-ray and palatographic data for /tʲ/, /dʲ/ and /nʲ/ in different Slavic languages (Boyanus, 1955; Koneczna & Zawadowski, 1951, 1956; Vihman, 1967; Wierzchowska, 1971) often reveal that the primary place of articulation for these palatalized consonants is mostly at the dental and/or alveolar zone and does not reach the prepalate. This is the expected outcome for a double articulation involving a tongue front gesture and a tongue dorsum gesture: the location of the tongue front closure or constriction needs to be front enough so that a dorsal gesture can be executed simultaneously and independently. Consequently palatalized dentalveolars are articulated with less extension of contact around the primary place of articulation than alveolopalatals. Blending is often possible in this case, and conveys the active involvement of the blade instead of the tip and some retraction of the place of articulation; the result is a combined articulation for the production of which "most of the fore part of the tongue, including the blade and the front, acts as a single articulating organ" (Jones & Ward, 1969).

An interesting language in this respect is Irish Gaelic which distinguishes phonemically dentalveolars (such as /n/), palatalized dentalveolars (such as /nʲ/) and alveolopalatals (such as /ɲ/).

Figure 19.3 shows linguopalatal configurations for these three consonants (one Irish speaker). Data were obtained across five repetitions of symmetrical VCV sequences with the vowels [i], [a], and [u] (Recasens, Farnetani & Ní Chasaide, 1991). It can be seen that /nʲ/ is produced with a postalveolar closure while /n/ is front alveolar and /ɲ/ is alveolopalatal. A more posterior place of articulation for the palatalized dentalveolar than for the alveolar can be attributed to some coupling effects caused by the tongue dorsum raising gesture in the case of the former consonant; the primary articulator has now become the tongue blade instead of the tongue tip. In comparison to /n/, the consonant /nʲ/ shows some central narrowing at the back palatal zone which is indicative of the presence of an active tongue dorsum raising gesture. The fact that lingual contact at the front palatal zone is much less for /nʲ/ than for /ɲ/ is consistent with the former consonant being produced with two independent gestures and the latter being produced with a single alveolopalatal gesture.

(b) The relative independence between the tongue front and the tongue dorsum for palatalized dentalveolars may result in some gestural dissociation in time. In particular, Estonian shows an "on"-glide palatalization effect from a preceding vowel into the consonant reflecting presumably a slight anticipation

/n/   /nʲ/   /ɲ/

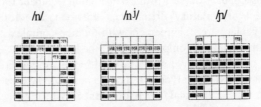

Figure 19.3. Linguopalatal configurations at the period of maximum contact for Irish /n/ (left), /nʲ/ (middle) and /ɲ/ (right) (One Irish speaker; Recasens *et al.*, 1991).

of the secondary tongue dorsum raising gesture with respect to the primary closing gesture (Lehiste, 1965; Eek, 1973; Sepp, 1987). Temporal dissociation in this case does not imply that the two gestures are temporally ordered in the way that a dentalveolar and a palatal consonant are ordered in a consonant cluster (e.g. /nʲ/ vs. /nj/). Maddieson & Ladefoged (1989) have shown a similar timing asymmetry in double articulations, such as labial-velars [k͡p] and [g͡b] with velar closure onset preceding very briefly labial closure onset. According to Vihman (1967), the timing asymmetry between the two lingual gestures in Estonian palatalized dentalveolars is associated with the degree of lingual pressure and tongue dorsum height. Indeed, Russian palatalized dentalveolars, which appear to be produced with more tongue dorsum raising than their Estonian counterparts, do not show an "on"-glide but an "off"-glide palatalization effect from the consonant into the following vowel (Derkach, 1975; Vihman, 1967). Scatton (1984) also refers to lesser tongue dorsum raising for palatalized lingual consonants in Bulgarian vs. Russian, and to dialectal differences in the degree of temporal overlap of the two elements of the palatalized consonant in the former language. As for /nj/ and /ni/ (see section 19.2), it should be possible to obtain complete temporal overlap, and thus complete blending between the gestures involved in the production of /nʲ/.

Recent EMMA (electromagnetic midsagittal articulometry) data collected at Haskins Laboratories (Recasens & Romero, submitted) are in support of the complex nature of palatalized dentalveolars and the simple nature of alveolopalatals. In comparison to Catalan /ɲ/, Russian /nʲ/ is produced with a significantly longer lag between the offset of maximum displacement for the tongue dorsum and for the tongue front articulators. Closure release at both articulatory regions is thus quasi-simultaneous for /ɲ/ (with a very short delay for the tongue dorsum release for reasons pointed out above) but clearly sequential for /nʲ/ (with a much longer tongue dorsum delay, between that for /ɲ/ and that for /nj/).

19.7 Conclusions

Alveolopalatal consonants and palatalized dentalveolars cannot be assigned the same phonological representation: alveolopalatals are simple segments while palatalized dentalveolars are complex. Gestural blending may apply to sequences with alveolar consonants and to palatalized dentalveolars: the resulting articulatory trajectory is intermediate between the two input lingual gestures and may be assigned phonological status. Clusters and palatalized dentalveolars differ among themselves in that the two gestures overlap to a larger extent in the realization of the latter vs. the former; gestural overlap for palatalized dentalveolars is not complete, which explains a clearer perceptibility of the [j] element for these consonants than for alveolopalatals. In the case of palatalized alveolars, this [j] effect is truly representative of an independent, actively controlled dorsal gesture which may appear at closure onset or at closure offset; for alveolopalatals, however, it is just associated with a transitional articulatory configuration occurring fixedly during closure offset. Several articulatory and perceptual processes can be explained assuming that alveolopalatals are simple segments.

Notes

*This work was supported by NINCDS Grant NS-13617 to Haskins Laboratories, and by project ESPRIT-BRA 6975 "SPEECH MAPS" and Working Group ESPRIT-BRA 7098 "ACCOR" from the European Community, and DGICYT project CE93-0020 of the Spanish Ministry of Education and Science. Our thanks to John Trumper and Joaquín Romero.

1 Alternations between the realizations [nj] and [ɲj] are also documented in languages in which /ɲ/ has phonemic status, e.g. in French dialects (*panier, union, grenier, n'y a pas, nièce, boutonnière*; *ALF: ALEC, ALEN, ALEFC, ALEAL, ALEB, ALEBRAM*) and in Argentinian Spanish (*opinión*; Malmberg, 1950).

2 This is so in Gascon (Millardet, 1910), Friulian (Iliescu, 1972; Marchetti, 1967; *ASLEF*) and Ladin (Zamboni, 1983).

3 The percentage of the F_2 vowel transition duration with respect to the full vowel duration is 74.9 (speaker DR), 84.4 (speaker JP), and 63.3 (speaker DP) in final position, and 41.7 (DR), 49.5 (JP), and 50.1 (DP) in intervocalic position. A smaller but consistent trend is also found in the EPG data.

4 It is documented in Gascon (prepausally and before the plural ending *s*; Bec, 1968), in Friulian (Marchetti, 1967; *ASLEF*), and in French dialects (*ALF: ALEN*; Ardenne, according to Bruneau, 1913).

5 This realization is found in Portuguese dialects (Lipski, 1989), French dialects (*ALF: ALEN*), Friulian (*jui* Latin IUNIUS "june"; *ASLEF*), Gascon (Millardet, 1910), Provençal (Ronjat, 1932), and Old Roumanian (*vie* Latin VINEA "vinyeard"; Nandris, 1963).

6 This is so in the following examples: Argentinian Spanish ['ɲuðo] (Malmberg, 1950) and Central Italian ['ɲudo], ['ɲuto] (Latin NODUS "knot")(Jaberg & Jud, 1928-40); Catalan dialects [ɲiu] *niu* (Latin NIDUS "nest"); French dialects [ɲuf] *neuf* (Latin NOVUS "new"; *ALF: ALEFC*).

References

Atlasul lingvistic romîn (ALR). 1956–72. Bucarest: Editura Academiei Republicii Socialiste Romania, 7 vols.

Atlante storico-linguistico-etnografico friulano (ASLEF). 1972–86. Padua: University of Padua, 6 vols.

Atlas linguistiques de la France par régions (ALF). Paris: Éditions du CNRS. *(ALEC) Atlas linguistique et ethnographique du Centre* 1971–, P. Dubuisson; *(ALEN) Atlas linguistique et ethnographique normand* 1980–, P. Brasseur; *(ALEFC) Atlas linguistique et ethnographique de la Franche-Comté* 1972–, C. Dondaine; *(ALEAL) Atlas linguistique et ethnographique de l'Auvergne et du Limousin* 1975–, J.C. Potte; *(ALEB) Atlas linguistique et ethnographique de la Bourgogne* 1975–, G. Taverdet ; *(ALEBRAM) Atlas linguistique et ethnographique de la Bretagne Romane, de l'Anjou et du Maine* 1975–, G. Guillaume & J.-P. Chauveau; *(ALEP) Atlas linguistique et ethnographique de la Provence* 1975–, J.C. Bouvier and C. Martel.

Avery, P. & K. Rice. 1989. Segmental structure and coronal underspecification. *Phonology* 6: 179–200.

Bec, P. 1968. *Les Interférences linguistiques entre gascon et languedocien (dans les parlers du Comminges et du Couserans)*. Paris: Presses Universitaires de France.

Bhat, D. N. S. 1974. A general study of palatalization. *Working Papers on Language Universals*, Stanford University, 14: 17–58.

Bothorel, A., P. Simon, F. Wioland & J.-P. Zerling. 1986. *Cinéradiographie des voyelles et consonnes du français*. Travaux de l'Institut de Phonétique de Strasbourg.

Boyanus, S. C. 1955. *Russian Pronunciation*. Cambridge, MA: Harvard University Press.

Browman, C. P. & L. Goldstein. 1989. Articulatory gestures as phonological units. *Phonology* 6: 201–251.

Bruneau, Ch. 1913. *Etude phonétique des patois d'Ardenne*. Paris: Librairie Ancienne H. Champion.

Connell, B. 1992. Tongue contact, active articulators, and coarticulation. *Proceedings of the International Conference on Speech and Language Processing 92 Vol. 2*. Edmonton: Priority Press, 1075–78.

Derkach, M. 1975. Acoustic cues of softness in Russian syllables and their application in automatic speech recognition. In G. Fant and M. A. A. Tatham (eds.), *Auditory Analysis and Perception of Speech*. New York: Academic Press, 349–358.

Dukelski, N. I. 1960. Cercetare foneticăexperimentalăasupra palatalizării și a labializării consoanelor romînești. *Fonetica și Dialectologie* 2: 7–46.

Eek, A. 1973. Observations in Estonian palatalization: an articulatory study. *Estonian Papers in Phonetics* 4: 18–36.

Farnetani, E. 1986. Lingual and velar coarticulatory movements in the production of /n/ in Italian: some preliminary data. *Quaderni del Centro per le Ricerche di Fonetica*, University of Padua, 5: 285–307.

Farnetani, E. 1990. V-to-V lingual coarticulation and its spatiotemporal domain. In W. J. Hardcastle & A. Marchal (eds.), *Speech Production and Speech Modelling*. Dordrecht: Kluwer, 93–130.

Farnetani, E. & D. Recasens. In preparation. Initial alveolopalatal and alveolar consonants: an EPG and acoustic characterization.

Hardcastle, W. J., W. Jones, C. Knight, A. Trudgeon & G. Calder. 1989. New developments in electropalatography: a state-of-the art report. *Clinical Linguistics and Phonetics* 3: 1–38.

Iliescu, M. 1972. *Le Frioulan à partir des dialectes parlés en Roumanie*. The Hague: Mouton.

Jaberg, K. & J. Jud. 1928–40. *Sprach- und Sachatlas Italiens und der Südschweiz.* Zofingen: Ringier, 16 vols.

Javkin, H. 1979. Phonetic universals and phonological change. *Report of the Phonology Laboratory*, University of California at Berkeley, 4.

Jones, D. & D. Ward. 1969. *The Phonetics of Russian.* Cambridge: Cambridge University Press.

Keating, P. 1988. Palatals as complex segments: X-ray evidence. *UCLA Working Papers in Phonetics* 69: 77–91.

Keating, P. 1991. Coronal places of articulation. In C. Paradis & J. F. Prunet (eds.), *The Special Status of Coronals*. San Diego, CA: Academic Press, 29–48.

Keating, P. 1993. Phonetic representation of palatalization versus fronting. *UCLA Working Papers in Phonetics* 85: 6–21.

Koneczna, H. & W. Zawadowski. 1951. *Przekroje Rentgenograficzne Glosek Polskich.* Warsaw: Panstwowe Wydawnictwo Naukowe.

Koneczna, H. & W. Zawadowski. 1956. *Obrazy Rentgenograficzne Glosek Rosyjskich* Warsaw: Panstwowe Wydawnictwo Naukowe.

Ladefoged, P. 1968. *A Phonetic Study of West African Languages.* Cambridge: Cambridge University Press.

Lahiri, A. & V. Evers. 1991. Palatalization and coronality. In C. Paradis & J.F. Prunet (eds.), *The Special Status of Coronals*. San Diego: Academic Press, 79–100.

Lehiste, I. 1965. Palatalization in Estonian: Some acoustic observations. In V. Kõresaar & A. Ronnit (eds.), *Estonian Poetry and Language (Studies in honor of Ants Oras)*. Stockholm: Vaba Eesti, 136–162.

Lipski, J. M. 1989. Spanish "Yeísmo" and the palatal resonants: Towards a unified analysis. *Probus* 1: 211–223.

Maddieson, I. & P. Ladefoged. 1989. Multiply articulated segments and the feature hierarchy. *UCLA Working Papers in Phonetics* 72: 116–138.

Malmberg, B. 1950. *Etudes sur la phonétique de l'espagnol parlé en Argentine.* Lund: Gleerup.

Marchetti, G. 1967. *Lineamenti di grammatica friulana.* Udine.

Millardet, G. 1910. *Etudes de dialectologie landaise.* Toulouse: Edouard Privat, 2 vols.

Miyawaki, K., S. Kiritani, I. F. Tatsumi & O. Fujimura. 1974. Palatographic observation of VCV articulations in Japanese. *Annual Bulletin, Research Institute of Logopedics and Phoniatrics*, University of Tokyo, 8: 51–57.

Nandris, O. 1963. *Phonétique historique du roumain.* Paris: Klincksieck.

Ohala, J. J. & H. Kawasaki. 1984. Prosodic phonology and phonetics. *Phonology* 1: 113–128.

Öhman, S. E. 1966. Coarticulation in VCV sequences: spectrographic measurements. *Journal of the Acoustical Society of America* 39: 151–168.

Pignon, J. 1960. *L'Evolution phonétique des parlers du Poitou (Vienne et Deux-Sièvres).* Paris: Editions d'Artrey.

Recasens, D. 1984. Timing constraints and coarticulation: alveolo-palatals and sequences of alveolar + [j] in Catalan. *Phonetica* 41: 125–139.

Recasens, D. 1990. The articulatory characteristics of palatal consonants. *Journal of Phonetics* 18: 267–280.

A production and perceptual account of palatalization

Recasens, D. 1991. *Fonètica descriptiva del català*. Barcelona: Institut d'Estudis Catalans.

Recasens, D. & J. Martí. 1990. Perception of unreleased final nasal consonants. *Journal d'Acoustique* 3: 287–299.

Recasens, D., E. Farnetani & A. Ní Chasaide. 1991. A study of the production of coarticulatory characteristics of palatal and palatalized consonants. *Periodic Progress Report*, ESPRIT-ACCOR BRA project of the European Community, vol. 2.

Recasens, D., J. Fontdevila & M. D. Pallarès. In press (a). Velarization degree and coarticulatory resistance for /l/ in Catalan and German. *Journal of Phonetics*.

Recasens, D., J. Fontdevila & M. D. Pallarès. In press (b). Palatal consonants as non-complex segments. *Catalan Working Papers in Linguistics*. Barcelona: Universitat Autònoma.

Recasens, D. & J. Romero. Submitted. An EMMA study of segmental complexity in alveolopalatals and palatalized alveolars.

Rohlfs, G. 1966. *Grammatica storica della lingua italiana e dei suoi dialetti*, Fonetica: 1. G. Einaudi.

Ronjat, J. 1932. *Grammaire historique des parlers provençaux modernes*. Montpellier, 3 vols.

Scatton, E. A. 1984. *A Reference Grammar of Modern Bulgarian*. Columbus: Slavica Publishers Inc.

Sepp, A. 1987. Acoustic variation and types of palatalization. *Proceedings of the XIth International Congress of Phonetic Sciences,* Tallinn, 4: 36–39.

Shibata, S., A. Ino, S. Yamashita, S. Hiki, S. Kiritani & M. Sawasahima. 1978. A new portable unit for electropalatography. *Annual Bulletin of the Institute of Logopedics and Phoniatrics*, University of Tokyo, 12: 5–10.

Straka, G. 1979. *Les Sons et les mots*. Paris: Klincksieck.

Vihman, M. M. 1967. Palatalization in Russian and Estonian. *Project on Linguistic Analysis Reports*, Phonology Laboratory, University of California at Berkeley, Second Series, 1: V1–V32.

Wierzchowska, B. 1971. *Wymowa Polska*. Warsaw: Panstowowe Zaklady Wydawnictwo Szkolynch.

Zamboni, A. 1983. I dialetti cadorini. In G. B. Pellegrini & S. Sacco (eds.), *Il ladino bellunese*, Istituto Bellunese di Ricerche Sociali e Culturali, Serie "Studi Ladini", 3, 45–83.

20

An acoustic and electropalatographic study of lexical and postlexical palatalization in American English

20.1 Introduction

In American English, alveolar obstruents (/t, d, s, z/) become palatoalveolars (/ tʃ, dʒ, ʃ, ʒ/) before the (palatal) glide /j/. Palatalization is obligatory at the lexical level, as illustrated by pairs such as *habit/habitual*, *grade/gradual*, *confess/confession*, and *please/pleasure*. Palatalization also appears to apply, optionally, at the postlexical level, as in the phrases *hit you*, *made you*, *press your point*, and *please yourself*. This paper argues, however, that lexical and postlexical palatalization are two different processes, requiring two different representations.

Other investigators have noted that a similar process, palatalization of /s/ before /ʃ/, may be gradient when it applies across word boundaries (Catford, 1977; Shattuck-Hufnagel, Zue & Bernstein, 1978; Zue & Shattuck-Hufnagel, 1980; see also Holst & Nolan, this volume, for British English). In the experiment reported here, acoustic and electropalatographic (EPG) data contrasting lexical and postlexical palatalization of /s/ before /j/ were collected. The data show that palatalization of /s/ before /j/ is also gradient when it applies across word boundaries, while lexical palatalization is categorical. It is argued here that the articulatory patterns found in postlexical palatalization suggest overlapping gestures, as in the theory of Articulatory Phonology (Browman & Goldstein, 1986, 1990, 1992). In a departure from Articulatory Phonology, however, it is further argued that lexical palatalization is best described in terms of features, and a mapping between features and gestures is suggested. Sections 20.2 and 20.3 discuss the methods and results of the experiment. Section 20.4 turns to the question of how the categorical and gradient rules should be represented.

Lexical and postlexical palatalization

20.2 Methods

20.2.1 Stimuli

Stimuli for this experiment contrasted underlying alveolars and palatoalveolars with both lexically derived palatoalveolars and alveolar + /j/ sequences occurring across a word boundary (Table 20.1A). Data for /t/, /d/, /s/, and /z/ were collected, but only the data for /s/ are analyzed here. In the alveolar + /j/ sequences, /j/-initial pronouns and content words were contrasted, and the boundary between alveolar and glide was varied (phrase break vs. none). Each condition was represented by two different lexical items, divided into sets 1 and 2. In order to obtain information on the articulation of /j/, data from a second set of lexical items was also collected, in which the first consonant in the sequence was a labial (Table 20.1B). Within each set, the preceding vowel and the stress pattern remained constant across conditions.

Table 20.1. Stimuli contrasting underlying /s/, /ʃ/, and /j/ with lexically derived /ʃ/ and /s#j/ sequences.

A. Fricatives:	Set 1	Set 2
1. underlying /ʃ/	mesh on	fresh analysis
2. underlying /s/ + /t/	confess to	press together
3. underlying /s/ + /t/, phrase break	confess, to	impress, to get
4. lexically-derived /ʃ/	confession	impression
5. underlying /s/ + /i/	messy	dressy
6. /s/ + you	confess you	press you
7. /s/ + you, phrase break	confess, you	press, you
8. /s/ + your	confess your	press your
9. /s/ + your, phrase break	confess, your	press, your
10. /s/ + /j/-initial content word	confess unitedly	press uranium
11. /s/ + /j/-initial content word, phrase break	confess, uniting	press, uranium

B. Palatal glide:		
1. /b/ + you	stab you	
2. /b/ + you, phrase break	stab, you	
3. /b/ + /j/-initial content word	stab Eugene	
4. /b/ + /j/-initial content word, phrase break	stab, Eugene	

Elizabeth C. Zsiga

Each lexical item was placed in a sentence. For presentation to the subjects, sentences were randomized within sets, over all consonants. For each subject five different randomizations of each set were created.

20.2.2 Data collection and analysis

Three native speakers of American English participated.

Acoustic and EPG data were recorded simultaneously, using the Rion palatography system (Shibata, Ino, Yamashita, Hiki, Hiritani& Sawashima, 1978). In this system, palates are not custom made; rather, the best fit is chosen from six available sizes. The arrangement of electrodes on the palate is shown in Figure 20.1. One data frame (the 63 electrodes sampled in sequence) is recorded every 15.6 ms.

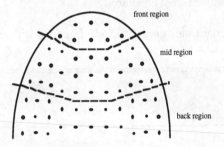

Figure 20.1. Arrangement of electrodes on the palate, showing the division into front, mid, and back regions.

In the acoustic analysis of the fricative tokens, the centroid of the fricative noise was computed for each EPG frame. (The centroid is the weighted average, based on amplitude, of all the frequencies present in the spectrum of fricative noise.) The times indicating the beginning and end of each EPG frame were marked in the acoustic signal, which was digitized at 20,000 samples/second. For each token, the spectrum of the fricative noise was computed from the first EPG frame showing full frication to the last, using a 12.8 ms Hamming window at 1 ms intervals. Centroid values over a range of 500 to 10,000 Hz were then computed for the window in the center of each EPG frame.

In the EPG analysis, patterns of palate contact for lexically derived /ʃ/ and for the /s#j/ sequences were compared with patterns of contact in utterances containing underlying /s/, /ʃ/, and /j/. The series of EPG frames that made up each fricative or glide articulation was isolated on the basis of the articulatory patterns. For each control utterance (i.e., underlying /s/, /ʃ/, and /j/: 1–3 in Table 20.1A for the fricatives, and 1–4 in Table 20.1B for /j/), an empirically-determined target pattern for the articulation was then located. Target was deemed to have been reached when the pattern of articulation remained stable over several frames (see Zsiga, 1993, for details). These target patterns formed the basis of templates, to which the other articulatory patterns were compared in terms of front, mid, and back contact.

20.3 Results

20.3.1 Acoustic results

Clear differences in the centroid values for the different fricatives were found. Figure 20.2 displays data for several sample utterances. These figures show the centroid values at each frame for five repetitions of underlying /s/, underlying /ʃ/, derived /ʃ/, and an /s#j/ sequence, aligned at the last frame of frication.

Figure 20.2A displays the centroid values for /s/ (in *press together*) and /ʃ/ (in *fresh*) for subject 1. The two fricatives are clearly distinct, and divide the figure into two regions, above 5200 Hz for /s/ and below 5200 Hz for /ʃ/. Lexically derived /ʃ/ (Figure 20.2B) falls completely within the /ʃ/ region. The pattern is different, however, for /s#j/ (Figure 20.2C). In the phrase *press your*, the centroid values begin like /s/, but fall into the /ʃ/ region by the end.

Figure 20.2D-F shows the same contrasts for subject 2. As can be seen in Figure 20.2D, this subject shows even greater separation between /s/ (in *confess to*) and /ʃ/ (in *mesh*). Figure 20.2E shows that the /ʃ/ in *confession* is not different from the /ʃ/ in *mesh*. The /s#j/ tokens, however, show a lot of variation, and often a large change over time. While all are fully in the /ʃ/ range by the end of the fricative, at the beginning tokens are either /s/-like, or in between /s/ and /ʃ/.

For statistical analysis, centroid values for all of the fricatives were compared at three points: the first frame of frication (onset), the last frame of frication (end) and the third to last frame of frication (−3 frames). The third from last, rather than the middle, frame was chosen for analysis because, as Figure 20.2 shows, the effect of a following articulation begins to be evident near the end of the fricative, but not necessarily half-way through. The hypotheses to be tested were (1) that lexically derived /ʃ/ does not differ from underlying /ʃ/ and (2) that the /s#j/ sequences show partial palatalization, evidenced by falling centroid values over the course of the fricative.

These hypotheses were tested by comparing /s#j/ and lexically derived /ʃ/ to underlying /s/ and /ʃ/ at the three measurement points. The two underlying fricatives are predicted to differ at each measurement point. It is predicted that lexically derived /ʃ/ will not be distinct at any point from underlying /ʃ/, while the /s#j/ sequences will show a gradient change, with values not distinct from /s/

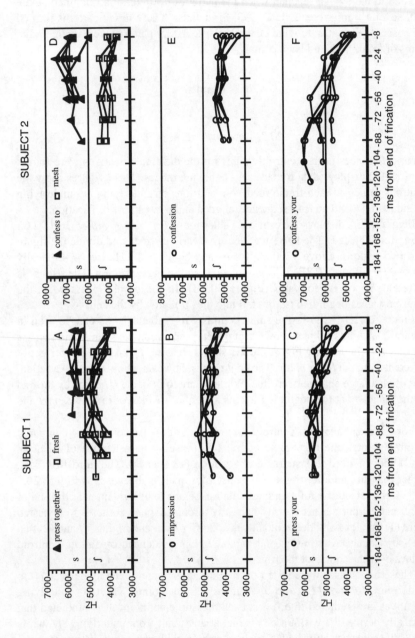

Figure 20.2. Centroid values for several sample utterances.

at the first frame, not distinct from /ʃ/ at the last frame, and possibly distinct from both /s/ and /ʃ/ at the third from last frame.

Figure 20.3 shows the mean values for each subject for underlying /s/ (in *dressy* and *messy*), underlying /ʃ/ (*fresh, mesh*), derived /ʃ/ (*impression, confession*), and /s#j/ (averaged across all conditions with no phrase break). The /si/ rather than /s#t/ sequences were used in these comparisons to control for differences at the end of the fricative that might be due to the effect of a following stop rather than a more open articulation.

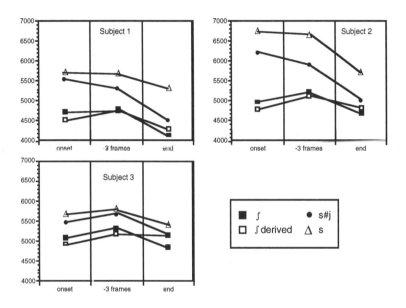

Figure 20.3. Mean centroid values for four fricative types.

As is evident in Figure 20.3, the fricative types were different overall, and they differed in the way their values changed over time. In a repeated measures analysis of variance, with factors set, fricative type, and frame, each subject showed a highly significant effect of fricative type, and of the interaction between fricative type and frame. (No subject showed a significant three-way interaction of fricative × set × frame.) As there was a significant effect of fricative for each subject at each frame, a Tukey test was used to analyze which fricatives differed from which at each of the three points. The predicted and actual contrasts among the different fricative types are shown in Table 20.2. In the table, conditions not significantly different at the 0.05 level are separated by an = sign, and where relevant (subject 3, end) are enclosed in identical bracketing.

287

Table 20.2. Predicted and actual contrasts in centroid values at onset, -3 frames, and end for four fricative types.

	Onset	-3 frames	End
Predicted:	s = s#j > ʃ-derived = ʃ	s > s#j > ʃ-derived = ʃ	s > s#j = ʃ-derived = ʃ
Subject 1:	s = s#j > ʃ-derived = ʃ	s > s#j > ʃ-derived = ʃ	s > s#j > ʃ-derived = ʃ
Subject 2:	s > s#j > ʃ-derived = ʃ	s > s#j > ʃ-derived = ʃ	s > s#j = ʃ-derived = ʃ
Subject 3:	s = s#j > ʃ-derived = ʃ	s = s#j > ʃ-derived = ʃ	(s= [s#j =ʃ-derived) = ʃ]

Underlying /s/ and underlying /ʃ/ were distinct at all three points for all three subjects. Underlying /ʃ/ and derived /ʃ/ were not distinct at any point for any of the subjects. The centroid values of these fricatives tended to be lower at onset and end (where amplitude was also lower) than at –3 frames.

In the /s#j/ sequences, subjects 1 and 2 fit the predicted pattern almost perfectly. For both subjects, although the centroid value for /s/ is lower at the end of the fricative than at –3 frames, the value for the /s#j/ sequences is lower still. For subject 1, there is substantial change over the course of the fricative in a /s#j/ sequence: at onset, /s#j/ is not significantly different from /s/; at –3 frames, /s#j/ falls in between /s/ and /ʃ/, and is significantly different from both; and at the end frame, /s#j/ is much closer to /ʃ/ than to /s/, although a significant difference remains between the sequence and underlying /ʃ/. Subject 2 also shows a large change over time. The /s#j/ sequence falls in between /s/ and /ʃ/ at both onset and –3 frames, although it is closer to /s/ at onset. At the end of the fricative, /s#j/ is not distinct from /ʃ/.

Results for subject 3 are less clear. Centroid values for underlying /s/ and /ʃ/ were more similar for this subject than for the other two, and overlapped to a greater extent. While the /s#j/ sequence shows lower values than /s/ throughout, it is not significantly different from underlying /s/ at any of the three points. At the end frame /s#j/ fell in between /s/ and /ʃ/, but is not significantly different from either. Note, however, that derived /ʃ/ is also not significantly different from /s/ at the end of the fricative. Derived /ʃ/ and /s#j/ have nearly identical values at this point, and even the difference between /s/ and underlying /ʃ/ was significant at the 0.05, but not the 0.01, level. This convergence of values at the end of the fricative makes the results for this subject difficult to interpret. He does show a tendency for /s#j/ centroid values to become /ʃ/-like at the very end of the fricative, but because the values for /s/ and /ʃ/ at this point are so close,

/s#j/ and /s/ are not significantly different. It may be that placement of the palate interfered with articulation for this subject (see section 20.3.2).

Overall, these acoustic results show that lexical palatalization is categorical. There is no acoustic difference between underlying and derived /ʃ/. For /s#j/, palatalization is gradient, in two senses. First, /s#j/ shows substantial change over time, from /s/-like at the beginning to /ʃ/-like at the end. Second, the acoustics for the /s#j/ utterances may show centroid values intermediate between /s/ and /ʃ/ throughout the fricative. As could be seen in Figure 20.2, there is considerable token to token variation in the /s#j/ sequences. Some begin like /s/ and fall over time, some are /ʃ/-like throughout, others are in between the two. While lexical palatalization is categorical and obligatory, postlexical palatalization is both gradient and variable in its application.

The next section turns to the patterns of articulation, and how these patterns are correlated with changes in the acoustics.

20.3.2   *EPG results*

Contact patterns at target for /s/, /ʃ/, and /j/ for each subject are shown in Figure 20.4. For /ʃ/, patterns are based on the steady state portion of the articulation in *mesh* and *fresh*, for /s/ in *confess to* and *press together* with no phrase break, and for /j/, in *stab you* both with and without phrase break. The number of times each electrode was activated at target over ten tokens is shown. Electrodes activated in 80% or more of the tokens are outlined. For the most part, the patterns shown here are qualitatively similar to those reported in earlier studies (e.g. Recasens, 1984, 1990; Hardcastle & Clark, 1981; Hardcastle, Gibbon & Nicolaidis, 1991). Some differences are discussed below.

For quantitative comparison, the palate was divided into three regions: front, comprising the first two rows; mid, comprising the middle three rows; and back, comprising the back three rows (see Figure 20.1). A one-way analysis of variance was performed on the target frames for each subject and region, with utterance as the independent variable and the number of electrodes activated within each region for each token as the dependent. The utterance effect was highly significant ($p < 0.001$) for all subjects and regions, except for front contact for subject 3, where the effect just reached significance ($p = 0.036$). A Tukey test was then performed to determine which articulations were significantly different in each region. Very few differences were found due to the presence or absence of a phrase break, or to set. The /j/ in *Eugene*, however, was found to show substantial coarticulation with the following affricate, and so is not used as a template (see Zsiga, 1993, for discussion). Differences between underlying /s/, underlying /ʃ/, and /j/ in *you* are summarized in Table 20.3. Differences not significant at the 0.05 level are separated by an = sign.

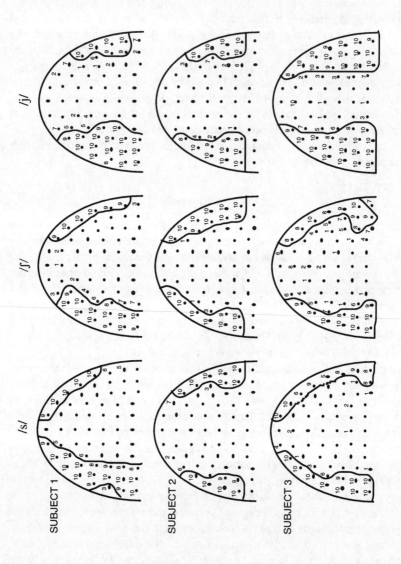

Figure 20.4. Target patterns for underlying /s/, /ʃ/, and /j/ for each subject, based on a steady-state portion of the articulation.

Table 20.3. Differences in the number of electrodes activated at target in each region of the palate for each subject.

	S1	S2	S3
front region	s > ʃ = j	ʃ > s = j	s = ʃ = j
mid region	s = ʃ = j	ʃ > s = j	s = ʃ = j
back region	s = ʃ < j	s = ʃ < j	s < ʃ < j

For subject 1, the target patterns are as expected for alveolars, palatoalveolars, and a palatal glide. The /s/ articulation shows more front contact and less back contact than any other: it is the only articulation showing contact in the frontmost row. /ʃ/ differs from /s/ in having less front contact, and from /j/ in having less back contact.

For subject 2, while /s/ and /ʃ/ show a significant difference in the amount of front contact, unexpectedly /ʃ/ shows the greater contact in this area. For this subject, the artificial palate was probably set slightly too far back, and failed to record contact at the frontmost edges of the subject's palate. (Recall that this subject showed the greatest acoustic difference between the two fricatives.) Due to the reversal in the amount of front contact for /s/ and /ʃ/ for this subject, and the fact that the two articulations do not differ in the amount of back contact, it is not clear that the patterns for /s/ and /ʃ/ can be reliably distinguished, nor is it clear how a /s#j/ sequence is predicted to differ from an underlying /ʃ/.

Subject 3 showed the least consistent patterns of articulation. As discussed above, his acoustic patterns were also problematic. Many electrodes are activated in fewer than half of the articulations. Several isolated electrodes, particularly in the center of the palate, appear to remain activated after release. (This can occur when the mouth is too dry.) For this subject, the articulations are clearly distinguished only in the back region.

Because of the difficulties in distinguishing the patterns in the control utterances for subjects 2 and 3, the rest of this discussion will focus on the articulatory data for subject 1. (See Zsiga, 1993, for a full discussion of all three subjects.)

The patterns for underlying /s/, /ʃ/, and /j/ serve as templates for examining /s#j/ and derived /ʃ/. Figure 20.5 illustrates, for subject 1, how the patterns of activated electrodes in derived /ʃ/ (from *confession* and *impression*) and /s#j/ (from *press you* and *confess you*) change over time. Filled dots indicate those electrodes activated in at least eight of ten repetitions at the first frame of frication, the third to last frame, and the last frame. (Grayed electrodes were on

Elizabeth C. Zsiga

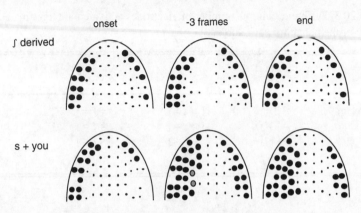

Figure 20.5. Change in contact patterns over time, subject 1. Electrodes shown in black were activated in at least eight of ten repetitions, those in gray, in seven of ten repetitions.

seven out of ten times.) Just as the acoustics do not change over time for derived /ʃ/, the pattern of palate contact remains stable throughout the whole fricative. The pattern for /s#j/, however, does not follow that for /ʃ/. At the onset of frication, there is very little contact at the back and center of the palate, but over the course of the fricative central and back contact fills in.

Figure 20.6 shows the pattern of electrodes for derived /ʃ/ and *s+you* at one point in time: −3 frames (the middle column in Figure 20.5). In each column of Figure 20.6, templates from the /s/, /ʃ/, and /j/ control utterances (corresponding to the outlined areas in Figure 20.4) are overlaid on the palate patterns. In the first column the template for underlying /ʃ/ is overlaid. This template corresponds almost exactly to the pattern for derived /ʃ/. For *s+you*, however, the /ʃ/ template is not a good fit: there is too much contact at the front and center of the palate. This poor fit illustrates that although the acoustics in the *s+you* sequence at this point in time may be /ʃ/-like, the articulation is not. Rather, as the set of template patterns in the second column shows, the pattern in the *s+you* sequence is what would be expected from an /s/ and /j/ being articulated at the same time. While the /s/ and /j/ templates do not fit the derived /ʃ/ articulation, they do account well for the front and central contact in the *s+you* sequence. Although not all the *s+you* electrodes are covered by the templates, it is likely that the tongue, if it made contact at both the front and back regions at the same time, would cover the areas of those electrodes as well. In the third column, the /ʃ/ and /j/ templates are overlaid on the *s+you* pattern. It might have been the case that /s/ did undergo a categorical change to /ʃ/, and that the difference in the patterns seen in Figure 20.5 was due only to the fact that the following consonant is /j/ in one case but /n/ in the other. However, the combination of the /ʃ/ and /j/ templates could not account for the pattern of front

292

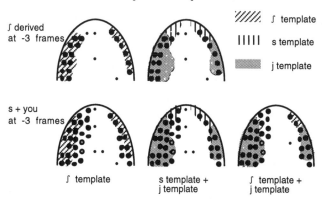

Figure 20.6. Templates from underlying /s/, /ʃ/, and /j/ overlaid on the patterns for *s+you* and derived /ʃ/ at –3 frames.

contact seen for *s+you*. It is the pattern produced by the overlap of /s/ and /j/ that fits the *s+you* articulation at -3 frames most closely.

Finally, a significant correlation was found between the acoustic and articulatory measures. The centroid values at onset, –3 frames, and end were correlated with the total number of electrodes activated in the front and back regions at those points. For subject 1, the amount of back contact accounts for 28% of the variance in the centroid values, and front and back contact, taken together, account for 45% of the variance (both significant at $p < 0.01$). Back contact, not front contact, better determines the centroid value. As contact in the back region increases, the centroid value falls. These findings are consistent with the hypothesis that in the /s#j/ sequences, increased overlap of the /s/ and /j/ gestures, and therefore more back contact during the fricative, leads to the lower centroid values.

20.4 Discussion

This experiment has shown a clear difference between lexical and postlexical palatalization in American English. Postlexical palatalization is gradient and variable. Lexical palatalization, on the other hand, involves a categorical alternation between /s/ and /ʃ/: underlying and derived /ʃ/ were not found to differ either acoustically or articulatorily. (The data presented here are consistent with the view that the coronal fricative in *confession* in fact *is* an underlying /ʃ/. It will be assumed here, however, that the regular lexical alternations relating words such as *confess* and *confession* should be expressed in the grammar as phonological rules.) This section examines the question of how the two different kinds of palatalization should be represented. Representations using autosegmental features and articulatory gestures are compared. It will be argued

293

Elizabeth C. Zsiga

that both representations are needed: phonological features best capture categorical alternations, articulatory gestures best capture gradient processes.

Consider first the featural representation. The featural representation of American English palatalization is bound up with the question of the best way to represent palatal consonants and glides. In the feature geometries argued for in Sagey (1986) and McCarthy (1988), /s/ and /ʃ/ are represented with the feature [ant] as a dependent of the [coronal] node (1a, 1b). The glide /j/ is represented with the features [+high] and [−back] as dependents of the dorsal node (1c). Borowsky (1986) formalizes /s#j/ palatalization as spreading of [+high] from the glide to the alveolar. In this formalization, a dorsal node to which the feature can attach must be interpolated, and then a special implementation rule must be invoked to interpret the resulting configuration as phonetically identical to that in (1a).

(1)   a. /ʃ/   b. /s/   c. /j/

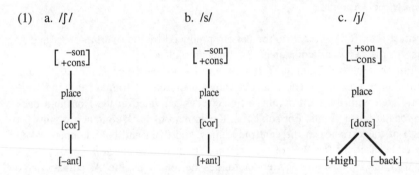

However, recent studies, both phonological (Clements, 1976, 1991; Hume, 1990, 1992; Broselow & Niyondagara, in press; Ní Chiosáin, 1991) and phonetic (Keating, 1988), have argued that /j/ should be analyzed as having a coronal component. (For an alternative view, see Recasens, 1990, this volume.) The representation of palatalization in (2) follows Keating in representing /j/ as a complex segment with both coronal and dorsal components. The [−ant] coronal component spreads from the glide to the alveolar, effecting a categorical change from /s/ to /ʃ/. As will be argued below, however, this representation is not appropriate for gradient palatalization.

Consider instead the gestural representation. The articulatory evidence presented here (at least for the subject for whom clear results can be obtained) suggests that gradient palatalization can be represented in terms of gestural overlap (following Browman & Goldstein, 1986, 1990, 1992). The palatal constriction for /j/ overlaps in time with the alveolar constriction for /s/ when /s/ and /j/ are adjacent at a word boundary. The combination of front contact due to the /s/ gesture and increasing back contact due to the /j/ gesture results in centroid values that fall over the course of the fricative.

294

(2)

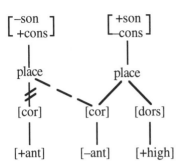

The gestural representation captures the gradience and variability seen in postlexical palatalization. For the period of time before the /j/ gesture begins, the articulation and acoustics will be that of a simple /s/. As overlap with the /j/ increases, the articulatory and acoustic influence of this gesture also increase. Many instrumental studies have demonstrated overlap among speech gestures (e.g. Öhman, 1966; Perkell, 1969; Hardcastle & Roach, 1977; Hardcastle, 1985; Marchal, 1988). Zsiga (1994) provides evidence for substantial overlap between consonant gestures at word boundaries in English. It may be that the pattern of overlap seen here is typical of the overlap between any two consonants at a word boundary. If so, then no postlexical rule of palatalization is required. The effect of palatalization would simply be the acoustic consequence of the normal pattern of overlap.

Both categorical and gradient palatalization can be seen as the imposition of the high tongue position for the glide onto the consonant. In categorical palatalization, the [–ant] coronal feature spreads from one root node to the next. In gradient palatalization, the /j/ gesture overlaps in time with the /s/ gesture.

The featural and gestural representations in fact correspond very closely. Compare the autosegmental representation in (3), argued for in McCarthy (1988), with (4), the "functional anatomy of the vocal tract" presented in Browman & Goldstein (1989). Both representations are based on articulators: the lips, the tongue tip, the tongue body, and possibly the tongue root. (See Browman & Goldstein, 1989; McCarthy, 1994 for discussion of the representation of pharyngeal articulations.) In both the gestural and the autosegmental representations, the nasal, laryngeal, and oral subsystems are separated. Browman and Goldstein (1989) have argued that the convergence on a single geometry from the direction of phonological patterning and from the direction of phonetic function provides strong support for the geometry's essential correctness.

(3)

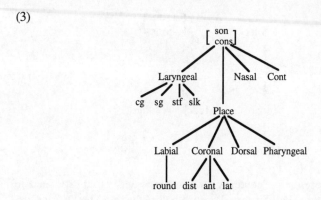

(4)

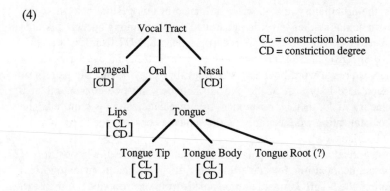

CL = constriction location
CD = constriction degree

There is an even more striking similarity to the feature geometry proposed in Padgett (1991). Padgett argues, on the basis of patterns of assimilation, that [continuant] and [consonantal] should be specified for each articulator, in an "articulator group", as shown in (5). These two features then correspond directly to the constriction degree and stiffness specified for each gesture. (In Articulatory Phonology, stiffness encodes the difference between vowels, glides, and consonants.) While smaller differences between the two geometries remain to be resolved (see Zsiga, 1993), a straightforward correspondence between the feature [labial] and a labial closing gesture, between the feature [nasal] and a velum opening gesture, etc., is evident.

Despite this close correspondence, the representations can not be collapsed. The different way that timing is expressed in the two representations makes features appropriate for expressing lexical contrasts and categorical alternations, and gestures appropriate for expressing gradient processes. Consider two simple examples that illustrate this point: the first example deals with lexical contrasts, the second with phonological rules.

(5)

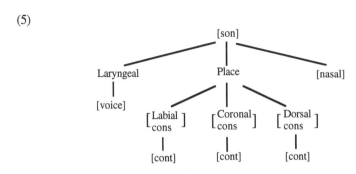

Compare the gestural and autosegmental representations of a labial–velar stop in Figure 20.7. Figure 20.7A shows an autosegmental representation, Figure 20.7B a gestural representation. Both representations involve two articulators: lips and tongue body (labial and dorsal). The most basic difference in the representations is how temporal organization is expressed. Features do not have specific durations, and the only temporal relations that can be defined in this representation are linear precedence and an unspecified amount of overlap (see Sagey, 1988; Bird & Klein, 1990). Association among features is expressed by linkings to abstract hierarchical nodes. Features associated to a given hierarchical node (and not on the same tier) are assumed by the phonology to overlap in time, but the degree of overlap remains unspecified. Thus, there can be no contrast between two kinds of labial–velars that differ only in timing: labial closure followed by dorsal (/b͡g/ and dorsal closure followed by labial (/g͡b/).

In contrast, gestures have inherent extent in time. Precise overlap relations can and must be specified, and are crucial for describing articulatory patterns. Organization among gestures is expressed through the direct specification of timing relations (phasing) between two or more gestures, not through linkings to abstract nodes. In the theory of Articulatory Phonology, phase relations can in themselves serve as the basis of phonological contrast: for example, the difference between aspirated and unaspirated stops is encoded in the phase relations between the glottal and oral gestures (Goldstein & Browman, 1986). Given that several different phasings are possible between the labial and tongue body gestures in a labial–velar stop, there is no reason the phase differences could not serve as the basis of lexical contrast. Thus Articulatory Phonology predicts a possible contrast between /b͡g/ and /g͡b/. The same holds true (as Clements, 1992, points out) of phasings between glottal opening and oral gestures. A gestural representation predicts many possible contrasts, for example

297

between pre-aspirated, unaspirated, and post-aspirated stops, when in fact no language has more than a two-way contrast.

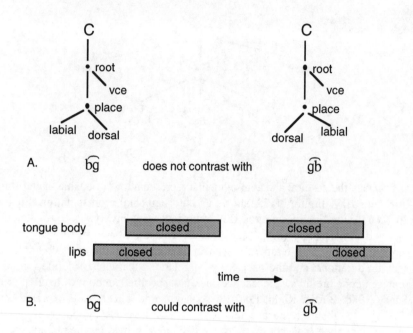

Figure 20.7. Representations of a labial–velar stop. A. Featural. B. Gestural.

In fact, /g͡b/ (dorsal closure first, labial closure second) is almost invariably chosen as the articulatory organization (Connell, 1991; Maddieson & Ladefoged, 1989). As Connell (1991) points out, the phase relations among the different component gestures are crucial for understanding the phonetic behavior of these stops, as well as their diachronic development. Therefore, a phonetic representation must be able to express the asymmetry of the dorsal and labial gestures. But any phonological representation that has the power to express that timing relationship makes wrong predictions about possible synchronic phonological contrasts. It also makes wrong predictions about possible phonological rules.

Consider two rules of nasalization, one categorical, the other gradient. Categorical nasalization can be represented as spreading of the feature [nas] from consonant to vowel (Figure 20.8A). Because there is no way for a feature to spread only part way from one root node to another, the result is categorical assimilation. To express partial nasalization, explicit timing must be taken into account.

Figure 20.8B shows a gestural representation of partial nasalization. Because gestures have extent in time, specific points in one gesture are timed with respect to specific points in another gesture. In this gestural score, maximum velic opening is timed to occur at the beginning of the tongue tip gesture for the final /n/. (Krakow, 1989, found this timing relation to hold for nasalized vowels in American English.) In order to achieve this timing with respect to the consonant, the velum opening gesture must begin during the vowel, resulting in partial nasalization. A gestural representation can also capture complete nasalization, by specifying a different timing relation. The vowel and the velum opening could begin at the same time, so that nasalization extends throughout the vowel.

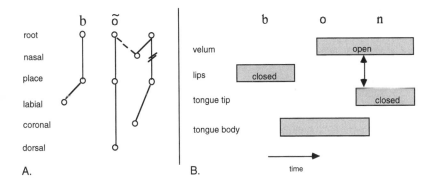

Figure 20.8. Two rules of nasalization. A. Categorical. B. Gestural.

The gestural approach thus uses the relation of overlap in time to describe complete as well as partial processes. Yet specific timing is unnecessary for the description of synchronic phonological rules. In the lexical component, where all rules are categorical, and where reference to abstract hierarchical nodes like the root node is necessary, a theory that allows specific temporal relations to be manipulated is too powerful. While specifying timing relations among gestures is appropriate for gradient rules, categorical rules require the all-or-nothing, plus-or-minus specification that feature spreading provides. However, because the two representations are so similar in respects other than timing, the mapping between them is straightforward. Gestural scores can be seen as feature trees with elaborated timing information, or feature trees can be seen as gestural scores underspecified for temporal relations.

This paper has argued for two different representations for lexical and postlexical palatalization: an autosegmental featural representation for the categorical lexical rule and a gestural representation for the gradient postlexical rule. Articulators form the basis for both representations. These differ

299

Elizabeth C. Zsiga

principally in the kind of temporal information that is available for manipulation: specific extent in time for gestures, only simultaneity and precedence, expressed in terms of linking to hierarchical nodes, for features. This simple correspondence between features and gestures leads to a simple correspondence between categorical and gradient rules.

Note

* This research was supported by NIH grant HD-01994 to Haskins Laboratories. I would like to thank Louis Goldstein, Draga Zec, and John McCarthy for invaluable input at all stages of this research; and Ken de Jong, Joaquìn Romero, and the reviewers and editors of this volume for helpful comments on the manuscript. The results and discussion presented in this paper are condensed from Zsiga (1993).

References

Bird, S. & E. Klein. 1990. Phonological events. *Journal of Linguistics* 26: 33–56.
Borowsky, T. J. 1986. Topics in the lexical phonology of English. Ph.D. dissertation, University of Massachusetts, Amherst.
Broselow, E. & A. Niyondagara. In press. Morphological structure in Kirundi palatalization: implications for feature geometry. To appear in F. Katamba (ed.), *Studies in Inter-lacustrine Bantu Phonology*. Cologne: Afrikanistiche Arbeitspapiere.
Browman, C. P. & L. Goldstein. 1986. Towards an articulatory phonology. *Phonology Yearbook* 3: 219–252.
Browman, C. P. & L. Goldstein. 1989. Articulatory gestures as phonological units. *Phonology* 6: 201–251.
Browman, C. P. & L. Goldstein. 1990. Tiers in articulatory phonology, with some implications for casual speech. In J. Kingston & M. E. Beckman (eds.), *Papers in Laboratory Phonology I: Between the Grammar and Physics of Speech*. Cambridge: Cambridge University Press, 341–376.
Browman, C. P. & L. Goldstein. 1992. Articulatory phonology: an overview. *Phonetica* 49: 155–180.
Catford, J. C. 1977. *Fundamental Problems in Phonetics*. Bloomington IN: Indiana University Press.
Clements, G. N. 1976. Palatalization: linking or assimilation? *CLS : Proceedings of the Chicago Linguistics Society* 12: 96–109.
Clements, G. N. 1991. Place of articulation in consonants and vowels: a unified theory. In B. Laks & A. Rialland (eds.), *L'Architecture et la geometrie des representations phonologiques*. Paris: Editions du CNRS.
Clements, G. N. 1992. Phonological primes: features or gestures? *Phonetica* 49: 18–193.
Connell, B. 1991. Accounting for the reflexes of labial–velar stops. *Proceedings of the XIIth International Congress of Phonetic Sciences,* Aix-en-Provence, 3: 110–113.

Lexical and postlexical palatalization

Goldstein, L. & C. P. Browman. 1986. Representation of voicing contrasts using articulatory gestures. *Journal of Phonetics* 14: 339–342.

Hardcastle, W. J. 1985. Some phonetic and syntactic constraints on lingual coarticulation during /kl/ sequences. *Speech Communication* 4: 247–263.

Hardcastle, W. J. & J. E. Clark. 1981. Articulatory, aerodynamic, and acoustic properties of lingual fricatives in English. *Phonetics Laboratory, University of Reading, Work in Progress* 3: 51–79.

Hardcastle, W. J., F. Gibbon & K. Nicolaidis. 1991. EPG data reduction methods and their implications for studies of lingual coarticulation. *Journal of Phonetics* 19: 251–256.

Hardcastle, W. J. & P. J. Roach. 1977. An instrumental investigation of coarticulation in stop consonant sequences. *Phonetics Laboratory, University of Reading, Work in Progress.*

Hume, E. 1990. Front vowels, palatal consonants, and the rule of umlaut in Korean. *NELS: Proceedings of the North East Linguistics Society* 20: 230–243.

Hume, E. 1992. Front vowels, coronal consonants, and their interaction in non-linear phonology. Ph.D. dissertation, Cornell University.

Keating, P. 1988. Palatals as complex segments. *UCLA Working Papers in Phonetics* 69: 77–91.

Krakow, R. A. 1989. The articulatory organization of syllables: a kinematic analysis of labial and velar gestures. Ph.D. dissertation, Yale University.

Maddieson, I. & P. Ladefoged. 1989. Multiply-articulated segments and the feature hierarchy. *UCLA Working Papers in Phonetics* 72: 116–138.

Marchal, A. 1988. Coproduction: Evidence from EPG data. *Speech Communication* 7: 287–295.

McCarthy, J. J. 1988. Feature geometry and dependency: a review. *Phonetica* 45: 84–108.

McCarthy, J. J. 1994. The phonetics and phonology of Semitic pharyngeals. In P. A. Keating (ed.), *Phonological Structure and Phonetic Form: Papers in Laboratory Phonology III.* Cambridge: Cambridge University Press: 191–233.

Ní Chiosáin, M. 1991. Topics in the phonology of Irish. Ph.D dissertation, University of Massachusetts, Amherst.

Öhman, S. 1966. Coarticulation in VCV utterances: spectrographic measurements. *Journal of the Acoustical Society of America* 39: 151–168.

Padgett, J. 1991. Stricture in feature geometry. Ph.D. dissertation, University of Massachusetts, Amherst.

Perkell, J. 1969. *Physiology of Speech Production: Results and Implications of a Quantitative Cineradiographic Study.* Cambridge, MA: MIT Press.

Recasens, D. 1984. Timing constraints and coarticulation: alveo-palatals and sequences of alveolar + /j/ in Catalan. *Phonetica* 41: 125–139.

Recasens, D. 1990. The articulatory characteristics of palatal consonants. *Journal of Phonetics* 18: 267–280.

Sagey, E. C. 1986. The representation of features and relations in nonlinear phonology. Ph.D. dissertation, Massachusetts Institute of Technology.

Sagey, E. C. 1988. On the ill-formedness of crossing association lines. *Linguistic Inquiry* 19: 109–118.

Elizabeth C. Zsiga

Shattuck-Hufnagel, S., V. W. Zue & J. Bernstein. 1978. An acoustic study of palatalization of fricatives in American English. *Journal of the Acoustical Society of America* 64, S92.

Shibata, S., A. Ino, S. Yamashita, S. Hiki, S. Hiritani & M. Sawashima. 1978. A new portable type unit for electropalatography. *Annual Bulletin of the Research Institute of Logopedics and Phoniatrics* 12: 5–10.

Zsiga, E. C. 1993. Features, gestures, and the temporal aspects of phonological organization. Ph.D. dissertation, Yale University.

Zsiga, E. C. 1994. Acoustic evidence for gestural overlap in consonant sequences. *Journal of Phonetics* 22: 121–140.

Zue, V. & S. Shattuck-Hufnagel. 1980. Palatalization of /s/ in American English: when is a /ʃ/ not a /ʃ/? *Journal of the Acoustical Society of America* 67, S27.

21
What do we do when phonology is powerful enough to imitate phonetics? Comments on Zsiga

JAMES M. SCOBBIE*

21.1 Two classes of palatoalveolar fricative

Zsiga demonstrates convincingly that English palatoalveolar fricatives fall into two classes, confirming instrumentally the clear impressionistic account of Catford (1977). One class encompasses both underlying and "lexically derived" /ʃ/ (*fresh* and *pressure* respectively), and the other case comprises the external sandhi of /s#j/ (*e.g. miss you*). This case is shown not to be subject to a rule /s#j/ → /ʃ/. Instead Zsiga argues that this gradient palatoalveolar results from coarticulation.

I will show, however, that given the excessive expressive power of phonological representations, the fact of phonetic gradience does not unambiguously indicate phonetic coarticulation. The source could be phonological assimilation producing a contour segment /sʃ/. Such a segment even finds support in Zsiga's data, as we will see. However, I will reject segments like /sʃ/ on phonological grounds and thereby reinforce the argument for a phonetic approach.

21.2 The problem of concreteness in phonology

Over the decades Generative Phonology has been heavily criticized for its overly abstract analyses recapitulating phonological history. Generative Phonologists are now more willing to accept that linguistic generalizations involving sound systems may instead be explained best by diachrony and allomorphy. A greater shift of perspective is now emerging: generalizations traditionally the stuff of phonological analysis, are being re-evaluated to see if they are, in fact, better analyzed as phonetic. Being "better analyzed" requires

303

• adequate and elegant analyses using the mechanisms of phonetics, and entails

• depriving the phonological formalism of structures the sole purpose of which are to express fine-grained phonetic detail.

Just because a phonological theory is expressively powerful enough to represent gradient, variable and detailed facts of phonetics does not mean that it should do so. The laboratory may well provide empirical evidence that a given phenomenon is characteristically phonetic, but if phonology is overly concrete, the phonologist can construct representations which partially echo the phonetic facts, as I will show. This "Concreteness Problem" simply parallels the problem of abstractness, by over-extending the remit of synchronic phonology.

21.3 The content of phonological surface structure

Zsiga asks whether lexical and postlexical rules of palatalization are the same or different. I would like to change the emphasis. In common with many phonologists, I see phonological rules not as string transformations, but exclusively as well-formedness statements on a phonological representation (e.g. Bird, 1990; Bird & Klein, 1990; Coleman, 1991; Scobbie, 1991; Local, 1992; Broe, 1993, amongst many others). This representation – "surface structure" – is composed of categories (hierarchical bundles of distinctive features) and well-formedness conditions constraining its form. Such a model of phonology is fundamentally "constraint-based". And, following Pierrehumbert (1990), I assume that phonetics is the semantics of the phonology. This interpretative relationship is not universal or strictly physically determined, so is truly cognitive and linguistic. Many variations within this framework are possible in the nature of the category structures or the constraints, not to mention the mechanism of constraint satisfaction (see Scobbie, 1993, for some discussion). These variations are not particularly relevant to the two general issues I want to discuss:

• What is the content of surface structure?

• How do we decide whether a given generalization in a language's sound system is encoded in surface structure (and thus assigned to the phonology), or is handled in phonetics?

Feature bundles represent different phonological categories. The essential purpose of a category is to express the patterns of lexical contrast. Most phonological theories employ categories beyond the bare minimum, enabling the representation in the phonology of *non*-contrastive patterning: allophonic variation. Given the sheer quantity of allophony and the gradient nature of many allophone classes, not every allophone can possibly be represented by a unique feature bundle, however. The two questions about surface structure above can therefore be combined:

• Which allophones (if any) are present in surface structure?

Some cases are relatively clear. The English words *sip* and *zip* contrast, so surface structure *must* provide feature bundles, say /s/ and /z/, to differentiate them. The /z/ in *buzz* is usually partially devoiced, being prepausal. General (but not necessarily universal) phonetic interpretation rules account for this, so we do not need a new feature bundle (phonological allophone) for "partly devoiced /z/".

Other cases are less obvious. Some English dialects have categorially distinct allophones for /l/ such that the vocalized [ɫ] of *pill* lacks a tongue-tip gesture, unlike clear [l]. Now, if we permit both dialect-specific phonetic interpretation rules, and phonological allophones, do we need two different feature bundles for /l/ or not?[1]

Turning to the English palatoalveolar fricatives in *fresh*, *pressure point* and *press your point*: are they contextualized phonetic interpretations of one phonological category or do we need different feature bundles for them?

21.4 Phonetic targets and phonological categories

Zsiga confirms that more than one type of phonetic behavior (target) is involved in English palatalization. If each contextualized phonological category conditions a target, there must be more than one phonological source of palatoalveolar, *if the context is held constant*.

Unfortunately, the triggering contexts of lexical and postlexical palatalization are in complementary distribution in General American; /s#j/ appears only *between* words, derived /ʃ/ only between morphemes *within* words. These contextual differences are sufficient to condition the observed phonetic differences. The study would therefore benefit from direct comparisons controlling for context. A (different) dialect with tautomorphemic /sj/ sequences would enable interesting comparisons between underlying /ʃ/ and /sj/ in lexemes like *shoot* and *suit* respectively. Even in General American there is the contrast /s#j/ vs. /ʃ#j/ in *mess your* and *refresh your* which could be addressed.

Given the lack of a picture of /sj/ in a variety of contexts, we need the rather strong assumption that if two phonological categories have indistinguishable phonetic targets, they must be the *same* phonological category. Consider underlying (U) /ʃ/ and lexically derived (D) /ʃ/. Though D-/ʃ/ only appears before /j/-initial suffixes (assuming a synchronic phonological palatalization rule is used), U-/ʃ/ does not seem to appear in this context. However, we can assume that, in *surface* structure, bimorphemic *pressure* and *fresher* have the same phonetic fricative *in exactly the same context*. Thus Zsiga's data does indeed show that U-/ʃ/ and D-/ʃ/ share a phonological feature structure.[2] Moreover, a different one is needed for /s#j/.

Note that it is not easy to determine the phonological categories conditioning phonetic behavior. Some English dialects with /dj/ and /tj/ within a morpheme have gradient amounts of affrication, from [dj] in careful speech to extreme "yod coalescence" approximating [dʒ] (Wells, 1982). In my Scottish English dialect the /dj/ of *dune* varies from [dj] in slow speech to [dʒ] in fast speech. However, there is free variation between initial /tj/ and /dj/ clusters and the phonemic affricates /tʃ/ and /dʒ/.[3] If *dune* has initial /dʒ/, then phonetically it is [dʒun] *even in slow, careful, monitored speech*. Consequently, *dune* with /dʒ/ is homophonous with *june*.

An affricate [dʒ] observed in a fast speech token of *dew* does not tell us whether the surface structure contains /dj/ or /dʒ/. A similar problem holds for postlexical palatalization, for at faster speech rates or in more relaxed styles the frication in *miss you* would probably become more and more [ʃ]-like due to increasing coarticulation.

Table 21.1. Examples of freely varying / dj/ ~/dʒ/ and / dʒ/.

Freely variable / dj/ or / dʒ/	Only / dʒ/
dew/due	jew
dune	june
deuce	juice
dual/duel	jewel

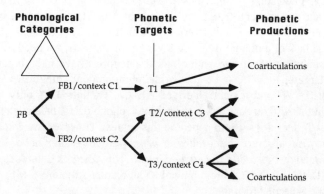

Figure 21.1. The relationship of phonetic targets to phonological categories.

But imagine for a moment that targets can be easily identified. It is then still necessary to decide whether the target is the *only* exponent of a phonological category, or one of many contextually determined targets. In both cases the actual articulation of the target will vary under coarticulation. Figure 21.1 shows a feature bundle, FB, specified further by the phonology in contexts C1 and C2 as the phonological allophones FB1 and FB2. These are interpreted phonetically. FB1 is assigned a single target, FB2 is interpreted in context C3 as target T2 and in context C4 as T3. The phonetic-target allophones T2 and T3 themselves have coarticulatory allophones. To identify a target is to go only part of the way in identifying its allophonic provenance as phonological or phonetic.

21.5 The acoustic analysis

Zsiga's results show that subjects 1 and 2 have statistically distinct centroid values for /s/, /s#j/ and /ʃ/, as identified from a point on the −3 EPG frame. For both, /s#j/ is closer to /s/ at the beginning and to /ʃ/ at the end. It is clear that for all speakers, /s#j/ and /ʃ/ are categorially distinct phonologically. But this does not justify the conclusion that "for /s#j/, palatalization is not categorical [*sic*]", as Zsiga claims. True, /s#j/ cannot become /ʃ/, but *other* categorial rules are possible, perhaps producing /sʃ/ (see below). /sʃ/ would behave differently from /ʃ/ and thus account for the acoustic data.

For subject 1 /s#j/ is not distinct from /s/ at the onset of friction, which appears to be strong evidence that an /s/ target is present initially. Unfortunately, /s#j/ is not acoustically distinct from /ʃ/ at the offset of friction for subject 2, so it appears that we should posit an /ʃ/ target. (Subject 3's results are less clear, and should probably be ignored, but are compatible with both points.) If these phonetic results are used to argue that phonologically *press your* includes an /s/ initially, then they also argue for an /ʃ/ finally. The same conclusion will be drawn from the articulatory analysis.

21.6 The articulatory analysis

Zsiga's Figure 20.5 shows recurrent contacts for three EPG frames, representing the onset, the end, and the near-end of friction (the −3 frame) for one subject. Zsiga examines this third-from-last frame to discover which target or combination of targets accounts best for the contacts found. She does this in her Figure 20.6 by overlaying templates abstracted from pronunciations of /s/, /j/ and U–/ʃ/.[4] Zsiga's template for U–/ʃ/ does not match the −3 frame of /s#j/ but matches D-/ʃ/ almost perfectly. The /s#j/ −3 frame matches quite well with the separate templates for /s/ and /j/ when they are simply overlaid, but this can be improved. As Zsiga puts it, "although not all the *s+you* electrodes are covered

Table 21.2. Estimated number and types of mismatch of templates at the –3 frame.

Templates	Under-coverage	Over-coverage	Total # errors
s & j (overlaid)	7	7	9
s–j combined	4	2	6
ʃ & j (overlaid)	9	1	10
ʃ–j combined	7	2	9

by the templates, it is likely that the tongue, if it made contact at both the front and back regions at the same time, would cover the areas of those electrodes as well". This informal and estimated *combination* of /s/ and /j/ templates is not itself a phonetic target in the same sense as the others. I have estimated the quantitative details in Table 21.2.

Zsiga's conclusion is that postlexical palatalization arises from the overlap of gestures conditioned by /s/ and /j/. Table 21.2 indicates that /s/-/j/ combined has the least number of errors. Consider now the other frames using this methodology.

Table 21.3 shows that the onset frame of the friction in *s+you* does *not* match the /s/ template better than the /ʃ/ template. We can only get the desired result if we modify the /s/ template. Making it smaller reduces the over-coverage. Discounting the electrodes activated eight times in Zsiga's Figure 20.4 gives a total error of four for /s/. Moreover, the figures above for the -3 frame are not affected – the electrodes omitted are contained in the /j/ template. There are no independent grounds for this suggestion, unfortunately, and it shows how arbitrary the abstraction of a target can be.

Table 21.3. Estimated number and types of mismatch of templates at the onset frame.

Templates	Under-coverage	Over-coverage	Total # errors
s	0	7	7
ʃ	2	4	6

Table 21.4. Estimated number and types of mismatch of templates at the end frame.

Template(s)	Under-coverage	Over-coverage	Total # errors
s & j (overlaid)	6	4	10
ʃ & j (overlaid)	7	2	9
j	9	1	10
s & ʃ (overlaid)	10	4	14
s	12	4	16
ʃ	14	2	16
s–j combined	5	6	11
ʃ–j combined	6	2	8

As for the end frame, Table 21.4 (using Zsiga's own Figure 20.4 template from S1 for /s/, not the revision suggested just above) shows that the best match comes from using the targets for /j/ and /ʃ/, whether combined or not.

Zsiga's articulatory methodology provides evidence that an /s/ target and /j/ target receive overlapping realizations during the fricative. It also seems to indicate that gestures realizing a /j/ target and a /ʃ/ target overlap at the offset of friction.

21.7 Revised conclusions on the external sandhi palatalization on the basis of phonetic evidence alone

Zsiga's methods show that there is no simple phonological rule replacing /s#j/ with /ʃ/. They show, if we are careful, that there is a standard /s/ target initially, and that during the course of the friction, the coarticulatory influence of the /j/ target increases. On the same basis, they additionally show acoustic evidence for /ʃ/ and articulatory evidence for /j/ and /ʃ/ targets overlapping at the very end of friction. There is therefore phonetic evidence for /s/, /j/ *and* /ʃ/ as phonological feature bundles. Although we might hope that the appearance of [ʃ] can be explained as part of the overlap of gestures, we should consider whether there really *is* a target for /ʃ/. In other words, we need to consider a phonological source of the observed [ʃ] frication.

309

21.8 Arguments against phonological palatalization in /s#j/

Consider the result of a partial phonological assimilation, /sʃj/. This is a surface structure configuration able to provide all the phonetic targets indicated above. In this section I will show that while the rules creating it are relatively simple, the resulting surface structure configurations are not. On that basis, I will argue against a phonological source of [ʃ] in the external sandhi case.

21.8.1 Assimilatory rules of palatalization

Zsiga gives in her (2) a rule of lexical palatalization for *pressure* and *fission*. It generates /ʃ/ by spreading a [−ant] coronal node from /j/ onto /s/. (/j/ must then be deleted.) Being a spreading rule, the source /j/ must be specified itself, in part, as a posterior coronal.

As for /s#j/, Zsiga rejects phonological assimilation. The reason is that simple /ʃ/ cannot account for the phonetic data. It is possible, however, to reject the over-simplistic postlexical palatalization /s#j/ → /ʃ/ whilst maintaining that a phonological assimilation rule is involved. All that is needed is a minor modification of Zsiga's (2). Lexical palatalization involves the deletion of the [+ant] which /s/ bears underlyingly, after [−ant] spreads from /j/. Postlexically, neither the [+ant] specification nor the /j/ is deleted, giving (1).

(1)

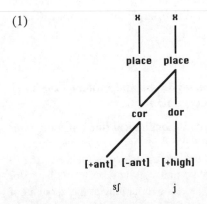

The first segment in (1) has gradient anteriority and is symbolized as /sʃ/. The second, a dorso-coronal, can be symbolized as /sʃj/ or /jsʃ/. Three articulatory targets would be assigned by (1), including a post-alveolar target (evidence for which has been revealed above). The targets will, just as in the phonetic account, be subject to coarticulation. The rule has two important characteristics:

- it creates new (non-phonemic) phonological categories like /sʃ/;

310

- the new categories have geometric properties which replicate aspects of the fine-grain temporal detail required by *phonetics*.

The phonological analysis accounts for the appearance of post-alveolar friction as a consequence of the parallel lexical and postlexical rules.

21.8.2 The expressive power of contour segments

This phonological analysis boils down to the use of "gradient" phonological categories in surface structure. It uses *contour segments,* i.e., segments whose root nodes (x) ultimately dominate a sequence of opposite-valued binary features on a single tier (in this case [anterior]).

The major problem contour segments pose for Autosegmental Phonology is that the phonological formalism can handle both categorial *and* gradient data. A phenomenon with proven fine-grained temporal and spatial coarticulation is not necessarily predicted to be phonetic. A partial phonological analysis is probably available using contour segments.

We must constrain this power. We could insist perhaps that contour segments be licensed by underlying representations, or otherwise limit their appearance as the output of rules. Rather than trying to elaborate a partial scheme like that, I will briefly consider the simple and radical solution of banning contour segments altogether. That is, we could follow Scobbie (1991) in permitting the multiple or "one-to-many" association of one autosegment to many roots, but not the sequenced "many-to-one" association demanded by (and only by) contour segments.

Though radical, this is not an unmotivated step. Taken together, the reasons to reject contour segments are: (a) they are rarely used but make it more complicated to formalize aspects of tier sequencing (Scobbie, 1991); (b) one major use they do have is simply to recapitulate non-contrastive, predictable and fine-grained temporal detail in surface structure; and (c) another major use, the representation of affricates, makes incorrect phonological predictions (Lombardi, 1990; LaCharité, 1993).

The solution is to confine phonological sequence to the root tier: this means features dominated by a single root cannot be sequenced relative to each other. Such a facility is not required for the bulk of nonlinear representations anyway: typically a single feature is shared by many roots or a root dominates a number of *different* features. Only rarely are opposite valued features dominated by the one root, and only in this case must non-root tiers be independently sequenced.[5] This is simply because the segment is internally inconsistent otherwise: [+ant] and [−ant] are incompatible unless they are ordered.

A contour-free phonology does permit a phonological analysis of *press your point* and the like, but /ʃ/ can be only be present if it (i.e., its root node) is epenthesized. Consequently, an assimilation analysis parallel to the lexical case is *not* available, so undermining the only argument in favor of a phonological analysis.

In general, contour segments allow dual analyses of many phenomena on the phonetics/phonology interface. This lack of predictiveness is a problem. For example, Clements (1987) analyses stop epenthesis in English *tenth* and *prince* with the phonological contour segments like /t̪t̪/, /t̪θ/, /nᵗθ/, etc. Yet Fourakis & Port (1986) report that the epenthesis has an overwhelmingly phonetic nature: it does not result in homonymy between *prints* and *prince*, it can create novel clusters not used phonemically, it is optional and it is gradient. See also Hayes (1992) who uses contour segments to revise Nolan's (1992) phonetic analysis of cases like *late calls* and *ten things*. Even if such representations are little used, they are always available for difficult cases, which are of course the very ones we want to study most.

21.9 Conclusion

A cautious line must be taken in constructing phonological interpretations of phonetic data. First, the gradience which Zsiga demonstrates is the most important thing, more so than the statistical coincidence of the end-points of that trend with target templates, because the nature of these is not fully understood. We cannot yet draw firm conclusions about which targets are present. Indeed we *should* not do so while the phonology is able to represent any resulting hypotheses using contour segments. Banning contour segments reinforces the basis for a phonetic account and counters the phonetic evidence for /ʃ/ in an interesting way. I follow Zsiga in looking for a likely account in the coarticulation of /s/ and /j/.

Notes

* I would like to thank the editors, three anonymous referees and Katerina Nicolaidis for their very helpful comments on an earlier draft. Thanks also to Fiona Gibbon and Bob Ladd for useful discussion of various points. Support from a SERC post-doctoral grant and MRC project G9 117453N is gratefully acknowledged.

1 This issue is addressed by Nolan's (1990: 458) commentary on Pierrehumbert (1990). Nolan claims that Pierrehumbert needs different categorial representations (in my terms, different feature bundles in surface structure) for each of the radically different phonetic targets for English /t/ arising in different syllabic positions and in different dialects (and, we might add, sociolects). This conclusion is based on the assumption that dialect-specific phonetic targets such as [ʔ] or [ɾ] demand dialect-specific categorial feature bundles. In fact, speakers might be employing dialect-

specific semantics of the single feature-bundle /t/. That both options exist in competition is the very issue I want to address.

2 The alternative is to analyze D-/ʃ/ as underived /s+j/. I reject this on the grounds that there should be a *gradual* and *incremental* change in the interpretation of /sj/ as the strength of the boundary between /s/ and /j/ increases. In dialects with tautomorphemic /sj/, the cluster has essentially the same pronunciation whether / sj / or / s#j /. The hypothetical /s+j/ of *pressure* is quite different. The interpretation of /sj/ would have to change from [sj] (*suit*) to [ʃ] (*pressure*) and back again to [sj] (*miss you*). This seems quite undesirable.

3 I do not know the sociolinguistic nature of the variation.

4 Abstracting patterns of contact or articulatory targets from actual EPG contacts is a difficult problem. See Hardcastle, Gibbon & Nicolaidis (1991).

5 If roots never dominate sequenced features the sequence of any tier is still available, because it can be derived from the root tier. Multiple association is not affected. Potential contour segments (such as the rare short diphthongs) must be reanalyzed given the clear predictions made by contour-free phonology. Following LaCharité (1993), Lombardi (1990) and others, affricates are phonologically stops, whereas contour tones require a sequence of roots with sufficient prosodic structure to bear the tones one per root (cf. Duanmu, 1992).

References

Bird, S. 1990. Constraint-based phonology. Ph.D. dissertation, University of Edinburgh.

Bird, S. & E. Klein. 1990. Phonological events. *Journal of Linguistics* 26: 33–56.

Broe, M. 1993. Specification theory: the treatment of redundancy in Generative Phonology. Ph.D. dissertation, University of Edinburgh.

Catford, J. C. 1977. *Fundamental Problems in Phonetics*. Edinburgh: Edinburgh University Press.

Clements, G. N. 1987. Phonological feature representation and the description of intrusive stops. In A. Bosch, B. Need & E. Schiller (eds.), *Papers from the 23rd Annual Regional Meeting of the Chicago Lingusitic Society. Parasession on Autosegmental and Metrical Phonology*. Chicago: Chicago Linguistics Society, 29–50.

Coleman, J. 1991. Phonological representations: their names, forms and powers. D.Phil. dissertation, University of York.

Duanmu, S. 1992. Re-examining contour tone units in Chinese languages. Paper presented at the 18th meeting of the Berkeley Linguistics Society.

Fourakis, M. & R. Port. 1986. Stop epenthesis in English. *Journal of Phonetics* 14: 197–221.

Hardcastle, W. J., F. Gibbon & K. Nicolaidis. 1991. EPG data reduction methods and their implications for studies of lingual coarticulation. *Journal of Phonetics* 19: 251–256.

Hayes, B. 1992. Comments on chapter 10. In G. J. Docherty & D. R. Ladd (eds.), *Papers in Laboratory Phonology II: Gesture, Segment, Prosody*. Cambridge: Cambridge University Press, 280–286.

La Charité, D. 1993. The internal structure of affricates. Ph.D. dissertation, Université d'Ottawa.

Lombardi, L. 1990. The nonlinear organization of the affricate. *Natural Language and Linguistic Theory* 8: 375–425.

Nolan, F. 1990. Who do phoneticians represent? *Journal of Phonetics* 18: 453–464.

Nolan, F. 1992. The descriptive role of segments: evidence from assimilation. In G. J. Docherty & D. R. Ladd (eds.), *Papers in Laboratory Phonology II: Gesture, Segment, Prosody*. Cambridge: Cambridge University Press, 261–280.

Pierrehumbert, J. 1990. Phonological and phonetic representation. *Journal of Phonetics* 18: 375–394.

Scobbie, J. M. 1991. Attribute value phonology. Ph.D. dissertation, University of Edinburgh.

Scobbie, J. M. 1993. Constraint violation and conflict from the perspective of declarative phonology. *Canadian Journal of Linguistics* 38: 155–169.

Wells, J. C. 1982. *Accents of English 1: An Introduction*. Cambridge: Cambridge University Press.

22

The influence of syntactic structure on [s] to [ʃ] assimilation

TARA HOLST and FRANCIS NOLAN

22.1 Introduction

This paper is about the phonetic facts of assimilation, its phonological modeling, and the effects of syntactic structure on its occurrence. The emphasis is on the first two. In some respects the paper leads on from an earlier paper (Nolan, 1992) and the commentaries on it by Browman, Hayes, and Ohala. Section 22.2 will review some of the points in that paper, which dealt with place of articulation (POA) assimilation in stops. Section 22.3 will then take up some suggestions which arose in the commentaries; and this will lead in to the main part (section 22.4) of the current paper, which will present new work on POA assimilation, this time in fricatives rather than stops.

22.2 Place of articulation assimilation in stops

The work reported in Nolan (1992)[1] starts from the question: "Does articulation mirror the discrete change implied by phonetic and phonological representations of assimilation?" For instance, in *red car,* does the /d/ at the end of *red* "change into" a /g/ as a phonemic, or even phonetic, transcription would imply? The experiments used pairs of sentences, such as:

(a) *They di*[dg]*ardens for rich people.*
(b) *They di*[gg]*ardens for rich people.*

where (a) provides a potential POA assimilation site at a word boundary – specifically an alveolar before a velar; and (b) provides a velar–velar control context. The basic instrumental tool used was electropalatography (EPG).

315

In short, the EPG analyses showed that speakers produce a continuum of forms for the "lexical" alveolar, ranging from complete occlusion at the alveolar ridge to a pattern with no contact further forward than that seen in the control (velar-velar) sentence. Forms between these extremes, having no complete alveolar closure, but nonetheless contact further forward on the palate than is present in the velar control, were referred to as "residual alveolars".[2]

22.3 Phonological interpretation

22.3.1 Problems with standard formalisms

Nolan (1992) argues that the kind of "gradual" articulatory behavior found with EPG is hard to accommodate in the discrete mechanisms of phonology. For instance in a "feature geometry" approach, both (1b) and (1c) below assume that the supralaryngeal node of the first consonant is linked to the place node of the second, but neither satisfactorily accounts for the range of forms discovered by the EPG studies.[3]

(1)

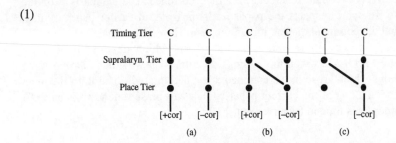

With delinking of the first consonant from its original place node, as in (c), there should never be any trace of an alveolar, so (c) is unable to account for a significant proportion of the EPG data (namely the "residual alveolar" forms).[4] Without delinking, as in (b), it was argued that although this configuration shows why the alveolar activity survives, the formalism gives no indication that the alveolar may be present in greater or lesser degree whilst the velar does not exhibit such variation.

Hayes, in his commentary, points to a different objection to (b): by analogy to tonal phonology the output should be a "contour segment", like a contour tone – sliding from alveolar to velar. Although such a sliding (or perhaps "rolling") articulation is possible, there is no evidence that it occurs. A consistent interpretation of the phonological formalism thus makes (b) incompatible with the observed data.

316

22.3.2 "Articulator nodes"

As a solution to his own objection Hayes takes up the proposal of Sagey (1986), and of Maddieson & Ladefoged (1989), that the place node should dominate three "articulator nodes" – LABIAL, CORONAL, and DORSAL. This allows one timing slot to have more than one otherwise contradictory feature values, e.g. [+ant] and [–ant], and thus permits the representation of double-articulations, as shown in (2). Note that in (2) the "daughters" are simultaneous; it may help to visualize the nodes in three dimensions, with DORSAL at the front and LABIAL at the back. The tree on the left simply shows the nodes which the place tier can dominate; the tree on the right shows the representation of an occurring sound, a labial–velar stop (e.g. [g͡b]).

(2)

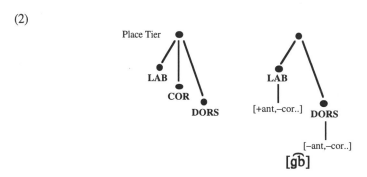

Given such a mechanism, POA assimilation would then produce a "complex segment" – the /d/ becoming a double-articulated (simultaneous) coronal–dorsal, as in (3):

(3)

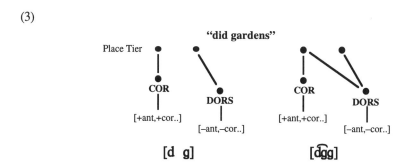

This leaves unresolved, however, the problem that the first segment, when detectable, is often only residually articulated.

22.3.3 Syllable-final weakening

To address this problem, Hayes suggests that two distinct processes are operating: assimilation proper, which is phonological and discrete, as in (3) above; and, separately, a general process of syllable-final weakening of coronals, which is phonetic and gradual, and yields the "residual alveolar" articulations.

Hayes admits (1992: 284) that the plausibility of this account depends in part on the coronal weakening process occurring in other contexts and hence being independently motivated. A good test case seems to be that of a following /h/, where there is no competing oral gesture. If syllable-final coronal weakening of the radical kind found at assimilation sites, where often little remains of the movement towards the alveolar ridge, is a general process, it should also happen in contexts such as *bad house*. If it turns out to happen only when a stop follows, it seems more appropriate to treat the weakening as integrally part of the phenomenon of assimilation.

Kühnert (1994) presents data directly relevant to this issue. Like the Cambridge projects, Kühnert's work examines POA assimilation in alveolars before velars, but she includes German as well as English, uses not only EPG but also electromagnetic articulography (EMA),[5] and her material includes alveolars before /h/, that is, examples of the *bad house* type. It emerges (Kühnert, 1994: 84–87) that whilst syllable-final alveolar stop articulations do weaken somewhat in faster speech before /h/, crucially they do not weaken to the extent that pre-velar alveolars do. There is always clear evidence of an alveolar gesture. Arguably this points to the radical weakening of syllable-final coronals found before velars being inherently part of the assimilation process, contrary to Hayes' proposal.

22.3.4 Assimilation within an articulator node

Hayes also raises the issue of place assimilation *within* a given articulator node, for instance between the adjacent *coronal* segments when an alveolar occurs before a dental (e.g. *get Thelma*). Here there is no question of a "complex segment" or "double articulation" in the same sense as with labial–velars. For instance, the articulation of a "canonical" alveolar, with the tongue tip/blade no further forward than the alveolar ridge, is incompatible with the simultaneous articulation of a dental. But Hayes asks whether instead the result is a "contour segment" (by analogy with tonal phonology – see section 22.3.1 above), where the articulator slides from the first specification to the second, or a "static target", where the articulator adopts the position of the second specification from the start. The "contour segment" and "static target" possibilities correspond respectively to Catford's (1977: 223) "gliding" and "shift" types of "accommodation".

Phonological representations underlying these two possibilities are given in (4) below. For both the outputs [t̪θ] and [t̪θ] the *coronal* node of the first consonant is linked to the feature specification of the second; in [t̪θ] there is delinking, resulting in a "static" articulation, while lack of delinking produces the "contour segment" [t̪θ]. Notice how in (4), unlike in (3) above, linking is taking place below the "articulator node", thereby making "same articulator" and "different articulator" assimilation formally different (a point made by Browman & Goldstein, 1989: 220). Hayes' intuition is that both [t̪θ] and [t̪θ] can occur in his own speech.

(4)

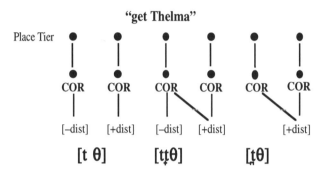

"get Thelma"

At this point, however, it should be remarked that a third outcome is articulatorily possible, namely a static articulation which is *between* alveolar and dental in place. This appears to be explicitly predicted by Browman & Goldstein (1989: 219). They view assimilations as resulting primarily from increased overlap in time of "gestures", which are the abstract control units underlying observable articulatory movements, and which serve as primes in their phonological representation, the "gestural score". In connection with "same articulator" assimilation, they write:

The hypothesis of gestural overlap, and consequent blending, makes a specific prediction: the observed motion of the TT [Tongue Tip] tract variables[6] resulting from overlap and blending should differ from the motion exhibited by either of the individual gestures alone. In particular, the location of the constriction should not be identical to that of either an alveolar or a dental, but rather should fall somewhere in between.

The results of the experiment to be described bear directly on the issue of what happens when adjacent segments have different specifications for the same articulator.

22.4 Assimilation and syntactic structure

22.4.1 Motivation from speech comprehension for studying assimilation

Although the experiment will provide information on the phonetic nature of POA assimilation *per se*, it is also motivated by the question of how listeners process the speech stream.[7] Following other work on connected speech processes, such as that of Scott & Cutler (1984), we may expect that some assimilations will be inhibited by syntactic boundaries. Given such a relationship, it seems fruitful to explore whether a phonetic effect which correlates well with syntactic boundaries, or their absence, can be exploited by listeners in the real-time comprehension of speech. For instance, if a particular assimilation never occurs across a major syntactic boundary, can a listener use the occurrence of the assimilation at the end of a word to infer that the following word, the "trigger" of the assimilation, should be integrated into the present constituent (a phrase, for instance), rather than being potentially the start of a new major constituent? That is, can the assimilation act as a "cohesion cue", in the sense of Grabe & Holst (1992)?

The experiment was a production experiment designed to find out where particular assimilations occur, and used sentences structured in such a way that they could form the material for a subsequent on-line sentence-comprehension experiment. In the present paper, though, the focus will be on the nature of the assimilations themselves.

22.4.2 The choice of /s/ to /ʃ/ assimilation

This assimilatory process was chosen for the following reasons: it is common; it is a relatively easy assimilation for a hearer to hear and so it has the potential to act as a cue in comprehension; and its effects are relatively easy to categorize acoustically. Furthermore it exemplifies the kind of "same articulator" POA assimilation discussed in section 22.3.4 above, and so the results of the production experiment may be expected to help resolve issues of the kind raised there.

22.4.3 Experimental design

Sentence pairs of the following type were used:
–CB: *Before a shop assistant restock*[s ʃ]*elves ‖ all old produce must be removed.*
+CB: *Before a shop assistant restock*[s ‖ ʃ]*elves ought to be at least half empty.*

The influence of syntactic structure

That is, sentences containing an /s/ to /ʃ/ assimilation site without, and with, a major clause boundary intervening (for convenience, –CB and +CB). The item ending in /s/ at the assimilation site was always an ambiguously transitive/intransitive verb ending in a voiceless stop.

There were 17 such pairs. These were distributed between two randomized blocks of sentences such that only one member of a pair appeared in a block. The blocks also contained a large number of other sentences of types required for other experiments. Each of 12 subjects read both blocks, in two sessions separated by a week. After exclusion of two pairs whose misreading went uncorrected in the recording sessions, 202 tokens remained for analysis in each category (+CB and –CB).

The subjects were four female and eight male speakers of southern British English. They were instructed to read each sentence through silently, and then read it aloud at a comfortable speed as fluently as possible.

22.4.4 Analysis technique

A Kay 5500 digital spectrograph was used to display 0–8 kHz wideband spectrograms of the utterances. Preliminary inspection of a substantial sample of the data suggested that the pattern of the voiceless fricative energy at the assimilation sites could be assigned qualitatively to one of a small set of categories. These categories are shown in Figure 22.1, where the shapes schematize patterns of fricative energy on a spectrogram (with time running from left to right, and increasing frequency up the vertical axis).

In type A, there are two essentially stable patterns of energy corresponding respectively to an [s] and an [ʃ], the latter differentiated by the lower cutoff of fricative energy in the frequency domain. Usually this pattern was associated with a silent pause, as indicated in the upper schema, but some pauseless realizations of this pattern were also encountered, as shown in the lower schema. Type A represents an absence of assimilation. (See Figure 22.2 for spectrograms exemplifying the different types of assimilation.)

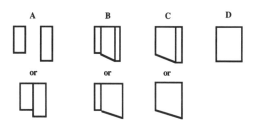

Figure 22.1. Categorization of abutting fricatives at assimilation sites. The shapes schematize the kind of energy patterns seen on spectrograms.

Types B and C show patterns of energy which glide between a more [s]-like energy distribution and a more [ʃ]-like distribution. In B, there is an apparent period of static [s]-like friction at the start of the block of friction, whereas in C the transition starts immediately. In both B and C there may be a stable [ʃ]-like phase at the end of the friction, as in the upper schemata, or not, as in the lower schemata. B and C represent successively increasing degrees of assimilation of the [s].

Type D is defined by a single spectrally stable period of friction. As the schema implies, this friction is, impressionistically, more like [ʃ] than [s], but this point will be discussed in more detail below. Type D represents the greatest degree of assimilation.

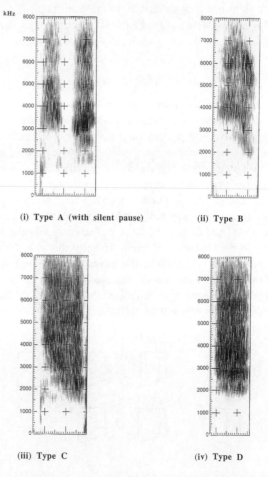

(i) Type A (with silent pause)   (ii) Type B

(iii) Type C   (iv) Type D

Figure 22.2. Spectrograms (0–8 kHz) illustrating the four assimilation types.

Notice that duration is not criterial for assigning tokens to the types, and the schemata are drawn so that the fricative portion of the spectrogram appears to be the same duration in each type. Systematic variation in duration between the types will be discussed below.

Before the main analysis, a number of tokens were judged independently by four members of the project, and the results were compared. Agreement was generally good, though it should be noted that many tokens are hard to categorize unambiguously. Subsequently the tokens with which the main analyst had difficulty were again subjected to independent analysis by three other members of the project, and differences of allocation resolved by discussion.

22.4.5 Results

22.4.5.1 Assimilation types by syntactic category.
Figure 22.3 shows the distribution of the types A, B, C, and D by syntactic category – whether or not a clause boundary intervened between the [s] and the [ʃ]. Where there is no clause boundary at the assimilation site (CB), there are fewest tokens in type A, and a steady increase to type D. When there is a clause boundary, the most striking finding is the apparent strong preference for type A. This is, however, not as straightforward as it seems, since a large majority of the tokens with a clause boundary at the assimilation site had some degree of silent pause.

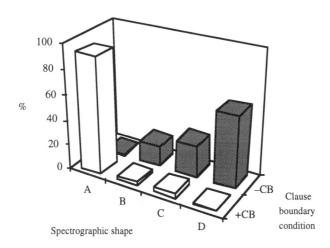

Figure 22.3. Distribution of assimilation types by syntactic category.

It would not be expected, *a priori*, that an assimilatory process would happen across a silent pause, and indeed the assimilation under investigation was not found to do so. Whether we are interested in the articulatory process, or in the possible role of assimilation in sentence comprehension, it would have been preferable to have avoided silent pauses. Their frequent occurrence reflects their naturalness as a marker of major syntactic boundaries, but also the length and complexity of the sentences. A future experiment would have to use shorter clauses, which would probably discourage pausing. Nevertheless it is useful, from the point of view of assimilation, to focus on the +CB tokens without a silent pause.

22.4.5.2 *"Pauseless" +CB tokens*

Only 20 +CB tokens showed no acoustic evidence of pause. Of these pauseless +CB tokens there are six of type A, six of type B, seven of type C, and one of type D. Though few in number, these tokens are of interest because they show evidence of reluctance to use type D assimilation across a clause boundary. Admittedly there is one token out of 20 which appears clearly to be a D; and indeed a second token, which, although originally classified as a C, and confirmed as such after panel discussion, was somewhat ambiguous between type C and D; and so it is not possible to rule out type D from the boundary context. Nonetheless, allowing the possibility that the one clear D could be the result, say, of a performance error, the data is suggestive of a strong hypothesis for testing in a future revised version of the experiment, namely: *type D assimilation, "full" assimilation, is blocked across a clause boundary.* The significance of such a hypothesis will become clearer after the discussion of the modeling of the assimilation types which follows in section 22.4.6.

22.4.6 *The modeling of assimilation*

In this section it will be concluded that type D assimilation is different from A, B, and C. Specifically, type D will be claimed to involve a phonological rule, whilst the others do not. Such a recognition of a fundamental difference underlying an apparent continuum of observed forms is in keeping with the spirit of a comment by Ohala (1992: 286) on the variety of residual alveolar articulations found in the "dig gardens" examples (see section 22.2.1 above): "In other words, I think there may be a huge gap between the faintest version of an alveolar stop in red car and the fully assimilated version [reg ka...]."

To reach this conclusion, however, it will be necessary to consider and reject the apparently more parsimonious view that all types of assimilation stem from the same source. Consideration will be given to the Articulatory Phonology approach of Browman and Goldstein, and to a more conventional phonological autosegmental approach, as discussed in section 22.3.4.

22.4.6.1 Articulatory Phonology

Articulatory Phonology appears to make the strong claim that assimilation, like other casual speech processes, can be modeled in terms of the overlapping of gestures and changes in their magnitude: "All changes are hypothesized to result from two simple mechanisms, which are intrinsically related to the talker's goals of speed and fluency – reduce the size of individual gestures and increase their overlap" (Browman & Goldstein, 1989: 220). The gestures, it should be remembered, are not the concrete observable movements of articulators, but, rather, the abstract specifications of segments which underlie the observable activity.

The Articulatory Phonology account of the data presented so far would probably look something like the schemata in Figure 22.4. Notice that, unlike in Figure 22.1, possible durational differences are implied in Figure 22.4. The assimilation types A to D would be regarded as a continuum of outputs, varying spectrally and durationally, which result from progressively increasing overlap of the [s] gesture and the [ʃ] gesture, represented by the thin and thick curves respectively. Type D results when the two gestures overlap completely in time, and there is no longer any evidence of the original sequential ordering of the two segments.

This is an elegant and attractive conceptualization, but there are two crucial pieces of evidence which suggest that it does not provide a comprehensive account of what is happening. Before examining these, however, we need to consider precisely what the prediction of Articulatory Phonology is for "same-articulator" assimilation. According to Browman & Goldstein (1989: 220), what

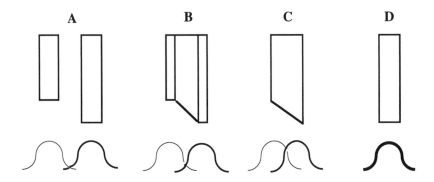

Figure 22.4. An Articulatory Phonology view of assimilation. Increasing degrees of overlap in time of [s] and [ʃ] gestures, represented by the thin and thick curves respectively, are associated with the schematic spectral patterns A – D. The fricative event is predicted to become progressively shorter as overlap increases.

is predicted for this kind of assimilation is gestural blending such that in the case of an alveolar followed by a dental (see section 22.3.4 above) "the location of the constriction should not be identical to that of either an alveolar or a dental, but rather should fall somewhere in between". As noted in section 22.3.4, this appears to predict a stable, intermediate articulation, which is neither Hayes' "delinked" all-dental, nor his alveolar-to-dental "contour segment". It is already clear from the existence of B and C forms that the gestural overlap hypothesis needs to be interpreted so as to accommodate a "contour segment" stage in articulatory reduction. In itself such a stage seems not to be incompatible with the gestural blending account.

The first substantive evidence that gestural blending fails to give a comprehensive account concerns the spectral properties of type D. Articulatory Phonology predicts an articulation intermediate between [s] and [ʃ], and hence presumably an intermediate acoustic output. The facts, however, point to type D forms being identical with [ʃ] and not at all [s]-like. Average spectra were calculated for 10 tokens of a speaker's "canonical" word-final [s] in non-assimilatory environments, for 10 tokens of "canonical" word-initial [ʃ] in non-assimilatory environments, and for all available type D tokens for the speaker (between nine and 15; two speakers with fewer than nine type D tokens were left out). To calculate each spectrum, the relevant fricative tokens were excised and concatenated, and the long term average spectrum of the concatenated sequence was computed. Figure 22.5 shows the results for the ten speakers for whom there were sufficient D tokens. In each case the D spectrum matches almost exactly the "canonical" [ʃ] spectrum. There is no evidence, then, that type D shows the effects of an intermediate articulation.[8]

At this point in the argument the gestural account might still be saved by appeal to non-linearities in the aerodynamics and acoustics of the fricatives. It might, for instance, be the case that [s] requires a very specifically formed groove at a very precise location, and that, in a way reminiscent of Quantal Theory, deviation more than a small amount away from that configuration results in a discrete switch to [ʃ]-like friction – hence the spectrum of type D. Such a defence would need to be argued in detail, and might well prove hard to sustain. As a phonetic exercise, at least, it seems that the articulators are quite capable of producing a continuum of fricatives between [s] and [ʃ]; and indeed the widespread occurrence in the data of type B and C, which involve a transition through spectral properties intermediate between [s] and [ʃ], suggests compellingly that speakers readily achieve such intermediate friction in real speech. There is, then, no reason for type D not to have intermediate spectral characteristics if it were the result of the intermediate articulation predicted by the gestural account. It does not, so some additional principle must be invoked in order, perhaps, to decrease the magnitude of the [s]-gesture and allow [ʃ] to dominate totally in type D.

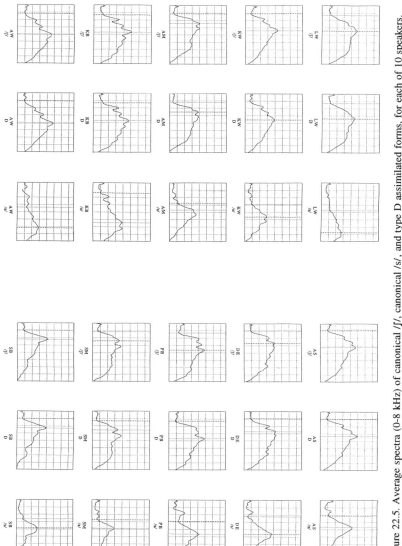

Figure 22.5. Average spectra (0-8 kHz) of canonical /ʃ/, canonical /s/, and type D assimilated forms, for each of 10 speakers. Each spectrum is a long term average spectrum computed over at least nine tokens.

But, even if a model is elaborated in this way, there is a second substantive piece of evidence against the Articulatory Phonology account. If we allow that types B and C result from increasing gestural overlap in time, but nonetheless exhibit characteristics of both fricatives involved, it must logically be the case that type D can only occur through total gestural overlap in time. Since it is the [ʃ] which "wins" in terms of spectrum, the duration of type D should be that of a word-initial [ʃ]. Table 22.1 shows the results of a spectrographic analysis of the duration of the fricative portion of all tokens (for type A, only tokens without a silent pause were included). To factor out differences in speaking rates between speakers, the fricative durations of each speaker were expressed as a proportion of that speaker's mean duration for "canonical" [ʃ], and these normalized durations were averaged across speakers.

Crucially, type D is longer than the canonical single word-initial [ʃ] (1.16 to 1.00), and this difference is highly significant ($Z = 6.08$, $p < .001$) on a Mann-Whitney test. This extra duration cannot be accounted for by simple gestural overlapping. The extra duration of [ʃ]-like friction in type D must mean that some duration "belonging", as it were, to [s] has been articulated as [ʃ] – that is, in a very real sense, a process of assimilation has occurred.

It seems, then, that the initially persuasive explanation offered by Articulatory Phonology fails to account convincingly for either the spectral or durational properties of the type D forms. It is therefore appropriate to see whether a more traditional phonological approach can offer a uniform account of the data.

Table 22.1. Mean normalized durations of fricative portion of different assimilation types.

Assimilation type	No. of tokens	Mean normalized duration
A (pauseless)	8	1.97
B	39	1.52
C	58	1.36
D	117	1.16
"canonical" [ʃ]	110	1.00

22.4.6.2 Autosegmental Phonology

The kind of formalism used in example (4) (*get Thelma*), section 22.3.4, to describe alveolar-to-dental assimilations can be directly adopted for [s] to [ʃ] assimilation, as shown in (5). Delinking, as on the right of (5), results in complete POA assimilation, as in the case of type D with its extra duration and uniformly [ʃ]-like friction. Failure to delink, as in the middle of (5), produces a contour segment, as in types B and C.

The main argument against this account for types B and C is one of economy. Types B and C appear to correspond straightforwardly to the kind of mechanical dynamic output of a device required to reach two incompatible targets in a short time. This, of course, is precisely the insight to which Articulatory Phonology gives qualitative expression, and the associated physical model of task dynamics gives quantitative realization. The crucial fact is that the speaker does not need to *do* anything to produce types B and C – they arise naturally from the characteristics of the articulators and their targets. There is therefore no motivation to invoke a specific cognitive operation, that is, a phonological rule, to model them. The kind of phonological configuration suggested for "contour segments" is therefore inappropriate and unnecessary. Phonological assimilation with delinking is, in contrast, appropriate for type D, precisely because there is no evidence of competing articulatory targets.

(5)

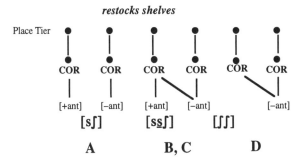

restocks shelves

[sʃ]	[ssʃ]	[ʃʃ]
A	B, C	D

22.4.7 Conclusion

It has been argued above that the mechanisms of Articulatory Phonology cannot account for type D assimilation, but they do account for types B and C. It has also been argued that it is supererogatory to devise autosegmental representations to express phenomena (such as B and C) which emerge from the workings of the articulatory mechanism. Type D, on the other hand, appears at

Tara Holst and Francis Nolan

this preliminary stage to exhibit a combination of spectral and durational characteristics which necessitate a rule of phonological assimilation.

We arrive, then, at the situation whereby an apparent continuum of assimilation involves two separate phenomena: gestural blending, in the case of B and C, and an explicitly cognitive phonological assimilation in the case of D. On the face of it, this may seem unparsimonious. But it fits in with a view of phonetics which embraces variation in production, perceptual reinterpretation, and sound change – as advocated notably by Ohala.

Phonologists are faced with a range of assimilatory phenomena, historically and synchronically. At one end of the range, we have apparently mechanical effects such as our Bs and Cs, and the process which blends /s/ and /j/ in *miss you* into, perhaps, [ç]. At the other end, we have the historically "phonologized" results of such effects, like the /s/–/ʃ/ alternation in *office ~ official,* where /s/ and /j/ became /ʃ/ historically, and the pronunciation cannot be other than [ʃ]. Phonologization of such articulatory effects is probably mediated by perception, as Ohala suggests.

As it happens, we have informal evidence on perception of our /s/ to /ʃ/ assimilations. The first author listened to the sentences, to decide where /s/ could be detected.[9] Even in careful listening to the sentences, a phonetically trained analyst could not hear /s/ in more than 50% of Bs and Cs. A reasonable perceptual interpretation for a naive hearer, then, is that these utterances involved the application of an optional phonological rule of assimilation. Such a rule in effect licences a speaker to scan ahead in an utterance and plan a number of conventionalized articulatory simplifications. When such a rule applies, there is no more reason to expect a trace of the original articulatory target than in the case of *official.*

In time, the assimilated form may oust other forms; but this is more likely word-internally than at word boundaries, since word-final sounds will be occurring in many contexts irrelevant for the assimilation in question. Here we may expect articulatorily blended, and phonologically assimilated forms to co-exist stably.

If it is a phonological rule of assimilation that produces D forms, it is reasonable to suppose that the rule may be sensitive, like other phonological rules, to higher levels of linguistic structure. Specifically, as anticipated in section 22.4.5 above on the basis of the small subset of "pauseless" +CB data which provides only one type D, the assimilation rule may be inhibited from applying across a clause boundary. Gestural overlap, on the other hand, will occur to yield types B and C wherever it is promoted by rhythmical factors – prosodic phrasing and speech rate, for instance – regardless of syntactic boundaries.

It should be emphasized that the interpretation of assimilation which has been outlined, and especially the view of the interaction of assimilation with syntax,

330

are more in the nature of hypotheses than proofs; some of the issues emerged only as the experiment progressed, as did its design flaws. Plans are in hand to augment the present experiment by one whose design more directly tests the issues discussed in this paper.

22.5 Summary

On the basis of previous and new work the following points have been made in this paper:

1. POA "assimilation" in stops yields a continuum of forms through partial loss to apparent total loss of an articulation.

2. Syllable-final "weakening" in coronal stops does not seem to be general enough to justify separating it from assimilation.

3. /s/ undergoes articulatory blending with a following /ʃ/ to yield a "contour segment," and this process can be modeled by gestural overlap, representing a "mechanical" effect.

4. /s/ may also become phonetically identical to a following /ʃ/ while retaining duration, and this process can only be modeled as a phonological rule, representing a cognitive operation.

5. The phonological assimilation rule, but not gestural overlap, is directly inhibited by a clause boundary.

Notes

1 This work was carried out in Cambridge, as part of various projects, by Paul Kerswill, Martin Barry, and Susan Wright.

2 There may still, of course, be a residual articulation which leaves no trace on the EPG palate.

3 *SPE* features are used throughout, but it is unlikely that any arguments would hinge on the exact features used.

4 Browman and Goldstein (1989: 220) make a similar point: "To interpret a delinked gesture as one that is articulatorily produced, but auditorily hidden, would require a major change in the assumptions of the [autosegmental] framework."

5 EMA is a technique in which the positions of small receiver coils glued to the articulators are tracked. The data is similar to that provided by x-ray pellet tracking systems.

6 Within Browman and Goldstein's (1989) articulatory model the TT "articulator set" is associated, in principle, with three "tract variables" for gestures of the tongue tip/blade, namely the degree of constriction, the location of the constriction, and the shape of the constriction.

7 The experiment reported here was carried out by Tara Holst. It forms part of a project "Post-lexical and prosodic phonological processing," held at the University of

331

Cambridge by Paul Warren and Francis Nolan (of the Linguistics Department) and Ted Briscoe (Computer Laboratory), and funded by the Joint Research Councils' HCI initiative under grant SPG 9030657, with Esther Grabe and Tara Holst as RAs.

8 Here it may be appropriate to note that the substantial number of D forms, with stable spectral properties consistent with [ʃ], brings into question Catford's assertion (1977: 223) that, whilst phoneticians have often represented the first sibilant in e.g. *this shop* as [ʃ] implying a complete shift in articulation, "[i]t is doubtful if this commonly occurs". The D forms are also out of step with the data and argumentation in Local (1992), where a small number of tokens of *This shop's a fish shop* are presented in which the first and second word-boundary fricative sequences differ spectrally and palatographically. Local argues on the basis of such incomplete assimilations for a "non-procedural" account, in which it is unnecessary, indeed inappropriate, to say that one segment "turns into" another. It is not clear how type D tokens would be accommodated in his account.

9 /s/ heard in context: **A 98%** (186/190), **B 46%** (18/39), **C 41%** (24 /58), **D 8%** (9/117) /s/ heard in isolation: **A 100%** (190/190), **B 92%** (36/39), **C 74%** (43/58), **D 5%** (6/117). Note: (i) it is easier to hear traces of /s/ for B and C types in isolation; (ii) B and C are similar in both conditions; (iii) there is a systematic correlation with the spectrographic categories; (iv) the (small) percentage of /s/ heard in D is almost certainly due to top-down processing (cf. /d/ heard in "dig gardens" control velar-velar sequences in Nolan , 1992).

References

Browman, C. P. 1992. Commentary on F. Nolan, "The descriptive role of segments: evidence from assimilation". In G. J. Docherty & D. R. Ladd (eds.), *Papers in Laboratory Phonology II: Gesture, Segment, Prosody*. Cambridge: Cambridge University Press, 287–289.

Browman, C. P. & L. Goldstein, 1989. Articulatory gestures as phonological units. *Phonology* 6: 201–231.

Catford, J. C. 1977. *Fundamental Problems in Phonetics*. Bloomington, IN: Indiana University Press.

Grabe, E. & T. Holst. 1992. Cohesion cues in the processing of connected speech. Paper presented at the Colloquium of the British Association of Academic Phoneticians, Cambridge.

Hayes, B. 1992. Commentary on F. Nolan, "The descriptive role of segments: evidence from assimilation". In G. J. Docherty & D. R. Ladd (eds.), *Papers in Laboratory Phonology II: Gesture, Segment, Prosody*. Cambridge: Cambridge University Press, 280–286.

Kühnert, B. 1994. Die alveolar-velare Assimilation bei Sprechern des Deutschen und des Englischen – kinematische und perzeptive Grundlagen. Ph.D. dissertation, Munich.

Local, J. 1992. Modeling assimilation in nonsegmental, rule-free synthesis. In G. J. Docherty & D. R. Ladd (eds.), *Papers in Laboratory Phonology II: Gesture, Segment, Prosody*. Cambridge: Cambridge University Press, 190–223.

Maddieson, I. & P. Ladefoged, 1989. Multiply articulated segments and the feature hierarchy. *UCLA Working Papers in Phonetics* 72: 116–138.

Nolan, F. 1992. The descriptive role of segments: evidence from assimilation. In G. J. Docherty & D. R. Ladd (eds.), *Papers in Laboratory Phonology II: Gesture, Segment, Prosody*. Cambridge: Cambridge University Press, 261–280.

Ohala, J. J. 1992. Commentary on F. Nolan, "The descriptive role of segments: evidence from assimilation". In G. J. Docherty & D. R. Ladd (eds.), *Papers in Laboratory Phonology II: Gesture, Segment, Prosody*. Cambridge: Cambridge University Press, 286–287.

Sagey, E. 1986. The representation of features and relations in non-linear phonology. Ph.D. dissertation, MIT.

Scott, D. R. & Cutler, A. 1984. Segmental phonology and the perception of syntactic structure. *Journal of Verbal Learning and Verbal Behaviour* 23: 450–466.

23
Assimilation as gestural overlap: comments on Holst and Nolan

CATHERINE P. BROWMAN*

The Holst & Nolan paper makes a welcome contribution to the work on assimilation. It is not, however, as definitive as one would like, given the relatively large number of subjects that were used in the study. In particular, the classification of their type D is problematic. They use acoustic durational data and spectral data, neither of which, I argue below, supports the conclusion they draw. In fact, although it is impossible to know for sure with acoustic data, the Holst & Nolan data might be consistent with an analysis of all the types – A through D – as increasing gestural overlap.

In addition to the above point, the Holst & Nolan paper purports to show that gestural overlap is not affected by syntactic processes. This claim is not supported either by their own data or by data from Hardcastle. That is, gestural overlap does appear to be affected by syntactic processes.

23.1 [s] to [ʃ] assimilation

Holst and Nolan present us with two kinds of analyses, analyses of the spectra and of the acoustic durations of sentence pairs like [with commas added – CPB]:

Before a shop assistant restocks shelves, all old produce must be removed.
Before a shop assistant restocks, shelves ought to be at least half empty.

They divide the spectra into four types, A through D, in which type A has two essentially stable patterns of acoustic energy, often separated by a silent pause, types B and C glide between a more [s]-like and a more [ʃ]-like pattern, and type D has a single pattern of acoustic energy. They argue that types B and C involve increasing gestural overlap, but type D is different, using delinking rules that involve removal of the phonetic material for [s] and assignment of its duration

334

(in some way) to the [ʃ], using both the spectral and durational analyses. In this section, I will indicate my doubts about both types of analyses, especially in the case of type D, and show how a gestural overlap analysis of type D would work.

23.1.1 Durational and spectral analyses

On the one hand, Holst and Nolan argue that, because the acoustic duration of type D is greater than that of a singleton [ʃ], there must be two root nodes, with no overlap, present in type D. While it is not possible to predict duration, either articulatory or acoustic, from feature geometry specifications, nevertheless I would expect that if type D has two root nodes and no gestural overlap, then it should have an acoustic duration more like an unambiguous type of two root nodes (type A) than an unambiguous type of a single root node ([ʃʃ]). But of course, this is not the case; rather, the acoustic duration for type D is much closer to the acoustic duration of the singleton [ʃ] than the acoustic duration of the two root nodes (type A), as can be seen in Figure 23.1. This figure, from the preprint version of the Holst and Nolan paper [see also Holst and Nolan, this volume, Table 22.1 – eds.], shows the mean normalized acoustic duration for each of the types A through D, compared to the normalized acoustic duration of 1.0 for [ʃ].

Let us consider type D, since it is this type that they suggest might not be increased gestural overlap, but rather a different kind of assimilation. Holst and Nolan show that D's mean normalized acoustic duration of 1.16 is significantly different from 1.0, the acoustic duration for the singleton [ʃ]. Of course, if 1.16 is significantly different from 1.0, 1.16 is very different from 1.97, the mean normalized acoustic duration for type A, the type with two unambiguous segments (and therefore two root nodes in feature geometry terms). Therefore, the Holst and Nolan analysis of type D as having two root nodes, but no gestural overlap, seems very unlikely to me. Rather, I would expect to analyze type D as

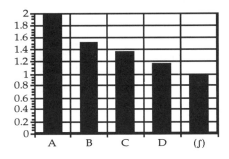

Figure 23.1. Mean normalized durations of types A-D and [ʃ] from Holst & Nolan (1993).

Catherine P. Browman

falling in a continuum with types A–C, so that type D would also be a type of increased gestural overlap between two gestures, with more overlap than in types B and C but not complete overlap (because the duration is greater than that for [ʃ]). (This assumes that type D is not bimodal, that is with most of the cases having duration of 1.0, and a few having a duration of 2.0, so that the mean normalized acoustic duration of 1.16 is typical of each case.)

On the other hand, because type D has a single acoustic signal, very similar to that for [ʃ], Holst and Nolan argue that type D is specified using only the phonetic material, or features, for an [ʃ]. This is a point that unfortunately cannot be proved from their data, which are acoustic. This is because, although there is a lawful relation between the articulation and the acoustic signal, this relation is not always linear, and therefore acoustic data alone canot be used to determine what is being controlled. In particular, the acoustic signal can be much more discrete than the articulation for [s] and [ʃ]. Data from Perkell, Boyce & Stevens (1979), in Figure 23.2, showed that as their speaker moved the constriction location of the tongue gradually articulatorily, nevertheless there was an abrupt change acoustically, from the spectrum for [s] to that for [ʃ].[1] They explained this by referring to Quantal Theory. Thus, even though the tongue articulation apparently changed quite gradually in this case, the acoustic signal did not show a comparable gradual change, but changed comparatively abruptly from one set of values to another set of values. Put another way, there may be many positions of the tongue that correspond to a single set of acoustic values for, say, [ʃ]. Therefore, it is not possible to know from the acoustic signal exactly what the articulation is. That means it is also not possible to use the acoustic signal to determine whether there is one underlying feature specification, or two nearly completely overlapping feature specifications.

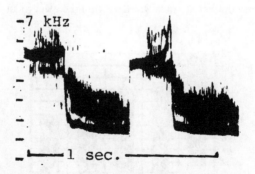

Figure 23.2 . Repeated spectra of [s] and [ʃ] given gradual tongue movement, from Perkell, Boyce, & Stevens (1979), Figure 3.

336

Assimilation as gestural overlap

23.1.2 A possible solution – type D as gestural overlap

Because it is not possible to know from the acoustic signal whether the articulation is the result of two (nearly completely) overlapping specified gestures that cause a resultant constriction location that is close enough to that of [ʃ], or whether the acoustic signal comes from a single specified gesture for [ʃ], and because the durational results show that the acoustic duration of type D is longer than that for a singleton, type D seems like a real candidate to be generated by nearly completely overlapping gestures. In this subsection I will show how it is possible to generate the durational results of type D using nearly completely overlapping gestures.

The result of interest is in Figure 23.3d; the rest of Figure 23.3 is setting up for (sub)Figure 23.3d. Figures 23.3a and 23.3b show the gestural scores, with the resultant articulatory movements and midsagittal sections, for the individual consonants pseudo-[s] and pseudo-[ʃ], generated by the computational gestural model at Haskins Laboratories (Browman, Goldstein, Saltzman, & Smith, 1986); note that these articulations are referred to as pseudo-[s] and pseudo-[ʃ], since they are not necessarily accurate (indeed, the spectrum for pseudo-[s] is flat, which of course is not correct). The single articulatory movement resulting from the overlap of several gestures, defined as Articulatory Phonology defines them (Browman & Goldstein, 1989, 1992), is shown in Figure 23.3c.

Figure 23.3a shows the gestural score and some resultant articulatory movements, with a (resultant) mid-sagittal section, for the singleton consonant pseudo-[s] in the utterance [ɛs.ɛ]; the gestural score used, along with the audio (or acoustic signal) generated by the vocal tract synthesizer, is at the bottom of the subfigure and the mid-sagittal section that occurred at the time of the end of activation (which is close to achievement of target) at the top. In this subfigure, as in all the subfigures, the boxes indicate the activated gestures. The movement curves resulting from the activation boxes are superimposed on the boxes indicating tongue tip constriction location and tongue body constriction degree and location; the two tongue body channels are for the vowels in the utterance and are included only to show that the vocalic influence did not change throughout the utterance, and therefore the vocal tract shape changes, for this pseudo-fricative, came only from the controlled tongue tip constriction location. The bottom two channels, for the vertical movement of the lower lip and jaw, are also included purely for information; neither of them is controlled at all in these utterances (note the lack of activation boxes). Figure 23.3b shows the same information for pseudo-[ʃ] in the utterance [ɛ.ʃɛ]. Figure 23.3c is the first of the subfigures in Figure 23.3 to have two (overlapping) consonant gestures, in the utterance [ɛs.ʃɛ]. The amount of overlap chosen is arbitrary, but less than the amount required for Holst and Nolan's type D. Notice that the movement curve for the tongue tip constriction location is fairly continuous, even given this moderate amount of overlap. That is, although the activation boxes representing

337

Catherine P. Browman

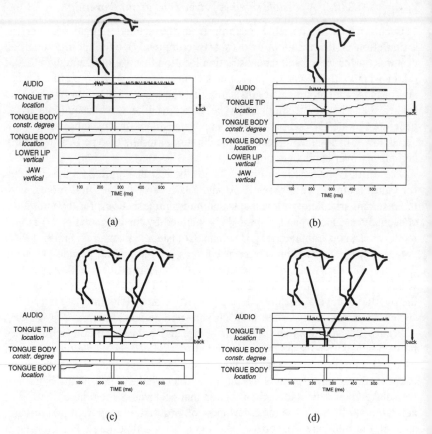

Figure 23.3. Gestural scores, articulatory movements, and mid-sagittal sections generated by a gestural computational model: (a) pseudo-[s] (in [ɛs.ɛ]); (b) pseudo-[ʃ] (in [ɛ.ʃɛ]; (c) moderate overlap of pseudo-[s] and pseudo-[ʃ] (in [ɛs.ʃɛ]); (d) nearly complete overlap of pseudo-[s] and pseudo-[ʃ] (in [ɛs.ʃɛ]).

the gestures are discrete, the movement curve resulting from the overlapping gestures (which are blended by the task dynamic model) is continuous.

Figure 23.3d again shows overlapping consonant gestures in the utterance [ɛs.ʃɛ]. However, the amount of overlap is greater than in Figure 23.3c, and is intended to provide a fairly close approximation of the amount of overlap in Holst and Nolan's type D (aiming for an acoustic duration of 1.2, that of [ʃ], given the quantization of the computational model). Note that the gestures overlap almost, but not quite, completely. Because of this large amount of overlap, the mid-sagittal sections at the ends of the activation boxes for pseudo-[s] and pseudo-[ʃ] are virtually identical (with a constriction location halfway

338

between those for the pseudo-[s] and the pseudo-[ʃ], as must happen given a constraint that the gestures are equally weighted; note that this constraint need not be imposed, and indeed may have to be relaxed if articulatory data show unequal influence of [ʃ] and [s]). The important aspect of this subfigure is that the movement curve for the change in constriction location of the tongue tip is completely continuous, as it is for the singleton consonants (especially [ʃ], in Figure 23.3b). That is, two nearly completely overlapping gestures (in the Articulatory Phonology sense) can be associated with a single articulatory movement, and therefore (presumably) with a single acoustic spectrum. Thus, the Holst and Nolan data could be consistent with all the types B–D being the same kind of assimilation, that of gradually increasing overlap of two gestures. Indeed, if the acoustic duration of 1.16 for type D reflects the individual cases, then gestural overlap is the only extant mechanism that will generate the observed durational data.

23.2 Gestural overlap and clause boundaries

Figure 23.4 (from Holst & Nolan, this volume) shows the relation between types A–D and presence or absence of clause boundary (only the data in which in general each type had more than 10 cases are discussed). In each type, there is a definite asymmetry between the number in that type that have clause boundary, and the number that do not – in type A, most of the members contain a clause boundary, while in types B–D, most of the members do not contain a clause

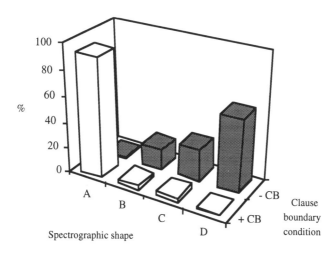

Figure 23.4. Percent with (+CB) and without (–CB) clause boundary in types A–D, from Holst & Nolan (this volume) Figure 22.3.

boundary. Notice that there also appears to be a progressive increase in the percentage without clause boundaries from B through D. Recall that types B and C are argued to be assimilation by increasing gestural overlap by Holst and Nolan. Therefore, gestural overlap appears to be negatively correlated with presence of clause boundary in these data, unlike the Holst and Nolan claim of no relation. And if type D is included (which, as argued above, may also be increased gestural overlap), then it is even clearer that there is a negative correlation between gestural overlap and the presence of clause boundary in these data.

Other data that show a relation between overlap and clause boundary come from Hardcastle (1985). These data are not about assimilation, but rather coarticulation between [k] and [l] using electropalatographic information. However, Hardcastle analyzes these data in terms of increasing overlap, as can be seen in Figure 23.5. (The boxes in the figure are schematic aids to help explain overlap, but could also be thought of as indicating Articulatory Phonology gestures.) Figure 23.6 displays some data selected from Hardcastle's Figures 8 and 11. Looking at the slow speech rate (the dark bars), one can see a marked effect of presence or absence of clause boundary in all four subgraphs, with the same negative correlation between presence of clause boundary and overlap as was seen in the Holst & Nolan data. Thus, if the Hardcastle data are

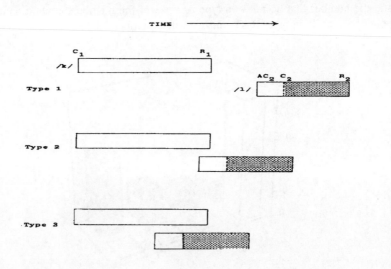

Figure 23.5. Schematic representation of articulatory events during a /kl/ sequence, after Hardcastle (1985), Figure 7.

indeed dealing with gestural overlap, then here (as well as in the Holst and Nolan data) gestural overlap is affected by presence or absence of clause boundaries. (Notice that the Holst & Nolan data are similar to the slow Hardcastle data; therefore, one might expect that assimilation data spoken at a faster rate might show overlap everywhere, as in the Hardcastle data.)

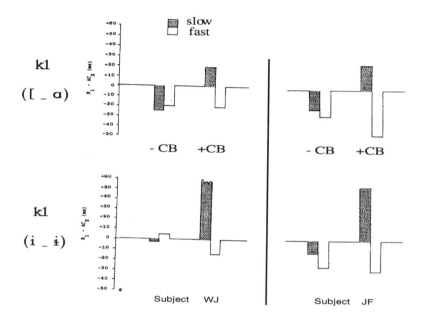

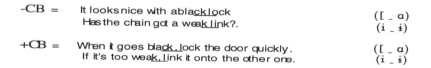

-CB = It looks nice with ablacklock   ([_ ɑ)
      Has the chain got a weak link?.   (i _ ɨ)

+CB = When it goes black lock the door quickly. ([_ ɑ)
      If it's too weak link it onto the other one. (i _ ɨ)

Figure 23.6. Means for /kl/ co-articulation measure (negative = overlap). Data from two subjects are shown, one on the left and one on the right. Data for low vowels are on top, and data for high vowels on bottom. –CB means no clause boundary and +CB clause boundary. Dark bars show amount of coarticulation for slow rates of speech, white (transparent) bars for fast rates. After Hardcastle (1985), Figures 8 and 11.

Catherine P. Browman

23.3 Summary

In summary, I have made two points. First, it does not appear to me that the Holst and Nolan data support two kinds of assimilation. Rather, even though it is not possible to say for sure given that the physical measure is acoustic, it is as or more consistent with the data to say that all the assimilation in the Holst and Nolan types has the same origin – increasing gestural overlap. Second, it seems that gestural overlap is in fact affected by the presence of clause boundaries, at least at slow rates of speech. This in turn means either that gestures are phonological (if only phonological entities are affected by syntactic factors such as clause boundaries), or else that the clause boundary effect is not restricted to phonological entities.

Notes

* This work was supported by NSF grant DBS-9112198 and NIH grants HD-01994 and DC-00121 to Haskins Laboratories.

1 After the Laboratory Phonology meeting in 1993, Sarah Hawkins ran a preliminary study with herself as speaker, and found a more gradual acoustic transition from [s] to [ʃ] for a gradual articulatory movement, although a transition she still characterized as "quantal" (personal communication).

References

Browman, C. P. & L. Goldstein. 1989. Articulatory gestures as phonological units. *Phonology* 6: 201–251.

Browman, C. P. & L. Goldstein. 1992. Articulatory Phonology: an overview. *Phonetica* 49: 155–180

Browman, C. P., L. Goldstein, E. Saltzman & C. Smith. 1986. GEST: A computational model for speech production using dynamically defined articulatory gestures. *Journal of the Acoustical Society of America* 80, S97.

Hardcastle, W. 1985. Some phonetic and syntactic constraints on lingual co-articulation during /kl/ sequences. *Speech Communication* 4: 247–263.

Perkell, J. S., S. E. Boyce & K. N. Stevens. 1979. Articulatory and acoustic correlates of [s–ʃ] distinction. In J. J. Wolf & D. H. Klatt (eds.), *Speech Communication Papers Presented at the 97th Meeting of the ASA,* Cambridge, MA, 12–16 June, 1979.

24
Orals, gutturals, and the jaw

SOOK-HYANG LEE*

24.1 Introduction

In Arabic, gutturals – uvular fricatives, pharyngeal fricatives and laryngeals – behave phonologically as a natural class in terms of some phonological phenomena such as co-occurrence restrictions and guttural lowering rules. The uvular stop /q/ does not pattern with gutturals with respect to these two phonological phenomena in Arabic.[1] As shown in Figure 24.1a, gutturals have traditionally been specified as [–anterior, –hi] in the *SPE* system. The features [low] and [back] distinguish the uvulars, pharyngeals, and laryngeals from one another. However, this analysis suffers from phonetic unrealism. The features [low] and [back] in the *SPE* system are defined in terms of tongue body position. Yet laryngeals, which are said to be [+low], cannot involve the tongue at all, and pharyngeals, which are said to be [+low, +back], involve the tongue root instead of the tongue body.

The specification of gutturals also provides problems in feature geometries developed within non-linear models of phonology, such as those of Clements (1985) and Sagey (1986). First, if we translate the *SPE* feature specifications directly into these frameworks, the use of [anterior] for gutturals is impossible since in these feature geometry frameworks, it is used for specifications only of coronal consonants. The more crucial problem for these frameworks, especially for articulator-based feature geometry frameworks such as Sagey's (1986), is that gutturals do not share a single major articulator.

Because of these problems, McCarthy (1994) proposes a [pharyngeal] place feature on par with [labial], [coronal], and [dorsal] in the articulator-based feature geometry, but defines [pharyngeal] not as involving any articulator but rather as the "orosensory pattern of constriction anywhere in the broad region of the pharynx" (McCarthy 1994: 199), which is introduced from Perkell's (1980) suggestion that distinctive features may involve such sensory feedback. Furthermore, to account for guttural transparency in vowel assimilation in Arabic, he proposes grouping the [labial], [coronal], and [dorsal] place features together under an Oral class node with both the Oral class node and [pharyngeal] being dominated by the Place node as shown in Figure 24.1b.

(a)

	ant	cor	high	low	back
labial	+	−	−	−	−
palato-alveolar	−	+	+	−	−
velar	−	−	+	−	+
uvular	−	−	−	−	+
pharyngeal	−	−	−	+	+
laryngeal	−	−	−	+	−

(b)

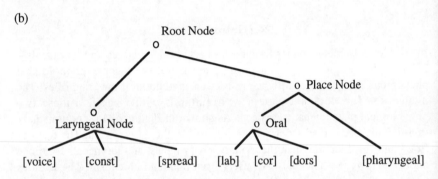

Figure 24.1 (a) Feature specification of consonants in the *SPE* system, and (b) feature geometry proposed by McCarthy (1994).

Goldstein (1994) questions McCarthy's proposal, listing some advantages of defining each basic place feature in terms of an active articulator. This view is compatible with the idea that speech is composed of "gestures formed by the independently controllable articulator sets within the vocal tract" as in Browman & Goldstein's (1990) Articulatory Phonology framework. Also, it is not clear whether [coronal] and [dorsal] can be defined in purely orosensory terms as well as in articulatory terms. He then proposes two alternative accounts, the more striking of which is that the jaw serves as the common articulator to differentiate oral consonants from gutturals although the jaw does not figure in the traditional phonetic specification. His claim is based on the assumption that the jaw has a common function in the coordinative structures for labial, coronal, and dorsal constrictions, but does not participate in the articulation of gutturals. Specifically, given the mechanical coupling between the jaw and the lower lip and between the jaw and the tongue, raising the jaw will contribute to constrictions of lips, tongue tip, and tongue dorsum.

This paper tests Goldstein's hypothesis by examining the jaw positions for consonants in VCV utterances. If his hypothesis is correct, we would expect the jaw to be high during oral consonants and to find some consistent movements during oral consonants out of and into the vowels but no jaw movements attributable to vowel contexts during gutturals.

24.2 Method

24.2.1 Subjects

Three native speakers each of Korean, Arabic, and French served as subjects. Descriptions of the speakers are given in Table 24.1.

Table 24.1. Description of the speakers.

Language	Speaker	Sex	Dialect	Educational level
Korean	K1	F	Seoul	post-doctoral
	K2	M	Seoul	graduate student
	K3	F	Seoul	graduate student
French	F1	F	Moroccan	graduate student
	F2	M	Belgian	post-doctoral
	F3	F	Belgian	elementary school teacher
Arabic	A1	M	Palestine	undergraduate
	A2	M	Palestine	graduate student
	A3	M	Palestine	undergraduate

24.2.2 Material

Obstruent consonants from each place of articulation from the three languages were chosen and put in intervocalic position in a VCV structure.[2] Voiceless consonants were chosen if consonants were in contrast with respect to voicing in the same place of articulation. For surrounding vowels, high and low vowels were chosen with the vowels being the same on either side of the consonant. I used existing words wherever possible. However, there were only few real

345

words available in each language and therefore most words used here are nonsense words. Target words were randomized across consonants and repeated 10 times in isolation. Four target words and two foil words were written on 4 × 6 inch index cards in the script of the language. On each card, two foil words with the same syllable structure as the target words (VCV) were placed before and after the four target words. For the foil words, the same syllable structure (VCV sequence) and consonants as in the target words were used and three mid vowels, /e, ø, o/ and /æ, o, ɤ/ were used for French and Korean, respectively. For the foil words in Arabic, I used all ten consonants and three high and low vowels (instead of mid vowels) again because short mid vowels are phonologically absent in Palestinian Arabic (Herzallah, 1990). The list of the consonants and vowels used in target and foil words, and the number of real words are given in Table 24.2 and Table 24.3.

Table 24.2. List of consonants used in target and foil words .

	Labial	Coronal	Velar	Uvular	Pharyngeal	Laryngeal
	Oral				Non-oral (guttural)	
Korean	p	t s tʃ	k			h
French	p f	t s ʃ	k	ʁ		
Arabic	b	t s ʃ	k	q χ	ħ	h ʔ

Table 24.3. List of the vowels used in the target and foil words.

		High			Mid		Low	Number of real words
Korean	target	i ɨ u					a	5/24
	foil				æ o ɤ			1/18
French	target	i y u					a	1/28
	foil				e o ø			8/21
Arabic	target	iː uː					aː	3/30
	foil	ɨ uː					aː	

346

Orals, gutturals, and the jaw

24.2.3 Data acquisition

A splint similar to those used in Edwards & Harris (1990) was attached to each subject's lower teeth. Using the splint magnifies jaw movement, since the splint is located farther away from the center of jaw rotation than the most anterior point on the jaw, thus allowing finer spatial measurement resolution. A plaster cast of each subject's lower teeth was made using dental impression material and acrylic was molded to the teeth with stiff round wire being embedded in it. It was trimmed to make a comfortable fit for each subject. Three points were marked on the wire with contrasting paint.

Video and audio signals of the subjects were simultaneously recorded in a double-walled sound-treated booth. A video-camera was used to take a profile view of the subject, as shown in Figure 24.2a. The camera angle was made perfectly horizontal using the bubble level on the supporting tripod. The distance between the camera and the subject's face ranged from 13 1/2 to 14 1/2 inches. The camera's zoom function was then used to make a much closer picture of the jaw and lips. For the calculation of the real distance, I used a plumb line hanging from the ceiling of the booth with the known length marked on it. It was placed in front of the mid-line of the subject's nose, positioned in the same sagittal plane as the splint.

The recording was done in one session for each speaker. The speakers were asked to put their jaw in the clench position before and after the recording. The lists of words were presented on cards held at eye level so that the subjects did not have to move their heads to read comfortably. Subjects' heads were secured to an Ear-Nose-Throat chair with a strap to minimize head movements. To assess and correct for any head motion, a white wire with two black points on it was attached to the subject's forehead with tape above the subject's nose, under the assumption that these points would not move if the subject's head did not move in normal speech situation.

24.2.4 Data processing

After the recording, frame numbers (1/30 sec.) were added in a space away from the measurement points to facilitate frame selection. I chose appropriate frames for the preceding vowel, consonant and following vowel by eye, i.e., a frame which shows the lowest point, and a frame which shows the highest point for vowels and consonants, respectively. The selected frames were digitized with the image processing boards, DT 2851 & DT 2858 and IRIS software. Using IRIS software, digitized images in IRIS format were converted to TIFF format for the measurement programs which were developed in the OSU phonetics laboratory. About 10 frames showing the marked plumb line were chosen from each session's recording. The positions of two points on the plumb

347

(a)

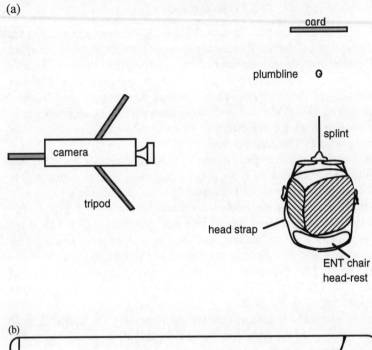

Figure 24.2 Schematic drawing of (a) the top view of the setting for data recording and (b) profile view played on TV monitor.

line (known to be 60 mm apart) were logged from the digitized video frames, and a pixel to millimeters conversion formula was developed and used to convert screen pixels for target points into distance in mm from the first point of the wire on the nose, which was chosen as the origin in a Cartesian space.

24.2.5 Correction of head movement

After all the positional values of the data points were converted to millimeters, they were corrected for head movement by using the reference points on the wire attached to the subject's nose. All measurements were taken relative to the position of the head and jaw in the clenched position for that speaker. The frame of the clench position for each speaker was used as the reference. The algorithm used for head-movement correction removes the effects of rotational and translational displacement in the sagittal plane only.

24.2.6 Statistical analysis

For each subject, Analysis of Variance (ANOVA) was used to examine the jaw position in consonants for effects of consonant identity and vowel environment. *Post-hoc* tests for differences between the mean jaw positions for different consonants were also performed.

24.3 Results

24.3.1 Jaw height

All speakers from all three languages showed a significant main effect of consonant with respect to jaw height ($p < 0.01$). (The significance level in this paper is $p < 0.01$ unless otherwise specified.) Mean jaw heights for all consonants for each speaker are given in Figure 24.3.

Although there were some inter-speaker differences, generally coronals, especially coronal fricatives and affricates had the highest jaw positions, bilabials, velars, and uvulars intermediate, and pharyngeals and laryngeals the lowest jaw positions.

24.3.2 Jaw protrusion/retraction

All speakers from all three languages also showed a significant main effect of consonant with respect to degree of jaw protrusion/retraction ($p < 0.01$), although the effect was clearly smaller for K2 and K3.

349

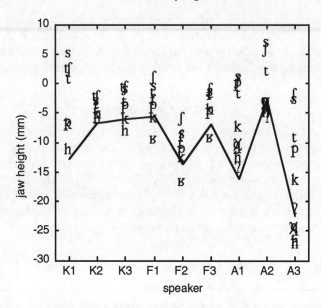

Figure 24.3. Mean jaw height for consonants across vowels for each speaker in all three languages. The solid line connects mean jaw heights of the preceding vowels.

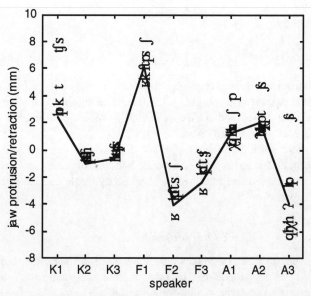

Figure 24.4. Mean jaw protrusion/retraction for consonants across vowels for each speaker in all three languages. The solid line connects mean jaw protrusion of the preceding vowels.

Mean jaw protrusion/retraction degree for each consonant for each speaker is given in Figure 24.4. Again although there were some inter-speaker differences, generally coronal fricatives showed the largest jaw protrusion, coronal stops, labials and velars intermediate, and uvulars, pharyngeals and laryngeals the smallest jaw protrusion.

24.3.3 Jaw position of consonants compared to the surrounding vowels

Comparison of the mean positions of consonants with those of the preceding vowels showed a general tendency for oral consonants to have a higher and more protruded jaw position than the preceding vowels. Gutturals and uvular stops had lower and more retracted jaw position compared to those of the preceding vowels even though differences were not always statistically significant.

As shown by the ANOVA results previously discussed, coronal fricatives and stops had a consistently high jaw position. Figure 24.5a shows that these consonants are affected relatively little by the vowel environment. In contrast, Figure 24.5b shows that, as expected, the laryngeal consonants /h, ?/ had no effect on the position of the jaw. Here the jaw stayed level throughout the VCV sequence. Comparing the jaw positions for the surrounding vowels for these two types of consonants shows that jaw position for the surrounding vowels for the coronals is higher than those for the laryngeal consonants. Patterns were clearest for speaker A3, but the other speakers showed similar trends.

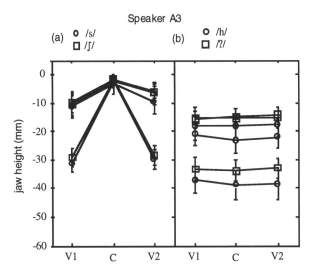

Figure 24.5. Means and standard deviations of jaw heights (a) during /s/ and /ʃ/, and (b) during /h/ and /ʔ/ in all vowel contexts for speaker A3.

Sook-hyang Lee

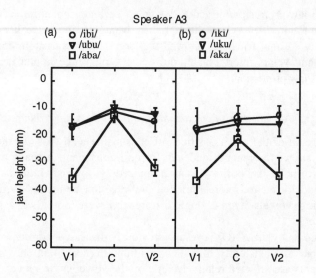

Figure 24.6. Mean and standard deviations of jaw heights (a) during /b/, and (b) during /k/ in all three vowel contexts for speaker A3.

Some consonants, such as labials, velars, and uvulars, had intermediate ranges of jaw position. As can be seen in Figure 24.6, the jaw positions in velars and labials were not as high as those observed in coronals. They also showed a larger effect of adjacent vowel though not as large as that for the laryngeals.

Figure 24.7 shows that the jaw positions in uvulars were lower than the jaw positions in high vowels but higher than the jaw positions in low vowels. I interpret this as evidence for a mid-height articulatory target that either involves the jaw directly or as a member of a coordinative structure that implements this target.

Pharyngeals, shown in Figure 24.8a and b, have a large coarticulatory effect of vowel environment, but they also show as consistent a change in jaw position as that associated with the pharyngeal consonant. Comparing Figure 24.5b with Figure 24.8a and b shows that the pharyngeal consonant has a jaw gesture which the laryngeal consonants do not have.

Again, inter-speaker differences were observed. For example, unlike the other two Arabic speakers, for A1, all consonants, even gutturals, showed either raising of the jaw or a level jaw throughout the VCV sequence. The velar stop for A2 showed a similar pattern to uvulars for A2 and A3, as can be seen in Figure 24.9, while the velar stop for the other speakers showed the same pattern as the other oral consonants. A3's uvular fricative and pharyngeal fricatives showed a more retracted jaw position than surrounding vowels in all vowel contexts although the differences were not always significant. As shown in Figure 24.10, the glottal stop for A2 always showed lower jaw position than the

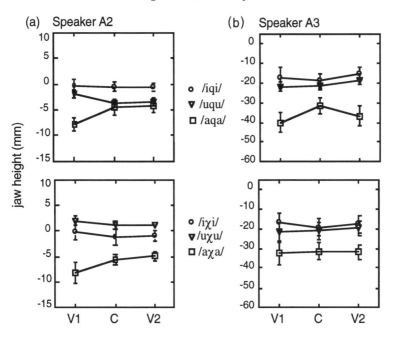

Figure 24.7. Means and standard deviations of jaw heights (a) during uvulars /q/ and /χ/ for speaker A2, and (b) during the same uvulars for speaker A3 in all three vowel contexts.

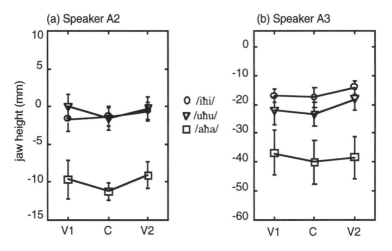

Figure 24.8. Means and standard deviations of jaw heights (a) during / ħ / for speaker A2, and (b) for speaker A3, in all three vowel contexts.

353

Sook-hyang Lee

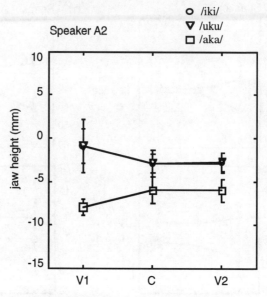

Figure 24.9. Means and standard deviations of jaw heights during /k/ for speaker A2 in all three vowel contexts.

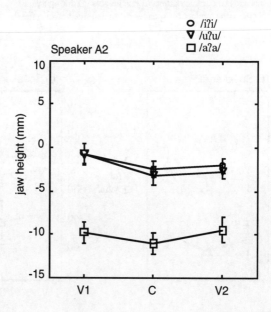

Figure 24.10. Means and standard deviations of jaw heights during /ʔ/ for speaker A2 in all three vowel contexts.

354

Orals, gutturals, and the jaw

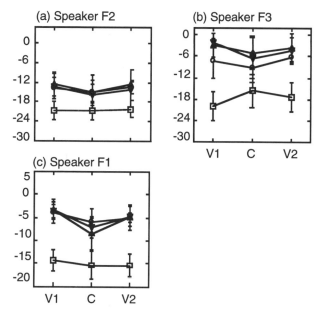

Figure 24.11. Means and standard deviations of jaw heights during /ʁ/ for all three French speakers in all vowel contexts.

surrounding vowels, which is very similar to pharyngeals for A3 and A2. For A2, differences in mean jaw height between the glottal stop and the preceding vowels were significant in the /u/ and /i/ contexts ($p < 0.01$ and $p < 0.05$, respectively).

The French uvular fricative /ʁ/ did not show much variation in horizontal jaw movement, though it did show a consistent pattern of vertical movement (see Figure 24.11). As in the uvulars from Arabic speakers, A3 and A2, the jaw moves downward from the high vowel and upward from the low vowels in the case of F2 and F3, as shown in Figures 24.11a and b. On the other hand, as Figure 24.11c shows, for F1, the jaw moved downwards from the preceding vowels in all vowel contexts, which shows a similar pattern to the Arabic pharyngeals for A3 and A2. Both patterns indicate that the jaw participates in the uvular fricatives, even though the direction of the movement of the jaw out of and into the vowel is different from the oral consonants in French.

24.4 Discussion and Conclusion

Even though some differences among speakers were observed, coronal fricatives and affricates (and the coronal stops for some speakers) showed the highest jaw positions, while pharyngeals and laryngeals showed the lowest positions.

355

Coronal fricatives also showed the most protruded jaw positions, while uvulars, pharyngeals and laryngeals showed retracted positions.

These results partially support Goldstein's hypothesis, in that orals showed higher and more protruded jaw positions than gutturals, even though the uvular stop (non-guttural) showed a similar pattern to gutturals. However, patterns of jaw movements for consonants turned out to be not as simple as Goldstein claimed. According to Goldstein, generally the jaw seems to serve to differentiate oral consonants from gutturals, in that the jaw has a common function in the coordinative structures for labial, coronal, and dorsal constrictions of raising, to augment the raising of a primary articulator (tongue or lower lip) toward the roof of the mouth or the upper lip. However, we do see some exceptions; the jaw lowers for the velars for A2, and for uvular stops for A3 and A2 in high vowel contexts. Moreover, the jaw also participated in some gutturals such as the uvular fricative and the pharyngeals for A3 and A2, which provides evidence against Goldstein's second assumption that the jaw does not participate in the articulation of gutturals. A more accurate characterization would be that rather than such a categorical binary distinction (the jaw does or does not participate), there is a continuum of degrees of participation and also varied roles. Two extreme cases were observed. Coronals, for some speakers, coronal fricatives, showed clear and invariant jaw specification with the narrowest window (Keating, 1990), and the jaw positions for their surrounding vowels were higher than those for the glottals, indicating accommodation of vowels to the jaw position of the coronals. The glottal consonants, except for the glottal stop of A2, had no jaw specification with the widest window, and took the jaw positions of the surrounding vowels.

Clear and invariant jaw specification for the coronal fricatives could be explained by a requirement of stiffness of the tongue for these consonants. Stone (1991), and Stone, Faber, Raphael & Shawker (1992) found that /s/ was produced with a midsagittal groove along the entire length of the tongue and much contact of the tongue with the anterior portion of the palate, and that /ʃ/ was produced with a midsagittal groove in the posterior tongue, but with an oblique tongue shape at the anterior and dorsal portions of the tongue and much tongue contact with the posterior portion of the palate. They speculate that the groove shape of the tongue and the bracing of the tongue against the palate for /s/ and /ʃ/ would be made by allowing the tongue to stiffen.

In addition to these two clearly contrasting cases, two intermediate cases were observed. The first case is jaw movements in labial and velar consonants seen in Figure 24.6. Although they did not show as invariant jaw targets as the coronals, still the jaw had some amount of movement out of and into the surrounding vowels. The jaw moved upward from the vowels and downward into the following vowels indicating that the targets of the tongue or the lower lip for the consonants are higher than those for the surrounding vowels. Similarly, the uvular stop (which is treated as a non-guttural) and the uvular fricative (which is treated as a guttural) showed some movement out of and into the surrounding vowels even though the direction of the movement was different from that for the labials and velars in high vowel contexts: the jaw moved downwards from the preceding high vowel and upwards into the following high vowel. This pattern indicates that the targets of the tongue for the uvulars are between the targets for the high vowel and the targets for the low vowels. In these cases, the jaw seems to cooperate with the tongue or the lower lip to achieve the target of the tongue or the lower lip for the consonants with accommodation of the jaw position of the surrounding vowels. The French uvular fricative showed a similar pattern to uvulars in Arabic. For F2 and F3, the jaw was lower compared to the surrounding vowels in the high vowel contexts, while it was higher than the surrounding vowels in the low vowel contexts. Another case of the jaw participation (but not of invariant jaw target for the consonants) is the pharyngeal fricative for A2 and A3 and the glottal stop for A2. These consonants for these subjects showed deflection of the jaw during the consonant even though the gesture is weak compared to those for oral or uvular consonants. Even though the gesture is weak, the pattern of the jaw movement out of and into the vowels is different from that for glottal consonants, which showed straight lines. The jaw seems to participate in such a way that it cooperates with the tongue to achieve the tongue target which seems to be lower than that of any vowels. We could apply Lindblom's (1983) analogy of window cleaning to these different degrees of jaw participation for different consonant groups. As a window cleaner moves his feet (jaw) as well as stretches his arm (tongue or lower lip) in synergistic interaction and shows continuously different degrees of trade-off relationships between the amount of movement of the feet and the arm, here, producing the speech segments showed a similar relationship between two mechanically coupled articulators, the jaw and the tongue or the jaw and the lower lip. For example, the production of coronals is at one extreme with a large amount of jaw raising and a small amount of tongue raising being involved in a cooperative way. The production of uvulars involved lesser jaw involvement than that of coronals, but the jaw still cooperated with the tongue to achieve the tongue target.

Some inter-speaker differences which are problematic for Goldstein's hypothesis were observed. Deflection of the jaw during the glottal stop in the case of A2 was not expected from its phonological description as "placeless". We might find the answer to this unexpected phenomenon in the realization of this sound as creaky voice instead of clear stop which was actually observed in A2's production of the glottal stop. Lowering the larynx to produce creaky voice might cause lowering of the jaw. Actually, Hirai, Honda, Fujimato & Shimada (1993) and Honda, Hirai & Kasakawa (1993) showed that lowering the larynx for lower pitch pulls on the hyoid bone which can lower the jaw. The velar stop for A2 showed a different pattern from the velars for the other speakers. Instead of raising the jaw for velars in all vowel contexts, A2 lowered the jaw in the high vowel contexts showing a pattern similar to that for uvular consonants. This inter-speaker difference might be explained by the different shape of the palates. As shown in Figure 24.12, A2's palate was short and the back of the palate curved downward, while A3's palate was long and flat at the back. Compared to other speakers, A2 does not have to raise his tongue and the jaw much to form the constriction for the velar stop. A2's labials also did not show raising of the jaw in high vowel contexts indicating some active compensation of the upper lip for lip closure for /b/.

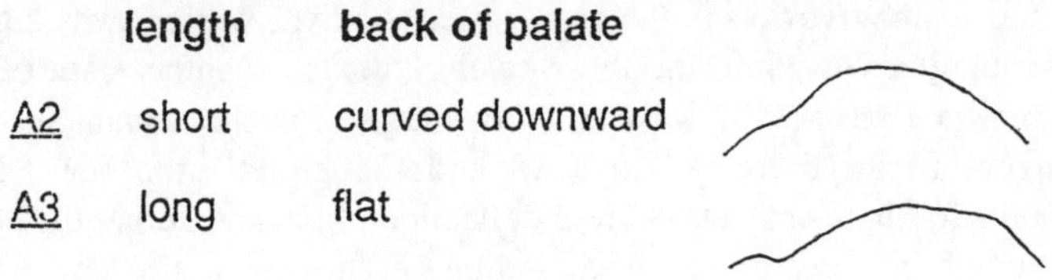

	length	back of palate
A2	short	curved downward
A3	long	flat

Figure 24.12. Schematic drawing of the palate for speakers A2 and A3.

In sum, the jaw's contribution in the articulation of consonants is not as simple as Goldstein (1994) claimed. Participation of the jaw was observed in the articulation of the oral and some guttural consonants, such as the uvular fricative and the pharyngeal consonants (A3 and A2) and the glottal stop (A2), where no contribution of the jaw was expected according to Goldstein's hypothesis. Consonants where jaw participation was observed showed some differences in the ways in which the jaw participates. Coronals showed invariant jaw targets which the surrounding vowels accommodate, while other consonants did not show invariant jaw targets, but cooperation with the tongue to achieve the tongue target, accommodating to the jaw targets for the surrounding vowels. In addition, there were some inter-speaker differences which seem to indicate accommodation to differences in palate morphology. Thus, whatever the phonetic basis of guttural vs. oral distinction, it cannot be simply that the jaw does not contribute to guttural articulation. However, results from this study can be interpreted as supporting Goldstein's claim by reinterpreting it in a more sophisticated way. Rather than postulating a binary distinction (participation vs. no participation), how the jaw participates in guttural vs. oral consonant articulation would differentiate them from each other: jaw raising for orals vs. no jaw raising (lowering or no participation) for gutturals. However, the problem of differentiating the uvular stop (oral consonant) from the uvular fricative (guttural consonant) in terms of how the jaw participates still remains unsolved.

Notes

* The preparation of this manuscript was supported by Grant IRI-8858109 to Mary Beckman. I thank Mary Beckman and Michel Jackson for their helpful suggestions on earlier drafts of this paper, and Michel Jackson, Sergey Zhupanov, and Yongkyoon No for writing many different kinds of programs for the data analysis of experiments done for this paper. I also thank the Center of Teaching Excellence at the Ohio State University for adding frame numbers on the video-tape.

1 Actually, uvular fricatives show dual pattern in terms of the co-occurrence restriction: they occur neither adjacent to other guttural consonants nor adjacent to some of the non-guttural consonants — velar and uvular stops.
2 In Arabic, /ʔVCV/ words were used because Arabic does not allow vowel-initial words.

References

Browman, C. P. & L. Goldstein. 1990. Tiers in articulatory phonology, with some implications for casual speech. In J. Kingston & M. E. Beckman (eds.), *Papers in Laboratory Phonology I: Between the Grammar and Physics of Speech.* Cambridge: Cambridge University Press, 341–376.
Clements, G. N. 1985. The geometry of phonological features. *Phonology Yearbook* 2: 225–252.
Edwards, J. & K. S. Harris. 1990. Rotation and translation of the jaw during speech. *Journal of Speech and Hearing Research* 33: 550–562.
Goldstein, L. 1994. Possible articulatory bases for the class of guttural consonants. In P. A. Keating (ed.), *Phonological Structure and Phonetic Form: Papers in Laboratory Phonology III.* Cambridge: Cambridge University Press, 234–241.
Herzallah, R.S. 1990. Aspects of palestinian arabic phonology: a non-linear approach. Ph.D. dissertation, Cornell University.
Hirai, H., K. Honda, I. Fujimato & Y. Shimada. 1993. Analysis of magnetic resonance images on the physiological mechanisms of fundamental frequency control. *ATR Technical Report* [in Japanese].
Honda, K., H. Hirai & N. Kasakawa 1993. Modeling vocal tract organs based on MRI and EMG observations and its implication on brain function. *Annual Bulletin of the Research Institute of Logopedics and Phoniatrics* 27.
Keating, P. A. 1990. The window model of coarticulation: articulatory evidence. In J. Kingston & M. E. Beckman (eds.), *Papers in Laboratory Phonology I: Between the Grammar and Physics of Speech.* Cambridge: Cambridge University Press, 451–470.
Lindblom, B. 1983. Economy of speech gestures. In P. F. MacNeilage (ed.), *The Production of Speech.* New York: Springer-Verlag, 217–246.
McCarthy, J. 1994. The phonology of Semitic pharyngeals. In P. A. Keating (ed.), *Phonological Structure and Phonetic Form: Papers in Laboratory Phonology III.* Cambridge: Cambridge University Press, 191–233.

Sook-hyang Lee

Perkell, J. S. 1980. Phonetic features and the physiology of speech production. In B. Butterworth (ed.), *Language Production*. New York: Academic Press.
Sagey, E. C. 1986. The representation of features and relations in non-linear phonology. Ph.D. Dissertation, MIT.
Stone, M. 1991. Toward a model of three-dimensional tongue movement. *Journal of Phonetics* 19: 309–320.
Stone, M., A. Faber, L. J. Raphael & T. H. Shawker. 1992. Cross-sectional tongue shape and linguopalatal contact patterns in [s], [ʃ], and [l]. *Journal of Phonetics* 20: 253–270.

25
The role of the jaw – active or passive?
Comments on Lee

FRANCIS NOLAN

Lee's paper is one which for me characterizes the spirit of the Laboratory Phonology Conference. It takes a class of sounds primarily defined in terms of their phonological patterning, and tests experimentally an essentially phonetic hypothesis about their relationship, the hypothesis being generated by a theory which attempts to unify phonetics and phonology.

In this discussion I will focus mainly on the following question: how reliably can we infer gestural structures from articulator movement? In particular, I want to ask whether Lee is correct to conclude from the fact that there was jaw movement for pharyngeals, in general, and for subject A2's glottal stops, that the jaw does participate in the coordinative structure for gutturals. I shall leave aside the uvulars, which are in any case problematic, since the fricative behaves as a guttural while the stop does not.

The data used to support the claim that the jaw contributes to gutturals are in Lee's Figures 24.8a (A2 [ħ]), 24.8b (A3 [ħ]), and 24.10 (A2 [ʔ]), where the jaw can be seen to dip in the medial consonant. There has to be a baseline against which these are compared, and Lee uses A3's laryngeals [ʔ] and [h] (Figure 24.5b) which she regards as showing no jaw movement. Lee says: "Comparing Figure 24. 5b with Figure 24.8a and b shows that the pharyngeal consonant has a jaw gesture which the laryngeal consonants do not have."

There are clearly some difficult issues of data interpretation here. Let us consider the uncontroversially oral consonants measured, that is the labials, coronals, and velars. The supportive raising of the jaw in the open vowel context can apparently be as large as 30 mm (at the measurement point), for instance in the case of A3's [asa] (Lee's Figure 24.5a). Where do we set a threshold, below which we consider there to have been effectively no movement? At 5 mm? At 1 mm?

361

Francis Nolan

Indeed, closer examination reveals that some of A3's glottals (Lee's Figure 24.5b) are not, as implied, totally free from apparent movement, and the movement is scarcely less than that of the pharyngeals in Figures 24.8a and 24.8b. Actually it turns out that glottals are not, as a class, free of jaw movement as might be expected *a priori* from their lack of place of articulation since, as noted above, A2's glottal stop shows a consistent, thou– ng. We need not, then, worry too much in practice about whether A3's glottals are truly without movement or show a slight lowering; but as a matter of principle work of this kind needs a rigorous criterion for defining where there is jaw movement and where there is not – even though such a criterion will be very hard to define.

However, let us accept that pharyngeals, and some glottals, show a degree of jaw lowering. This is interpreted by Lee as counter-evidence to Goldstein's hypothesis that the jaw does not participate in the coordinative structure for gutturals. But notice that if we adhere strictly to the concepts of Articulatory Phonology, what we observe in the data is a jaw *movement*, and not a jaw *gesture*, contrary to Lee's claim that, "the pharyngeal consonant has a jaw gesture". We can *infer* a gesture underlying an observed movement, but it is precisely this process of inference that I want to examine.

To do this we need to take a closer look at the musculature affecting the jaw. First, Figure 25.1 shows a rough sketch of the jaw as the speech production modeler would ideally have it. Note the single muscle dedicated to raising the jaw, and the single muscle dedicated to lowering it. No other muscles attach.

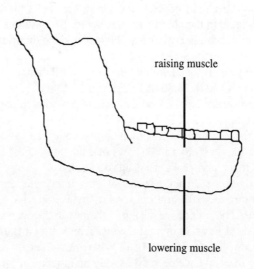

Figure 25.1. The speech production researcher's dream jaw.

362

The role of the jaw – active or passive?

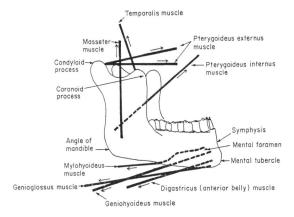

Figure 25.2. Lateral view of mandible showing the main structural parts and the movements of the mandible when the various mandibular muscles contract from fixed origins. Reproduced with permission from Hardcastle (1976, Figure 30).

Now of course in reality there is no muscle pulling directly up or down on the jaw as shown, and many different muscles contribute to both raising and lowering. Hardcastle (1976: 107) lists the following as contributing to raising: pterygoideus internus, masseter, temporalis; and, more importantly here, the following as contributing to lowering: pterygoideus externus, geniohyoideus, digastricus (anterior belly), mylohyoideus, genioglossus. These are shown in Figure 25.2, taken from Hardcastle (1976, Figure 30).

Clearly the real picture is more complex than that shown in Figure 25.1, with a large number of interactions between muscles being possible. But the full potential for interactions becomes clear only when the jaw muscles are seen in a wider context. Particularly significant is the fact that, of the various muscles attaching below the jaw, the geniohyoid, the mylohyoid, and the digastricus, are attached to the hyoid bone in the neck. This can be seen in Figure 25.3, again reproduced from Hardcastle (1976, Figure 18). In a sense, the hyoid hangs in a muscular hammock, the muscles being attached posteriorly to the skull and anteriorly to the jaw. Note also that the Middle Pharyngeal Constrictor Muscle has its origin in the (greater and lesser cornu) of the hyoid bone.

Let us now consider what interactions might occur in a sound articulated in the pharynx. Pharyngeal constriction presumably requires contraction of, among other muscles, the Pharyngeal Constrictors. Contraction of the Middle Pharyngeal Constrictor would tend to pull the hyoid backwards, and indirectly (via the digastricus, mylohyoid, and genioglossus in particular) exert some pull on the jaw. Here, then, is a mechanism which might promote "passive" (rather than intended) jaw lowering in pharyngeals.

363

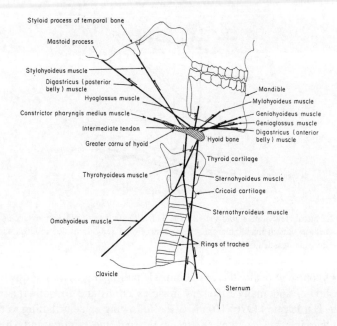

Figure 25.3. The extrinsic laryngeal musculature showing the direction of movement of the hyoid bone when the muscles contract from fixed origins. Reproduced with permission from Hardcastle (1976, Figure 18).

Furthermore, I would claim there is a natural association between pharyngeal constriction and larynx raising. Nolan (1983, Figure 4.11), reproduced here as Figure 25.4, shows X-ray tracings of the author producing a neutral vowel with extreme raised, lowered, and neutral larynx positions. It is striking that the higher the larynx, the narrower the laryngopharynx – possible through a kind of "concertina-ing" of the tissues.

There seems to be a constellation of features which naturally occur in voice quality adjustments: on the one hand, raised larynx, tense phonation, and pharyngeal constriction; and on the other, lowered larynx, lax phonation, and pharyngeal expansion. Admittedly Trigo (1991), writing about languages with "voice quality" or "register" contrasts, argues against a necessary conflation of the features [± ATR] and [± LL][1] into a single feature of [expanded/constricted pharynx], but the fact that Trigo has to argue such a case arises from the fact that these dimensions, together with phonation type, in her words "frequently co-occur or work together as a team" (1991: 113). My expectation, therefore, is that pharyngeal consonant constrictions are likely to be associated with larynx raising.[2]

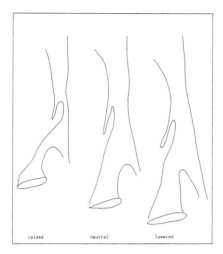

Figure 25.4. Tracings from X-ray pictures of the larynx and pharynx in neutral, extreme raised larynx, and extreme lowered larynx settings. Reproduced, with permission, from Nolan (1983, Figure 4.11).

To return to the jaw, larynx raising is achieved in part by raising the hyoid bone, from which the larynx broadly speaking is suspended, via contraction of muscles including the digastricus and geniohyoid (see Figure 25.3). As in the case of the Middle Pharyngeal Constrictor muscle, the contraction of these muscles again would tend to exert a downward pull on the jaw. I hypothesize, therefore, that the small downward movements of the jaw seen for the pharyngeal fricative in Lee's Figure 24.8a and b are merely the passive consequences of some of the muscular contractions needed for the pharyngeal constriction. The data does not, therefore, tell against the hypothesis that the jaw does not contribute to the coordinative structure for gutturals.

My claim that Lee's Figure 24.8a and b shows *passive* lowering is supported by the fact that the observable lowering is as great, or greater, in the context of open vowels. There is no sense of the jaw lowering contributing to the attainment of a target, as there is in Lee's data showing jaw raising for oral constrictions; on the contrary, it may be that the lowering is greatest in the cases where the jaw is already low. Perhaps in the case of the close vowels the muscular action required to raise the jaw to support the vowel articulations "braces" it against passive lowering in the consonant, whereas in the context of open vowels there is no raising gesture in the environment and therefore no resistance to passive lowering.

Francis Nolan

It is at first sight less clear why glottals should be associated with passive jaw lowering, as appears to be the case in the data from A2's [ʔ] (Lee's Figure 24.10). To resolve this we need more information on the articulatory activity realizing the glottal stops. Lee suggests that A2's realization is creaky voice, and assumes that this will be achieved by the kind of larynx lowering associated in general with low fundamental frequency. She then adduces evidence that larynx lowering is associated with a lower position of the hyoid bone, and hence (presumably through the muscular connections between the hyoid and the jaw) of the jaw.

But it is not necessarily the case that creaky voice can result only from an extreme of fundamental frequency lowering. The term "glottal stop" probably covers a range of realizations all of which may be associated with perturbed phonation, from brief creaky voice alone, through actual full-glottal closure, to glottal closure reinforced by closure of other structures above the true vocal folds. The reinforcing closure may involve the ventricular bands (Catford, 1977: 163) or the aryepiglottic folds (Trigo, 1991: 131), or both. Trigo says: "According to Lindqvist (1969, 1972) there are two different kinds of laryngeal constriction: one at the level of the vocal folds and one higher up at the level of the aryepiglottic folds." The aryepiglottic folds run from the sides of the epiglottis to the tops (apexes) of the arytenoid cartilages, and function protectively in swallowing.

Some Caucasian languages even contrast "deep pharyngeal" or aryepiglottic sounds with both true glottal and with upper pharyngeal sounds; Catford (1983: 347) cites the Burkikhan dialect of the Dagestanian language Agul as having (upper) pharyngeal /ħ ʕ/, glottal /h ʔ/, and "deep pharyngeal" (aryepiglottal?) /ʜ ʢ ʡ/. In languages with fewer guttural contrasts there may be scope for variation in the realization of "glottal" sounds. It is tempting to suspect the Arabic glottals of straying in the direction of the aryepiglottals because of their phonological patterning with pharyngeals – both sets would involve constrictions in the pharynx. Trigo, however, says (1991: 131) "the claim that the laryngeals which pattern after pharyngeals are aryepiglottal has not been substantiated".

If A2's glottal stop were aryepiglottal, however, such an articulation might well bring with it a complex of activity promoting larynx raising and pharyngeal constriction. Trigo (1991: 118–119) cites evidence on the relation of larynx raising and approximation of the aryepiglottic folds in languages with "register" contrasts; and larynx raising is intrinsic to swallowing, the primary occasion of aryepiglottic closure. Do true glottal stops involve larynx raising? It would certainly not be surprising, given the development of high tones before them, and the close association of larynx raising with increased pitch.

The above explanation of jaw lowering in A2's glottal stop seems preferable, then, to Lee's (lowered larynx) explanation, because it constitutes a unified account for similar jaw lowering in glottals and pharyngeals, and because it fits

366

The role of the jaw – active or passive?

in with external facts (specifically, tonal developments). But to resolve the issue finally we will need evidence of larynx height during the consonants.

In summary, I have argued in this commentary that any observed lowering of the jaw in pharyngeals and glottals could be explicable in terms of passive effects on the jaw of muscular contractions centrally involved in the articulation of those sounds, and so the lowering need not be evidence against Goldstein's suggestion that the jaw is not involved in the coordinative structure for these sounds. The general points to be made are that even when good data is available on articulatory movements, as in Lee's paper, inferences about articulatory organization should still be approached with considerable caution; and that we have a particular need for more information on the mechanical interactions within the vocal apparatus.

Notes

1 ATR = Advanced Tongue Root; LL = Larynx Lowering.
2 Unfortunately I do not know if any data exist on larynx height in pharyngeals.

References

Catford, J. C. 1977. *Fundamental Problems in Phonetics.* Edinburgh: Edinburgh University Press.
Catford, J. C. 1983. Pharyngeal and laryngeal sounds in Caucasian languages. In D. Bless & J. Abbs (eds.), *Vocal Fold Physiology: Contemporary Research and Clinical Issues.* San Diego CA: College Hill Press, 344–350.
Hardcastle, W. 1976. *Physiology of Speech Production.* London: Academic Press.
Lindqvist, J. 1969. Laryngeal mechanisms in speech. *Quarterly Progress and Status Report, Speech Transmission Laboratory, Royal Institute of Technology* 2–3: 26–32.
Lindqvist, J. 1972. A descriptive model of laryngeal articulation in speech. *Quarterly Progress and Status Report, Speech Transmission Laboratory, Royal Institute of Technology* 2–3: 1–9.
Nolan, F. 1983. *The Phonetic Bases of Speaker Recognition.* Cambridge: Cambridge University Press.
Trigo, L. 1991. On pharynx-larynx interactions. *Phonology* 8: 113–136.

26

The phonetics and phonology of glottalized consonants in Lendu

DIDIER DEMOLIN*

26.1 Introduction

Lendu, the language of the Ɓālē, is spoken by about 500,000 people in various areas of the Ituri Province west of Lake Mobutu, in north-eastern Zaïre. This language belongs to the Central Sudanic subgroup of the Nilo-Saharan language family. Several researchers have paid attention to the rather complex set of implosivesand glottalized consonants in this language, most of them giving a personal interpretation of the system. Descriptions made by Lendu speakers – Ngakpa-Ndjali (1977), Dhejju (1977), Dirive (1981) and Dz've (1982) – present a distinction between voiced and voiceless implosives (or preglottalized consonants) in their inventory. Trifkovic (1977) gives an inventory of five implosives [ɓ, ɗ, ƥ, f, ʃ]. Mertens (1978) gives four voiced implosives [ɓ, ɗ, ʃ, g͡ɓ] and four voiceless implosives, [ƥ, f, c̓, k͡ƥ]. Dimmendaal (1986) posits two implosives [ɓ, ɗ], a set of three preglottalized consonants [ʔ͡b, ʔ͡d, ʔ͡j] and two preglottalized glides [ʔ͡j, ʔ͡w]. Goyvaerts (1988) presents data showing contrasts between voiced egressive, voiced implosive, and preglottalized consonants at three articulatory positions: labial, alveolar and velar. He suggests three possible solutions to account for the set of preglottalized stops: they are either preglottalized, or ejectives, or voiceless implosives. Finally, Kutsch Lojenga (1991) presents an inventory of eight consonants pronounced with a glottalic airstream mechanism: five voiced implosives, [ɓ, ɗ, ʃ, ʔ, ʔ͡w] ([ʔ, ʔ͡w] being historical developments of *ʔg and *g͡ɓ), and three voiceless implosives, [ƥ, f, c̓]. Furthermore, Goyvaerts (1988) and Dhejju (1977) present velar consonants which are not taken into account in the other inventories. This situation being rather confusing, one aim of this paper is to present a detailed phonetic description of the implosive consonants found in Lendu. Diachronic aspects concerning the inventory of implosives in Central Sudanic languages and their possible influence on tonogenesis are also examined.

26.2 Lendu implosives

The data in (1) show contrasts between voiced and voiceless stops, as well as voiced and voiceless implosives. These data correspond to those studied in Mertens (1978).

(1)

bà	"to obtain"	bĭ	"to burn"
ɓà	"to abandon"	ɓĭ	"to be eaten by insects"
ßà	"to tie"	ßĭ	"to omit"
pà	"swing"	pĭ	"to lower"
dà	"to pass"	dĭ	"to settle boundaries"
ɗà	"long"	ɗĭ	"to taste"
fà	"good"	fĭ	"to cut"
tà	"to catch"	tĭ	"to speak"
ʃà	"to deform the lips"	ʃɛ̆	"to vomit"
cà	"to weave"	cà	"to look aside"
ʒà	"to announce"	ʒɛ̆	"to split in small parts"

Thus, the inventory of Lendu implosives is as in (2):

(2)

	labial	alveolar	palatal
voiced	ɓ	ɗ	ʃ
voiceless	ß	f	c̓

There are, therefore, three voiced and three voiceless implosives, but none is velar – contrary to statements made by Dhejju (1977) and Goyvaerts (1988). Similarly there are no labial–velar implosives, whether voiced or voiceless, contrary to what is stated by Mertens (1978). Close examination suggests that the voiced alveolar implosive is really postalveolar as shown by the tracings made from magnetic resonance images given in Figure 26.1.[1]

In order to determine how these implosives are produced, their production was examined from both an articulatory and an acoustic point of view. Thirty-seven words and sentences containing voiced and voiceless implosives were recorded by three speakers of the same dialect. The recording apparatus used was the Physiologia system, which allows several signals to be gathered at the same time.[2] In Figures 26.2, 26.5 and 26.6, the plots identified from 1 to 7 represent, respectively: (1) audio signal, (2) electroglottograph signal, (3) oral flow, (4) nasal energy, (5) a neutralized signal, (6) nasal flow, and (7) pharyngeal

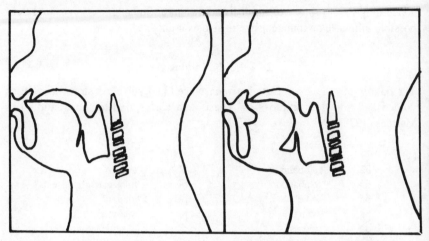

Figure 26.1. Tongue positions for the alveolar stop [d] and the postalveolar implosive [ɗ]. The tracings are left facing sagital views; bony structures (e.g. the teeth and mandible) show up as gaps.

pressure. The recordings were also used to determine F_0 plots and spectrograms.

In Lendu, the main parameters distinguishing voiced implosives from voiced stops are: a lowering of the larynx, which generates a negative pressure in the pharynx, and a progressive increase of the voicing amplitude towards the following vowel. The importance of the negative pressure is variable. Nevertheless, with one notable exception (see section 26.3 below), it is almost always possible to identify this negative pressure in the measurements. The voicing amplitude is generally greater during an implosive than during a corresponding voiced stop, where the amplitude of the voicing gradually decreases towards achievement of closure. This fact has also been shown by Lindau (1984) for languages such as Degema and Kalabari, spoken in Nigeria.

In addition to these well known factors, an interesting phenomenon can be observed for all Lendu implosives, on the oral flow plot. At closure release, there is almost always a drop in the oral flow. The same phenomenon has been observed in Mangbetu (Demolin, 1992: 229), and a similar drop in oral air pressure has been observed by Ladefoged (1964: 6) to sometimes occur in languages spoken in West Africa. The oral airflow plots in Figures 2a, b, and c show that there is a ingressive airflow at the moment of release in the Lendu voiceless implosives. The small drop of oral flow at the time of release is due to the fact that when the closure is released, the pressure inside the mouth is still slightly lower than the atmospheric pressure.

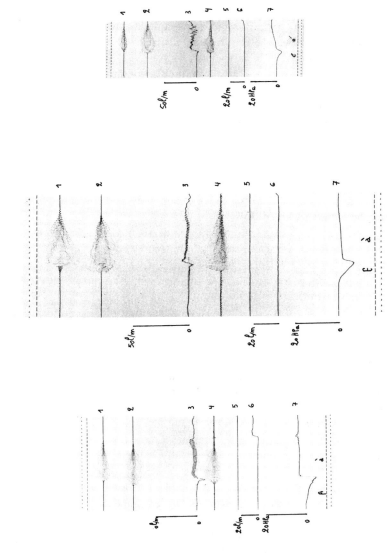

Figure 26.2a, b, c. Aerodynamic data for Lendu voiceless implosives: (a) /ɓà/ "to obtain", (b) /fà/ "good", and (c) /có/ "to weave".

This drop in oral flow is very similar to what happens at the release of labial velars, yet its causes are different for implosives and for labial–velars. For implosives, the drop of oral flow is caused by glottal suction resulting from of the lowering gesture of the larynx. For labial–velars, the drop is precipitated by the increase in volume of the cavity between the two closures in the mouth, which results in velaric suction. This fact may explain why Mertens (1978) confused the voiced labial–velar [g͡b] with an implosive.[3]

A crucial difference between labial–velars and voiceless implosives is that during the latter, the glottis remains closed from the start of the closure up to the release, when the larynx starts to rise to recover its initial position. Immediately after the lip closure, the lowering of the larynx and the following expansion of the pharynx begin. Pharyngeal pressure decreases progressively to reach its minimum before the end of the closure. The raising of the larynx is sudden, giving an almost vertical tracing on the plots. The difference between the upward and downward movement is sharp in most cases. The lowering of the larynx is generally progressive, while the raising is more sudden. This raising of the larynx, in the case of voiceless implosives, starts only at the release of the oral closure, the moment where ingressive air flow also starts. The delay in the rise of pharyngeal pressure, after the oral closure release, confirms that the oral cavity is still larger than normal. Figures 26.2a, b, and c present data showing three words containing the voiceless implosives [ɓ, ƒ, ƈ] examined from an aerodynamic point of view. Figures 26.3a, b, and c present the same words from an acoustic point of view.

The aerodynamic data suggest the following articulatory mechanism for the labial, post-alveolar, and palatal voiceless implosives. After the initial closure of the stop, the glottis remains closed for a period of time before the larynx is lowered. During this downward movement of the larynx, the glottis remains closed most of the time and therefore no voicing results. The fact that pharyngeal pressure decreases (see plot 7 in Figure 26.2a, b, and c) presenting aerodynamic data) confirms that the glottis is closed. Before the larynx starts rising to recover its initial position, voicing of considerable amplitude appears up to the release of the oral closure. This prevoicing, which is one of the main cues for identifying voiceless implosives, is clearly seen on Figures 26.3a, b, and c. The end of this prevoiced interval is shown by the bursts on the spectrograms. Note that the voiceless palatal implosive in the word /ƈó/ "to weave" seems to behave like a voiced sound. However, in the data used for this experiment, this word was in contrast with the word /ʃó/ "finely."

This description of the voiceless implosives corresponds fairly well to the impressionistic description given by Dimmendaal for what he identifies as preglottalized sounds. While emphasizing the need for instrumental analysis, Dimmendaal describes the three sounds as [ʔ͡b], [ʔ͡d], [ʔ͡j], saying they "almost always sound like geminates when pronounced without any word preceding

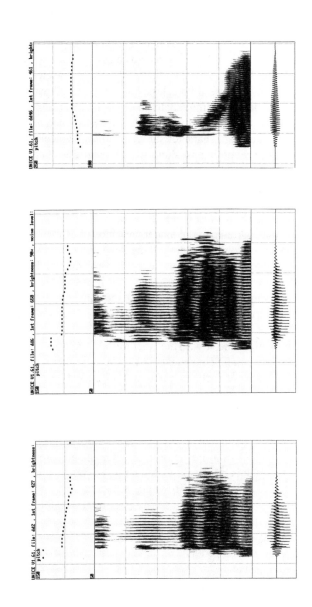

Figure 26.3a, b, and c. Spectrogram, F0 plot and audio signal for (a) /ʃà/ "to obtain", (b) /fà/ "good", and (c) /có/ "to weave".

them but when a particular word (or syllable) precedes, the glottal stop is heard"; and that, "the stops involved probably do have a voiceless onset, but one can still observe a short voicing while the glottalized consonant is pronounced, i.e., one hears [ʔpb], [ʔtd], [ʔcj]" (Dimmendaal, 1986: 172). Kutsch Lojenga (1991), in rightly claiming that these sounds are voiceless implosives instead of preglottalized consonants, states that "a minimal degree of voicing seems to be an articulatory necessity" to produce voiceless implosives. Furthermore she adds that "this would explain the fact that in the set of voiceless implosives the first part of the sound is indeed voiceless, but in the second part the feature voiced is necessarily added at or immediately before the release of the closure" (Kutsch Lojenga, 1991: 83). Like Dimmendaal, Kutsch Lojenga has identified the slight prevoicing as the main characteristic in identifying voiceless implosives. It is the fact that this prevoicing is short which identifies them as voiceless. Both descriptions, although different, are in accordance with the aerodynamic and acoustic data presented here.

The overall gestures involved in the making of a voiceless implosive can be schematized as shown in Figure 26.4a, b, and c. The schematic gestural scores add a new tract variable to the model presented by Browman & Goldstein (1989, 1992): the larynx, corresponding to the downward or upward movement (for an ejective) of the larynx in the oral tract. In Browman and Goldstein's model of articulatory phonology, each tract variable is associated with a specific set of articulators whose movements determine the value of the tract variable. Thus the larynx tract variable corresponds to the vertical movement made by the larynx in the vocal tract. The constriction degree descriptors for a larynx tract variable have values high and low. This tract variable allows one to account for the realization of glottalic consonants in Lendu and other languages. Note that the possible inclusion of such a variable was suggested by Browman and Goldstein (1989: 208) to account for these vertical movements of the larynx. The TB (tongue body) tract variable has a wide pharyngeal value due to expansion of the pharynx subsequent to both the lowering of the larynx and the advancement of the tongue root. This advanced tongue root position can be observed on the schemas obtained from magnetic resonance images presented in Figures 26.1 and 26.7 where it is compared with the tongue root position for a corresponding non-implosive consonant.[4] Browman & Goldstein (1989: 208) suggested the inclusion of an independent tongue root tract variable to represent the TB constrictions in the third dimension. This tract variable has not been included here since it is difficult to determine whether the tongue root advancement is an automatic or an independent articulatory movement in the realization of the voiceless implosives.

Since the glottal closure is always followed by a lowering of the larynx and therefore by negative pharyngeal pressure, there is no doubt about the implosive character of these voiceless consonants. Without the downward movement of the larynx, these consonants would only be preglottalized. The high amplitude of the prevoicing, which can appear with the bilabial and the postalveolar, is explained by high transglottal air flow. This prevoicing corresponds to an opening of the vocal folds before the oral closure release and before the larynx executes its upward movement (see section 26.5 for further details).

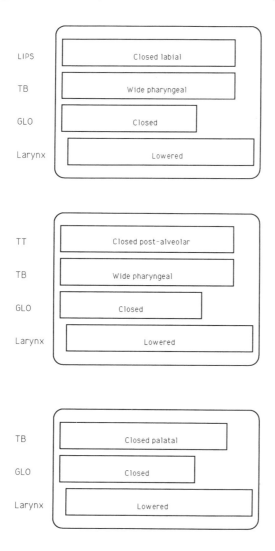

Figure 26.4a, b, and c. Schematic gestural scores for (a) a voiceless bilabial implosive, (b) a voiceless postalveolar implosive, and (c) a voiceless palatal implosive.

26.3 The voiced palatal implosive

As discussed above, there is disagreement as to the inventory of voiced implosive stops in Lendu: Dimmendaal (1986) gives a bilabial and an alveolar, Kutsch Lojenga (1991) presents these and an additional, palatal, implosive, while Dhejju (1977) and Goyvaerts (1988) also recognize a third implosive, but identify it as velar. Clearly, the phonetic nature of this third consonant presents a problem: it is difficult to identify and to localize its exact point of articulation. Figure 26.5 shows aerodynamic data for the word /ʃà/ "to deform the lips".

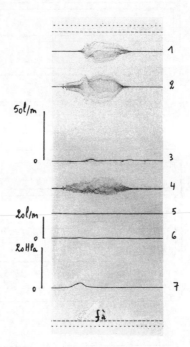

Figure 26.5. Aerodynamic data for the voiced palatal implosive [ʃ].

Plot (7) in Figure 26.5 shows that the pharyngeal pressure is increasing instead of becoming negative, as expected for an implosive. In fact, there is an increase of pharyngeal pressure just after the closure, and a drop towards the end of the closure. This rather unexpected fact might explain why this segment was not identified by Dimmendaal as an implosive. If the only characteristic to identify an implosive is a negative pharyngeal pressure, then it is clear that the palatal consonant is not implosive. In all the measurements made in the examined data, there was no negative pressure for the consonant presented as palatal implosive. But if we look at the electroglottographic data of plot (2) in

Figure 26.5, there is a clear increase of voicing amplitude, which is characteristic of an implosive consonant. If this consonant were a simple stop, one would expect a gradual decrease of voicing towards the end of the segment. There is, therefore, an apparent contradiction between pharyngeal pressure data and electroglottographic data.

In fact this consonant may not actually have an ingressive airstream. Ladefoged (1964) and Ladefoged, Williamson, Elubge & Uwalaka (1976) have suggested that in languages with voiced implosives, the flow of air through the vibrating vocal cords is often sufficient to compensate for the decrease in oral pressure due to the downtrend movement of the larynx. This seems to apply for the voiced palatal implosive of Lendu.

26.3.1 Origin and diachronic evolution of the Lendu implosives

As far as the present data allow us to reconstruct the original consonantal system of the Eastern Central Sudanic languages, it appears that voiced implosives were already present in Proto-Eastern Central Sudanic. One of the questions about the proto-system concerns the palatal consonant, which is not always present in the languages of the neighboring Mangbetu language group. It is difficult to know, therefore, if a voiced palatal implosive has to be reconstructed. Concerning the labials, Greenberg (1970) and Kutsch Lojenga (1991) suggest that [ɓ] can arise from a previous [g͡b] by loss of the velar closure. But Greenberg's examples come from the Mande languages, not from Central Sudanic, and Kutsch Lojenga gives no evidence for her claim. Such an origin for [ɓ] would leave open the question of the origin of [ɗ] and [ʄ], and there is no reason to doubt that at least [ɓ] and [ɗ] are found in Proto-Eastern Central Sudanic.

The data from pharyngeal pressure measurements in Figure 26.6 show an interesting variation in the realization of the bilabial implosive [ɓ]. While in most cases of [ɓ] there is a decrease of pharyngeal pressure after the oral closure, there is sometimes an increase of pressure before the lowering of the larynx which produces the negative pharyngeal pressure; this suggests that a closure is briefly realized in the oral tract. The obvious explanation for this variation is that lip closure is made before the lowering of the larynx. I want tentatively to suggest a second explanation, though one that is much weaker than the first. This second hypothesis is to account for an observed variation between [ɓ] and [g͡b]. Ladefoged (1964) has shown that a backward raising of the tongue accompanies the bilabial implosives in Igbo. The same phenomenon has been observed in Mangbetu (Demolin, 1992: 231). Figure 26.7 shows the tongue position during the production of a bilabial implosive [ɓ] compared to the tongue position during a bilabial stop [b].

377

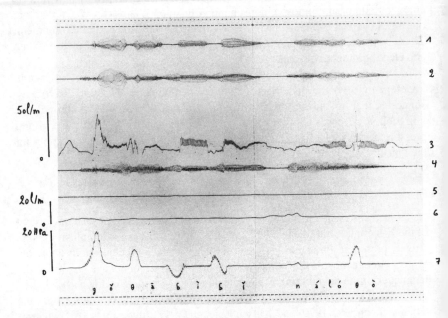

Figure 26.6. Aerodynamic data showing variation in the realization of the voiced bilabial implosive [ɓ] in the sentence: gŏdhā ɓìɓî ná lò dhò gŏdhá ʔŏ njŭ nzǐ "Beans don't taste good because they are eaten by insects".

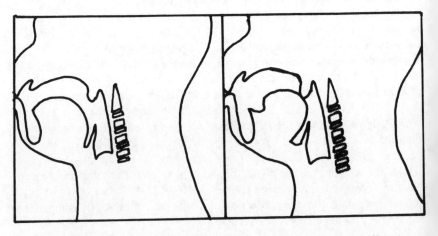

Figure 26.7. Tongue positions for the bilabial stop [b] (left) and the bilabial implosive [ɓ] (right).

These tracings, obtained from magnetic resonance imaging, show that the tongue dorsum is in the velar region, in contrast to its position for a non-implosive bilabial stop. The position of the tongue in the velar region suggests that a brief closure could happen shortly after the lip closure, before the downward gesture of the larynx. This realization of [ɓ] suggests a variation of [ɓ] with [ɡ͡b] and therefore a possible evolution of [ɓ] to [ɡ͡b]. Note that the evolution of a labial consonant to a labial–velar is not exceptional in the world's languages. For example, Malmberg (1971) shows that there is abundant evidence that the Spanish sequence bue is replaced in many dialects and in the popular language of different regions by güe. There are many examples of the type: *bueno > güeno, buey > güey* in the popular Andalusian literature, as well as in American Spanish. Michailovsky (1988), in discussing the origin of [ɓ] in the Nepalese languages Sunwar and Bahing, shows many correspondences between [ɓ] and labialized velar consonants. He suggests two possible origins for the implosive [ɓ], first, that it could represent a preglottalized manner-series, or second, that it could have developed from a labialized velar. Whatever the origin of Sunwar and Bahing [ɓ], the interesting fact is the correspondence between the implosive [ɓ] and labialized velar consonants in neighboring and genetically related languages as shown in (3). (Data from Michailovsky 1988: 32.)

(3) Bahing /ɓa/ "chicken"; Sunwar /bwā/; Khaling /bā/; Kulung /wā/ "hen"
     Magar /gwā/
     Bahing /ɓa/ "yam"; Sunwar /reːkbe/ "potato"; Khaling /ki/; Kulung /khe/;
     Chapang /goyʔ/ "potato"
     Bahing /ɓar/ "wound"; Sunwar /gār/; Khaling /kwaar/; Kulung /kher/;
     Kham /gəyh/
     Bahing /ɓarde/ "hawk"; Sunwar /bwāde/; Kham /gā/; Chepang /kwar/;
     "owl" E. Tamang /kwat/

Ronjat (1980) also gives examples in Provençal of variations between [w-, gw-] and [bw-] produced by a single speaker. Examples of labials changing into labial–velars or labialized velars can also be observed between Indo-European and Italic: PIE *peŋkwe "five" > Italic *kwiŋkwe. The same process appears in Tupi-Guarani: Proto-Tupi-Guarani *pwar "finger" > Tupi *kwar. All this suggests that the secondary velar character of labial consonants is found in other languages and that the evolution towards a velar is not uncommon. Thus this could suggest an evolution from [ɓ] to [ɡ͡b], rather than the reverse. This would certainly be more likely if the labial–velar consonant was an implosive [ɡɓ], as it is the case in neighboring Mamvu (Vörbichler, 1974). But this is contrary to the observations made by Ladefoged *et al.* (1976) and Connell (1994) for some Igbo dialects, though Connell also discusses a

Didier Demolin

development from labialized-velar to labial–velar elsewhere among Igbo dialects, and in other languages. Similarly, Hombert, Medjo & Nguema (1989: 140) have argued that for Fang, the origin of labial–velars is the following: *bw > [g͡b], and *kw > [k͡p], an evolution from labialized stops to labial–velars. Thus the evidence is that neither direction of change i.e., [ɓ] > [g͡b] or [g͡b] > [ɓ] is preferred to the other. This is due to the nature of labial–velars which have to be considered both as labial and as velars. Ohala and Lorentz (1977) have shown that there is a universal tendency for labial–velars to come both from labials and velars. More comparative work is needed to solve this problem in Lendu.

Finally, another claim made by Kutsch Lojenga (1991) is that the glottal stop [ʔ] originates in *ʄ. This is difficult to test because no language in the Central Sudanic family presents such a consonant, and because nothing in the data allows us to postulate such a reconstruction. Dimmendaal (1986) tentatively concludes that there is some evidence for an original glottalized consonant *ʔk or *ʔg which has been lost in Lendu. But no evidence confirming this claim has been found by comparing Lendu and Mangbetu as Dimmendaal does. Contrary to Larochette's (1958) claim, Mangbetu does not have glottalized velars; this fact seriously weakens the arguments in favor of an original glottalized velar. Therefore we would suggest that Lendu, with a three-term system, avoids the velar place of articulation. Maddieson (1984) has shown that languages having such three-term systems generally avoids the velar place of articulation. Lendu seems to fit into this kind of system.

26.3.2 Origin of voiceless implosives

Contrary to the voiced implosives found in Proto-Central Sudanic, phonemic voiceless implosives seem to be an innovation in Central Sudanic found only in Lendu. Hackett (ms) has mentioned that in Mangbetu there is a voiceless bilabial [ɓ̥] occurring in free variation with the voiced bilabial implosive [ɓ]. Our data show that similar variation occurs with the postalveolar [ɗ̥] and a palatalized [ɗ̥ʲ]. Figure 26.8 shows EGG (plot 1), audio signal (2), and pharyngeal pressure (plot 3) for the word /nɔ́ʊ̌ɗʲɔ́ʊ̌ɗʲɔ̌/ "to speak badly", in Mangbetu. Plots (2) and (3) for the realization of the first palatalized [ɗ̥ʲ], show that voicing is almost completely interrupted during the lowering of the larynx. This is also detectable on the electroglottogram (plot 1), where it can be observed that voicing has ceased at a time corresponding to the lowest pressure in the pharynx. The difference between the two implosives of the word shows that there may be considerable variation in the realization of implosives. Such variation is not uncommon in Mangbetu and other languages genetically related to Lendu.

380

The phonetics and phonology of glottalized consonants

Writing scan 1   High Speed Recorder   File:D:TEST21.NEM

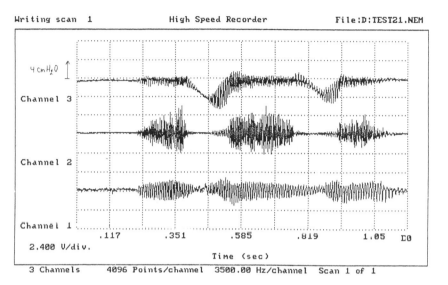

Figure 26.8. EEG (1), audio signal (2), and pharyngeal pressure plots for the Mangbetu word /nɔ́ʊ́dʒɔ́ʊ́dʒɔ̀/ "to speak badly".

Dimmendaal (1986: 176) states that in "Avukaya and other languages of the Moru-Madi cluster, the phonemic contrast between implosive and preglottalized stops [our voiceless implosives – D.D.] has been lost; implosion has become the phonetic norm, but in rapid speech implosives may be realized as preglottalized consonants i.e., ɓ becomes ʔb and ɗ becomes ʔl." The variation observed in Mangbetu and in other related languages suggests several hypotheses as to the origin of Lendu voiceless implosives. First, voiceless implosives in Lendu may have developed from earlier voiced implosives. Second, voiceless implosives may have developed from voiceless stops which would have become preglottalized before becoming true voiceless implosives. Third, the contrast between the two sets of implosives in Lendu is a retention from Proto-Central-Sudanic. In the absence of compelling evidence to the contary, the third hypothesis seems most plausible. The variation between [ɓ] and [ɓ̥] in Mangbetu, then, is seen as a remnant of an erstwhile contrast. Correspondences between Lendu and other Central Sudanic languages suggest that Lendu has preserved an old contrast, given the lack of a conditioning factor as the comparison with Avukaya in (4) shows. Although the third case is the most likely, much more comparative data is needed to establish firmly this hypothesis.

Didier Demolin

(4) Lendu   ɓã   "village"   Avukaya   bà
           ƥá   "be attached to"
     Lendu   ɗɛ̌   "young"   Avukaya   ɗɛ̃
           tɛ̌   "fall"

26.4 Effect of implosives on fundamental frequency

Lendu has innovated, compared to other Central Sudanic languages, in another way. While most Central Sudanic languages show a tonal system with either two or three tones, Lendu shows phonologically at least four level tones and maybe a fifth.[5] Kutsch Lojenga (quoted by Dimmendaal, 1986) has shown the existence of an extra high tone, in addition to the three other tones (low, mid, and high). If we compare Lendu and related languages, we find word correspondences which show abundant evidence that a higher tone occurs on a vowel when it is preceded by a voiced implosive.

(5)

"what?"	Mangbetu	àsèɗʋ̀	Madi	aɗʋ̄	Lendu	kāɗʋ̄
"fish"	Lendu	bɛ̀	Kaliko	ɛ̄bī	Lugbara	èɓí
"to swim"	Madi	ɔɗɛ̄	Mangbetu	nèɗɛ́ɗá		
"new"	Lombi	máɗǐ	Madi	ɔdǐ		
"to say"	Mangbetu	nɔ́djɔ̀	Madi	oʃō		
"to kill"	Madi	dǐ (kà)	Lugbara	dǐ (zà)		
"village"	Mamvu	ùbò	Lendu	ɓā		

Mazaudon (1977) has shown similar facts in some Tibeto-Burman languages (Lahu, Lisu, and Sani) where the tones that developed after glottalized consonants are higher than the tones found after both the voiced and the voiceless stops.

Such facts have also been mentioned by Greenberg (1970: 133) who has indicated that implosives "are always less productive of tone lowering than the corresponding plain voiced stops." The tone raising after implosives is puzzling given that voiced obstruents tend to be tone depressors (Hombert, 1978). Ohala (1976) has proposed an explanation, suggesting that although they differ only from voiced stops by a larger oral cavity, voiced implosives induce an elevated pitch on the following vowel. Ohala (who attributes this claim to Ladefoged) explains this by suggesting that the rapid lowering of the larynx during implosives causes higher than normal glottal flow and in this way raises F_0 (see also Hombert, Ohala & Ewen, 1979).

F_0 plots observed at the release of voiceless implosives show that the fundamental frequency can be very high during the characteristic prevoicing of these consonants. This high F_0 can continue on into the following vowel. Compared to what is observed after the release of a voiced implosive, the pitch is slightly higher after a voiceless implosive. These facts can be seen on the F_0 plots of Figure 26.3a and b.

This higher fundamental frequency during prevoicing and the onset of the following vowel is due to the fact that before the end of the lowering of the larynx, accomplished with a closed glottis and therefore with no trans-glottal airflow for a short moment, there is an opening of the vocal folds before closure release. During this opening of the vocal folds there is a high rate of glottal airflow. This high rate of glottal airflow gives for a short moment raises the pitch higher than normal. This pitch elevation does not happen for the voiceless palatal implosive (Figure 26.3c). In the data analyzed, at the onset of the following vowel F_0 has the lowest frequency following a plain voiced stop or a voiced implosive. F_0 is higher after voiceless implosive, except a palatal; finally F_0 is the highest after a voiceless stop.

26.5 Conclusion

This paper has presented a study of implosive consonants found in Lendu from an aerodynamic and acoustic point of view. The data have been examined in light of diachronic and variation factors, in order to account for the shape of the Lendu phonological system. Ohala (1990) has urged phonologists to incorporate known principles of aerodynamics, acoustics, and other psychoacoustic factors when they try to give adequate representations of sound structures. Taking into account the parameters of pharyngeal pressure and oral flow as well as EGG, it is possible to explain the functioning and behavior of implosives consonants in the Lendu phonological system. Moreover, the aerodynamic data allow us to derive a gestural analysis of these consonants and to propose the integration of another tract variable, i.e., the larynx, within the Articulatory Phonology model proposed by Browman & Goldstein (1989, 1992).

Notes

* I want to thank Dheda Djailo for his collaboration and his patience during the experiments. Bernard Teston has helped gather the data presented in this paper, and has permitted the use of his laboratory facilities at the Université d'Aix-en-Provence. In addition, I want to thank Jean-Marie Hombert, Gerrit Dimmendaal, Bruce Connell, and an anonymous reviewer for helpful comments. Finally, my thanks to Christoph Segebarth for helping gather the magnetic resonance data, and to René de Jonckeere for helping gather the aerodynamic data for Mangbetu presented in this paper.

1 The magnetic resonance images were taken with the speaker holding the position of the consonant. Therefore they can induce overcompensation which is not controlled. As little variation was observed in the realization of the implosives during the experiments, they have been incorporated in the study. The tracings given in Figure 26.7 raise an interesting question about a possible link between larynx lowering and tongue root advancement. This phenomenon has also been observed in neighboring languages but more, and dynamical, data are needed to answer this question.

2 Details about this machine can be found in Teston (1991).

3 This characteristic is common for the labial-velars examined in Lendu, whether voiced or voiceless, and for the labial-velars found in Mangbetu.

4 This seems to confirm the claim of Maddieson (1984: 119) that an expansion of the supralaryngeal cavity by tongue movement is plausible during the production of implosives.

5 Trifkovic (1977) notes that there is a non-contrastive extra-low tone.

References

Browman, C. P. & L. Goldstein. 1989. Articulatory gestures as phonological units. *Phonology* 6: 201–251.

Browman, C. P. & L. Goldstein. 1992. Articulatory Phonology: an overview. *Phonetica* 49: 155–180.

Connell, B. 1994. The structure of labial–velar tops. *Journal of Phonetics* 22: 441–476

Demolin, D. 1992. Le mangbetu: étude phonétique et phonologique. Thèse de doctorat, Université Libre de Bruxelles (to be published by Rudiger Köppe Verlag).

Dhejju, L. 1977. Documents sur la langue lendu, dialecte tadha. Thèse présentée en vue du diplôme de l'EPHE, IVème Section, Paris.

Dimmendaal, G. J. 1986. Language typology, comparative linguistics, and injective consonants in Lendu. *Afrika und Übersee* 69: 161–192.

Dirive, L. 1981. Elements de la morphologie lendu. Travail de fin d'études présenté pour l'obtention du Diplôme de Gradué en Pédagogie Appliquée. Université Nationale du Zaïre. ISP, Bunia.

Dz've, D. 1982. Essai d'onomastique lendu: étude toponymique. Travail de fin d'études pour l'obtention du Diplôme de Gradué en Pédagogie Appliquée. ISP, Bukavu.

Goyvaerts, D. 1988. Glottalized consonants: a new dimension. *Belgian Journal of Linguistics* 3: 97–102.

Greenberg, J.H. 1970. Some generalizations concerning glottalic consonants, especially implosives. *International Journal of American Linguistics* 36: 123–145.

Hackett, P. Unpublished field notes. Ms.

Hombert, J.-M. 1978. Consonant types, vowel quality and tone. In V. Fromkin (ed.), *Tone: a Linguistic Survey*. New York: Academic Press. 77–111.

Hombert, J.-M., P. Medjo & R. Nguema. 1989. Les Fangs sont-ils Bantu? *Pholia* 4: 133–147.

Hombert, J.-M., J. J. Ohala & W. G. Ewan. 1979. Phonetic explanations for the development of tones. *Language* 55: 37–58.

The phonetics and phonology of glottalized consonants

Kutsch Lojenga, C. K. 1991. Lendu: a new perspective on implosives and glottalized consonants. *Afrika und Übersee* 74: 77–86.

Ladefoged, P. 1964. *A Phonetic Study of West African Languages*. Cambridge: Cambridge University Press.

Ladefoged, P., K. Williamson, B. Elugbe & A. A. Uwalaka. The stops of Owerri Igbo. *Studies in African Linguistics* Supplement 6: 147–163.

Larochette, J. 1958. *Grammaire des dialectes mangbetu et medje*. Annales du Musée Royal du Congo Belge, Sciences de l'Homme, Linguistique, Vol. 18. Tervuren.

Lindau, M. 1984. Phonetic differences in glottalic consonants. *Journal of Phonetics* 54: 147–155.

Maddieson, I. 1984. *Patterns of Sounds*. Cambridge: Cambridge University Press.

Malmberg, B. 1971. *Phonétique générale et romane*. The Hague: Mouton.

Mazaudon, M. 1977. Tibeto-Burman tonogenetics. *Linguistics of the Tibeto-Burman Area* 3: 1–123.

Mertens, F. 1978. *Dictionnaire Bba-dhà français*. Ddrøddrø.

Michailovsky, B. 1988. Phonological Typology of Nepal Languages. *Linguistics of the Tibeto-Burman Area* 11: 25–50.

Ngakpa-Ndjali, N. 1977. Un essai d'étude de quelques proverbes lendu-djadha. Travail de fin d'études présenté pour l'obtention du diplôme de Gradué en Pédagogie Appliquée. Université Nationale du Zaïre. ISP, Bunia.

Ohala, J. J. 1976. A model of speech aerodynamics. *Report of the Phonology Laboratory* 1: 93–107. Berkeley.

Ohala, J. J. 1990. The phonetics and phonology of aspects of assimilation. In J. Kingston & M. E. Beckman (eds.), *Papers in Laboratory Phonology I: Between the Grammar and Physics of Speech*. Cambridge: Cambridge University Press, 258–275.

Ohala, J. J. & J. Lorentz. 1977. The story of [w]: an exercise in the phonetic explanation for sound patterns. *Proceedings, Annual Meeting of the Berkeley Linguistic Society* 3: 577–599.

Pinkerton, S. 1986. Quichean (Mayan) glottalized and nonglottalized stops: a phonetic study with implications for phonological universals. In J. J. Ohala & J. J. Jaeger (eds.), *Experimental Phonology*. Orlando: Academic Press, 125–139.

Ronjat, J. 1930. *Grammaire historique des parlers provençaux modernes*. Vol. I. Montpellier. Société des Langues Romanes. (Reprinted by Slatkine Reprints Geneva, Marseille. 1980.)

Teston, B. 1991. Station de travail ORL-phoniâtrie: caractéristiques techniques. *Phonologia*. IIRIAM Technopole de Château Gombert. Marseille: Europarc.

Trifkovic, M. 1977. Tone splitting: Lendu. *Studies in African Linguistics* Supplement 7: 223–234.

Vörbichler, A. 1971. *Die Sprache der Mamvu*. Glückstadt: Augustin.

27

Lendu consonants and the role of overlapping gestures in sound change: comments on Demolin

LOUIS GOLDSTEIN*

Demolin's analysis of Lendu consonants as including a series of voiced and a series of voiceless implosives is quite convincing. I would like to raise only two small points: one about the details of the analysis of voiceless implosives, one about the plausibility of a sound change in which labial consonants develop into labial-velars.

27.1 Timing of events for voiceless implosives

A schematic gestural score for a (labial) voiceless implosive, similar to the one presented by Demolin, is shown in Figure 27.1a (for simplicity, tongue root expansion, which appears in Demolin's score, is omitted) The right edge of each box in such a score represents the end of active control of the particular constriction gesture, and thus is roughly the point of time at which the articulators begin to move away from the most constricted position, i.e., the "articulatory" release of the constriction (the acoustic release generally occurs somewhat later). The sequence of gestural releases implied by this score (and discussed) by Demolin is as follows: (1) release of glottal closure, (2) release of larynx lowering (i.e., onset of larynx raising), (3) release of labial closure.

There are two problems with this interpretation of the timing of release events. First, in Demolin's aerodynamic traces, the oral release seems to be occurring at a moment in time at which pharyngeal pressure is at a minimum. This would imply that the larynx was still lowering right up to oral release, and that larynx raising, then, does not begin until after oral release. This would imply a timing organization like that shown in Figure 27.1b.

Overlapping gestures in sound change

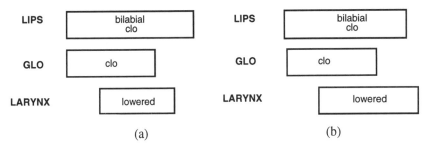

LIPS	bilabial clo		LIPS	bilabial clo
GLO	clo		GLO	clo
LARYNX	lowered		LARYNX	lowered
(a)			(b)	

Figure 27.1. (a) Demolin's proposed gestural score for [ɓ] in Lendu. (b) Suggested revised gestural score.

Secondly, Demolin notes a feature in the spectrograms of the labial and coronal voiceless implosives that he describes as high amplitude "prevoicing". He attributes this to the "release of oral flow, which is blocked for a short moment behind the closed glottis". Presumably he means flow from the subglottal to supraglottal cavities, since he assumes that the oral constriction is still in place at this moment in time. However, these "prevoicing" intervals are odd in showing significant energy in regions corresponding to the second and third formants of the following vowel. Exactly how such relatively high-frequency cavity resonances are radiated from a closed vocal tract is not clear. However, Lindau (1984) found similar cavity resonances at the *beginning* of the closure interval for voiced implosives in Bu̲mo. She interpreted these resonances as the acoustic result of tightly adducted vibrating vocal folds being lowered. If the cavity resonances in the Lendu spectrograms are caused by a similar mechanism, this would suggest that the larynx is still lowering during these prevoicing intervals. This would be consistent with Demolin's aerodynamic traces, and with the gestural organization shown in Figure 27.1(b).

27.2 Labials > Labial-velars: a case of gestural addition?

Demolin hypothesizes a historical development in Eastern Central Sudanic languages in which [ɓ] develops into [ɡ͡b]. In fact, the development seems quite plausible, given that, as Demolin shows, [ɓ] (in Lendu) is produced with the tongue dorsum raised and backed toward the soft palate. Thus, [ɓ] (despite its transcription) is, in fact, a labial-velar (although the tongue body gesture in [ɓ] appears not to be as constricted as it is would be in [ɡ͡b], so perhaps labial with secondary velarization would be a better description). However, in discussing the change, Demolin describes it as a change from "a labial consonant to a labial-velar", and asserts (with following examples) that such a change is "not exceptional in the world's languages." It is this assertion (and examples) that I would like to examine critically here.

387

A change from a labial consonant to a labial-velar would involve adding a new articulation (velar constriction of the tongue body) that was not there (in the relevant words) at an earlier stage. Browman & Goldstein (1991) have hypothesized that adding new articulations is a relatively rare form of sound change, and they present a wide variety of changes that can be analyzed as involving no additional articulations. They propose that from the point of view of gestural structure, sound changes can be seen to result from three sources:

(a) variation found in normal casual speech production; this involves reduction in gestural magnitude (up to and including complete deletion), and increase in gestural overlap (up to and including complete "hiding" – and subsequent deletion – of overlapped gestures).

(b) gestural misparsing; this results from possible variation in how language learners parse the continuous motion of articulators into discrete, active gestural units.

(c) interactions among overlapping gestures; these involve reassignment of gestural attributes (specific values of the constriction location and degree descriptors) among overlapping gestures.

In some particular cases where the traditional description appears to involve addition of a gesture, the evidence presented in Browman & Goldstein (1991) shows that a form of the putatively added gesture is already present before the change in the "environment". In such cases, the change involves a *reassignment* of gestural attributes (parameter values of constriction location and degree) among a set of partially overlapping gestures (source (c), above).

Why should such reassignment occur? In general, listeners (or language learners) are able to recover the pattern of gestures that gives rise to the acoustic signal, even though gestures overlap substantially in time, and the acoustic signal is determined by the combined effect of all the overlapping gestures (e.g. Fowler & Smith, 1986; Liberman & Mattingly, 1985). In some circumstances, however, listeners may fail to pull apart the overlapping gestures correctly, and changes in the gestures' attributes may result. This kind of change has been described by Ohala (1981) as a "listener-based" sound change.

A good example of gestural reassignment is the change in Middle English of final velar fricatives to labial fricatives ([x] > [f]), discussed in Browman & Goldstein (1991). This change is commonly analyzed as one motivated by the acoustic similarity of labials and velars. From that perspective, a labial gesture is being added, in the course of the change, replacing the earlier tongue dorsum gesture. However, a more detailed analysis of this change by Pagliuca (1982) presents a very different picture (see also Pagliuca & Mowrey, 1987). Pagliuca shows that this change takes place only following diphthongal vowels with rounded offglides. Thus, he notes, there are labial and dorsal articulations in

388

close proximity *before* the change. The change involves primarily weakening of the velar constriction and increased overlap with the labial articulation of the vowel offglide. Following the change, the vowel is monophthongal (which is not accounted for by the more usual analysis of this change), and the labial articulation (that was rounding before the change) is now a fricative.

The analysis of this change is terms of (partial) gestural scores can be seen in Figure 27.2, for the word "cough". The hypothesized gestural score before the change is shown in (a). Oral constriction gestures are shown for the tongue body (TB) and the lips for [oʊx]. The {bilabial narrow} LIPS gestures represent rounding (it is an oversimplification to describe them this way – see, e.g. Browman, 1994; Goldstein, 1991 – but this does not affect the present point). The {velar crit} TB gesture is for the final fricative; {crit} stands for that degree of constriction that will have critical aerodynamic consequences. The {wide} glottal opening (GLO) gesture for the voiceless fricative is also shown.

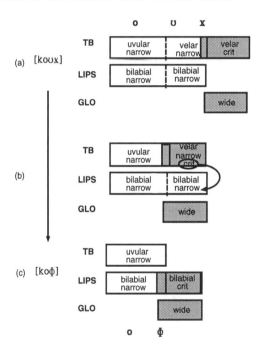

Figure 27.2. Analysis of sound change of Middle English [oʊ] > [oɸ]. Gestural scores are shown for three different stages. In each gestural score, rows correspond to distinct articulatory "tiers", boxes represent activation intervals of gestures. Terms within boxes are the gestural descriptors specifying the constriction degree (and location, for oral constrictions) for each gesture: (a) state before the change; (b) increased overlap of final consonant gestures with preceding vowel; (c) near-final state, resulting from reassignment of the {crit} specification, and weakening of velar gesture. (After Browman & Goldstein, 1991).

389

The first stage of the change (shown in (b)) involves increasing overlap of the TB {volαr crit} and GLO {wlde} gestures with the gestures constituting the preceding glide. There are now two TB gestures, {velar crit} and {velar narrow}, that are roughly synchronous. Note that this results in some "weakening" of the TB {velar crit} gesture since it presumably blends with the TB {velar narrow} gesture somewhat. The crucial next stage is represented by the arrow in (b): the {crit} descriptor is "reassigned" from the tongue body gesture to the lips gesture. Why should this reassignment occur?

One possibility would be as follows. Note that in (b), the GLO {wide} gesture now overlaps with the LIPS gesture, as well as the TB gestures. Having a wide open larynx (and thus greater airflow) would probably result in turbulence being generated at the lips, turbulence that would not be generated under voiced conditions for the same degree of lip constriction (cf. Catford, 1977). In addition, Ohala and Lorentz (1977) have argued that turbulence at the lips dominates turbulence generated within the vocal tract, both acoustically and perceptually. Thus, once the turbulence at the lips is generated (through increased overlap) it is easy to see why listeners might reassign the {crit} descriptor to the LIPS gesture. The last stages of the change involve the ultimate erosion of the TB gestures.

This account, then, shows that there is a plausible explanation of the change in Middle English that does not involve addition of any gestures – only reassignment of attributes among overlapping gestures. A similar analysis can be proposed for the Spanish example presented by Demolin as evidence of labials developing into labial-velars. The sequence *bue* is replaced by *güe*, e.g. *bueno* > *güeno* (Malmberg, 1971). Here again, however, both lip and tongue body gestures are present at all stages of the change. The original "labial" consonant has a labial-velar offglide, so the velar gesture of the tongue body is not, in fact, added, but has been there all along.

A gestural analysis of this example is illustrated in Figure 27.3. In (a), a partial gestural score is shown for the stage preceding the change. There are two LIPS gestures: a closure {clo}, followed by a {narrow} rounding gesture, and a single TB gesture, a {narrow} velar constriction for the [u] glide. The change would involve a reassignment of the {clo} from the LIPS gesture to the TB gesture. The reason for the reassignment in this case is probably very similar to the explanation that Ohala (1981) has given for a number of (similar) cases of dissimilation. At the release of the initial stop, the listener (presumably) successfully detects information specifying that there have been constrictions of the tongue and of the lips. However, the perceived lip information is (mistakenly) attributed to the ongoing rounding gesture, so the {clo} is attributed to the tongue body gesture instead. Again, there is no evidence for a gesture being added here. Similar considerations apply to the examples from Provençal that Demolin presents.

Overlapping gestures in sound change

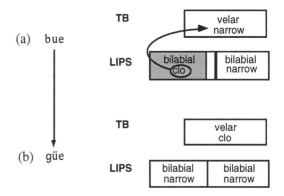

Figure 27.3. Analysis of sound change of Spanish *bue* > *güe*. Gestural scores (see Figure 27.2) are shown for two different stages: (a) state before the change; (b) after reassignment of the {clo} descriptor.

Finally, the possibility of [ɓ] developing into [g͡b] in Eastern Central Sudanic can be analyzed in a similar way (see Figure 27.4). Since Demolin shows that there is a velar constriction (not a stop) associated with [ɓ] (at least in Lendu; see Ladefoged, 1964, for similar data from Igbo), the gestural score (for oral constrictions only) would include both LIPS and TB gestures. The change involves assigning the {clo} descriptor to the TB gesture, as well as the LIPS gesture. Here, unlike the Spanish case, the {clo} specification is maintained on the LIPS gesture as well. The reason for that may be that here there is no rounding gesture to which perceived labial information can be misattributed. In general, more details about the environments of the proposed change need to be known to fully address this. Whatever the reason, the change can be analyzed as reassignment of attributes among temporally overlapping gestures.

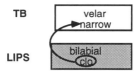

Figure 27.4. Gestural analysis of possible sound change [ɓ] > [g͡b].

391

Louis Goldstein

Notes

[Editors' note: Louis Goldstein's comentary is based on Didier Demolin's conference presentation. Subsequent to the conference, and following the comments offered by Goldstein, Demolin's paper was slightly modified. The comments included here do not take account of those modifications.]

* This work was supported by NSF grant 8820099 and NIH grants DC-00121 and NIH grant HD-01994 to Haskins Laboratories.

References

Browman, C. P. 1994. Lip aperture and consonant releases. In P. A. Keating, (ed.), *Phonological Structure and Phonetic Porm: Papers in Laboratory III.* Cambridge: Cambridge University Press, 331–353.

Browman, C. P. & L. Goldstein. 1991. Gestural structures: distinctiveness, phonological processes, and historical change. In. I. Mattingly & M. Studdert-Kennedy (eds.), *Modularity and the Motor Theory of Speech Perception.* Hillsdale, NJ: Erlbaum, 313–338.

Catford, J. C. 1977. *Fundamental Problems in Phonetics.* Bloomington, IN: Indiana University Press.

Fowler, C. & M. Smith. 1986. Speech perception as "vector analysis": an approach to the problems of segmentation and invariance. In J. Perkell & D. Klatt (eds.), *Invariance and Variability of Speech Processes.* Hillsdale, NJ: Erlbaum, 221–232.

Goldstein, L. 1991. Lip-rounding as side contact. *Proceedings of the XIIth International Congress of Phonetic Sciences,* Aix-en-Provence, 1: 97–101.

Ladefoged, P. 1964. *A Phonetic Study of West African Languages.* Cambridge: Cambridge University Press.

Liberman, A. & I. Mattingly. 1985. The motor theory of speech perception revised. *Cognition* 21: 1–36.

Lindau, M. 1984. Phonetic differences in glottalic consonants. *Journal of Phonetics* 12: 147–155.

Malmberg, B. 1971. *Phonétique générale et romane.* The Hague: Mouton.

Ohala, J. J. 1981. The listener as source of sound change. In C. Masek, R. Hendrick & M. Miller (eds.), *Papers from the Parasession on Language and Behavior.* Chicago: Chicago Linguistic Society, 178–203.

Ohala, J. J. & J. Lorentz. 1977. The story of [w]: An exercise in the phonetic explanation for sound patterns. *Proceedings, Annual Meeting of the Berkeley LinguisticsSociety* 3: 577–599.

Pagliuca, W. 1982. *Prolegomena to a theory of articulatory evolution.* Ph.D. dissertation, SUNY at Buffalo. Ann Arbor: University Microfilms International.

Pagliuca, W. & R. Mowrey. 1987. Articulatory evolution. In A. C. Ramat (ed.), *Papers from the VIIth International Conference on Historical Linguistics.* Amsterdam: John Benjamins, 459–472.

Subject index

vowel-to-vowel timing, 208, 209, 212, 213, 223, 228

Weight-tier Theory, 168
word blends, 141, 157, 161
word duration, 171, 191, 193, 195

Index of names

Index of names

Index of names

400

Index of languages

402

Index of languages

Kalabari, 370
Khaling, 379
Kham, 379
Khoisan, 91
KiNdendeule, 175, 176
Korean, 84, 151, 153, 157, 158, 165, 235, 242, 245, 254, 255, 345, 346
Kulung, 379

Lahu, 382
Latin, 89, 91, 275
Lendu, 368, 370, 374, 377, 380, 381, 386, 387, 391
Lisu, 382
Luganda, 169, 170, 171, 173, 174, 175, 178, 179, 181, 183, 184, 188, 189, 190, 191, 192, 193, 194, 195, 197, 198

Magar, 379
Majorcan Catalan, 270
Malayalam, 231
Mamvu, 379
Mandarin, 158
Mande, 377
Mangbetu, 370, 377, 380, 381
Mayan, 91
Middle English, 388, 390
Moose Cree, 169
Moru-Madi, 381

Ngwo, 269

Ojibwa, 169
Old Japanese, 164

Palestinian Arabic, 346
Portuguese, 159
Proto-Bantu, 176
Proto-Central Sudanic, 380, 381
Proto-Eastern Central Sudanic, 377
Proto-Tupi-Guarani, 379
Provençal, 379, 390

Roumanian, 267
Runyambo, 169, 170, 171, 173, 174, 175, 178, 181, 184, 185, 188, 189, 190, 191, 192, 193, 194, 195, 197, 198
Russian, 265, 275, 277
Sani, 382

Scottish English, 306
Spanish, 152, 153, 157, 158, 265, 269, 274, 275, 379, 390, 391
Sukuma, 174, 190
Sunwar, 379
Swedish, 89

Taiwanese, 165
Taiwanese Mandarin, 159
Tupi, 379
Tupi-Guarani, 379

Uto-Aztecan, 91

Yoruba, 170

403